EIN VOLK
EIN REICH

During a cross-country journey to a field hospital some shots were heard near a village. No one knew whence and why, but at once several hundred SS men surrounded the village and shouted to me that Polish snipers were hiding there. Every house was broken open and all the Polish men were driven into the church, which was set on fire with its human contents and completely burnt.

I was shocked and appalled by this summary justice. ... But I had learnt well enough not to burn my fingers when the SS or Gestapo were stewing a broth.

Dr Franz Wertheim

He had a strange nervous twitch in his face when he spoke. But the most marvellous thing was his eyes; they were very large and radiant, with a peculiar gleam lighting them with an uncanny power. I had to summon all my strength to look into his eyes. But then I knew surely and certainly and calmly that whoever looked in his eyes would be ready to die for him.

From that day I knew that the Führer possessed supernatural powers over men.

Eric Dressler

No one amongst my friends could take the Nazis seriously. The economic foundations of the Nazi programme were both vague and crude. ... The nebulous, vague and hardly comprehensible tone of their speeches, slogans and propaganda might serve to stir up certain sections of the population or to inflame unstable youths; but a businessman had no time for this kind of Valhalla hysteria.

Herman Voss

What could one say in school about the 'poets' who now found themselves hurled into an undreamt-of popularity and whose literary value was less than nothing? Every poem was a marching song. Interminably they sang the Führer's praises in every stanza, every line, every foot. With sickly lumps in their sickly throats they bleated the words 'Homeland, Fatherland, Germany, Race, Generosity, Blood, Soil, Honour, Mother Earth, Sorrow, Breeding, Sacrifice, Reproductive Force, Earthlove, Flags, Standards, Faith in Ancestry, Faith in Kindred, Faith in the Führer, Faith in Fate' – which just about composed their complete vocabulary.

Verner Harz

I was never afraid of Goering or of any of the high-up Nazis whom I knew personally. They were not in the least touchy on the subject of their credo. In fact I was always amazed at their cynicism about most of the Nazi philosophy. They admitted quite freely that the Hitler salute, the blood and soil, German sacred destiny, Jewish-communist world domination and the innumerable oaths of allegiance, were nothing but so much eyewash; necessary only for the masses, to keep them marching blindly in the right direction.

Baroness Mausi von Westerode

LOUIS HAGEN

EIN VOLK EIN REICH

NINE LIVES UNDER THE NAZIS

SPELLMOUNT

I dedicate this book to the memory of my brother K.V. Hagen, former officer of the American DSS who was killed on the Berlin Air Lift.
Louis Hagen

'Ich hatte einst ein schones Vaterland: es war ein traum …'
Heinrich Heine

This book would not have been republished were it not for the encouragement and conviction of my late mother, Anne-Mie Hagen. She had an unshakeable belief in my father's ability to relate these stories without prejudice and to give full weight to their historical importance. This edition is dedicated to her memory.
Caroline Hagen-Hall, England, 2011

This book was originally published in 1951 by Allan Wingate Ltd under the title *Follow my Leader*.

This edition first published 2011 by
Spellmount, an imprint of The History Press
The Mill, Brimscombe Port
Stroud, Gloucestershire, GL5 2QG
www.thehistorypress.co.uk

British Library Cataloguing in Publication Data.
A catalogue record for this book is available from the British Library.

ISBN 978 0 7524 5979 0
Typesetting and origination by The History Press
Printed in Great Britain
Manufacturing managed by Jellyfish Print Solutions Ltd

CONTENTS

ABOUT THE AUTHOR

Louis Hagen was born in Berlin in 1916, the second son of a wealthy Jewish banker. The family lived in an imposing Bauhaus-style villa on the banks of the Jungfernsee in Potsdam. In 1934 he was apprenticed at the BMW factory founded by his grandfather, but he was later dismissed for being non Aryan. One day he sent his sister Carla a joke on a postcard: 'Toilet paper is now forbidden so there are even more Brownshirts.' She left it lying around and it was picked up by a maid in the Hagen household; this maid had been caught stealing jewellery and was about to be sacked. She threatened to give it to her SS boyfriend if the family did not withdraw the accusation of stealing, but they would not be blackmailed. A few months later Louis, who was only sixteen at the time, was taken to the concentration camp in Schloss Lichtenburg.

While imprisoned Louis saw the true nature of the political giant that was taking control of Germany. Drunken guards would wake him at night, strip him naked and beat him with riding whips. He also watched as four other prisoners were forced to swim back and forth across a pond until they drowned.

Family connections were Louis' salvation, a school friend told his father of Louis' imprisonment. The latter was a judge and Nazi Party member, who wasted no time in driving to the camp in a chauffeur-driven BMW, asking to see the commandant, and taking Louis home. Louis had been forced to sign a document saying he had been well treated.

Louis' parents realised that their children would have to flee the country – but thousands of other Jews were also desperately trying to leave. It was eighteen months before a business friend, Sir Andrew McFadyean, arranged for him to emigrate to England. In 1936 Louis left Germany, intending to go to the US, but he ended up staying in England and took a job with the Pressed Steel Company near Oxford. He spent several happy years in the city rubbing shoulders with people such as Robert Graves, Nye Bevan, Stephen Spender and Sir Peter Medawar. Meanwhile, back in

The Hagen family before the war. Louis Hagen stands third from right.

Germany most of the Hagens had fled, and the family home was seized by the Nazis. Five of Louis' relatives would die in concentration camps.

As war loomed, Louis lost his job; new rules stated that no foreigners could work in factories engaged in war work. He transferred to Prestcold Refrigerators in London, but lost that place too once war broke out, as he was classed as an 'enemy alien'. He was called to a tribunal to ascertain whether he should be interned, but Sir Andrew McFadyean came to his rescue once again, testifying on his behalf. However, he was later arrested as a deserter for not having reported for military service. This was because he had no fixed address for his call-up papers to be sent to.

Louis joined the Pioneer Corps and in 1943 became a pilot with the Glider Pilot Regiment, No.22 Flight, D Squadron, No.1 Wing, changing his name to Lewis Haig to avoid problems in the event of his capture. On 18 September 1944 he was ordered into action, being amongst the first to take off. When his Horsa aircraft landing on the outskirts of Arnhem, he and the rest of the crew were greeted by ecstatic Dutch civilians. His conduct was more than impressive, especially since this was his first experience of combat. Louis attempted to destroy a machine-gun post single-handed, and managed to run to within 20 metres of it before he was forced to take cover. The Germans manning the post knew that he was there but not that he could understand every word of their bickering, which revealed how low their morale was. He was eventually able to report his information to an officer. He was wounded on the 24th when a splinter severed a vein in his hand as he manned a Bren gun, but he refused to leave the front line. When the Division pulled out, he and a friend, Captain Ogilvie, made their way to the banks of the Rhine for evacuation. With the embarkation point under fire and no boats to be seen, they decided to swim for it. Louis made it to the far bank but Captain Ogilvie drowned in the attempt.

On his return to England he was decorated for his bravery by King George VI, and later remembered the then Queen Elizabeth staring at him, amazed, he felt, to discover a German in her palace. During his leave he wrote his first book, *Arnhem Lift*. It was an immediate success, selling over 150,000 copies in the first years, and was adapted into a film. He was posted to a glider unit in India and was then transferred to the staff of *Phoenix* magazine, travelling widely as a war correspondent. He wrote *Indian Route March* about his experiences.

After the war he was sent to Germany as a news correspondent, first by the *London Sunday Express* and then by Odhams Press. It was during this time that he collected material for the book that would become *Ein Volk, Ein Reich* (first published as *Follow My Leader*). He then translated and edited a book on gliding, wrote a biography of Joseph Goebbels called *Evil Genius*, and translated the books *The Schellenberg Memoirs* and *Berlin*. His next title was a book based on the diary of Alfred Boeldeke, *With Graziela to the Head Hunters*, tracing Boeldeke's journey across South America along the Amazon river.

In 1950 he moved to north London with his Norwegian wife Anne Mie, a painter, with whom he had two daughters, Siri and Caroline. He set up a company, Primrose Film Productions, producing films with Lotte Reiniger – who had been engaged in 1923 by Louis' father as a private art teacher to his children – and at the same time making *Prince Achemd*, the first full length animated film. Together at Primrose Films, they made over 24 animation films, several of which won international awards, including first prize for children's films at the Venice Film Festival.

In 1964 he went to Germany to represent the Advertising and Documentary Film Division of the Rank Organisation. While there he collected the material for his 1969 book *The Secret War for Europe*, the story of espionage in Germany since the Second World War.

Louis Hagen died on 17 August 2000, at the age of 84. The day before he died, at a birthday party for his daughter, he declared that he had had a marvellous life. Death, he added, held no fear for him. He rests at Asker in Oslo, Norway.

FOREWORD

It was largely straightforward curiosity which prompted me to return to Germany as soon as possible after the war; curiosity and also some stirrings of an ignoble wish to see the great German eagle dethroned, stripped of its feathers and with its talons drawn. But when I got there it was too big for me. The appalling, relentless fact of 80 million people in the grip of famine, pestilence and despair left little room for exultation – none for idle curiosity. It is glib and easy to say 'This must not happen again'; but it must be said, and meant. And to resolve that this tragedy must not come again means that one must know how and why it happened at all.

I had lived in Germany until 1936 and had witnessed and been involved in the opening scenes. The development of the action and the tragic climax I had seen only from outside. And although distance can lead clarity to a cold assessment of political factors, this was more than a political interlude. Politics anyway are only a mechanical projection of the wills and thoughts of the people. And this German tragedy was an evil nightmare projected from the minds of people I had known as kind, industrious and civilised. It was a political disease which had attacked the people themselves – a cultural cancer which had overwhelmed the once healthy minds of the German men and women.

I wanted desperately to know what it had felt like to suffer from this 'German malady,' or at least what it was like to have been an inmate of this political fever hospital; to have lived cheek by jowl with the disease and its carriers. I did not set out to find a cure. I realised from the start that it would take me all my time to discover the nature of the disease – although I have lived three-quarters of my life in Germany. I realised, too, that it was no use merely studying the leaders and the events they precipitated, or which precipitated them. The theory that the leaders were responsible for the people's character, or lack of it, that Goebbels governed their thoughts, Hitler their actions, is an over-simplification of a much more involved problem. Unfortunately this theory is a very convenient one both for Germans and the Allies

Louis Hagen in later life.

alike. It is an ideal excuse for the Germans to evade their own personal responsibility, and the Allies find it very convenient to explain the actions of tens of millions in terms of tens.

Nor could an answer be found by submitting a haphazard cross section of the people to a questionnaire and thus formulating a post-mortem Gallup poll. This would have been as unsatisfactory as was judging the average standard of nutrition by random weighing-machines on the streets of Berlin. The only hope was to reconstruct in detail the everyday lives of a number of ordinary people. This was the only way of finding out what Herr Schmidt thought about events; what he said to his family and friends; how he felt when he saw his Jewish neighbours being collected by the Gestapo; how enthusiastically he hung out the flags when Germany absorbed Austria and Czechoslovakia; what he did when his daughter in the BDM told him that Christianity was a Jewish decadence, and planned procreation the German woman's ideal.

In surveys and histories, biographies of the leaders and newspaper articles, this story remains untold. It is the story of a highly civilised and moral people, industrious, gifted and efficient, who managed within twelve years to destroy not only Germany but also their own minds. Every German is part of this story – and this story is part of every German. I decided to tell the story – not as it seemed to me – but as it actually occurred in the lives of a number of Germans. This could not be the whole story: but through these lives the shape of the whole might be discovered.

I found it necessary to pick my representative characters amongst people I had known before I left Germany; amongst people I had known and observed before 1933 and during the first three years of the Nazi regime. This knowledge of their previous lives and characters would be my principal safeguard against being misled by conscious or unconscious misrepresentations of the past. Every conversation was taken down word for word as it happened. Afterwards I checked every fact carefully through cross-questioning of common acquaintances, examining official records and by further questioning. I am now sure that these stories depict the feelings, emotions and reactions of the people concerned as accurately and as truthfully as possible.

Nine people emerged as representatives of the whole. Each typifies a class, a kind of character, a group of motives, a way of thinking. Three are Nazis, from a simple SA man to a fashionable physician; three are non-Nazis, but fellowtravellers: a regular officer, a business man and a politically minded socialite; two are anti-Nazis: one by accident of birth, the other from sincere inner conviction. There are no Jews amongst these biographies: they are no more representative than the high-up Nazis and atrocity fanatics who also find no place in this book. Much has been written about the Jews, and those who are left are being looked after. Much has been written about the master criminals, and most of them have been looked after too. These – the full blacks and whites – present no problem compared with the millions of ordinary men and women in their varying shades of grey who are going to be the citizens of the Fourth Reich – if there should be a Fourth Reich.

For reasons of policy, I have had to change the names of my nine characters, and in certain cases it has been necessary to alter some unimportant details to ensure their anonymity. This in no way affects the basic truth of these stories; every thought, action and event recounted is, to the best of my knowledge, true and accurate. It should be remembered that these opinions are their own opinions, freely and honestly expressed. I believe them to be completely sincere – not only from my own knowledge of my characters, but also because, on re-reading their stories objectively, their innate sincerity seems to be too obvious to need stressing.

I leave the reader to judge for himself where the responsibility lies, and who contributed most to the ruin of these people's Fatherland. At least these nine stories will, when viewed as representative parts of a greater whole, give some idea of the nature of the German disease. It may, after all, not be solely a 'German' disease. One may have to look for the symptoms not only in Germany, but in the world; not only in the wreckage of the Third Reich, but also in Britain, France, Russia and America; not only in the black hearts of the Nazi sadists, but also in the hearts of our own countrymen – perhaps even in our own hearts.

1

FRITZ MUEHLEBACH

I have known Fritz for as long as I can remember; he was the brother of our gardener Karl Muehlebach. Fritz used to come to Potsdam at irregular intervals to see Karl. He was the 'sailor brother,' and possessed a certain glamour for us children. Whenever he came we used to spend a good deal of time at Karl's cottage at the end of the kitchen garden, plying Fritz with questions; he was reserved but quite friendly and always ready to answer in his rather serious way. Being friends with Fritz, and talking to him 'man to man' about his experiences at sea, made us feel grown up. He had seen the world, and besides he was always so spruce and tidy. There was a shiny, scrubbed look about him which we admired as being thoroughly nautical.

Then, in 1932, I remember hearing that Fritz had joined the SA. When we asked Karl what he thought about this, he shrugged and said that as Fritz was out of work and times were hard, at least it meant that he would be making a bit extra over his unemployment relief.

It was some time before I had a chance to ask Fritz what it felt like to be a storm trooper, and when eventually he did turn up he had changed a lot. He was still serious but nothing like as reserved, which was surprising, as I had expected him to be stand-offish. He was as friendly as ever and certainly not anti-Semitic so far as my family was concerned. He was also bursting with enthusiasm and was only too anxious to tell me anything I wanted to know about his life in the SA.

Time went on and things got more and more difficult for us. Fritz continued to visit his brother and was always friendly and even sympathetic. He never actually said anything against the Party line, but he was full of vague consolations such as 'they'll never do anything to you; you're not the sort of people we are after,' and 'you've been in Germany for centuries, it's the Jews from the East that we've got to get rid of,' or 'Your father was an officer in the last war, and anyway none of you looks Jewish.'

When I saw him after I came out of a concentration camp he was genuinely sorry, because it was me. He said so rather awkwardly in a way which embarrassed us both, but he added rather feebly that 'there must have been a reason for it.' of course in 1934 to Fritz, the SA man, there was a very good reason for everything his party did. He was a good party member; so he had nothing to worry about.

When I met him again in 1946, poor Fritz had plenty to worry about. At first – apart from looking ten years older and rather as it he had shrunk in the wash – he seemed to have altered very little. His suit was shabby, but looked impeccably tidy and neat, and he still had the scrubbed look.

He was very hang-dog at first, but when I eventually got him talking, he did so quite freely, provided we were alone. Soon an urgency and passion crept into his voice. It was as if he felt that talking about the past might help him to solve his innermost problems. But although telling his story seemed to help him for the moment, he was as crushed and bewildered as ever when we said goodbye. He reminded me more than anything of a child whose illusion of his father's infallibility had been shattered. In a strange, dark world with no one to guide him, Fritz was utterly lost, with no idea what to do or think.

Fritz Muehlebach, born 1907

My father was a market gardener in Weissensee. Although my brother Karl carried on the family tradition when he left school I felt that it did not lead anywhere. When I left school I got a job as assistant to a chemist, but, owing to the bad times, that did not last long. After my father passed away I would have liked to have stayed at home with my mother. But there was no work to be had, so I finally decided to try my luck at sea. I left home at the age of twenty – that was in 1927 – and went to Rotterdam. There was a lot of unemployment there too, but I was lucky enough to get a ship right away.

For the next five years I was a sailor and enjoyed myself very much. I went all over the world, saw foreign countries and foreign people and brought back souvenirs and curios from all over the place: Chinese beads, snakes in bottles, painted coconuts, native weapons and brass idols. My mother was very proud of them and used to show them off whenever one of the family came to an evening meal.

In 1931 we were in the North Sea when there was a bit of a rough-house between several lads and some of the older seamen. As the youngsters seemed to be getting the worst of it, I sided with them. I got a broken wrist and a torn ear, but we got the better of them and when the mate caught us we got two of the older fellows locked up. I never did find out the reason for the row.

When we landed at Stettin I was told by two of the youngsters that they were in the Hitler Youth. To show their gratitude, because I'd helped them in the fight, they asked me to come to one of their gatherings at what they called their *Sturmlokal* [a pub in which Party members regularly met]. Here I was introduced to other Party members and men who were in the SA.

Until then I had only heard vaguely about the National Socialist doctrine. Now, I began to realise that it was a very large party and its leaders really did know what they wanted, not like all the other parties.

One of the lads called Erwin Eckhart took me back to his flat. As we had been signed off and it looked as though I would have to stay ashore a bit, I rented a room from Erwin and used to share his kitchen. He told me a whole heap of things about politics that I never knew before. We hadn't talked about politics at home. I suppose my mother and father were only simple, old-fashioned people and they couldn't grasp the new, modern ideas about politics. Erwin knew it all and used to jaw away by the hour. And then he started taking me to the Party meetings and lectures. It's wonderful how it broadens your mind to think about important things like politics. I was bowled over by some of the lectures – I was beginning to get my eyes opened to a few things: the way all the other parties were just muddling through because they hadn't got one ideal and one leader and the way our German industry was being smothered by Jewish moneylenders. And the way the other countries were trying to pin the war guilt on the German people. We had to throw the Versailles lie back in their teeth, and throw over all the unjust burdens which the Treaty had laid on us. Socialism was the answer – finish the class struggle, and no one must earn more than a thousand marks a month. Put Germany in the hands of the Germans and throw out the Jews and foreigners.

At these meetings there was often a good deal of heckling by communists and other political groups. It annoyed me that people holding different political views should disturb these lectures. I, for one, wanted to know what the Nazis stood for, so that I could form an opinion. The shouting and heckling often made it impossible for the speaker to complete his speech. The SA men always tried to keep order, and I always used to give them a hand with the disturbing elements so that the lectures could continue undisturbed. Quite often it led to serious fights.

In the Sturmlokal near the place where I lived I met a lot of students and unemployed SA men. I went there a lot and the talk was mostly on political problems. I enjoyed these discussions which were interesting and always to the point. But the others were much better talkers than I was for I had not had any political training. But I liked the general atmosphere of comradeship and in the end, I decided to send in my application forms for the SA. It was time for me to belong to an organisation and take an active part in shaping the future of my country. I felt that this party was on the right road and that I would learn a great deal about politics in its ranks. I wanted to know what was going on; I wanted to be able to answer questions and have the strength and confidence which all the other SA men seemed to have.

As soon as my wrist was better I went to sea again. Whenever we put into a German port I found my way to the nearest Sturmlokal and spent what free time I had there. Wherever I went I found the same comradeship and sense of purpose. I was more and more proud and happy that I was part of this movement.

Back in Stettin I was very disappointed to learn that I had not been accepted by the SA. In my absence, in April 1932, the SA had been prohibited and they were having to be very careful about new members. And they didn't know anything about my past and thought I might have been a spy for the communists or for the police. I was very sorry, of course, but it did mean that the party was very alive to the dangers. Every member had to show his worth and reliability before being accepted. This really made me admire them more than ever.

I couldn't get a ship after this and was again out of work. Times were bad and I was very depressed. When I realised that there were six million workless in the same position as myself the responsibility of getting a job seemed completely hopeless. Depression and panic were in the air; some of the biggest banks had closed and no one could see any end to it. Of course Moscow started making mischief in this atmosphere of unrest and discontent, and almost six million people went over to the communists. The Reds were busy with strikes and the picketing of offices and factories and intimidating the workers. They were at the back of all the street brawls and shootings. The government was always changing and couldn't do anything, and the police didn't seem to care. They were all making it easy for the communists to terrorise the whole German population.

In July 1932, three of the local SA men were murdered by the Reds. This strengthened my resolve to try again to join the SA and avenge them. I was careful to get references from home, and Erwin vouched for me. This time it worked.

It was wonderful to know at last that I was taking an active part in the welfare of my fatherland. We SA men were the soldiers of the movement. It was our job to maintain order at all Party meetings. The speakers and leaders were protected by the SS, which was a special corps of picked SA men limited to ten per cent of our strength. Members of the SA and SS were strictly forbidden to make speeches or take part in public discussions. All that was entrusted to the political leaders and those members of the Party who had received special political training. We were not trained to talk and argue, but it was up to us to make the best possible impression through our discipline and military bearing.

Life was still tough. Ninety per cent of our Sturm [roughly equivalent to a company of soldiers] were unemployed, but now we had something to fight and live for and this made it so much easier for us all to bear the hardships. We were all in the same boat together. I got 8.40 marks a week unemployment benefit. Five marks went on rent and the remaining 3.40 had to pay for all my living expenses. Thirty pfennigs were spent on tobacco, ten pfennigs I paid towards the Party insurance fund in case I was disabled whilst fighting for the Party. When I drew my benefit I just spent one mark on eleven small sausages from a stand outside the labour exchange. They cost ten pfennigs, but you could get eleven for the price of ten. The free sausage I ate immediately. The rest I kept for my breakfasts and suppers for the rest of the week. Another 1.20 marks I kept for buying bread and other things. For my main meal of the day I was able to go to the SA home where for only ten pfennigs we got a really good midday meal. The well-to-do party members made regular contributions to the SA home. We often had real butter, and also venison and wild pork from their shooting estates, and in the season we often got jobs as beaters and loaders. Whenever a big pot came to the Sturmlokal we got a free meal and free beer all round. Being members of the Party they weren't a bit stuck-up and stand-offish, but talked to us man to man and made us see that we all had the same ideas and the same hopes for Germany. My membership fee was paid by what we used to call a 'Godfather,' who owned a shoe shop. Once I was really on the rocks and he lent me some money. When I wanted to pay it back in weekly instalments he wouldn't have it, and let me off the whole amount. Many of us had party godfathers – people we could always go to when we were in trouble, and who would invite us to Christmas and other festivals.

I was very badly off for clothes, because you never needed much on board ship and I had never bothered about them. Now, of course, I had no money and I couldn't even afford a uniform. I felt rather ashamed of this. Most of the men in our Sturm wore at least part of a uniform, and all I could do was to wear a swastika armlet. In November my only pair of boots gave out and a heel came off in the snow. When I limped to the Sturmlokal my *Sturmbannführer* took me straight to the SA offices and saw to it himself that I was given a complete uniform free of charge. I was very happy to get the uniform in time for the big November [1932] elections, because now I was able to undertake more important public duties, such as standing in front of the polling booth with a sandwich-board. The results were very disappointing because we got even fewer votes than last time. But the leaders weren't at all downcast. They explained to us that this was really a victory for us. What it meant was that the luke-warm elements had now shown themselves in their true colours and left the Party. Now we knew where we stood. And those of us who were left would be true to their ·oath and their Führer.

The elections were the excuse for renewed outbreaks of violence on the part of our opponents. We had fights every day and several hospital cases each week. I got my nose broken with a knuckle-duster during a scrap with the *Kampf Ring Junger Deutsch Nationaler*, the military youth organisation of the German National Party.

Each party had its own fighting force; the communists had the *Rot Front Kämpfer Bund*, the social democrats had the *Reichsbanner*, and so on. And they all did every-thing they possibly could to provoke us. There was not one large-scale meeting that was not disturbed in some way or other, and not a single propaganda march that took place without a disturbance. But now and again we got our own back.

I remember a large communist rally where 150 of our people entered in ordinary clothes and took up the end seats on each side of the centre gangway right down the hall. When all the speeches were well underway one of our men slipped a stick of cordite into the stove. There was a fine explosion, the windows were shattered and the whole hall was filled with thick sooty smoke. At the moment of the explosion we all stood up, put on our armlets and SA caps and stood to attention giving the Hitler salute. The Reds were taken completely by surprise. They started shouting and dashing round the hall like a lot of scalded cats. Then, as the smoke cleared away and they saw the solid wedge of disciplined SA men standing shoulder to shoulder down the whole length of the hall, they squealed with terror and made a rush to the doors. Then we all seized chairs, smashed them as we had been taught, and, armed with the legs, waded into them. We always had to work fast and scientifically as the police were against us and were always liable to turn up. They were always pro-Red and beat us up whenever they could catch us. I remember once we broke up a Deutsch National meeting at the Stettin Kaiser Garten. The police got word of it and surrounded us. We had to come out through a long narrow corridor; the police had lined up all along the passage, and as we tried to get through they thrashed us with rubber truncheons, and some of them weren't above using their feet. I was ill for a week after that meeting.

What made it worse was that we had strict orders not to resist the police, and we weren't allowed to carry guns. Anyone caught with a gun was expelled from the SA. All we were allowed to do was to defend ourselves against insults with our fists. There was a lot of grumbling about the unfairness of this, but our leaders explained to us that we mustn't give the government the chance to get us banned. They were really terrified of us and would take the first opportunity. We just had to put up with it as best we could while our enemies tried their very best to incite us. Many of our comrades were murdered by the Reds, and we couldn't lift a hand to avenge them. But we were able to stick it out because we knew our time would come.

We were not allowed to wear our uniform or badges when we went to the labour exchange, where we had to get our cards stamped each day. Waiting in the queue, arguments would break out and they often led to fighting. By the end of 1932 things had got to such a pitch that a man couldn't go to the labour exchange without being beaten up if it was known that he was in the SA or a Party member. To avoid trouble and protect ourselves the whole Sturm used to go together in a group. That usually kept the troublemakers quiet.

Everything we did now had to be organised in groups. Regularly, after midnight, parties armed with ladders, paint brushes and pails went out until dawn sticking up posters and slogans on walls and houses. Then, after we'd finished, we used to march through the town chanting in chorus: 'All power to Adolf Hitler.' Smaller groups of four to six men were busy all day pushing leaflets and party newspapers through letterboxes. We were always told to begin at the top of the house as fights usually started if the people on the lower floors had time to give the alarm. Then members of the *Haus Schutz-Staffel* [Military self-protection squads organised for the protection of houses and blocks of flats against rival political parties] would sometimes lie in wait for us at the entrance and grab our leaflets and attack us with clubs and knuckle-dusters. Another group was specially detailed to escort SA members home who lived in streets mainly inhabited by our opponents. Pommersdorf, for example, was a hotbed of communists, and if we hadn't escorted home the only two SA men who lived there they would certainly have been attacked, and probably murdered.

The struggle continued and our ideas spread, and by the end of 1932 we had the satisfaction of knowing that we were by far the strongest party. We all felt that final victory was just round the corner and the decision could no longer be delayed. General von Schleicher's government was all the time on the edge of a crisis, and it was obvious that nothing could save it. Then in January of the new year we heard that our Führer had been asked to join this government, obviously in a last desperate effort to keep it on its feet. This was a terrible moment for us. We were scared that he might get compromised and go with the reactionaries. But we needn't have worried, for this was followed by the news that the Führer was prepared to take all or nothing. He would not prop up anybody else's government but was perfectly willing to form his own. We hung on from day to day with our excitement rising to fever pitch, and then, on 30 January, standing round the wireless in the Sturmlokal, we heard the news we were waiting for. Reich president Feldmarschall von Hindenburg had charged the Führer with the formation of a government.

We had been waiting for it. We had always known it had to happen and yet, when it came, it hit us like an explosion. We were beyond happiness. We sang the Horst Wessel song, we shouted 'Heil!' until we were hoarse – and then we drank to the Führer till our throats were clear again, and then we dashed into the streets, where groups of other brownshirts and Party members had already begun to gather. Swastika flags had appeared as if by magic. The day went by in a fever of activity, and a great torchlight procession was organised for the evening.

That night, as we marched singing through the streets, we had it all our own way. Now the police were on our side and guarded our procession. Our enemies were lying low and there were no fights until we came to Pommersdorf. There, in spite of our strict order not to leave formation, a few of our more enthusiastic members could not resist the chance of getting their own back on the Reds. Some of them were afterwards expelled from the SA for lack of discipline.

During the months that followed there was a sudden stream of newly converted Party members. The German National Party had already come over to us, and after the March elections the so-called March casualties started pouring in. We had a pretty poor opinion of them and I heard of cases in Berlin where the Sturms, particularly in the north, were now made up almost entirely of former communists. My own Sturm in Stettin was certainly not what it had been; 40 per cent of it had recently been Reds, 10 per cent Social Democrats and a lot were ex-Stahlhelm, Free Corps and old Landsknechte. These people had turned their coats just in time to reap the rewards of the victory for which we had fought. But we realised that it was high time that all these parties should be liquidated and that the Führer was right, as always, when he passed the law forbidding them, as there was no further need for them and they were only a hindrance to progress. By the time of the Reichstag fire, our enemies were too late to rally against us. We were now too strong for them. This act of terrorism might have split the country and plunged it into war, but it was no more than the final wriggle of a beaten foe. And whether the Communist Party had really employed the halfwit Dutchman Van der Lubbe to do the job, or whether they had nothing to do with it at all, was no concern of ours. The Führer knew what he was doing, and this was his chance to get rid of such communists as had been so silly as to stick to their guns, including all the Red members of the Reichstag. The Red terror had to be broken. And what had to be done was more important than the way it was done.

In the spring of 1933 I was still unemployed and I decided to go on an SA auxiliary police course. This meant that I would receive free meals as well as my benefit. Then, when this course came to an end, during September, I got a job in a Sauerkraut factory through the help of my *Ortsgruppenleiter*. When the cabbage season came to an end I was out of work again and started working as an honorary clerk at the SA headquarters. The SA paid me a monthly assistance of 20 marks, which, added to my 8.40 marks a week unemployment benefit, meant that I was not too badly off. I was able to eat at the SA house where our meals were now paid for by the *Nationalsozialistische Frauenschaft* [women's organisation of the Nazi Party] and that was a great help.

During the winter one man from every SA brigade was selected to go on a medical orderly course which was held at the big Reichswehr training camp at Doeberitz. As I had some medical knowledge from having once worked as a chemist, I was picked. I found the training very interesting and got on pretty well. But I was not much use at the PT and drill that went with it, although I did my best. Here we were always in trouble about our marching. We never managed to get the smartness we had in the Sturm in Stettin. The trouble was that the Bavarians and Westphalians were accustomed to march at quite a different speed, and the result was a terrible muckup. Because of this we were all given such punishments as bellycrawling and physical jerks; but this made no difference and our marching continued as ragged as ever. Then one day when we were out on a route march, someone started the Horst Wessel song. This was forbidden, as the song was sacred and only allowed to be sung on the most important official occasions. Nevertheless, everybody joined in and we suddenly found we were marching properly. It swept us along in spite of ourselves.

The Horst Wessel song was our battle hymn and our national anthem. It completely replaced the old 'Deutschland, Deutschland Ueber Alles' which smelt too much of the past. After this we always sang on the march and it did make a big difference. I was always very fond of singing and was often told I had a good natural voice. We had many patriotic and marching songs written by our own members which said in song what the Party stood for. 'In Soviet Russland' wasn't a very serious song but did show some our ideas about the Jews.

In Soviet Russland high up north,
The long-nosed Jews go bravely forth:
And plunder shops and rob the farms,
And kill the Russki babes-in-arms.

But here the Jews are gentlefolk,
And in the Bourse their noses poke,
And talk of par and bulls and bears
And things a gentile never hears.

Hi-de-hi and ho-de-ho:
Ikey Moses has the dough:
You can't keep a bad Jew down;
Ikey Moses rules the town.

When Jews were in the desert land,
They chewed their garlic in the sand.
When they found there was a drought,
Moses belched and the water came out.

Sara walking on the shore,
Fell in the sea and bumped her jaw.
'She drown, she drown,' cried Finklebaum,
But Sara swam back safe and sound.

Hi-de-hi and ho-de-ho:
Ikey Moses has the dough:
You can't keep a bad Jew down;
Ikey Moses rules the town.

'Brother Everywhere' was much more serious and moving:

Brothers in mines and brothers in ships and brothers behind the plough,
Brothers from factories, offices, shops, follow our Leader now.
Stock Exchange robbers and Stock Exchange Jews poison our Fatherland:
Our wish to work like honest men they'll never understand.
Hitler is our leader true and spurns their proffered bribes:
He'll kick the faithless Juden swine back to their heathen tribes.
And soon the glorious day will come, the day when we are free,
And German men in German land stand strong in unity.

Load the empty rifles, polish the gleaming knives,
Strike down the Jewish traitors who juggle with our lives.
We are loyal to our leader, Adolf Hitler, stern and strong,
He is our champion and our hope and will fight against the wrong.
Brothers in mines and brothers in ships and brothers behind the plough,
Brothers from factories, offices, shops, follow our Leader now.

My favourite was a sad song about one of our murdered comrades and how we
would avenge him. It was called 'Dawn was Breaking':

Dawn was breaking, sad and brown,
In the little country town;
The tramping feet went up and down,
Hitler's regiment is marching.

The bugles rang out loud and clear,
Like echoes of a dying year;
Requiem for a comrade murdered here;
Hitler's regiment is marching.

Dawn is breaking in the world;
Traitors from their lairs are hurled;

The Nazi banners are unfurled;
Hitler's regiment is marching.

Some people said these were our hymns, but I think they were more real than that.
We hadn't time for hymns and that sort of thing. There was too much to be done. The
Church had always been a danger in politics, and there was now no place for it. The
Party freely admitted the existence of God but we were not allowed to talk about
religion. Most of us were Lutherans; the rest were nothing. Most of these had been
communists. It was quite easy not to talk about religion, because none of us thought
about it very much.

We did not care much for the regular army people who were all too old-fashioned
and snobbish. And, after all, it was we who had done all the fighting in the recent
years, and it's fighting that counts – not just swaggering about in military uniforms.
The old army ideas were a thing of the past just like the monarchy – even though
Prince August Wilhelm had joined the party. We had a good laugh about him and
said: 'I hope they checked his references.'

We used to talk about our leaders a lot. Hess was very popular. Everybody said
he never put on airs, and acted just like an ordinary person even though he was the
Führer's right-hand man. Ley wasn't very popular, though. There was even a rumour
that his real name was Levy. Von Papen and Hugenberg were also unpopular; they
smelt too much of the old aristocracy and big business. Hindenburg was just a dod-
dering old man. There were many good jokes about the leaders and many of them
had nicknames; Goering was known as 'Lamette', Hermann as 'Tinsel' and Goebbels
as 'club-foot'. Hitler was never spoken of as anything but the Führer. We never joked
about him. Occasionally some of the very old fighters referred to him as Adolf, but
the younger men would never have dared to refer to him in this way. His name was
sacred. I remember during the training course a man called Waldfart said to me that
Adolf Hitler has done less for the world than Moses. I was completely staggered, and
my first thought was that such a man was not fit to be in the SA and that he should
be reported. But I didn't report him as I didn't really understand what he meant.
I don't think he did either. I think he was just trying to show off. But I often wonder
if I should have reported him.

In general, people were careful not to go too far when arguing. There was always a
danger that someone wouldn't understand and would make a report. If you really felt
someone was on the wrong track, you might try to argue, but it was safer to shut up.
Anyhow, we were all agreed on the main things, although we differed a bit on certain
topics. For instance, I approved of all the Party ideas but I wasn't so sure about some
of the methods. Of course, you've got to exclude all Jewish influence from the life
of the State, but some of the things seemed a bit cruel. Naturally, you can't help not
liking the Jews. After all, they had entered the Fatherland after the war and had sucked
it dry with their foreign money and commercial skill. But I didn't hate the Jews – not
all the Jews, although I was quite pleased to see them disappear from Germany again,
leaving behind them the wealth they had robbed. But there were also Jews who had

fought bravely in the last war and who did not act and look like Jewish people. My brother was working for Jews and they treated him very well and didn't look like Jews at all. Whenever I sang the songs like 'Throw out all the Yiddish gang' and 'When on the knife the Jew blood spurts' I never really meant all Jews. Of course they shouldn't have been allowed to hang on to all the good jobs for themselves like doctors, university teachers, wealthy merchants, big business men, actors, writers and lawyers, but I realised that this was largely a question of intelligence and education. A great deal of trouble lay in the fact that Germany's upper classes, who could have trained their sons to become doctors, merchants and lawyers, were proudest if their sons became officers. Of course Jews couldn't be officers, so they spent their time getting into all the other good jobs. I didn't really believe that the Jews were to blame for all our misfortunes past and present, as they were during the Middle Ages. Of course the pollution of the German race was rightly forbidden by law. And, equally, life had to be made unpleasant for the Jews so that they would get out. But the very crude attacks on them they always printed in *Der Stuermer* weren't right. I did not agree with the methods of Gauleiter Streicher. I couldn't understand that the Führer could tolerate a man like this in a prominent position in the Movement, and I really thought that sooner or later he would get rid of him and his like and order a general purge in the interest of all truly socialist elements.

There was only one man, Hans Stulpe, whom I made friends with during the course, whom I could talk to freely, and vice versa, about things of this kind without the fear that one of us would split. Hans and I did not have many opportunities for private conversations of this type and, when we did, we always suffered from a slight feeling of guilt, in spite of the knowledge that all that was said remained strictly between us two. We knew that the private opinions of the rank and file like us could be harmful to our movement as a whole. If everyone started airing his private opinion, the Party wouldn't be standing firmly shoulder to shoulder, and this was our greatest strength over our enemies. Hans and I knew that we could talk and still stand firm by the Party, but everybody wasn't to be trusted, and it was right that we weren't allowed to argue and make criticisms.

The next spring the Ortsgruppe sent me as an honorary assistant to the labour exchange, which meant that I lost the twenty marks a month which I got for my work at the headquarters. This was a blow, but orders were orders and I think I was as willing as anyone to make sacrifices. But I had no desire to have anything to do with the labour exchange, as I knew from my personal experiences it was being run in an unsatisfactory way.

The last time I asked for a job I had been told that my turn had not yet come, as my membership number was too large, and yet the officer who had told me this was himself such a new member of the Party that he hadn't got a membership number at all. But he had already got himself a fat job. After that, I never bothered to ask for a job again.

When I took up my new duties I found out that the men who had had my job before had had to be replaced on an average of once a week. That meant it had taken them about a week to get themselves a good job which in fact it had been their duty to pass on to an unemployed man. I felt very strongly that this behaviour was quite unworthy of the followers of the Führer, and I was determined to do the job conscientiously for as long as I was needed.

In the giving out of jobs, it seemed to me far more important to find work immediately for non-Party members. In this way they would realise that the Führer's promise to stop unemployment was being honoured. I felt that the Party members should only be considered after the disbelievers and waverers had been given jobs. But I seemed to be the only one who saw it this way, and they used to make jokes about me and laugh when I said it. I think I was the only Party member at the labour exchange who wasn't thinking only about how to fix himself a good job. In spite of all this I found the work very interesting. It brought me into contact with human affairs and enabled me to do my bit in rebuilding the country, which I found very satisfactory. It kept me busy till late at night, and so the time at my disposal was very limited and I couldn't spend much time at the SA.

Nowadays I had no time for any Sturm duties and I was only able to take part in the formal marches and parades. There was one big SA parade – it took place in June of that year – that I shall never forget. Ten thousand of us, that is three brigades, marched out to a field where we fell in in blocks of about 300 men. When each block had been lined up, inspected by his march-block Führer and then re-inspected to the satisfaction of the Sturmführers, we stood to attention waiting for the arrival of the Gruppenführer, Peter von Heiderbeck. At last he arrived, mounted on a white horse, and rode from block to block, looking at each man in turn and occasionally pausing to shout something to his storm troopers as he rode past. When he came to our block, he suddenly reined in his horse and said:

'My horse tells me that the SA is a wild, revolutionary horde. Is this true?'

At the top of their voices our block shouted:

'Yes, we are!'

To my astonishment and horror, I heard myself shout 'No.'

As I was in the first row, the Group Leader also heard me. He ordered me to fall out and asked me my name. My particulars were written out and I was told to report to him at the staff building the next day. I was very upset by my behaviour and rather afraid of what the consequences might be after the parade. I was sent for by my block leader who asked me what the hell I thought I was doing making an exhibition of myself and letting the whole block down. He was very angry, and by the time he had finished with me I felt worse than ever. I couldn't imagine what had come over me and made me shout 'no' when the others had all shouted 'yes.' I spent a miserable night and arrived very frightened at the staff building next day. After waiting all afternoon, I was told I was to go as the Group Leader could not see me, and so the matter was closed and I heard no more about it.

Later on I was able to think about it more calmly and I then saw that my answer to the Group Leader's question had been the right one, for it expressed my honest opinion. I believed the SA to be revolutionary, but I had not thought it was a wild and undisciplined horde. On the contrary, it was the well disciplined fighting force of Adolf Hitler, and I decided that I would have to answer 'no' again if ever the question should be put to me. When I had reasoned all this out, I wished that I could have had a chance to speak to the Group Leader, whom we all admired very much, and tell him what I thought. But, of course, the opportunity never occurred.

About ten days after the parade, I had something more exciting than myself to think about. Stettin was to receive a visit from the Chief of Staff himself, Hauptmann Roehm. I had never seen him before but – like all the rest – I had a very great respect for this man who had so successfully formed and led the Führer's Brown Army. We were all lined up on the large field where our parades were held, and it said in orders that when the Chief of Staff arrived he would be lifted on our shoulders and carried in triumph to his tent. I was with those who were detailed for cordoning-off·duties. Roehm did not arrive until after dark, and just before his arrival the arrangements for his reception were changed; he was no longer to be carried, we were forbidden to touch him, and the cordon was to precede him with their faces turned towards him and see to it that the men who came out of their tents kept their distance. This meant that I was able to get a good look at our chief.

He was a little fat man who looked rather like a butcher or a farmer. He had a red face with duelling scars and was smiling. Two things about him rather disappointed me. He was wearing the SA uniform coat which the storm troopers always looked down on, and he had on a white collar. A white collar to the SA was like a red rag to a bull. Did this mean that the upper-class was going to oust our good old brown shirt? These were my thoughts as I walked slowly backward in front of the Chief of Staff. But as the crowd behind me got thicker and thicker and the shouting and cheering grew louder I forgot about them. All I thought was: here was our Chief of Staff and I was taking part in a very great occasion. Everybody was so crazy with shouting and cheering that however hard we pushed we couldn't get a way clear for him through the crowd. At last a *Standartenführer* had the brilliant idea of hoisting one of the men on his shoulders and making several others around him shout 'Heil! Heil!' All the men at the back thought this was Roehm, and crowded round him and were able to get the real Roehm to his tent. A few days later he came to Stettin again, but this time I was not on duty. A fortnight later he was shot.

At this time I was in a pub opposite the brigade headquarters having a few pints with two comrades. Two of us didn't wear uniform but the third, Otto Schmidt, a *Sturmhauptführer*, wore his. There seemed to be some commotion outside and we went to the door to see what went on. A crowd had collected in front of headquarters and we were surprised to see several SA men and SA Führers being marched off by SS men. We started across the road to find out what the matter was When an SS man came across to us and arrested Schmidt, who was so surprised that he didn't say a word. We went back into the pub to find out if anyone knew anything, and as nobody did, we decided to go over to our own Sturmlokal. Our way led us past the railway station, and there we overheard a man who had just arrived from Berlin, telling someone that Roehm had been arrested. We decided that the informer must be one of the dangerous rumourmongers who deserved strict punishment. We asked him to accompany us to the nearest police station. Our informer repeated his assertion in front of the police officer and even added that there was a large-scale conspiracy against the Führer and that the SA was deeply involved. But the police didn't seem to want to do anything so we had to let him go. Then we went to the oldest Sturmlokal in Stettin and found a whole crowd of SA men excitedly discussing the rumour that had spread through the town like wildfire. They seemed quite mad and were saying that the SA had revolted against the Führer and the Chief of Staff had broken his oath to Hitler.

Later on the same night we heard all about the shooting on the wireless. We were deeply shocked and completely flabbergasted when we heard the death roll of so many well-known SA Führers and old fighters who were involved in the plot and accordingly punished for treason. But most of all the death of our Group Leader, Peter von Heiderbeck shocked us; he was sincerely loved and esteemed by every SA man and none of us ever believed that he of all the SA men could have gone against our Führer.

My comrade, Otto Schmidt, and many other SA officers who had been arrested came back two weeks later. All of them had been suspects, and they had only escaped being shot by the failure of the Stettin police to send them to Berlin the same evening. They were sent the next day and by the time they arrived at the Columbie House, where all the executions were carried out, the Führer had stopped the executions.

We never learned exactly what took place, as the suspected SA Führers never talked about it; neither did we learn exactly how many men were shot, but some of my comrades, who were better informed than I was, put the figure as high as several thousand.

The SA never really got over this terrible blow, and every member of the Führer's Brown Army was seized by a spirit of dejection. On 1 July all the old SA men who had received the dagger of honour from the Chief of Staff inscribed on one side 'All for Germany' and on the other 'In cordial comradeship – Ernst Roehm' handed them in, and later, when Roehm's inscription had been ground off, the daggers were handed back again.

Soon after we were forbidden to wear our SA uniform, but we still kept our old brown shirts and we older SA men still wore our chevron of honour on our arms. Some time later we were again allowed to wear our uniforms. But it wasn't the same. The old fighting spirit, the pride, the comradeship had gone. To us old fighters it looked as if we were nothing else but a shooting club; we couldn't see the purpose, and it seemed as if we were not wanted and of no use. The SS increased its membership many times over. Now it was the fashion to join the SS, it no longer had anything to do with the SA. The SS men were swaggering about in smart black breeches, polished jackboots, showy-looking jackets and army-type peak caps. No one seemed to care a hang for the simple brown shirt. The old fighters who had done the dirty work, before these young SS men had even entered the Hitler Youth, were forgotten and pushed into the background.

From now on, Himmler's SS and Gestapo forged ahead. Only the oath of allegiance which we had sworn to the Führer prevented me, and I am sure thousands of others, from leaving the SA. There now seemed very little reason for remaining. I found something useful to do when I was appointed a paid clerk at the labour exchange and at the same time honorary welfare officer for the Sturmbann. I had now become what was called in the SA a Staff Louse. But now that the Brown Army had lost its original purpose I much preferred this new social work. Every day fresh human problems had to be solved and my job gave me almost unlimited opportunities for furthering the national socialist ideals. As SA welfare officer I was also responsible for finding suitable employment for the men in the Sturmbann, and in my capacity as clerk in the labour exchange I was able to do this part very efficiently.

It had only been eighteen months since the Führer had taken control of all State affairs, and during this short period he had pulled Germany out of the most terrible economic crisis and achieved what the Weimar Republic had failed to do over a period of five years. Every month unemployment figures fell by hundreds of thousands, and some districts of the Reich had even been declared free of all unemployment. At my own labour exchange, the long queues had vanished, there were no more fights and shouting in the courtyard. In the office, my work had almost been reversed. Now our difficulty was to find men for the many jobs going, not as in the past, to find any old job for the thousands of men waiting. The Führer's genius had brought light and new life to millions of his people, and I put my whole heart and energy into the task of translating his laws and decrees into practice.

The four-year plan was brought in to nurse Germany back to economic health and increase her powers of production. The labour exchanges were entrusted with a number of new and important laws and had a lot more power. Labour had now to be directed in such a way that there was no unemployment amongst the older classes of workers; these classes were also to be placed in the best positions. The young men who had been replaced in their jobs by the older workers were to be directed to the poorer paid jobs as well as all those without work in the lower age groups. In this way, all labour was to be utilised. I felt that apart from the economic advantages this was a truly social law.

Very soon after this law was put into practice, we found that there were not enough jobs for the young men, and we had to direct them to the *Arbeitsdienst* [National Labour Service] and this counted as being employed. In practice this meant that there was now full employment, and young men were taken out of ordinary jobs and put in the Arbeitsdienst. This prepared the way for later on when the Arbeitsdienst was made compulsory for all young men and was followed by military service.

All this, of course, caused many cases of genuine hardship. I tried my very best, and became the expert in these matters for the whole office. I saw my duty in having good jobs for the older unemployed men and only directed the very young to the Arbeitsdienst, taking their private and family affairs into consideration. In this matter I came for the first, but not the last, time into collision with members of the Party in the office, whose one idea was to direct as many men as possible, quite apart from

their suitability, into the Arbeitsdienst. I considered this practice unworthy of followers of the Führer and I continued to fight as best I could; but I stood quite alone in
this and was especially hampered by my immediate superior, who did all he could to
make things difficult for me.

He was a short, tubby little man with a face like a red turnip. He was in an especially strong position, as he had the Golden Party Badge of Honour and was a
Gruppenführer, whereas I had had no advancement in the Party since I came to the
labour exchange, owing to my infrequent attendance at parades and social functions.
Only through the representations of my Sturmführer was I given the SA Sports Medal
and a teaching certificate in sports. For my promotion to the rank of Sturmführer
I still needed the Golden Sports Medal which could only be got by going several
weeks on a course at the SA Leader's Institute in Dresden. I decided against taking the
course, firstly because I was too busy at the labour exchange, secondly because I was
no use at sports, and thirdly because I had no real enthusiasm nowadays for this kind
of semi-military training which was not the real thing. I just did not think it served
any purpose. So my promotion to the rank of Sturmführer fell through as I was not
considered to have enough combat spirit.

At first I had not intended to stay with the labour exchange for very long, because
in my low-grade appointment I saw little opportunity of promotion, but since the
Roehm trouble, this now seemed to be a job worth doing, and I therefore changed
my mind and took evening classes to prepare for a higher-grade examination.

Eleven Party members, of both sexes, including my superior with the Golden Party
Badge of Honour, who just like myself had come into office only after the assump-
tion of power, were taking the same course. Some of those people had already stepped
into good jobs as the result of all non-Aryans being dismissed under paragraph four
of the Civil Service Legislation. This preparatory course had to be taken out of office
hours and required a great deal of hard work. This was too much of a sweat for many
of my colleagues, including my superior, and one by one they dropped out before the
date of the examination. They couldn't understand why I insisted on staying for it, for
they had suddenly decided that as Party members we were entitled to hold our positions without bothering about an examination run by a civilian body.

My argument was that the principle of the NSDAP from its earliest beginning had
always been against fiddling the good jobs for yourself and your friends just because
you were in the Party. I did not want to be a bad example about which one might
say that he did not practise what he preached. Whatever the others did, I made up
my mind to take the examination. They accused me of being a goody-goody and a
crawler. What was the use of being in the Party if I did not know how to make use of
it?. This gave rise to an unpleasant atmosphere between me and my colleagues. I was
not deterred, and went on preparing for the examination although I knew that many
of them would be higher-grade civil servants before me – and they were.

I could not brood much because great things were happening all the time and
I was happy to be able to be a part of them, in no matter how small a way.

The next big milestone for us all was the declaration of general conscription in

1935. This was a great step that could surely bring nothing but good from every point of view. It had always worried me that there were still young men hanging about the streets in the evening with nothing constructive to do with their spare time. Conscription meant a new and fuller life for them. They would be living all the time under the best possible conditions. It seemed to me that military service would be particularly good for the working classes, not for military reasons but from the point of view of education, and all classes, from the highest to the lowest, welcomed this decision of the Führer.

Once more we were a nation with a proud army, a nation which need no longer buckle under to the rest of the world, and other people could no longer dictate to us. The rest of the world had plenty of time to disarm if they really wanted to. The miserable army of 100,000 men that they had allowed us could not possibly make any difference to their decision as it was incapable of menacing anyone. As the democracies and Russia had not disarmed, they were still more than capable of menacing us. As our achievements grew, so was their jealousy and enmity likely to grow in proportion, and our achievements were growing by leaps and bounds. The four-year plan was going to make us self-supporting and independent of other countries; before long we would be producing all the raw material we needed. We were heading for the time when no lack of foreign exchange or economic fluctuations of the outside world would affect us. And how was the outside world going to take this? What would America do when we were producing all our own motor fuel? What would England and all the other rubber and cotton producing States do about our ersatz rubber and our cellulose wool? And what about our disregard of the gold standard? This was another smack in the eye for them. No one was going to be able to make any money out of us – as they did in the bad old days – so we were going to be pretty unpopular. It looked as if we were going to need our army as a precaution against our envious rivals. We also needed an air force, a navy and an armament industry, and these we began to develop with all our energy and enthusiasm. Now at last we stood on our feet and laughed at the Versailles Treaty, which had hung around our necks like a millstone for fourteen years. We could afford to march into the Rhineland and man our frontiers, and we could wash our hands of that silly and time-wasting institution, the League of Nations.

It was not long before our new weapons and young soldiers had their first taste of the real thing when they were sent to Spain. At first we could not quite see what it mattered to us if it was Franco or Negrin who ruled there, but we were very pleased to know that German arms showed themselves superior to those of France and Russia. When we heard of the frightful atrocities the Reds had committed we all felt great satisfaction that Germany should have helped Spain to regain her inner balance.

There was no doubt that every German at this time had a deep sense of pride and even deeper feeling of gratitude to the Führer; but everyone was a little worried about the reactions of the outside world. We wondered if Germany was going to be able to rise from her knees without stirring up a hornets' nest. But nothing happened, and Adolf Hitler, by reason of his superhuman intuition, had known it all the time.

I remember feeling deeply ashamed for my cowardice and my doubts. Some people were so astonished at the lack of opposition encountered that they firmly believed the Führer must have had a secret agreement with some of the outside powers. This was an endless topic of conversation in the office, at the Sturmlokal, in the pubs, wherever you went. Comrades would laugh and slap you on the back and say, 'Hitler was right again.'

All through the months that followed I worked harder than ever. The feeling that I was living and taking part in history spurred me on. The pinpricks and rivalries that went on around me at the office worried me less and less, for the routine of the labour exchange went like clockwork.

Instead of all the queues of men wanting work, now we had the employers almost fighting each other to get hold of men. In these circumstances, labour might easily have taken advantage of the boom and asked for bigger wages, but the *Sondertreuhänder der Arbeit* [Party-appointed representatives for the worker] saw to it that the fixed wage scales were kept to. Strikes were, of course, illegal. But this was necessary in the interest of industrial peace and the success of the Third Reich. It was, therefore, quite right, and the logical outcome of our policy which did bring prosperity for all.

At the end of 1936 I took my examination and got my promotion. This was a source of great satisfaction to me, as it widened the range of my activities and put me in a better position to see the great events which were taking place all around me.

We had in 1938 yet another proof of our Führer's infallible judgment, by his amazing knowledge of the feeling and tempers of those outside Germany as well as inside. When our Army marched into Austria there was little to indicate how it would be received. One could not help wondering if there would be bloodshed, but the Führer knew. Our troops were received with open arms, they were pelted with flowers: in fact the Anschluss was known as the 'Battle of Flowers'.

There was, of course, a great deal of speculation as to how Italy would take our march into Austria. There had never been much love lost between the Italians and ourselves; we had never trusted them since they turned their coats in the Great War, and we did not like the methods of Mussolini and his Party, who were known to be hostile to the workers. They were a nasty lot and unreliable, just like all southern races, but once more Adolf Hitler was right and Italy did nothing against our invasion; they even signed a pact with us later on. We still didn't like them any better.

The Anschluss marked the beginning of Adolf Hitler's Greater German Reich, and as the full realisation of what this meant began to dawn on us, we looked forward with ever-increasing pride and joy to the time when we should be one with all German-speaking people.

Our Führer had taught us that it was not enough to think of ourselves, the lucky ones inside Germany. If he could find time to think of our brothers in Czechoslovakia, in Poland, in South and North America and all over the world, so could we. The next wrong that needed righting was the position of the cruelly oppressed border population in the Sudetenland. This time the Führer had to decide the possible reactions of half-a-dozen different European countries, when he demanded the return of the

Sudetenland to its rightful place. This was his most difficult task to date; the Czechs were a hard, cunning and unyielding people and they had some powerful friends. We followed each move breathlessly as our Führer pitted his brains against the finest diplomats in Europe, and our excitement grew every day as prime ministers hopped about Europe like a lot of scalded cats. At last they realised that he had completely beaten them. The Munich agreement was another proof – not that we needed any more proofs – that our leader was unique amongst statesmen. Everyone had ranted and raved and shaken their fists at us, but again we had achieved our right without a shot being fired.

But now it did seem that tempers in the outside world were rising. Added to their jealousy of our success and strength they were all the time quarrelling and accusing amongst themselves. They blamed us for our success, but they blamed each other even more. Russia blamed France, France blamed Britain, Britain blamed Russia. It seemed that they just could not stand the sight of a really happy and united nation, working out its destiny. The outcry over the Sudetenland had hardly ceased when a new howl went up over our decision to put a stop to the petty squabbling amongst the Czechs, Slovaks and other national groups.

Placing Czechoslovakia under our protection, the automatic solving of her internal strife, was such an obviously sensible and logical step on the part of the Führer that only nations intent on picking a quarrel with us would have bothered to make an issue of it. At this time, Czechoslovakia was very much in need of protection, Poland, greedy as always, was trying to take advantage of her inner strife to steal some of the bordering country, but we got there first. Now the Poles, who had been getting increasingly cocky, took it out of their German minorities.

The treatment of these minorities in Poland had been causing anxiety for some time. There had been articles about it in the papers, and we knew that the Führer was biding his time, watching for a suitable moment when he could bring Danzig and the Corridor, with their German populations, back into the Reich where they belonged. But this was not going to be so easy. This was going to take even more skill, patience and tact than Munich, because things had now got to such a pitch, especially with the Poles, that the smallest move on our part was liable to be pounced on by the Poles and used as an excuse for our enemies to attack. For it was now quite obvious that we were surrounded by enemies, all of them arming as fast as they could.

It was a dangerous time, and we knew that war was in the air. We talked about it all the time at the office and in the Sturmlokal. But even the most confirmed pessimists agreed that whoever attacked us was going to get a rude shock and was not likely to go on attacking us for very long. In other words, there was not much to worry about. I based my view that there would be no war on what I had seen during my time at sea. I had never been much impressed by the Poles, Englishmen and Frenchmen whom I had seen on my travels and nothing that I heard about them since had altered my view. It was obvious that they were all jealous of us, and they were also jealous of each other in spite of the numerous pacts which pledged them all to sink or swim together if the balloon went up. It was just possible that the Poles with their strong military ideas might be stupid enough to start something, but England and France with their degenerate pacifist factions and perpetual internal strife were in no position to take action, and I was sure that they knew it themselves. Shouting was one thing, but making war on the finest war machine in the world was another.

However, the very fact that we were being threatened at all meant that we had to be ready. Rearmament was now absolutely number one priority at the labour exchange and, now that I had passed all my examinations and had a little more time, I devoted all my spare time to *Luftschutz* [ARP] work. There had been Luftschutz courses since 1935, but now this had obviously grown in importance in proportion to the external situation. I went on a four-week course to the *Luftschutz Hauptschule* [Central ARP School] and on my return became chief organiser at the labour exchange and of surrounding districts. It was a tough job, by far the most complicated I had ever tackled. I had to see that everybody, men, women and children, had their proper training, so that each one knew his appointed task, place and rank within the Reichluftschutzbund.

The organisation of the Luftschutzplan, as worked out by the authorities, was absolutely foolproof as long as everybody did his job. Nothing was going to be left to chance, and our enemies were not going to find any chinks in our armour.

This was very important. We had to show the world that we were ready for anything. There was no feeling of worry amongst us when we carried out our Luftschutz exercises. We didn't feel, or at least I certainly didn't, that outside influences had forced or frightened us into this. It was more like the exercises of a well-trained athlete. We were just showing what we could do.

During this time came the sudden announcement that we had signed a pact with Russia. Russia was so much our traditional enemy that the idea of this pact was like a blow between the eyes. My reaction was one of complete bewilderment. I had complete faith in the Führer, but whereas before I had always been able to understand, had always been pleased by the logic and rightness of his decisions, this last one baffled me completely. But I felt it my duty to reserve judgment. Some of my comrades, however, were more hasty, and there were outspoken arguments and talks that bordered on criticism. There were some things said which I should have felt called upon to report if I had not been so much in the dark as to the meaning of the pact. It was quite usual for the Führer to keep the world guessing; now he had us guessing too. We had to wait until 31 August 1939 for our answer when it was announced: 'It is now no longer the Poles alone who shoot. Since five fifteen this morning, we return their fire.'

Now that we knew we were at war we saw clearly just how clever our leader had been. We had only to look at the map. We stood behind him like one man, shoulder to shoulder, and ready for anything.

I regarded England's and France's interference and declaration of war as nothing else but a formality. There was no doubt that as soon as they realised the utter hopelessness of Polish resistance and the vast superiority of German arms they would begin to see that we had always been in the right and it was quite senseless to meddle in our private business. But of course we had to let these warmongers know that this was the last time that Germany would stand for any sort of foreign interference. It was only as a result of their guarantee of something that wasn't their business that the war had ever started. If Poland had been alone she would certainly have given in quietly.

Otherwise, we had no quarrel with France or England. Our West Wall was perfectly secure, and we never thought that we would have to invade these countries or fight them actively. When, after only four weeks, Poland was completely defeated and we offered peace to France and Britain, I was greatly disappointed they did not accept. Surely, any reason they might have had to pledge assistance to Poland didn't exist any more, as Poland didn't exist any more? But if they insisted, the Führer would be only too glad to oblige and teach them their lesson the hard way. Denmark and Norway learned their lesson all right, and only resisted very little. The Führer had been told that the British were plotting an invasion of these neutral territories, and had gone one better and got in first. When at last the Führer had finally assured himself that every possible chance of a peaceful settlement with Britain and France had been tried, he saw himself forced to order the attack.

Of course there was never the slightest doubt in our minds about the invincibility and superiority of German arms, but we were amazed at the lightning speed of the advance and the way we won battle after battle. When finally complete victory over France was announced in Stettin, we were all wild with joy. But the deepest and most moving feeling was the gratitude and love for the Führer. Every single one of us realised that he alone had changed our Fatherland from the deepest humiliation and raised it victoriously to never-dreamt-of greatness and power. Germany, through his genius, had at last won its rightful place in history. France, who had tried to stand in her way, had been totally defeated, and Britain received such a beating that she had retired from the European mainland, having dropped out of the battle.

There was indescribable rejoicing when our victorious armies returned. The whole of Stettin was a sea of flags; I had never been so happy in my life, nothing would now stand in the way of the most wonderful and glorious future. Everybody felt the same, now that victory had been gained and peace had come. I do not think there was a single person in our town who didn't share this happiness with me, and even the most convinced pessimists now knew that the Führer was the saviour of the Fatherland.

From now on, everything was going to go smoothly up and up. I was sure that we would now be able to satisfy all our demands peacefully, have our colonies returned, receive all the raw materials we needed and get a fair share of the world's export market. Of course Alsace-Lorraine was still an open question. But now, if the population wanted to return to the Reich, there was nothing to stand in their way, and no one was in a position to victimise them.

I and all my comrades were sure that there would soon be peace with Britain, and we never thought that we might have to fight and subdue that country. No danger could come from there, so we could choose our own time to settle things finally with them, or forget about them until they came to us suing for peace – as they certainly would have to sooner or later if they did not want to starve.

About this time pictures of Rudolf Hess were taken down from the Sturmlokal and everywhere else, and there were all sorts of rumours. Some said he had gone to England on a secret mission, and others that he had revolted against the Führer. In spite of what the papers said later, I couldn't believe he was a traitor. But Hess was hardly mentioned amongst us in the SA, although I was surprised that there was no special order forbidding discussion. Sooner or later we would get to know the real reason behind this going to Scotland, but everything was so wonderful and exciting now that there was no time to worry about things like that. We were on the brink of something so vast that no ordinary man could have foreseen it – something that the Führer with his genius and Godlike intuition had been working towards ever since he came to power. This was not just a new future for Germany or even Greater Germany; it was the future of Europe. Adolf Hitler's New Order. Every European country was going to be purged of inner strife and economic difficulties and fall into step with us and march with us shoulder to shoulder along the road to prosperity. This was our greatest moment.

There was one minor fly in the ointment, but this was rather a joke than anything else to us. The Italians were being a nuisance again. The moment the war was as good as over they had come rushing to join us, hoping for a share of the pickings. It had been quite easy for the Führer to discourage them from joining in as long as there was any fighting to be done, but now that victory had been won, Musso was determined to pinch as much as he could of our glory. We all considered his last-minute attack on the already beaten France a thoroughly mean and typically Italian trick. But what was really a pity about all this was the fact that we were now drawn into a war with Greece – a country that had never harmed us – and a war with Yugoslavia with whom we had recently made a pact of friendship. Without our help the Italians would have had the daylight beaten out of them by both the Greeks and the Yugs. Winning our own war was one thing, having to get the Italians out of their own mess was another. There were a lot of jokes going round at this time. One of the best was the Führer sitting at his desk deep in thought. Keitel enters the room ...

'My Führer.'

'Well,' says Adolf, 'what is it again?'

'My Führer, Italy has entered the war!'

'Send two divisions,' says the Führer. 'That should be enough to finish them.'

'No, my Führer,' says Keitel, 'not against us, but with us.'

'That's different,' says the Führer, 'send ten divisions.'

During the months that followed, the war was as good as over for most of the German people. Our armies were only out for occupation and mopping-up purposes. But we, in the North, were soon reminded that we still had to liquidate England, when they began bombing us again. We had a very nasty raid before the fall of France but now, since the British had withdrawn with their forces beaten and shattered, this bombing of towns and civilian habitations was nothing else but the last spiteful wriggle of a dying foe. Air-raid warnings became quite frequent, and there were some very unpleasant attacks.

The people in general were exceedingly scared and upset by these raids, especially as they came as a complete surprise. No one had imagined that England would go on bombing us after it was all over – and, anyway, our anti-aircraft protection around Stettin was said to be very strong. There was a good deal of discussion in the Sturmlokal about this. Some said that the Command was not properly informed, others that the gun crews drank too much. There was no question of the Luftwaffe being inferior to the enemy. But on the whole we decided that the reason was spies amongst the foreign workers, and now we had thousands and thousands of these going through the labour exchanges.

In the Luftschutzbund I found a great lack of team spirit now it had come to the real thing. I could not excuse this. They had first-class training and they all knew what to do, and they knew themselves to be on the winning side. There was every reason for them to behave in a proud and well-disciplined manner, and yet they frequently shirked their duties, put their own safety first and were so busy looking after their own homes that they had to be threatened very seriously before they would do their duties. This would have probably worried me even more if I hadn't been comforted by the thought that our enemies were getting much more back than they gave us. And Britain couldn't go on forever, nor could the air raids, I told myself. We must just grin and bear it; it wouldn't be long now.

Then, suddenly, we were at war with Russia. This was the last thing that anybody had expected. I didn't like it at all. It was not until we realised the Russians had been double-crossing us all the time that the reason for this new war became clear. It was the same old story of the Führer as usual being a jump ahead, his attack on Russia was simply getting in first. Churchill and Stalin had been busy behind our backs, and Russia was getting ready to attack our rear as soon as we started our big offensive against England. The Führer was wise to the dangers, and his decision to deal with his enemies one at a time was right, as our immediate and staggering success on the Eastern Front proved.

The first doubts that this might not be quite as easy a war as we had thought came with the sudden arrival of the Russian winter, when whispered rumours began to go round that all was not well.

There were tales of soldiers frozen to death in their thin summer uniform. Equipment that was useless and frozen solid. Murderous raids by Russian partisans behind our lines and differences of opinion between the Führer and his generals. These were the most serious rumours I had ever heard, and I was shocked to find so many people who believed them and passed them on. Rumour-mongering had always seemed to me one of the most low-down offences against the State, and I considered it my duty as a good citizen not only to turn a deaf ear to what I heard but also to report the offenders when I came across them.

Then in February Erwin came back and he told me the same. Both his feet were badly frostbitten and he said things were even worse than the rumours. Thousands of our comrades had been butchered and the transport had all broken down and they had lived on iron rations for days on end, and every night they had to huddle in a big circle or the Russian bandits crept up in the snow and cut their throats. When Erwin heard I had tried to join up he told me I was crazy. His one prayer was that he'd be crippled so that he wouldn't have to go back to the front.

Of course, this shouldn't have made any difference to my attitude to the rumour-mongers. But somehow I couldn't bring myself to report them any longer, although I felt very guilty about it. Apart from Erwin, I never listened to these stories and took care never to be drawn into discussions, but it was all very worrying.

The Army communiqués had always been very short and businesslike when they announced our victories. As winter went on they became longer and longer. They explained very carefully why we had to draw back to our inner lines of defence, and also why these lines had all the time to be shortened to make it harder for the Russians. When General Guderian and the others were chucked out everyone started arguing like mad and criticising. Then it was announced that the Führer himself had taken over the command of the whole German Army, and of course everyone was very relieved. There had been enough shilly-shallying. Now everything was going to be different.

Collections of clothes were made and were a tremendous success. We saw news-reels of the speed with which the clothes reached the front and were distributed there. It was wonderful to see the rallying effect all this had on the men and it cheered us to think that we were doing our bit to help things out there. This was a further proof that we were all in it together. It looked as if it was going to take longer than we had thought but, after all, victory was worth while waiting for.

In March 1942 I had another shot at joining up. I felt that as a member of the NSDAP it was only right that I should be in at the kill, now that we were advancing again and there was not so much time left. Third time lucky. I finally managed it and was sent to Denmark for my training. Our company was stationed at Esbjerg. Besides training, it was our duty to guard the airport against enemy paratroopers.

We were prepared for a landing, and had continual alarm exercises. The Danes were a sensible sort of people. Some of them were a bit cool but not really unpleasant. They knew we had a job to do and were prepared to put up with a bit of inconvenience. Now and again there was a bit of trouble, one of our sentries was beaten up and a gre-nade was thrown in one of our pubs, but these were probably only young hotheads.

From Esbjerg we were moved to a new sector on the coast where we were put to work to build fortifications. We put up beach obstacles and dug ourselves in on the downs. Here we sat waiting for an invasion which everybody knew couldn't come. Even if they tried, they wouldn't stand an earthly as the country behind us was bris-tling with our forces, especially with artillery. But during the winter we had plenty to do and little time to talk and, as the months went by, the old stories about the Russian winter began to crop up again. We were very glad we were in Denmark. Stalingrad was a bit worrying, but the Führer himself explained it all. The reverse of Stalingrad had a historical significance, and was only an apparent reverse because it would con-tribute to the achievement of final victory. Of course, to the ordinary soldiers it was a little hard to see just what the Führer meant, but we all knew that he knew what he was doing. After all, he had proved it often enough in the past.

I do not exactly remember when it was, but some time during the summer General Dittmar said that we had now passed to the defensive, which was rather depressing. We all wondered what the Führer had up his sleeve. I was sure he was playing for time and had his own reasons for prolonging the war. We knew very well that our scientists were not wasting their time either. For all we knew, the course of the war might be changed overnight with the introduction of a new weapon. It was quite possible that we had to shorten our lines of defence before such a weapon could be used. It was very likely that the Führer had got something like this in mind, without telling the generals, and that was why there were so many rumours about disagreements.

After this there were a lot of accidents to generals. First Todt had a fatal accident. Then Jeschonneck, General Chief of Staff of the Luftwaffe, shot himself and afterwards it was said he suffered from an incurable disease. Then we heard that Lutze, Chief of Staff of the SA, was dead, and then Noelders. These were worrying and caused a lot of argument. We began to wonder if the enemy might not, after all, try something, and perhaps we weren't sitting there for nothing, and we spent the spring adding to the fortifications. And, when the invasion did start in Northern France, we were more relieved that it hadn't happened to us than worried because it had happened at all. It certainly didn't depress us half as much as when I heard that the Russians had crossed the Polish frontier and that General Dietl had died in a plane crash. This meant that there was something very wrong on the Eastern Front.

How wrong was suddenly brought home to us all when the attempt on the Führer's life was announced on the wireless on 20 July. When the whole story of the revolt of so many high-ranking aristocratic officers was brought to light, a whole lot of things became clear. All our troubles there were due to sabotage by the old conservative and reactionary generals: one had only to look at the many names that were mentioned and one could recognise at a glance that they were the German Nationals, the big landowners from the East, the Prussian officer families and the reactionary aristocrats who had thrown in their lot with the Führer's National Socialist Party only when the going was good, and they were sure of plenty of promotion, glory and advantages. And now that the going was bad and their loyalty and honour were tested, they became weak and wanted to back out of it, leaving their Fatherland a hopeless prey to the ruthless enemy. It was just like the last war, when Germany was stabbed in the back, and these officers and reactionary aristocrats fled or retired to their estates, leaving the country undefended. Only when Adolf Hitler had paved the way and cleared the ruins they had left behind, had they come out of their retreats and reaped the reward. But this time they did not get away with it; each one of them was hunted down and paid the price of high treason.

After the first shock, and only after we could comprehend that any German could sink to such a depth of selfishness as to wish for the destruction of his own Fatherland and the death of the Führer to whom he had sworn holy allegiance, did we understand, how, with one stroke, the Führer had cleared his country of all inner strife and set the stage of history for Germany's final victorious battle. Now there was no one to undermine the Führer's plans. Himmler, the Chief of the Gestapo – one of his most trusted officers – was going to take charge of the whole Army and would not tolerate the slightest interference of regular Army officers, and it was the Führer followed by his loyal Party that would save Germany.

We all felt very optimistic about these last changes, the regular Army officers had been too arrogant for too long. They were only interested in their own comforts, and they were inefficient and snobbish. They received a wonderful shaking, and we enjoyed noticing it and felt pleased when the order came out that they had to use the Hitler salute to remind them all the time who was the real master in Germany.

But the revolt did me personally a bit of good. I was picked out to attend a course for reserve officers at Gnesen in the Warthegau. On the same course were many other reliable and well-tried SA men and Party members, and we were going to be trained as soon as possible to take the place of the many officers who were removed in the drastic and full-scale purge by the Führer and Himmler of all anti-Nazi elements in the Army which had been successfully completed by the beginning of August. I put all I had into this training.

On the front things were still going badly, but we realised that the damage done by those unreliable officers could not be wiped out from one day to another as the whole Army, from the top downwards, had been polluted with a poison. The Reds kept advancing, and had only been halted after they had reached East Prussia. The British and the Americans had broken out of Normandy and were advancing through Belgium, Holland and France towards our borders. We realised what an immense and almost superhuman effort the Führer and his loyal Party followers would need to stem the tide. But I believed that soon the new leadership and reorganisation would take effect, and with the use of our new wonder weapons the Führer would force a decision. There was a lot of talk about the wonder weapons. We learned that our scientists had developed entirely new types of planes with four to five times the present speed, and these were now ready waiting for the Führer to give the order to go into action. And the real 'wonder' weapons had shown during their trials that their power of destruction was so immense that anything we had developed before was a joke in comparison. That was why we were almost crazy with joy when we heard that the first secret weapon, the V1, was at last being used against Britain. There was panic in London, the town was in flames, and we saw again how the Führer had kept his word. It was now only a matter of his wonderful intuition when the final onslaught was going to take place to force the proud British on to their knees and make a vast desert out of their country.

Any fears we might have had when the final decision did not come immediately were soon dispelled when the news came through that the V2 had come into action as well as the V1. The range of this self-propelled bomb seemed to be so fantastic that it could be fired from the Fatherland itself and reach accurately every part of the British island. It was said that very soon the bombardment of America would start with an improved model. As usual, there were the grumblers and the fault-finders who made fun of our sincere and honest hopes, but the morale of the whole people was lifted tremendously. They knew that the effect of these weapons could not fail to turn the course of the war.

When the Führer decided not to speak for the first time since the birth of the Party on the anniversary of the Beer-cellar putsch on 8 November, I understood his motives. He did not want to face his people whilst the Fatherland was still suffering from the terrible shock it had received from the treachery which was directed against him, but for which he – as the leader of all Germans – felt himself responsible all the same. Only when this dark chapter of German history was completely wiped out would he face his people again. And then, suddenly, just before Christmas, the news we were all waiting for came at last. The German Armies in the West had gone over to the attack in the Ardennes, and within a few days broken right through the enemy lines, sweeping them away towards the sea. This was the happiest Christmas I had ever had; it was as if I had awoken from a nightmare. The Führer had at last given the word. He had bided his time, waited patiently, collected immense forces, thousands of planes and tanks, putting them up behind the lines, keeping them back in spite of danger and provocation, until he was certain that the moment for attack had come. Now, he was leading us to final victory. First the Americans and the British would be driven out of France and then, with the help of our victorious Western Armies, he would throw the Russians out of Europe. In our mess we drank our Christmas toast to success and victory and laughed as we had not laughed for years – all would turn out well in the end so long as we trusted and believed in the Führer. That was a Christmas I shall never forget.

Then our course was suddenly cut short, and we were bundled off to the front in East Prussia before they even had time to give us our commissions. I arrived there the day before the great Russian offensive. Everything seemed to be in rather a muddle. They told me that there were Finnish and Rumanian troops on either side of us, and when the Russians broke through next day and we found ourselves retreating in the direction of Koenigsberg, almost before we had fired one single shot, we knew that, as usual, the foreign troops guarding our flanks had given way.

After that, we stayed put a bit, just sitting in our holes in the ground, with nothing to do but listen to the announcements which came from the loudspeakers in the Russian lines – not that one believed what they said since they were enemy propaganda, but they helped to pass the time. Our organisation was in a muddle and provisions came up very rarely and it was very cold. There was no doubt that the chief reason for this was the incompetence of the officers, although there must have been a certain amount of sabotage going on as well. What caused a great deal of bad feeling was the fact that during large operations the officers all vanished behind the lines to take part in conferences, while the companies were left in charge of NCOs, and as things got more disorganised there was talk of clearing out. My company, the seventh, was different. We were still disciplined, and our Colonel saw to it that we stuck to our positions long after the others. It was said that this was because he was after the *Ritterkreuz* [the Knight's Cross of the Iron Cross, a high military decoration], but even he could do nothing against the general muddle and breakdown.

We never knew in those days whether food and supplies would turn up, but we had a bit of luck and came across a huge store near Eilau. There was every sort of luxury food here: sardines in oil, chocolates, champagne, liquor and every sort of comfort such as furs, linen, cigars and clothing. Most of the stores were marked as being from the last clothing and comforts collection at home, and there were even things here from the previous years. So much for the efficiency of those whose job it was to distribute comforts for the troops. One thing was certain, the Führer could not have known of this. We were very disgusted and helped ourselves to everything that we could carry away. The rest we left. We destroyed nothing as we retreated; guns, ammunition, petrol, everything was left behind. We had strict orders not to destroy anything, and this was a good sign as it meant that we were coming back. It was said that once we started advancing we would turn the Russians out of East Prussia in three days.

I was guarding a bridge with another comrade at Zinten when an attack started. I had only just got my helmet on when there was a tremendous roar and everything went black. When I came to I was in hospital in Berlin. I don't know how long I was there but the news still seemed to be rather vague, although the wireless said that Berlin was being attacked, but a relief army, under General von Wenk, was advancing towards the city. It said once that the Western Allies were combining with us against the Russians and that the Führer had some terrible wonder weapon at his disposal which he was only prepared to use when all else had failed, because of the frightful effect it would have.

One evening the matron came into the ward and called for silence. When everyone had settled down she announced in a quiet voice, almost in a whisper, that the Führer was dead. No one uttered a sound, we all stared at each other. It was like after a thunderstorm, all was suddenly hushed and still. No one said anything – there was nothing to say; it was the end, that was all, there was no use in going on fighting now, there was nothing to fight for now.

After I got better I worked very hard in the hospital as an orderly, and when all Nazis were told to register I didn't do anything about it. It was very hard work and there wasn't much food, but I didn't seem to care. The English and Americans were very kind and even the Russians seemed to be quite human, though a bit wild. They found out about me not registering later, and I was called in front of an Allied Court and was sentenced to five months' imprisonment. Now I am waiting until there is room for me to go, as all the prisons are full.

2

DR FRANZ WERTHEIM

I first met Dr Wertheim at one of the big Schmeling fights at the Sportspalast in Berlin when I was about fifteen. [Max Schmeling was heavyweight champion of the world 1930–32 and, blameless himself, became a propaganda tool for the Nazis – one which backfired in the rematch with Joe Louis in 1938 when Schmeling was destroyed in the first round.] He was a medical colleague and fellow boxing-fan of my uncle Ernst Levin, who usually took my brother Karl-Victor and me to the big fights.

Wertheim was a swarthy, stocky little man with beady eyes and bushy eyebrows. He talked too much and was too breezy and boisterous for my liking, but he got on well with my brother, who was four years older than I.

I think it must have been Karl-Victor who asked the doctor to Potsdam to watch the boxing in our private ring. Anyway, after that Wertheim came out quite often with Uncle Ernst. If he was anti-Semitic he certainly never showed it and although, as far as I remember, he made no bones about his association with the SA, it had no effect on his liking for Uncle Ernst – at least up to the time when I left in 1936.

Not that I saw very much of Wertheim after Karl-Victor left early in 1934, but I bumped into him occasionally in theatres and restaurants. He was never with the same girl twice, and it was obvious that he specialised in 'hot numbers'. He always greeted me heartily, wanted to know if I was keeping up my boxing and asked affectionately after Karl-Victor. Just before I left Germany in 1936, he attended my grandmother during her illness, and I remember Uncle Ernst comforting my mother by saying that if anyone could have saved Granny it was Franz Wertheim.

In 1947 I heard of him again from some American friends, two of whom were being treated by him for recurring boils, which had become known in Berlin as the 'American disease'. The local American doctors were, it seemed, altogether too slapdash and inexperienced to cope with this painful complaint, and Wertheim, thanks to some remarkable cures, was collecting new English-speaking patients every day.

When I called at his surgery near the Gedechniskirche to ask him to dinner, the atmosphere was so 'Harley Street' I could hardly believe that I was still in Berlin. There was nothing make-

shift here; everything was of the very best, from the quietly luxurious furnishings and glittering medical equipment to the two ravishing nurses – one blonde and one red-head.

Wertheim was as ebullient and self-confident as ever; he had even managed to retain his pre-war waistline. He accepted my invitations to drink and dine with great alacrity, but 1 think it was not so much for old times' sake as because I was a good listener. His reminiscences and opinions poured out of him in a never-ending stream. He was one of the happiest Germans I came across, due to his unshaken belief that he was still a jump ahead of everybody else.

Dr Franz Wertheim, born 1897

My first perceptions of this life were from a massive carved wood cradle standing in the garden of a rambling eighteenth-century house in the Black Forest. From the high gable windows one could see the Rhine winding far below in the deep valley, and in the distance the soft undulations of the Vosges. I remember little more of my birthplace; before I went to school my father had moved to the Bavarian town of Augsberg, where he took over a larger medical practice.

As father's time was mostly taken up with his work he had little time for me and my two younger sisters. On the whole he was nice, understanding and fairly generous. My mother, on the other hand, was inclined to be rather niggardly, both in affection and in practical things.

I went to a Benedictine School in Augsberg, where the standard of education was very high. From the first I was passionately interested in physics and chemistry but was always weak on languages. I never knew how I could get through matriculation, but fate took a hand in this.

I was seventeen and still in the Unterprima when the First World War broke out. As I wanted to volunteer I was pushed through a special emergency matriculation and just managed to pass. Then, having got father's signed permission and mother's bless-ing, I rushed headlong to the colours and the defence of the Fatherland.

I got my training with a Bavarian field-artillery regiment, after which I was first sent to Italy and then to France. It was an uneventful war for me. My first wild enthu-siasm soon abated and I was drafted from base to support and from support to base and hardly ever heard a shot fired in anger. My chief discomfort was that the distant rumbling of the guns gave me insomnia.

When the war ended I was in the region of Cambrai. I was dozing in the miserable flea-pit of a music hall when all the lights were switched on and the fat local com-mander appeared blinking and grinning on the stage like a tipsy primadonna. He managed to silence the ironic applause and told us that the war was over. We rushed back into the village shouting, and got disgustingly drunk, more as a matter of form than anything else.

It was, of course, a relief that the war was over, but we found it hard to realise that we had lost. In my view we could easily have won the war if the civilians at home had not stabbed the fighting men in the back. The flight of the Kaiser appalled us. We could neither understand nor approve of it. Now everything was over and lost. Our world had gone under and we could only very gradually orientate ourselves to the new reality.

When we were disbanded I was confronted with the difficult question of what to do next. I had already made up my mind that I would follow my father's profession, and I decided to go to Munich to study.

There was no money, for my parents were already dead and had left me precious little. I took the cheapest lodgings I could find and always fed in college on the inadequate fare provided for the more impecunious of us. One day a taximan suggested that I might work in my spare time, He took me along to his employer, who engaged me on night-shift. During the day I attended my lectures; what sleep I needed I took sitting in the taxi waiting for fares. I was paid little but did quite well in tips and my standard of life improved considerably.

At that time, February, 1919, the 'Spartakus' riots broke out in Germany. These were inspired by the militant communist organisations who overthrew the remnants of the Imperial Government in Bavaria and set up workers' councils. House fronts were plastered with innumerable posters and proclamations. One day I idly glanced over some posters and walked on. I had gone about twenty yards when two men grabbed me and dragged me to a police station. They accused me of having defaced the posters. Two policemen hustled me off to the town hall where I was thrown into the naval guardroom and beaten up before even being asked my name. Then I was taken to the officer on duty who, as luck would have it, was an old friend of my father. He gave me a surreptitious smile, and kept me quietly in a corner until the guard was changed, when he indicated that I could slip out safely.

I had thought little about politics up to now, but the treatment I had received at the hands of the communists gave me a decided inclination to the right wing. And, as a property owner – I possessed a large and very comfortable leather armchair – I could not approve of the communists' idea of common ownership. I thought now that I had better get out of Munich, and I also thought it was time I did something with my new political convictions. An anti-communist Free Corps under Ritter von Epp was being formed in Weilheim, and once again I flew to the colours and changed my civilian clothes for field grey.

But I soon had to change back again, for I was given a post in the espionage branch and sent back to Munich to gather information about the location of artillery and machine-gun posts likely to offer resistance. Dressed in shabby clothes and equipped with genuine communist passes I got through the chain of Red guards without difficulty. They were mostly a rabble of ex-soldiers who had lost their jobs after the war and were now ready to do anything.

I managed to get a room with some people I knew in Pestalozzistrasse and was able to get a great deal of valuable information. On 2 May I was woken up by fierce machine-gun fire. In the streets men with white arm badges were manning hastily constructed barricades. I rushed down to them and found that an anti-Red Citizens' Guard had occupied the Ministries of Justice and Transport and the Ring Hotel. But they were outnumbered a hundred to one and could not hold out long. A message had to be got through to the Free Corps Headquarters, and a gnarled old clockmaker called Butz was chosen by lot and set off immediately on his bicycle.

In the meantime the Whites held on to their positions against furious but thoroughly inaccurate rifle fire, which mostly killed neutral civilians and inquisitive children. Towards nightfall Butz returned with the news that the Free Corps had already started the assault on the city district of Pasing. I hurried off in that direction and on my way witnessed an unforgettable sight: a field-artillery battery, galloping through a street, had run into machine-gun fire and been killed to the last man. As soon as the last shot had died away men, women and children ran out of the houses with knives and began to saw off large chunks of horses' flesh from dead and dying animals alike.

In the city centre a bloody struggle was going on on the Stachus and the main-line railway station. Communists were heavily barricaded and were resisting fiercely. But a Free Corps armoured train had run up very near to the station and now bombarded the station buildings. With the help of mortars the last remaining resistance was overcome. The communists were crushed.

After the victory came the vengeance. Communists and their supporters were shot wholesale. On my return to Pasing I witnessed the shooting of 48 Russian prisoners-of-war in a gravel pit. They had joined the Red Army as volunteers and had been captured by the Free Corps Epp bearing arms. They spoke no German and were weeping and pointing to their wedding rings and making pantomime gestures for mercy. But a salvo from the machine guns silenced them. Justice in those days was rough and ready. Both sides, Red and White, were still drunk with war.

When, after a few weeks the town had been restored to order I thought of continuing my studies, and resigned from the Free Corps. I went back to the university and back to my taxi-cab, but at the same time kept up my political life by joining the 'Organisation E', a monarchist home-defence force, whose object was to safeguard Bavaria. We went on duty only once a week, for which we received fifteen marks. Every now and then we marched, but our main duties were drinking and singing.

Owing to the acquaintance which I had struck up with a bank employee, my private life now underwent a considerable change. This man used to exchange for me the pounds and dollars which foreigners sometimes paid me for their taxi fare. When the inflation started he opened my eyes to the financial possibilities, and I now turned my attention to foreign currencies. Within a short time I had amassed a 'fortune' of 65 dollars, which was then sufficient to buy several houses. I said goodbye to my taxi, moved into one of the houses and in 1922 I took my first medical exam.

At this time I joined the Stahlhelm – an association of ex-frontline soldiers whose object was to save Germany from the Red deluge which, already powerful in the Ruhr and central Germany, threatened to flood the whole country. In the local group of Leim I was received with open arms by my old battery commander Brandhuber who, after I had served on probation for eight weeks, put me in charge of training the *Jungstahlgruppe* [The youth organisation of the Stahlhelm]. We met every Thursday evening at the pub 'Zum wilden Bock' and studied military exercises in a relief model of the countryside in a sand box, and learnt how to deal with any situation that might arise in the forthcoming war against the Reds.

Before taking the state examination I transferred to Marburg University, for it had come to my knowledge that the examining professors there were all Stahlhelm men, and my academic studies had been so disrupted by politics that I was going to need political assistance to get me through my exams Of course, Marburg's medical school was a very celebrated one. Here the corps, student and sports association were still full of the thoughts of the good old days, which they hoped shortly to bring back. I took my state examination without trouble in 1925 and was well on the way to a distinguished academic career, which I helped by getting engaged to the daughter of my professor.

Unfortunately, I slipped up with a nurse in the university clinic, and was presented with a distressing ultimatum. I had to marry her rather hurriedly and, as I had by now exhausted my inflation fortune, we moved into a furnished room and I had to sell my watch to pay the first month's rent. Ilse earned our living by working as a private nurse, while I obtained considerable, though involuntary, experience in child welfare.

My private misfortunes also seemed to injure my reputation in Marburg Stahlhelm circles. Instead of completing my surgical training, I now had to spend all my time earning money. I scraped small and irregular pocket money by cramming, preparing students for their exams and assisting in a minor capacity in the operating theatre.

From time to time I found work as a locum in the country. One country doctor for whom I deputised for some time introduced me to the Nazi Party and pointed out that as an SA man I could soon obtain a salaried position. He gave me a copy of Hitler's *Mein Kampf* and explained to me the aspirations and ideas of his Party.

On comparison with the Stahlhelm this party impressed me with the resolute manner in which they faced the toughest internal and foreign problems. What had I to lose? Nothing! And what to gain? A decent job at least. Before I took my leave of my host I had become a Party member and medical officer in the SA.

In this capacity I found plenty of work to do, especially during the frequent election campaigns, for scalp wounds, broken arms and battered noses were only too frequent. A large number of the Marburg undergraduates belonged to the SA and took part in indoor battles.

In 1929 I had a considerable rest from these duties as I became a patient myself, having nearly become a corpse. I was in the middle of a private festivity when I was sent for urgently to treat two of our men who had been ambushed and beaten up by Reds. I said goodbye to Putzi and leapt into my car. My brain was not as clear as it might have been and I took a rather fast left-hand turn into the back of a twenty-ton lorry and trailer. I was thrown clean out of the driving seat, and landed head first on the pavement. I was badly concussed and was unconscious for five days. However, it's an ill wind, as I was to discover many years later.

My Marburg SA commander was transferred to Munich after one year, and so I was unexpectedly brought back to my first university town, where I also received my first fixed appointment.

I became medical officer to a SA Standarte [SA Company] for which my remuneration was 400 marks a month, besides free quarters and expenses allowances. My duties included attendance at all the large public gatherings, where I often heard the Führer of the Party, Adolf Hitler.

Anyone who heard him at that time must have found his arguments very convincing. I was highly impressed with his sweeping plan to attack the increasing unemployment in Germany and to re-establish Germany's military sovereignty. This was just the very plan for me, for I had known well enough what it meant to be unemployed. Every true German was thoroughly sick of seeing how all the small neighbouring nations, such as the Poles, Czechs, Letts, Estonians and Lithuanians were tearing out little chunks of German territory at will, ill treating and victimising the German inhabitants.

His speeches also gave me a new light on racial theory, about which I, as a doctor, had heard very little so far. This theory, which Hitler backed up with forceful quotations from Professor Gunther and other authorities, seemed to me perfectly convincing. If biology can give an exact proof of the law that in a mating of two racially different animals or plants the racially inferior characteristics become dominant, it did not seem too far-fetched to draw the same conclusion about the human species. And I had indeed come across cases of highly neurotic miscegenates in my work which bore out the theory.

Here I must mention a sore point in my life, which made my position in the SA difficult from the very beginning and continued to give trouble for quite a long time. Not only was my name Jewish-sounding, but by some freak – I had absolutely no Jewish blood in me – my appearance seemed slightly Jewish. This was a tremendous disadvantage in the Party. By upbringing and conviction I am actually an anti-Semite – mainly on 'aesthetic' grounds, for I am in favour of preserving racial purity and consider that as a race the Jews are inferior.

My Munich activities lasted only eight months, after which I followed my brigade commander to Berlin. There I soon made the acquaintance of the newly appointed Gauleiter Goebbels, who consulted me about an abscess on his leg. Owing to this connection a private clinic was set up for me out of Party funds in 1932.

The clinic, which was situated in Bleibtreustrasse, had 36 rooms, two operating theatres and an X-ray laboratory. My first surgical operations were of a cosmetic nature. SA men who had suffered injury in fighting at political meetings came to me to have their nose-bones straightened, to have ears stitched on and broken jaws set and teeth straightened. But the main department of the clinic, which later absorbed most of my interest, was concerned entirely with operations for embolism. I wished to become pre-eminent in this field and directed all my energies to this end, and finally did reach a position of worldwide authority. Every time a surgeon makes an incision there is always the danger of a clot getting into the bloodstream. At first it may circulate, but if it should enlarge it becomes an embolus. Should this embolus become lodged in the pulmonary artery between the heart and the lungs this artery is completely blocked up, with consequent danger to life. The bloodstream suddenly stops, the patient is unable to breathe and the heart stops beating before the surgeon has a chance of getting his knife to it.

I was one of the few men in the world who could undertake an operation to relieve this condition. This operation can only be successfully performed if two conditions obtain; the operating theatre must be controlled so that it has the same air pressure as the inside chest pressure of the patient; and the whole operation must be done with lightning speed by a team of assistants who have been thoroughly trained to work together. As soon as the embolism alarm-bell sounded through the whole clinic, everyone concerned with the operation rushed to his prearranged place. Oxygen tubes are already down the patient's windpipe to slow up his respiratory exertion. A quick glance to see that everyone is in place – anaesthetist, blood-transfusion, pressure regulator. Then I make an incision on the left side at the fourth rib; my assistant pulls back the skin on either side with retractors; I snip through with heavy bone forceps and completely remove the rib. The perioestrum is now exposed, and another incision reveals the dark red pericardium and the pulmonary artery. This is the most critical part of the operation. A swift longitudinal incision, and forceps grip and remove the embolus – sometimes as thick as a thumb; the embolus gone, the artery is sewn and the heart massaged till it resumes beating. Catgut sutures secure the perioestreum and the overlying skin. If the breathing is sluggish when the oxygen tube is removed, the patient has an injection of adrenalin and the operation is over.

My success in this sphere not only considerably increased the number of patients in my clinic, but I was frequently asked to be in attendance at operations where there was a danger of embolism.

Soon after my Party had come into power in 1933, Goebbels appointed me prison doctor to the Berlin Police HQ and medical officer of Brandenburg's concentration camps. These camps were springing up like mushrooms all over the place, to be filled with hundreds of opponents to the new regime. Of course, the prisoners had a very tough time herded together in crumbling castles and derelict farm buildings. None of them had had a trial and a large proportion were there simply as a result of personal vengeance by a Party member – but then what else can one expect just after a revolution!

'Investigations', taking the place of trials, were usually a brutal affair. The prisoner was called into a Gestapo office and punched fiercely in the face before knowing where he was, so that he would fall over the furniture. Then he was accused of damaging State property and given more kicks and punches. In some cases he was then thrown out of the window into the courtyard and later reported as 'killed whilst trying to escape' or he was carried out of the room, and thrown into a cell from which he was automatically dispatched to a concentration camp.

These practises were not to my taste, and I drafted a detailed memorandum with much documentary evidence, and addressed it to the Führer and Reich Chancellor. In it I asked that political prisoners should at least be put on the same footing as criminal prisoners.

It goes without saying that my memorandum never reached the Führer. But the consequence of this step was that I lost my position as chief medical officer for the concentration camps. Nevertheless, I still kept my position as prison doctor.

The scenes I had witnessed at Gestapo hearings drove me to seek advice of several of my colleagues. This showed me that many doctors by no means fully endorsed the ideas of the Third Reich. I remember in particular the indignation of our first *Reichärzteführer* [Leader of Reich Doctors], Dr Wagner, who expressed himself in very clear terms. Soon after he was taken ill with a curiously vague 'disease of the kidneys', and died. Amongst the initiated it was said that 'Reichsheini' Himmler had had a hand in it.

This was a warning to all of us and though I am certain that in their hearts most of the medical profession disapproved, they now openly condoned the 'methods of the State'. No one risked discussing the subject in the presence of more than one other person. When there were only two of us together one could be more outspoken; there were no witnesses and should the necessity arise there was no harm in denying or even accusing the informer.

My prison work was interesting but scarcely medical. In every pocket I carried several packets of cigarettes and handed out anything up to ten cigarettes, according to the impression the prisoner made on me. This was really all that I was able to do for them. I soon found out that medical instructions were completely ignored by the prison authorities. To complain about such malpractices was not only useless but might even have prejudiced my own position. The responsible authorities had only one reply: 'Whatever we do or omit doing is done in the interest of the State.' I have had written orders prohibiting all medical attention to certain prisoners. The more that died, the less trouble they were.

It is my firm conviction that Hitler knew nothing about these methods. But it must be admitted in justice that we were in the midst of a thorough-going revolution and 'you can't plane wood without dropping shavings'.

Some of these shavings could be compared with the many Jewish doctors who lost their means of livelihood and were no doubt a heavy loss to German medicine. But at least the Aryan doctors would now have not only twice the work but also twice the income. I had long recognised that the ability of Jewish doctors to enter everywhere into the best positions was chiefly due to the extensive connections they upheld with the press, intelligentsia and government offices during the period of the Weimar Republic. It was outrageous that despite their small percentage in the population the Jews should have occupied so many and such leading positions in the medical profession. The time had come for Aryan doctors to show that without unfair advantages they would be as good if not better doctors.

The Nazis' intransigent methods were now beginning to bring their benefits in external affairs, and in 1938 Austria was incorporated in the Third Reich. In my opinion this should have happened in 1866. At any rate our Führer had brought off in a few months what Bismarck had never been able to do. Britain's protest made little impression on us, for she was quite unable to make war. France would not make war, since the Führer had tactfully renounced his claim to the old German territory of Alsace-Lorraine.

I was now, together with a considerable portion of my SA comrades, drafted into the Wehrmacht. I was made chief medical officer of the first battalion of the 114th Infantry Regiment, and in this capacity witnessed the victorious march into the Sudetenland. It was a great disappointment to me to see that the Führer contented himself with those small border territories instead of swallowing the whole fat lump of Czechoslovakia at once, as he could have done. But during the Munich negotiations I saw that the Führer's strategy had been right. We were now in possession of the Skoda arms works, and the other powers, including Britain, were now in a weaker position tactically as well as diplomatically.

When the war broke out my only regret was that the Führer had waited so long. As a nation we were grossly overcrowded and had to have room to expand and grow. A year earlier our military prospects had been much brighter, because the other nations were not then prepared. France, Britain and Russia had now had a year to re-arm.

After the victorious conclusion of the Polish campaign I went to the surgical section of a military hospital in Krakow with the rank of surgeon-major. Here I saw for the first time how the racially inferior Poles lived in both town and countryside.

During a cross-country journey to a field hospital some shots were heard near a village. No one knew whence and why, but at once several hundred SS men surrounded the village and shouted to me that Polish snipers were hiding there. Every house was broken open and all the Polish men were driven into the church, which was set on fire with its human contents and completely burnt.

I was shocked and appalled by this summary justice. I felt that there should have been at least an investigation into the origin of these shots, which might just as well have come from our side. The method of the SS ran counter to my whole conception of justice. But I had learnt well enough not to burn my fingers when the SS or Gestapo were stewing a broth.

After about six months' service in Poland I returned to Berlin, but shortly before the offensive in the West I was posted to a small village near the West Wall. There were more doctors than patients, and so we spent the days playing cards.

Our work began with the invasion of Holland. Every day trains carrying casualties passed through our village. Heavy cases remained in our hospital; lighter casualties were at once bandaged and sent on. Eight days after the capitulation of France I crossed the Rhine in a rubber dinghy and was very disappointed not to be given the Iron Cross like most of my colleagues.

Then followed a very pleasant period in the well-furnished Rueil hospital near Paris. This was quite another show after lice-infested Poland. Nothing like the song from the operetta we used to sing in Krakow.

The Pretty Polish doxy
You have to bed by proxy.

Which was quite as near as any of us wanted to bed her. She was far too dirty and unhygienic. But here we discovered our appetite again. The French girls were delightful companions: highly developed for pleasure, though utterly spoilt for child-bearing. And although their depravities elicited my professional disapproval, my personal interest in them was more than aroused.

There were actually plenty of nurses and Wehrmacht girls in Paris but we were not so keen on them here; they somehow did not fit into the Parisian atmosphere. This was rather tough on them because it deprived them of their foremost reason for joining the Army. Furthermore, they found it exceedingly risky to go out without military escort into any of the remoter streets or districts. Some of them were fished out of the Seine or had their hair shorn; the French had no scruples in waging war against defenceless people.

This, of course, resulted in reprisals, and hostages were removed for shooting from a prison to which my duties occasionally took me. At first I was against this harsh policy, but when I learned that the men who were selected had been caught stealing Wehrmacht stores or using arms in guerrilla warfare, I agreed that as proven criminals they were fit for the gallows; without stern measures there was no hope of keeping order.

Later I was transferred to the little resort of St Jean de Luz in the south of France. Our advance in North Africa was going very well and every day I expected to be transferred to Rommel's Afrika Korps. Our period of waiting was dull and boring. To amuse ourselves we experimented with a little private pharmacology. We began in the morning with a tumbler of cognac and two injections of morphine. Midday we found cocaine useful and at night we usually finished off with hyoscine. Our interests were not entirely scientific, and we had to watch each other carefully for symptoms of addiction.

Twice weekly we went to Biarritz where, after one particularly gay evening, I woke up in the arms of a KDF [*Kraft Durch Freude*: Strength through Joy Organisation] actress to discover for the first time a woman who attracted me more in the morning than the night before. I arrested my habitual escape to the bathroom, asked her name and proposed to her. Gretel was her name. Six months later I was divorced from Ilse, and the next day I married Gretel.

But in the meantime the Führer had crossed the Russian border; I went east, and not to Africa. This clash between National Socialism and Communism was inevitably necessary and right. The Führer, with his usual genius, had foreseen the menace from the east and now met it in good time.

Before leaving for the new theatre of war I applied for several months' leave on professional grounds. I spent my afternoons in the clinic and my mornings with Gretel. Berlin was having its first air raids, which, at the beginning, made no very strong impression upon me; but there was a very wide indignation amongst the people. The papers said rightly that these were raids on an open city and a defenceless population, while our own raids on Britain were confined to fortified places and military objectives.

I watched the first bomber raids with perfect calm from the balcony of my flat, really rather enjoying the free fireworks display. But when heavy bombs devastated a block of houses near us I concurred with my wife's dictum that caution was the better part of valour, and thereafter went to the shelter with her as soon as the sirens went. My colleague Dr Wiesel, a fittingly named eye specialist, who not only looked like a weasel but was always first in the shelter, reserved seats for us on a bench in a safe corner between two buttresses. Here I listened quietly to the voice of the people. Air-raid shelters were the places where many rumours, secret information and whispered jokes were originated and disseminated. It was said that a man who came in saying 'Good morning' had slept already, if he said 'Good evening' he had not yet slept and if he said 'Heil Hitler' he was still asleep. This and many other jokes and stories I carefully remembered. To have a good Nazi joke in one's repertoire was the thing in SA as well as medical circles.

The weasel always wrinkled a terrified nose and put his finger warningly to his mouth when I told him the latest about 'Tinsel' Hermann or little 'Clubfoot' Josef. He was like a weasel on hot bricks when I told Gretel how the film actor Gerhardt Jolie had found 'clubfoot' in bed with his wife and had slapped his face. I comforted my colleague with the remark that the SA and other reliable Party members were entitled to exchange ironical comments at this great time, a concession which could not, however, be safely granted to ordinary citizens.

Characteristically enough, these subversive jokes hardly ever touched the Führer's person. He seemed to hover remotely above the clouds of irony and mockery. But Goering and Goebbels were fair and frequent game. Goering was said to be an eager collector of all stories about himself and had offered his valet 50 marks for each new one. Most of these originated in SA circles; for this body, to which I was still loyally attached, felt increasingly slighted and offended by the growing importance of the SS.

At first life was dull in Russia as we moved steadily forward through barren devastation with villages, fields and even woods ruthlessly burnt by the retreating moujiks. There was little sign of life; only the distant firing of the two armies as one advanced and the other retreated.

But then the winter came upon us and they advanced and we retreated. The cold was unbelievable. The guards outside our hospital had to be changed every quarter of an hour. Almost every injury proved fatal after the frost had got it. The SS poured water over Russians or Jews and placed them at road junctions, their arms stretched out like signposts; frozen solid they relieved, it was said, the timber shortage. I don't know if these prisoners were murdered in this way, but I suspected the worst since it seems to me almost impossible to get limbs into these positions after death.

In contrast to our leisurely life in French hospitals we now had to work like blazes, being on duty day and night and taxing our strength to the uttermost. Long trains of ambulance and Red Cross cars rolled past full of wounded and sick. The greater part of them suffered from frostbite. The noses, cheeks, ears and hands of these poor fellows had frozen and their pain was ghastly. Diagnosis and prescription were words from the past. We worked to an automatic routine. The bodies rolled in one side of

the operating theatre for ten CCs morphine intravenous injection, twenty minutes'
wait, sounding and amputation. Overtired, I thought mistily of a gigantic modern
slaughter house where sheep on a steady conveyor belt received the stunning blow,
the severed jugular, the skinning of the pelt, changing from live sheep to dead mutton
in a never-ending stream. Most of our cases too became dead mutton, which was a
sad waste of morphine. Bodies were heaped up in the backyard of the hospital, as the
frozen ground made it impossible to bury them. Then our supplies of medicine, dressing and food were running short and much of our urgent needs had to be dropped
by plane.

The removal of patients fit for transport gave us a major headache. All that had
remained of our car pool were three lorries, for in all the other cars the radiators had
frozen. Moreover the roads which in the autumn had turned to craggy formations of
clay under our tyres had now frozen into iron barriers. I cannot understand how our
lorry drivers managed time and again to get through to the railway station.

From time to time our grim routine was interrupted by alarm shots fired by our
patrols outside the village. Rubber gloves were peeled off and we changed scalpels for
rifles, and took up our position behind the barricaded windows. The Russian partisans did not treat our garrisons with kid gloves, nor was our Red Cross a safeguard
against these barbarians.

End of December we were given the long-awaited order to evacuate and retreat,
and before we had been able to arrange the transport of even a small number of
patients the first disorganised crowds of frontline troops were rushing headlong
through our village.

This was more than a retreat: it was a regular flight without any leadership, without
a chance of stemming the withdrawal at any point. The soldiers, wrapped in blankets,
oilskins, sacks and straw, had thrown away their arms, long frozen into uselessness.

We had no alternative but to leave everything and run for our lives. Whoever could
walk or crawl squeezed into one of the two lorries still remaining and then we went
bumping cross-country in the bitter east wind. We pressed close together for protection – there was no warmth. I had put two bottles of cognac into my overcoat pockets
and every now and then took a good draught; but the stuff filtered through my throat
like water, neither warming nor stimulating.

After eighteen hours our lorry landed comparatively safely in Pinsk, where we
slowly thawed in the sheltered 22nd military hospital. Our second lorry was never
seen again. Fortunately I could stay on in the Pinsk hospital which was desperately
short of surgeons.

Some of my colleagues were worried by the panic and lack of courage of our
troops during the retreat. They wondered whether the German soldiers had been
over-praised. But I was sure that the retreat was due to no weakness in our troops. It
was simply that the inhuman cold had been too much for them. I was sure that in the
spring the tables would be turned again. A few hundred miles signified little in this
vast country; and if cold and frost caused us casualties they could have done no less to
the other side. The only advantage the enemy had was his short lines of supply, which

enabled him to move men and materials quickly to the front, and, most of all, that he had been prepared for a Russian winter and we had not.

As soon as spring came, thawing the frozen roads, my expectations were fulfilled. With a powerful thrust the newly gathered troops threw themselves on the enemy and pressed him far back in mighty battles. Now endless trains of prisoners began to pass our hospital again, and the majority of our patients now came from the other side.

And unbelievably primitive people they were who now came under my knife! We had to economise in the use of anaesthetics which we saved for our own troops. But these near-animal creatures dumbly submitted to our operations without speaking and almost without wincing. I felt more like a vet than a doctor, and the primitive conditions under which I worked as we followed our advancing troops seemed less incongruous than they would if I had been working on ordinary civilised and sensate beings.

In July 1942, I was placed in charge of the surgery of the military hospital in Odessa. This port was rather more civilised than the open country. Many of the inhabitants spoke French and some of them English, and I could make myself understood. Most of the inhabitants had remained in the town, thus saving their homes and property and enabling a peaceful existence to be quickly resumed. I made contact with a fine-looking schoolteacher called Olga. She lived with three other girls who were almost frightening in their respectability. But Olga was different. She was wonderfully built and enveloped me with the warmth of her charms during the chill Odessa nights.

With the coming of autumn and winter our victorious progress once again came to an end. But the large objectives of the summer offensive were either attained or, at any rate, within our immediate grasp. The Caucasus had been occupied and the capture of Stalingrad, where the final mopping-up was in progress, would crown the offensive of that year.

Then, like a stunning blow, came the news that the entire 6th Army had been sur-rounded near Stalingrad and, after heroic resistance, had been annihilated. I began seriously to wonder about the possible outcome of the war. Odessa no longer seemed the right place for witnessing a second winter's retreat. I sent my batman to Berlin to get the case history of my car accident and, when it came, studied it with great attention. This accident suggested to me the reconstruction of an illness which even first-rate doctors in possession of all the facts can diagnose only with great difficulty. At any rate I was clearly suffering from the early stages of locomotor ataxia. It was made a little clearer by a discreet diet of barbitol tablets.

In view of my fully documented medical history I was declared unfit for service and discharged with expressions of deep regret that I should not be able to be with the vanguard of our troops when the hour of final victory came. I received the red discharge card and was sent back home. I took with me several cans of Ukrainian poppy oil, a few parcels of butter and a very clear notion about Russia and the war in general.

A few days after my arrival Tommy dropped a few tons of explosives on my house which sent the clinic with its valuable installations and 36 patients to hell. But a benign providence ordained that I should have spent the night with one of Ilse's girlfriends with whom I had formed a rather more than platonic attachment. Gretel had been evacuated in Breslau, the Reich funkhole, a few months before my arrival.

As I was now homeless I moved to the place of a former student, whose defeatism had made an unpleasant impression on me ever since the beginning of the war. Now he very kindly offered me shelter as one doctor to another. He was quite sure that we were going to lose the war and I was now rather inclined to share his opinion. I began to make preparations for the kind of victory that I now suspected was coming.

With this end in view I let my mind range carefully over the many quiet resorts in the remote uplands of Bavaria where I had spent my youth. In the end my choice fell on Woerishofen Spa where I removed forthwith for treatment and refuge. I joined there a charming and extensive circle of fellow sufferers who had also retired from the fray.

The food was good, the air exhilarating, the local girls were willing and the flesh was weak. I was back in my own bed by 4.30am, when a lusty peasant girl walked in with a bucket of cold water and a sponge and gave me an invigorating and reju-venating bath. She was a sprightly girl and sometimes left me more tired than she found me. Then back to sleep again until a merry trumpet blast called us out into the garden for our daily dozen. After an enormous breakfast we spent the remainder of the morning with more respectable water cures. The afternoons and evenings we carefully exhausted ourselves to be ready for the next day's cure.

Most of my companions were experienced staff officers or high-ranking officials who had been canny enough to leave off drinking vodka in good time and to make their way by arduous and various routes to this haven. A common feature was that in spite of most careful treatment they never seemed to get better in Woerishofen, and on the contrary grew worse month by month.

Of course none of them had been so raw as to try to regain the blessed soil of the Fatherland by an obvious act of self mutilation, as so many of the common soldiers had done. Something better than that was required; and so far as my trained eye could judge most of them were quite able to meet this requirement. Occasionally, of course, someone tried to be too clever and overdid things and soon aroused the suspicions of the medical board, politely known by us as the 'murder commission'.

My table-fellow, Buchholz, was one who suffered in this way. He started with a nice honest sciatica. But he lost faith in this and over and above it contracted diabetes by means of sugar injections. And although people were beginning to whisper about him, he ate large amounts of mepacrin until he was as yellow as a Chinese. Jaundice on top of the others did for him. Buchholz had forgotten that although mepacrin colours the skin yellow it leaves the whites of the eyes unaffected, and the examining staff doctor was unkind enough to point this out. He accused him roundly of malin-gering and gave him the choice of shooting himself here or getting shot in the front line. Buchholz made a lightning recovery and was back in action in three days. This was an object lesson to me and I gave up toying with the idea of an auxiliary migraine and rested quietly on my laurels and my locomotor ataxia.

A large part of the patients were medical men who were, of course, in the best position to perpetuate their stay. But everyone was rigidly discreet and to this day

I cannot tell which of my fellow shelterers in Woerishofen was genuinely ill and which was malingering.

I tried to avoid all mention of my own case. I didn't want to start an epidemic of ataxia. Because of the rareness of my disease I was a special case offering little cause for suspicion. I was determined to hold out till the bitter end and to that purpose I made friends with the doctors on duty by offering to assist them in their work.

These doctors were not so well off either. Any day the dreaded order calling them up for military duty might take them away from their comfortable jobs here. Hence it was necessary for them to prove their indispensability where they were by throwing an occasional passenger to the wolves, or rather back to service. I gave them a helping hand in this task.

It gave me particular satisfaction to catch out some narrow-minded, inveterate Nazi who had gone off the straight and narrow path. Of course it was not easy to push off some of these fellows who were sticking like limpets to their stories and the easy life; many of them had the highest connections, and so our medical findings had to be absolutely sure.

My first victim was SA Brigadier Passarge. Short and fat, with a bull's neck and an alcoholic face, he was too much of a bore with his incessant patriotic speeches. He would like to have been fit enough to engage each enemy soldier in single combat. With grim zeal he advocated the shooting of all parachuted enemy aviators. If we objected that a Tommy who jumps out of a damaged plane and lands in full uniform can neither be regarded as a spy nor a partisan, and had the same rights as every fighting man, he replied that they were mad dogs attacking defenceless women and children and like mad dogs they must be destroyed. Coventry was an exploit of his heart's content.

'That was our rightful revenge,' he shouted, with an ecstatic face, hitting the breakfast table with his fist.

'Revenge,' I said, 'for what?'

He thrust his purple nose into my face.

'You are a defeatist. You ought to be hanged!'

I now knew where we stood and marked him down as Number 1 on my list of deportees. In my view Passarge was one of the few men here who were really ill. He was suffering from some form of heart disease which he had either developed through drink or had acquired in some other way while serving the Führer. I gradually managed to bias the senior medical officer of the 'murder commission' against him. 'It was a shame that men like this brigadier were idling here instead of leading their troops into action on behalf of the Führer. His heart disease could not be of such a serious nature if he could stand such a strenuous course of drinking and whoring.' At the next examination the little fat drunkard was declared 'fit for garrison duties', which meant that he went straight into the front line. When I said goodbye I congratulated him on his recovery and his great good fortune in being able to serve the Führer more actively at last. But all the fight had gone out of him now and he merely grunted and patted me on the shoulder.

While fighting went on in the cauldron of Caen, the home front was tightened with an unprecedented rigour. One of the patients, a very decent fellow called Probst, ran by chance into an old girlfriend on the station. Of course the conversation soon turned to the war, and Probst said that he wasn't sure it could still be won. A few hours later he was arrested as he was having dinner with us, and taken away. Three days later he was dead. Executed for demoralising the war machine.

This depressed every one of us. We had known Probst as a good and upright German and wished that the wretched female who betrayed him had been executed herself. I took his fate as a last and unmistakable warning. Until then I had eagerly taken part in all discussions and had freely expressed my opinion. Now I imposed a rigid censorship on myself. Whenever armchair strategists prognosticated the course the fighting would take, whether the Western Wall would hold out, or whether the Volkssturm would come up to expectations, I either nodded seriously or shook my head with a thoughtful mien, as was required, without adding a word to the conversation.

Shortly before Christmas I got a wire from my wife saying she had escaped from Breslau just before the Russian onslaught and was staying in Berlin for the time being with friends. I was beginning to be bored by the spa life and had been locking my door against the early morning bath woman with her dreadful sponge. I had a strange desire to see Gretel again and so organised myself an official post in Berlin. But by the time I reached the capital the situation was looking serious. Berliners were living underground, leaving their cellars only for the most urgent purposes. After my first pleasure at seeing Gretel again I began to long for Woerishofen. But there was no going back, and, living a subterranean life, we came through the bombardment, the street-fighting and, in the end, the capture of the city by the Russians.

When the popping of guns had ceased for some time and nothing stirred outside I cautiously put my head out of the cellar door. I saw ruins, rubble and dust, and no living soul. Then I ventured a little farther into the street, where I met an old lady who had lived in our house. She told me in a bashful but rather pleased whisper that she had already been raped twice.

Shortly afterwards I came across different cases. Girls of eleven or twelve were brought in with torn ligaments and punctured bowels who quickly bled to death under my fingers. A woman was brought who had been shot through the temples for having cried while she was being raped. One man had a bullet in his head because he had not produced a watch quickly enough. They carried in another with compound and impacted fractures of both thighs. Russian soldiers had thrown him out of his third-floor window because he had tried to keep them from his wife.

The good old Dr Wiesel, who had been put in the Volkssturm and had run away after half a day, was back home and had Russians billeted on him for several weeks. He told me they washed their faces in his chamber pot and emptied their bowels in his bath tub. But this was a very welcome improvement on the first days, when they relieved themselves wherever they happened to be. This was not done out of malice, or spite, but simply because they knew no better and had obviously never been housetrained.

When the first Russian battalion marched through I simply had to hold my breath. These were athletic types with prize-fighter shoulders who marched at a very fast, springy pace. The latter arrivals were less prepossessing, but all had a tremendous vitality. They still have the elemental strength of a half-savage people, an immunity against the horrors of war which leaves civilised races far behind. If necessary they will subsist on their shoe leather. All they need is a kick in the behind, two onions a day, and off they will go wherever they are told.

The barbarian invasion improved only when, after several weeks, the Western allies moved into the city. With all other available doctors I was summoned to the town hall and, being homeless, I was given the deserted flat of a Nazi who had fled. I procured surgical instruments from hospitals and recovered some from the ruins of destroyed laboratories, while others were brought by my patients.

Now came the warm months of June and July. Berlin was without drainage, light, water or gas. Refuse of all kinds as well as human excrement was dumped in the streets or amongst the ruins. The stench was appalling. Wherever one stood or moved one was escorted by hundreds of bluebottles. The danger of deadly epidemics was imminent, and preventive action was more or less impossible.

My consulting hours brought a throng of patients, many more than I could ever deal with in a day. Many of them had venereal disease and in view of the lack of all medical supplies I could only advise them to clear out to the west, for nothing could be done for them here. There was an uninterrupted flow of women pregnant by Russians who wanted to get rid of this shameful result of their violation. Abortion had been strictly forbidden, but these were different and I aborted them in nearly every case. In any case, there was absolutely no baby food. Babies born in those days could only perish. It was by no means exceptional to see two or three babies die in the arms of their enfeebled mothers while they were waiting in the queue outside my consulting room. There had been no milk for months and little enough food for adults.

There was an inexpressible feeling of relief when we saw the first Tommy in our streets. Fortunately my flat was in the newly created British sector. At least one could now cross the street in daylight without fear. As long as the Red Army was stationed here it was best to remain within one's four walls to prevent being snatched away to disappear forever in the Russian steppes. Several of my colleagues were taken from their homes and have never been heard of since.

After nightfall it still remained very risky to step out of one's house, for well-organised gangs plundered and stripped any unwary pedestrians. Naked and partially clad persons at police stations were a common feature of Berlin's night life.

The Western powers now sent medical supplies to the city, not before time. The typhus syringe never cooled in my hands. Two girl assistants did nothing but open ampoules and refill the syringe for eighteen to twenty hours every day.

The food situation continued to be critical. Though we were given food cards with a ridiculously small allocation we could never be sure that they would be honoured. The black market alone saved most of the citizens from starvation, and so we should not be too indignant about the profiteers today. True, they took our last money and valuables, but they brought food into the city under great personal risks.

One day one of my assistants brought in two Russians to see me during consulting hours. They were wearing the smart uniforms of the Stalin Cossacks. She had been unable to cope with them outside, since neither of them spoke a word of German. They had asked their way equipped with a piece of paper that bore my name and the words 'clap' and 'penicillin' underneath. One of them had a large parcel in his arm, which he proceeded to unpack, disclosing a magnificent display of ham, butter, flour, cigarettes, besides two large black Russian loaves. I was unable to resist such a temptation. I asked the two strangers to take a seat, ran across to a chemist I knew and returned with a box of penicillin ampoules which he had unlocked from his safe. The Russians now got their injections, but this did not help them to get better, for after the second injection one of them had to be taken to hospital with severe symptoms of paralysis, while the other was only just able to drag himself to his commanding officer.

I was apprised of this surprising result when a gang of Russians carrying machine pistols instead of food parcels appeared at my door and dragged me to a Russian military station. The penicillin had been phoney. Luckily for me neither of them died of the injections, and after I had been able to explain how I got the penicillin the Russian commandantura handed me over to British military police who committed me for trial in Spandau prison.

Here at any rate I could receive *Sprecherlaubnis* [permission to speak and make request] and got decent treatment. But I got little comfort from the fact that penicillin offences were punishable with several years in prison. My only chance of escape was to betray the name and address of my supplier. The Russians had, strangely enough, left him in peace, but he soon occupied a cell next to mine. Having turned King's evidence, I received sentence of only four months' imprisonment and was put on probation for 'ignoring a military government order'. During the trial my former membership of the Nazi Party came to light and now I had to submit to denazification, a ridiculous business.

The first thing was to establish whether I had been implicated in Party offences of a criminal character. As this was not the case and as, moreover, several political prisoners came forward voluntarily to give evidence about my medical work at police headquarters, the commission was already swayed in my favour. And good old Dr Wiesel swore that he had never heard me say a word in favour of the Nazis. The scales were tipped by the fact that for several years I had employed an assistant who was a half-Jewess, a fact which now came to my knowledge for the first time. I was impertinently classified as a petty hanger-on and was allowed to continue my practice.

Amongst the Americans I made a welcome re-acquaintance in the pleasing shape of a pre-1933 girlfriend. Virginia had weathered the years gracefully and, with her trim WAAC uniform and her long hair swept back off her high forehead, she looked the picture of health, and put most of our sallower Berlin beauties in the shade. She was as pleased to find me again as I was to see her. The American men had no interest whatever in their own countrywomen, and ran exclusively and incessantly after the

German girls. Gretel was a little jealous, I think, but Virginia was so kind and generous and was able to give her stockings and make-up and all those things which are really so much more important to a woman.

Virginia came from a good family and had a large private income. She had come over because she was interested in Germany, and was acting as an interpreter at the Nuremberg trials. When I met her she was already operating an extensive traffic in cigarettes and coffee, and I was able to help her to some extent in this by introducing her to colleagues whom I knew could afford to pay her prices. In six months she was able to make a small fortune and we never lacked any luxury.

Berlin hospitals were in a terrible state during the first year after the war. Most were destroyed, and much had been stolen from the others. Emergency hospitals were established in undamaged premises, so that the patients had at least a bed and a roof over their heads. Field kitchens provided one warm meal a day. Those who were lucky enough to find a bed were infinitely better off than the many thousands of sick men and women who had to spend their last hours in half-destroyed houses without any attention whatever. The dead bodies were wrapped up with paper and string and interred in mass graves. Several times each day I was sent for to make out a death certificate for these 'parcels'. The greatest mortality fell on old people and young children.

The crisis reached its peak in the winter of 1946. The cold paralysed everything. Pipes were frozen, there was no light or coal or water or sanitation. Hospital wards registered temperatures of ten degrees below freezing point, and many private houses must have been lower still. Furniture, banisters, ceiling joists and often every second stair were ripped out and broken up for fuel.

Mortality curves reached an unprecedented height. People who died were left in the natural cold storage of their homes for weeks, for neither the municipality nor the commandantura had any facilities for removing them. In the end they were thrown on wheelbarrows and dumped outside the city.

My consulting hours were not long enough to cope with the number of patients. They overflowed into the long corridor and down the staircase right to the main door. Most of them really wanted medical advice, some just came for the warmth, for doctors had received an allocation of five hundredweight of coal a month. The black market price for coal-dust briquettes varied inversely to the height of the thermometer and reached the record figure of 100 marks per bag which represented an average wage for a fortnight's work. The only advice that I could give to the innumerable patients who came to me with frozen limbs, was to wrap themselves up in newspapers, move as little as possible and stay in bed, preferably two or three of them together to preserve their body heat. And although in normal times this might have been dangerous prescription from a moral standpoint, it was perfectly safe in this weather. I could understand now why the Esquimaux, unlike all the rest of *homo sapiens*, had a rutting season in the summer only.

An alarming feature of that winter was the disappearance of children. Ever since the end of the war, children had been vanishing from Berlin, never to reappear. The monthly police reports always contained the routine paragraph of the disappearance of between 120 and 150 children. Apart from the parents, few people gave much thought to the matter. It only began to make sense to me when, by pure chance, I mentioned this to a colleague from the health office. It appears that these children were not just kidnapped, for no one was fool enough to add to the difficulties of feeding himself by burdening himself with other people's children. They were simply slaughtered and sold as veal on the black market.

The most common disease amongst my patients was TB. The weak and undernourished bodies, the unhygienic conditions, the filth and the lack of soap and underclothes afford an ideal breeding ground for TB bacilli. The cold winter accounted for the rest, for people huddled together in their homes and for weeks let in no more fresh air than they could. Better suffocate than freeze.

The Berlin municipality tried to send their TB cases to health resorts. Because of the zonal division the Harz was the only possible district. There was plenty of good air there, but nothing to eat, and the patients were even advised to bring their own potatoes. In such conditions the victims might just as well stay in the towns.

It made me mad to read in the papers that Mrs Roosevelt had declared that she had not seen any underfed children in the streets of Berlin. If one is driven in a Lincoln from one dinner to another it is quite possible not to see underfed children. I personally have never seen an American general — but I don't thereby try to give the impression that they don't exist. There are more ways of lying than by telling an untruth. Other international philanthropists tried to make sure by erecting weighing machines in the streets and recording the weight of passers-by, to determine the average measure of under nourishment in Berlin. But this is mere childish frippery which can lead nowhere. The undernourished and starving were not to be found in the streets, but lying gasping in their beds trying to conserve their fading energy.

While all Germany had only one thought: namely to keep alive somehow from day to day, the Allies had nothing better to do than start on the denazification of Germany. In one stroke they created fifteen million pariahs, making a quarter of all living Germans outcasts and outlaws. The statesmen should have realised that by treating the Nazi Party as a still existing power they were encouraging fanatics to try again. The German people have an outstanding organising ability. Once bitten, twice shy — I would be an idiot to burn my own fingers again. But I have eyes and ears and know that illegal organisations are not just tales out of a story book. It happens not infrequently that old Party members invite me to some 'harmless' reunion. These small circles do not dream of a new war, an expulsion of the occupying powers, or similarly violent measures. They are content to act for the time being as a mutual welfare organisation. Unity is strength — and an unjust blanket revenge makes for unity.

The Nazis against whom there were really serious charges managed to disappear at the right moment. Every now and then I run into one in a distant district, for Berlin is a large place, and his name is now no longer Singer but Braun. All his neighbours will swear that they knew him by that name long before the Nazis came into power.

Some others have made their way into the Western zones, leaving their Party membership book behind, and probably having corrected their birth certificate.

When they come before the 'de-lousing commission' one will protect the other; sufficient evidence can easily be produced for the defence and the black sheep leave the courtroom white and pure.

Plenty of unimportant Party members have managed to keep their old posts, others have moved to new districts, assumed new identities and new positions. They are efficient, acquire influence easily and look after their old comrades. This esprit de corps, born as much of adversity as of idealism, makes new Nazi strongholds under the very eyes of the democratic and wary masters of the new Germany.

Amid the most distressing conditions of hunger and cold the Americans came out with an order calling on all Nazi doctors, without any investigation of their previous personal history, to leave their consulting rooms and start on demolition work. On my way to the town hall when I was going to prove my own denazification, I met three highly qualified colleagues at work on a ruin, shovelling and sorting out bricks. One of them had run a private hospital, the other two were very successful GPs. I was horrified and commiserated with them, but when I saw them after a few days they were quite resigned and even enjoying their freedom from responsibility. It was healthy work; they had a hut with a stove in it. And every night they took home a surreptitious bundle of firewood. I was almost tempted to join them, but one has to take a longer view, and I felt my duty to my patients and the future to be more important.

3

ERICH DRESSLER

My younger sister, Carla, had a nursery governess called Dressler. And Fräulein Dressler had a favourite nephew called Erich. A large tinted photograph in a silver frame on her dressing table made the most of his china-blue eyes, saffron hair and sullen expression. He was the same age as my sister, and Fräulein Dressler's great idea was that Carla and Erich should become friends. She made several attempts to bring it off, but it never worked out satisfactorily. Erich was invited to one or two of Carla's parties, but always stood about with a sulky and superior air. A year or so later she left us, and with the passing of the tinted photograph, Erich was forgotten.

Amongst the Americans I met in Berlin in 1947 was a Joe Richards. The first time I dined with him in Wannsee he sent his car to fetch me. The chauffeur was a handsome, sulky-faced youth in Afrika Korps shorts and shirt with a heavy gold cross round his neck. He clicked his heels and bowed as I got in the car, and when he took off his opulent-looking hogskin gauntlets he disclosed a heavy gold identity bracelet and an onyx signet ring. I had not been in the car five minutes before he offered to supply me with all the women I needed — blonde, redhead or brunette according to my fancy. When I politely declined he asked whether he could not accommodate me in other ways: he assured me he could get me anything I wanted. What I did want just then was material for an article on the black market, and so I asked him if he could get me some petrol.

It was not until our second meeting in his flat that I discovered that he was the sulky beauty of the silver photograph frame. He told me that his aunt was still alive and living in Spandau, and later I visited her to check his story, which she was only too delighted to tell me. There was no question of my ever having to prompt him or encourage him to give his frank opinions. All I had to do was to stop him being too longwinded about it, and to keep him to the point.

Erich Dressler, born 1924

There isn't much to be said about my childhood. I was born in 1924 in Kieler Strasse, in Steglitz, a suburb to the south of Berlin, the only child of my mother's second marriage. Her first husband had been an army captain who was killed in the First World War – fighting the English in the tank battle of Cambrai. She came from a military family and my grandfather, whom I never knew, had been regimental sergeant-major in the famous Alexander Grenadiers in Berlin.

Mother hadn't had an easy time of it during the inflation years when her small pension of less than 200 marks a month became practically valueless. The Weimar Republic never did anything for the families of those who fell in the World War, and so she just had to help herself as best she could. At first she was a shorthand typist and later became manageress of a laundry. She was a very good business woman, but of course she hated having to work; after all, an officer's wife is above that.

So when she married my father in 1923 it was probably because she didn't want to go on demeaning herself. Father was an executive at the Reichsbank, and quite well off. When they married they moved into a flat in Kieler Strasse and there I was born. It was a very large, comfortable, five-roomed flat, with wide balconies where we used to eat in summer.

I have never been on particularly good terms with my father. In any case the modern generation, reared under National Socialism, had little point of contact with the reactionary and hidebound generation of the Great War and the Weimar Republic. But for me it was particularly difficult.

To begin with my father had never been a soldier. He hadn't been in the war because of a stomach ulcer. I had often felt ashamed when my schoolfellows and friends talked about their fathers, of the battles in which they had taken part and the medals they had got. Often I couldn't bear to let myself down in front of the other boys and I used to make out that my father had been a cavalry officer like mother's first husband. It's not very good for one's self-respect to be ashamed of one's own father.

And he made it worse. He seemed to glory in his cowardice. I believe he was actually proud that he had never fought. And yet he always asserted that he was a good German! He didn't like the French, that is true; but that is no more than natural, and there is surely no merit in hating one's hereditary enemy. Father often used to speak contemptuously of 'playing at soldiers' – that is how he referred to the honour of serving under the flag.

The real trouble was that he was a fanatical Christian, and used to get his ideas from the Church. This only proves the national socialist conviction that Christianity is a decadent Jewish ideology and undermines the national sense of honour. He could trot along to church every Sunday and shout hallelujahs, but when it was a case of defending his Fatherland in the hour of need all he could do was to trot out his stomach ulcer.

From 1930 to 1934 I went to the elementary school in Lepsiusstrasse. I was, of course, too young to be fully conscious of the national revolution. But in the following year, a group of the *Jungvolk* [Hitler youths of ten to fourteen years] was founded in Steglitz. The reactionary element was then still so strong amongst the older people that the Jungvolk had to masquerade as a 'non-political sports group.' They didn't wear uniform, had no flags or pennants and at first had no drill or roll-calls at all. They used to camp in the woods around Berlin, and they also went on excursions.

I first heard about this from a schoolfellow who wanted me to join. I was very keen but I did not dare to say anything about it at home, for I knew my father would do all he could to stop me. For at that time he still used to natter about the National Socialists, whom he used to call the Swastikids. And he used to say the most shocking things about the Führer. So I did not tell him anything about the Jungvolk patrol, but I joined it all the same – and with it began for me the greatest experience of my life.

For the service of the Führer and the new revolution was the most important thing in my life – whether as a boy in the Hitler Youth or later as a soldier in the fight against the Bolshevik gangs or against the Jewish democracies of the West.

When I look back today, and think of those early days, I am always full of admiration for the steady purpose with which our education was directed with a view to our future needs. A German boy would one day have to become a German man, and the German man is first and foremost a warrior. He must be hard, and he must know how to obey. And to obey is the most important thing. One must have learned to obey in order to be able to command.

We had group meetings with community singing, story-telling and reading. And whatever was read to us was well chosen. It was almost invariably picked from German history, and, as is only proper, most of it was about the many great soldiers which our nation has produced.

The hero of my childhood was the famous Albert Leo Schlageter. He was one of the few who, at the time of the French occupation of the Ruhr, when Germany had reached the most ignominious depths, did not lose courage and remained faithful to his oath to the flag. Schlageter was the heart and soul of the German resistance movement against the French. With his men he blew up bridges and railway lines and destroyed trains carrying reparation goods into France. One day he was caught and sentenced to death. With a cigarette in his mouth he himself gave the last order to the firing squad. That is how a German man meets his death.

Of course our service to the Jungvolk did not only consist of group meetings. We used to carry out regular military exercises in the woods round Berlin, and we always thought this the high spot of our duties. We used to make dummy machine guns with a ratchet and a can at the end of the barrel so that we could make a real rattling noise, while the belt of ammunition was represented by a leather strap which moved slowly across as we were firing. We enjoyed playing about with these tremendously, and especially when some war veterans from an SA detachment came along to direct our operations. We were given real strategic tasks, like the defence of a hill or a road crossing, and we soon learned how to read ordnance maps and work out compass directions.

When we were out we were not allowed to slouch along like a Sunday school. We marched in formation, like soldiers, with vanguard, column and rearguard. On short marches we loaded our rucksacks with stones, for these marches were not meant for fun, but to develop our toughness and powers of endurance.

Thus we learnt at an early age all things a soldier must know – the regulation way of rolling the blankets and groundsheet in the rucksack, the correct way of tightening the straps, of dealing with shovels and entrenching tools and the chief drill movements.

Of course these things only started in earnest when we joined the Hitler Youth; but even in the Jungvolk we learnt a good deal and were slowly weaned from the softening influence of our homes and families. My father soon had to approve of my joining the Jungvolk. He himself had applied for membership of the NSDAP. But I suspect he only did it to save himself trouble at the Reichsbank.

In 1934, when I had reached the age of ten, I was sent to the Paulsen Realgymnasium. This was still a regular old-fashioned place with masters in long beards who were completely out of sympathy with the new era. Again and again we noticed that they had little understanding for the Führer's maxim – the training of character comes before the training of intellect. They still expected us to know as much as the pupils used to under the Jewish Weimar Republic, and they pestered us with all sorts of Latin and Greek nonsense instead of teaching us things that might be useful later on.

This brought about an absurd state of affairs in which we, the boys, had to instruct our masters. Already we were set aflame by the idea of the New Germany, and were resolved not to be influenced by their outdated ideas and theories, and flatly told our masters so. Of course they said nothing, because I think they were a bit afraid of us, but they didn't do anything about changing their methods of teaching. We were thus forced to 'defend' ourselves.

This was rather simple. Our Latin master set us an interminable extract from Caesar for translation. We just did not do it, and excused ourselves by saying that we had been on duty for the Hitler Youth during the afternoon. Once one of the old birds got up courage to say something in protest. This was immediately reported to our Group Leader who went off to see the headmaster and got the master dismissed. He was only sixteen, but as a leader in the Hitler Youth he could not allow such obstructionism to hinder us in the performance of duties which were much more important than our school work. From that day onwards the question of homework was settled. Whenever we did not want to do it we were simply 'on duty,' and no one dared to say any more about it.

Gradually the new ideas permeated the whole of our school. A few young masters arrived who understood us and who themselves were ardent national socialists. And they taught us subjects into which the national revolution had infused a new spirit. One of them took us for history; another for racial theory and sport. Previously we had been pestered with the old Romans and such like; but now we learned to see things with different eyes. I had never thought much about being 'well educated'; but a German man must know something about the history of his own people so as to avoid repeating the mistakes made by former generations.

Gradually, one after the other of the old masters was weeded out. The new masters who replaced them were young men loyal to the Führer. The new spirit had come to stay. We obeyed orders and we acknowledged the leadership principle, because we wanted to and because we liked it. Discipline is necessary, and young men must learn to obey.

After military sovereignty had been re-established in Germany it was agreed that I should become an officer. There are only two walks of life really acceptable to a Germanic man: the land and the army. Everything else is morbid and decadent. I had told my father of my intention, and now he said nothing against it, although we both remembered his jibes about 'playing at soldiers'.

And now it became clearer every day that the Führer had been right in everything. Austria returned to the Reich and the Führer was welcomed in his home country with indescribable joy. The streets of Vienna had turned into a sea of flags, and our soldiers were greeted with flowers. Never before had Germany been so strong and great!

Then my attention was absorbed by the heroic struggle of our legion Kondor in Spain. This small band of brave volunteers accomplished wonderful results in their fight against the Reds. I had bought the largest available map of Spain, hung it up on my wall, and on it followed the military operations by marking the positions of the Nationalists and the Reds with pins. The fall of Teruel made me completely delighted. [The battle of Teruel was fought December 1937–February 1938 and ended in Nationalist victory. The Republicans never really recovered, unable to replace the lost arms and men.]

In 1938 I was transferred to the Hitler Youth. I had been a Jungenschafts Leader in the Jungvolk, but now I had to start again as an ordinary Hitler Youth. This made me all the more ambitious, for I knew that I had a gift for leadership in me, and I wanted to advance rapidly. I had long been interested in all technical matters, and I reported to the motorised Hitler Youth, Bann 200 in Steglitz. Later I intended to join the Wehrmacht in a Panzer regiment. The best preparation for this was service with the motorised HJ, where we were instructed in everything to do with motors, and trained to ride motorcycles. We were trained by men of the NSKK [Nazi Automobile Association]. The time of games with the Jungvolk had come to an end. Now we were in earnest.

Our training was more thorough than that given to the ordinary Hitler Jugend. We learned not only the mechanical side but also to shoot with small-calibre guns, and with army pistols. Our exercises now turned into serious manoeuvres, and all the time we were waiting for the real thing which we called Plan X. On one occasion we really went into action – a planned offensive against Jewry.

Of course, following the rise of our new ideology, international Jewry was boiling with rage and it was perhaps not surprising that, in November, 1938, one of them took his vengeance on a counsellor of the German Legation in Paris. The consequence of this foul murder was a wave of indignation in Germany. Jewish shops were boycotted and smashed and the synagogues, the cradles of the infamous Jewish doctrines, went up in flames.

These measures were by no means as spontaneous as they appeared. On the night the murder was announced in Berlin I was busy at our headquarters. Although it was very late the entire leadership staff were there in assembly, the Bann Leader, the sub-Bann Leader and about two dozen others, of all ranks.

I was told that an important confidential discussion was in progress. In the corridor the sub-Bann Leader called me and asked how old I was. Then he said: 'Well, you're a bit young still, but you'd better come all the same: Come with me.'

I had no idea what it was all about, and was thrilled to learn that were to go into action that very night. Dressed in civilian clothes we were to demolish the Jewish shops in our district for which we had a list supplied by the Gau headquarters of the NSKK, who were also in civilian clothes. We were to concentrate on the shops. Cases of serious resistance on the part of the Jews were to be dealt with by the SA men who would also attend to the synagogues.

But there was little resistance. We carried out our orders in competent military fashion. We went in groups of up to twelve men with clubs to break the shop windows. And the night was full of the music of smashed and splintering glass, and the chorus of our Anti-Jewish songs – 'I am a Jew, do you know my nose,' and 'Ikey Moses has the dough.' Only one Jew, the proprietor of a large lingerie store, dared to turn out in his nightgown and start caterwauling; but he didn't stay there long! Or rather, he did stay there but he didn't caterwaul for long.

One thing seriously perturbed me. All these measures had to be ordered from above. There was no sign of healthy indignation or rage amongst the average Germans. It is undoubtedly a commendable German virtue to keep one's feelings under control and not just to hit out as one pleases; but where the guilt of the Jews for this cowardly murder was obvious and proved, the people might well have shown a little more spirit. This should have been a test case, calling for firm and decided action. Nothing of the kind was done. The Jews were let off with a punitive levy; only a few of them were put in a concentration camp, the rest were tamely allowed to emigrate. I felt the whole thing to be rather an unsatisfactory expression of Socialist ideals.

But my disappointment at our molly-coddling of the Jews was soon forgotten in the greatest and most joyful event of my life. In the spring of 1939 I met Adolf Hitler personally – face to face. It was a lucky accident – perhaps more than that. I think it must have been my destiny once in my life to see my Führer and speak to him.

It happened when a mixed group of my H.J. Bann went for a journey through Bavaria and the lower reaches of the Danube, in the course of which we had to pass through Berchtesgaden. Of course we were all wildly excited by the chance to have a look at the Berghof of the Führer. We had absolutely no idea that he was at Berchtesgaden himself, for, according to the papers, he was in Berlin at that time.

It was a gloriously bright and warm day in March and about a hundred of us were marching along the high road leading to the Berghof, when three large motor cars approached from behind us. The sub-Bann Leader, who was marching at our head, ordered us to step to the side of the road. Suddenly there were feverish shouts from the end of the column. The boys had recognized the Führer's standard on the first car. We all stiffened to attention like one man and raised our arms in the German salute.

The leading car slowed and halted. The car following also pulled up. Out of the corner of my eye I saw an adjutant call our Bann Leader over to the first car and he spoke to the figure inside. Suddenly our wild joy and excitement got the better of our discipline. We broke formation with a wild shout and swarmed round the car. The sub-Bann Leader and the Leader were shouting at us, but the Führer and the SS officer laughed, and then he got out of the car.

I saw him there for the first and the last time. I noticed that his face was more wrinkled and his hair greyer than one could tell from his photographs. And he had a strange nervous twitch in his face when he spoke. But the most marvellous thing was his eyes; they were very large and radiant, with a peculiar gleam lighting them with an uncanny power. I had to summon all my strength to look into his eyes. But then I knew surely and certainly and calmly that whoever looked in his eyes would be ready to die for him.

From that day I knew that the Führer possessed supernatural powers over men. His look was like an electrical discharge, an impelling force which none could withstand. I have read the same thing about Napoleon, but who was he to compare with the man whom destiny had sent to re-design the face of the earth! In my view the Führer was the greatest man of all time.

He spoke a few words to some of those nearest him, asked where they came from, whether they had enough to eat, and what their accommodation was like, and then he shook hands with them. His voice was strangely subdued and a little hoarse, but very full and masculine. Then he turned towards me.

'What career have you chosen for yourself?'

I could not speak properly, my throat was tight and throbbing.

'Officer,' was all I could say. The Führer nodded, looked at me silently for a moment, and then said, 'Very good' and pressed my hand.

After this he spoke to a few others, but I heard nothing of it. I was as though in a trance. In the end he made an adjutant give our Bann Leader 500 marks, with which we should go and see Vienna. He returned to his car; we stood taut and shouted 'Heil!' until the car was out of sight. The memory of this day has never faded and will be with me all my life. From this time I set myself religiously to follow the maxims which Adolf Hitler had laid down, especially his dictum 'Youth must be led by youth.'

But the harder I tried to realise the Führer's ideas the more I noticed the resistance of the members of the Hitler Youth. In a district like Steglitz, which was largely inhabited by small officials and shopkeepers, most of the boys had a secondary school education and should have been leaders in the Hitler Youth. But this was not the case. The leaders were drawn from pupils of elementary schools who were now training for jobs or had become workmen or were just full-time members of the Hitler Youth. These boys worked off their inferiority complexes by favouring the apprentices and young labourers of our group, while making sneering jokes about the 'high school men.' They used to call us in front of the whole group 'la-di-da gents … velvet boys with polished finger nails … you Latin twerps' and so on. And these boors were not able to say a single German sentence correctly.

I was particularly unpopular with them. I read too much for their taste, and also knew more about service matters than they did. When we had our group evenings they could not do without me, but at all other times they humbled me whenever they could. As I had been a Jungenschafts leader in the Jungvolk I should have been due for promotion, but they managed to stop that. They used to carry tales about me to the Bann headquarters, and whenever the Bann Leader took inspections he either picked on me or completely ignored me. In time they went from bad to worse until finally something happened which made my position in the Bann impossible. For some time I had noticed that there was something fishy about our monthly subscription lists. The lower ranks, whose job it was to deliver the money at the Bann, had invented quite a simple procedure by which they left a couple of fellows' names off the list, and kept their subscriptions for themselves. As the total number of members was constantly fluctuating on account of transfers and removals, this would be quite unnoticed. I had only found out about it because, being rather weak in the 'Three Rs', they had a few times appealed to me for help in completing the lists.

I could not make up my mind at first whether to report this or not; but as they continued to behave so abominably to me, I sent a written report to the Bann.

The results were not what I had expected. I was ordered before the Bann Leader, who in a furious rage called me a low-down grumbler, a crafty sneak who wouldn't fit in, who always wanted his own way, who showed no comradeship, and who was now going so far as to accuse his superiors. I tried to get a word in, but that was impossible. I asked to be confronted with the persons concerned, but he did not even allow that. So I arrived at the only possible explanation, which was that he himself took his cut. He now confronted me with the alternative of having the case tried before the court of honour of the Hitler Youth, in which case he would be witness to my 'bad, isolationist behaviour' or else I could volunteer to be transferred to another Bann or wherever I pleased. I could go to the dogs as far as he was concerned. All this was shouted in a screaming, malicious voice.

After this he grew very affable. He told me to let this be a lesson to me never to bring wanton charges against my comrades again, and to bear myself like an upright German boy. He thought for a moment, and then he told me that the foreigners' service of the *Reichsjugendführung* [Reich Youth Leadership] had asked for a few boys with qualifications as linguists. 'That is something up your street, you are one of those educated ones, aren't you!'

My new duties were pleasant, interesting and important. I was allocated to the district staff for Berlin. Our duties were to look after deputations of foreign youth organisations who were visiting Berlin and to guide them round the city; of course not every fool could undertake that, and so they had chosen a few especially able and clever people, who had to pass an intelligence test before they were admitted.

Of course all this took up much time, and it was really the sort of work which one should only take on if one has no other obligation. In my case, school had to suffer and as I had already missed my exams once, father made a lot of fuss saying that I should at least have asked him. But I did not pay any attention to the old man's grumbling. I had no further interest in my school work. An elementary school education was quite good enough for an officer, and if I got the *Einjahrige* [A German examination taken in high school at the age of fourteen] that was as much as I could wish. And I thought that I would get through that without much trouble.

The youth deputations whom we had to guide were mostly Italians and Spaniards; once I had some Slovaks and occasionally a few Dutch.

We liked the boys of the Falange best of all. The Spaniards suffer from an ill-deserved reputation; for they are a disciplined and warlike nation with a great past, who showed in the civil war against the Red thugs that they will also have a great future. The boys were all of them very neat. It is true they did not spend as much time on athletics as we, but against that even the youngest of them had already borne arms or had at least fought as dispatch riders. They consequently seemed rather more grown-up than the majority of German boys of their age. I made friends with one of them, Juan Gomez of Santander. As long as he was in Berlin he stayed with us, which was actually forbidden. He meant to become a naval officer, and hated the British on account of Gibraltar. I got on very well with him, and we corresponded until 1942; since then I have not heard from him any more.

The Italians were quite different from the Spaniards. I never had a great liking for the macaronis, and the boys of the Balila were such types as to make me really hate the whole lot of them. They were great braggarts, showing off their uniforms, which were indeed smarter than ours, but fit only for parades, not for duty. It is like everything with them; a fine exterior and nothing behind it. Without doubt the Duce was a great man, but his band of braggadocios could never be turned into heroes and soldiers, as the war in Abyssinia had shown. The heroes of the Balila knew everything and could do everything. It was our duty to be courteous and friendly, but I must say it was not always easy with them.

But it was a good feeling to know that one occupied an important post, and that one was at the same time an advertisement for one's country. We took great trouble over our work, and our schooling had to suffer. Consequently, after eight months I had to ask for leave again, or I should have missed my exams. This we could not afford, for school fees were expensive and we were not exactly rich. But before I could begin to think about school the war broke out.

My parents had told me often enough about the general rejoicings in 1914, but nothing like that could be noticed now. On the contrary many people, above all the older ones, were pulling long faces.

The mobilisation was carried out swiftly and secretly. I saw no more soldiers in those days than at any other time. Perhaps we were helped by the circumstance that we had just completed manoeuvres in East Prussia when the Poles launched their cowardly attack, and so most of our troops were already where they were needed. All the same our mobilisation was a masterpiece of German precision, punctuality and organisation. But of course all this paled in comparison with the victories that were then to come.

I was not entirely happy about our lightning victories. I was fifteen and my most ardent desire was to be a soldier myself and to be allowed to fight. But everything went off with such maddening speed, and before I could think of it the Polish campaign was over and the enemy utterly beaten! What was to follow? It was quite clear to me that the war would be over before my time came. At that rate we could have conquered half the globe before I had reached the age of eighteen and could join in.

From the beginning I had a special interest in the tank formations. The Führer had once said that tanks were the successors of the cavalry. They were the cavalry of the modern war. That was true; and since it had been my boyhood dream to serve with the cavalry it was not surprising now that I saw myself as a tank commander, installed in my turret and giving the order to open fire.

I got on very badly at school, and now when instruction became irregular owing to the call-up of a good many of the younger masters, I almost slipped back to the last place in the form.

Often our classes were interrupted and we were hurried into the great hall to hear a special communiqué. Sometimes masters came on leave and told us about their experiences in Poland, or talked to us generally about military life. I was always wildly jealous because they were allowed to be out fighting while I had to sit swotting at school.

At night the senior boys had to do fire-watching duties under the supervision of a master. This was very boring, for nothing ever happened. Those few tired British fliers who got through to Berlin every now and then were hardly worth mentioning, and nobody ever bothered to go into the cellar on their account.

At that time we were still reaping our greatest victories. The Nordic States were occupied in a twinkling and then came the French campaign. And now there was no holding us back. The snooty Britons at Dunkirk had taken such a beating that they left all their war material behind and most of them were miserably drowned! Then our U-boats made sport of their fleet and not a day passed without special communiqués announcing the sinking of British ships!

Those were great days and I had nothing but contempt for the grumbling of many of the older people, including my own parents, who, in the face of such events, found it possible to complain of the rations, or that they could no longer travel as much as formerly, or that they had to buy fewer clothes and all that kind of thing. All this was trifling and unimportant in comparison with these great events.

I had resumed service with the Hitler Youth. Visits from foreign youth organisations became more frequent again. We had members of the National Socialist movements of Holland, France, Belgium and Norway. To be quite honest, I liked none of them. They were all of them far too submissive, trying to ingratiate themselves with us. The Norwegians were not quite so bad, but then they are a Germanic brother race. The French were very vain and never stopped talking. I really could give only half my mind to the matter. What an absurd business, leading chattering Frogs round Berlin, while our boys were bleeding at the front!

When the war against Russia began it seemed as though that, too, would go like all the others. But soon we found that the Reds were tougher than we had expected. In addition, America now entered the war, and although at the outset our Japanese allies gave the Yanks enough trouble we were certain that before long the American Jews would try to poke their long noses on the Continent, using Britain as a base.

I was now seventeen, and as I expected my call-up fairly soon, I managed to avoid any more school work by joining a training course of the Hitler Youth in Pomerania. This course had been arranged by the infantry regiment Grossdeutschland, to enable senior Hitler Youth boys to receive proper infantry training. On reaching the minimum age they could transfer directly to the regiment. I had other plans, for I wanted to enter the tank forces; but a thorough infantry grounding is never wasted.

The training was in Meseritz and was in the hands of officers and NCOs of the 'Grossdeutschland'. The only unpleasant thing was the terrible cold. Everything else was good, although our training certainly was very tough. We were treated like real recruits and nothing was spared us. We wore ordinary army uniform with an armlet bearing the inscription 'Grossdeutschland' – of which we were very proud.

This training proved very useful later on. We learned all the things that an infantryman needs to know, including the heavy machine gun. But I noticed that we were pestered with many things that were quite superfluous. We had to spend evenings at political instruction, where we had addresses on the German colonies, Eastern politics, racial theory and things of that kind. In my view if a man had not grasped these things before leaving school he would never learn them. What mattered now was that a man should know how to handle a 98mm gun, read a map and be able to distinguish at long distance between a Mustang and a Spitfire. Who would worry now about German East Africa or the German population in Rumania?

At the end of our course I should have gone back to school, but in the meantime I had volunteered for the forces, for which reason I was eligible for the so-called emergency matric. This exam was child's play; I know of no one who did not pass it. As soon as I returned to Berlin I put my name down for another course; this time at the Luftwaffe medical school at Spandau.

This was hopelessly dull, but still better than maths or French, and at least I was in military surroundings and was not treated like a schoolboy. I did learn quite a lot with those first aid boxes that was to be useful to me later.

As I have already said, the emergency matric was a farce. We were set a few questions which a third-former could have answered. Then our old head made a moving speech. He called us heroic young men and told us that a hero's death in the face of the enemy was the highest virtue. I have thought about this speech more than once, especially when I heard that he shirked the Volkssturm in 1945 and was shot as a deserter. No doubt he thought a hero's death in the face of his own countrymen is the second highest virtue.

I was attached to the fifth tank regiment in Neuruppin. Here, too, we were treated to a speech as soon as we had got our kit, but the speaker was the regimental commander and what he told us was a little different from the sob-stuff of our old head. He told us the man in the tank force should be as bold as a cavalryman, as tough as an infantryman and as capable as an artilleryman.

Almost all of us were of my age or slightly above, and this was brought home to us during our training. When older men are present there is usually some easing up, but we were drilled until we nearly dropped. It was unbelievably hard at first. Our only comfort lay in our smart uniform – black, open collar and a death's head on the lapel – Almost as smart as an SS uniform. But during the first few weeks we hardly ever got out of our fatigue overalls.

For weeks we practised the slow march, fast march and goosestep. We knew our rifle drill backwards, and our shoulders were blue from sloping arms. What interminable barrack and cupboard inspection by night as well as by day!

One Sunday afternoon I had to clean the corporal's mess room eleven times with a tooth brush because during the dress inspection I had a few grains of dust under the turning of my sleeve. This was one of their favourite fatigues. They were very good at this sort of thing. But, strange as it may seem, many of us were unable to take a gun to pieces to remove an obstruction in its loading mechanism. We were paraded for many hours because someone had not saluted a lieutenant smartly enough, but we had no instruction about making use of natural features, and a bump in the ground had to be at least a metre high for us to know how to take cover behind it.

Of course, such trifles did not really matter. We had an ideal to fight for, while the British or Russian soldiers were being driven into disaster by the international Jews. But such irritations do mount up and can help to embitter a man. I felt that all of us would have been much more enthusiastic soldiers if we had been treated a little better.

But one hardly had any time to think, let alone worry about fundamental questions, and when our training was over all of us heaved deep sighs of relief. We were given a short spell of leave, and then we were posted; I and a few others went to a tank detachment in Brittany. Of course, our training continued but it was far better than in barracks in Neuruppin.

A few days after our arrival we were examined for fitness for tropical climates, from which we concluded that we were about to be sent to Italy or Greece. Naturally we preferred that to action in Russia; no one was very keen to go to the Eastern Front. Losses there were enormous, and the Russians were known for their barbaric fighting methods. No, I must say we preferred Greece to that.

Indeed we had not been wrong; we were soon to be on our way. First we went by train all across France and Germany and through the Brenner Pass; then by lorry from Florence, until we reached Pisa, and from there we were put on board Italian transports and went by sea to Sicily. We had rough weather on the way and most of us, including myself, were very seasick. All the same we were thrown into action as soon as we had reached land at Palermo.

We had hardly refuelled and been issued with ammunition when the order to go into action came through. Freshly landed British troops, strongly supported by the RAF: and naval artillery were attacking our positions with superior forces. This was my first battle, and at the same time it was one of the hardest in which I have fought.

The heat was intense. We hadn't the foggiest notion of the ground on which we were fighting, and knew nothing whatever about the way our positions were drawn up, or about the lines of supply. We had nothing to eat for twenty-four hours and, what was even worse, we had nothing left to drink. Dressed in bathing-trunks and steel helmets we stood behind the guns and fired.

At first I did not notice the bomb and shell hits at all. But when the gun next to ours, about fifty metres away to the right, got a direct hit and two of our men were hurt by bomb splinters, I realised the danger. As far as I could see there wasn't a single

German anti-aircraft battery, not a single German plane. The British bombers flew
as low as they pleased. Occasionally a tank would try vainly to get them down with
machine-gun fire.

The British artillery fire was intensified after three hours, from which we concluded that the attack was now to be launched. If they had not been such cowards
they could have had us long ago. The British are cowards. They do not like to attack,
and only do attack when they are in superior force and when enemy positions have
been softened by artillery and bombers.

In these three hours we had lost more than half our complement. If the Tommies
had known how matters stood here they wouldn't have taken such a long time over
it. But in the end they attacked. First came the tanks, then, in thin rows, the infantry
swarmed out. Their fire was terribly inaccurate. Their machine-gun volleys were far
too high; one could see that they were nervous and could not properly judge the
distance. In hilly country like this, machine-gun fire must be kept low.

We shot up nine or ten of their tanks. Then they were on us. The tanks stopped, and
the infantry went forward. We were in utter chaos; there was no communication with
the base, our lieutenant was killed, the sergeant-major had lost his head. We primed
our hand grenades.

Then the order came to withdraw. With more grit the Tommies could have finished the whole lot of us. We started our engines up. The crew of a tank was dragging
wounded men in through the turret while the commander sat on top and fired from
his hip. British shock troops went in. Now, I thought, it is all over. But for some reason
or other they suddenly stopped.

I still can't think why they did; maybe they wished to spare their men, or perhaps
they had suddenly lost interest in the war. Whatever the reason their artillery only fired
again when we had already withdrawn three kilometres. But we had no further losses
and reached prepared positions without hindrance. These positions were in the abattoir
of Palermo, which we defended for five days, in fact as long as was humanly possible.
The British had cut us off from the main fighting line. Our colonel had taken over the
sector and tried desperately to restore communication with the division – but it was
impossible. Our air force was hopelessly outnumbered. We hardly ever saw anything of
it, and when we did there were five British or American planes to every one of ours.

We had no provisions, little water, no dressings for the many wounded. Soon
ammunition became short, and petrol almost non-existent. We suffered most from the
heat. When the colonel at last ordered us to break out in the direction of Catania we
were completely finished. We had lost almost all our tanks and a great number of field
guns and our chances were very bad.

All the same most of us got through. The British tanks were just as cowardly as their
infantry and turned round as soon as they came within our range. Since our range
was greater it was comparatively simple to break through in spite of attacks from low-
flying aircraft.

Everything went well until, far behind Catania, on the road to Messina, we came
under the fire of British 75mm. We got a direct hit which blew up the remainder of

our ammunition. Only one other man escaped besides myself. He had a splinter in his leg and one in his chest while I received only a few superficial scratches.

From now on it became a real gipsies' scramble. But we had luck on our side and met no one, except Italians, who were openly hostile. We had to get water, bread and fruit at pistol point in villages. Most of the villagers gazed at us dumbly. They were sitting outside their houses and watched us as we passed. No help could be expected from them.

When we reached the coast we learnt that we were amongst the last Germans still in Sicily. That was why it had become so quiet. The last units of our fleet had already left. As the sea was perfectly calm and we had no desire to be taken prisoner, we went off in a little open motor boat. This boat was designed to hold ten men only. We were twenty-three, but as the sea was so calm we managed it. Out at sea we met several motor cutters and open boats, all of them filled with dispersed troops making for the mainland.

Everything went well until we came with a few metres of the coast. Then British corvettes intercepted us and opened fire. We got a hit in the stern and the boat sank rapidly. A few men were drowned, but most of us reached the coast. From there a lorry took us as far as Naples where we were re-mustered. I was posted as a gunner on a No. 4 tank, the precursor of the famous Panther. As I had received no training on this model I had great difficulties with it at first, which was especially unfortunate as we were immediately thrown into the Battle of Salerno.

Here we got our first taste of what superior material force really meant. We saw no soldiers at all. First came low-flying bombers in such close formation that one could not distinguish the individual squadrons, whilst artillery and mortars plastered us for hours. Then, finally, and of one accord, scores of Sherman tanks broke out of their deep camouflage. These tanks were so superior to ours that it was senseless to engage them, particularly as we soon ran out of petrol.

Now we learnt the whole extent of Italian cowardice. They swarmed over to the Americans in whole battalions, leaving tanks which were still intact, throwing down helmets and arms. More than once we fired into this rabble from the back, but it was no good. They fled as soon as they had a chance.

Our evacuation turned into a rout. The enemy forces were far too superior. On the retreat our gun jammed and I had to get out of the machine to try to fix it. I was just climbing back when I was hit in the leg. I was dragged through the turret and came round to find that I had a clean penetration of the right thigh, leaving the bone mercifully untouched. I was taken to the dressing station and then to a military hospital, which was in progress of being moved back into the interior, and then aboard a hospital ship.

This was an Italian ship, the *Aquileia*. Here we had another proof of the honour of the Americans who always boasted of their high regard for international agreements. The *Aquileia* had been painted white and was marked with three enormous red crosses. Nevertheless, they attacked us with Lightnings just off Livorno.

I was brought back to Germany, into a hospital in the northern part of the Black Forest. It was a former nunnery of the Franciscan Order, and it was rather funny to have nuns about me every day. I had never had much time for that sort of thing, and nuns and monks are really a bit of a joke, but they did their work well and took great care over us. They did not even ask whether we were believers, but perhaps this was just a put-up show because they were afraid of the Gestapo.

My wound was soon cured and I left hospital with an Iron Cross of the second class and six weeks' convalescent leave, which I spent in Berlin.

I had already noticed in the Black Forest how many soldiers there were still left in Germany, and this became even more evident on the journey to Berlin. Some of them were no doubt on leave, but the greater part of them belonged to reserve contingents or were travelling 'officially' over the country. Out at the front there was not only a shortage of material, there was also a lack of soldiers, particularly infantrymen. All these men should have been out in the fighting lines. If they had been we should not always have had to retreat. Later on when the army reserves were placed under the command of Himmler, orders to that effect were issued, but then it was already too late.

I found that my parents had aged. Father especially was very sickly and I cannot say that they displayed any marked enthusiasm for the war. As soon as Berlin had received its first heavy air attacks their belief in ultimate victory just faded away. During my stay with them, in November 1943, the British made their dastardly and cowardly attacks on the city without regard for the defenceless women and children. I think my parents were rather afraid. To be quite honest, it gives a man a better feeling to be behind a gun, however intensely he is fired at, than to sit in a cellar and be unable to do anything except await what is coming.

In December 1943, I was posted to a reserve contingent in Erfurt. I had quite a pleasant time there. I had a girlfriend in the town, a ripe young BDM girl who had been to Paris and knew her way around. But otherwise, life was very dull and our duties very tiring. I was glad when, in the beginning of 1944, I was ordered to the military academy at Rennes in France as an instructor.

My first brief stay in France had given me a very unfavourable impression of the people, which I could only confirm now. The German soldiers in France were all of them infected by them, completely demoralised and corrupted. This went not only for the other ranks but also for the officers and, painful as it is to have to admit this, officers were the worst.

There were two factors which ruined our men in France: women and drink. It is impossible to form too bad a picture of the French women. They were living examples of the degeneration which results from the mixing of races. Thousands of German soldiers so far forgot their honour as to have illicit relations with these women. These crafty females got our men drunk and drugged them with filthy aphrodisiacs. Their reasons were only too clear. The women were all of them in with the partisans, and their only interest was to find out military secrets and destroy our men's value as fighting soldiers.

A black market flourished in France. Every imaginable object was trafficked in, and most of our men joined in the game and sent fat parcels home. They had black dealings in petrol, vehicles and even arms against which they acquired food, textiles, shoes, etc. Here again it grieves me to say that the officers were the chief culprits.

But here, too, we were pestered with all kinds of drill and training, but it was very little use. There was no petrol to take our tanks on practice drives. We were trained on different vehicles from those which we used in action, and all this was going on when the invasion could have been expected at any moment.

Air raids became more intense. The attitude of the French became more and more hostile. And at the decisive moment we had nothing but old weapons, no Panthers and Königstiegers, not a single tank. Was this entirely due to chance?

Of course none of us gave the war up for lost. We all waited confidently for the wonder weapons of which we had been told. As far as we were concerned the war might have gone on for another couple of years. But the easy time was now definitely past.

As the great alarm had been given several times for practice we were not much surprised when another such alarm was given at the beginning of June 1944. We didn't hurry much. No one believed this to be the actual day. But when we were given live ammunition we knew that the hour had struck. We were put on board a train, which, under continual low-level air attacks, took us in the direction of Normandy.

Most of the men in my unit were youngsters of eighteen to twenty-two years, just come from Italy, who had seen at most a fortnight's action. Having been hustled all across France by train for several days they were fit for nothing, and we now went straight into battle. Our tanks were ordered to push forward in the direction of St Lô. But we never got as far as that.

For the first days a few German fighters careered about in the air, but the Allies were so strong that our planes were nearly all shot down during the first 24 hours. Then we were ordered to withdraw in a south-easterly direction. At first there were no signs of this being a general retreat, but suddenly word came that American tanks had broken through and were only 30 kilometres behind us. We had to leave behind an increasing number of tanks because no petrol came through. We got little sleep and little food and were soon utterly exhausted. So far we had not sighted the enemy.

We were almost relieved when at last we were told that British units had struck close to our lines and that we were to prepare for a counter-thrust. No sooner had we taken up position than a new report followed, saying that we had been encircled and must break out, which cost us eleven out of our 42 vehicles.

The retreat gained in speed and in chaos. The country was impossible to survey. Woods and moors, quite unsuitable for tanks. It occurred to us that our leaders must have lost command of the situation.

From now on no supplies came through at all. Nothing could be got from the French population except at pistol point. Allied parachute units continually harassed our rear. The French now fired on us when we passed through their villages at night. Being without maps we had to take our bearings from the sun. We continued in a north-westerly direction as far as we could.

But soon it was impossible to get any farther and we had to blow up our tanks. Enormous numbers of infantry, some of them without arms, were retreating in a state of utter demoralisation. Rumours amongst the French had it that Paris had already fallen. I joined a few other chaps from my unit and we got hold of a French car. Owing to the complete rout of our troops we had to career all over France, constantly attacked by low-flying planes. Nevertheless we got through to Strasburg, where we were stopped and our car taken from us. Vast numbers of lorries were lining the streets stacked with textiles, food and other goods. From Strasburg we were sent back to our reserve unit in Erfurt.

Back in Erfurt I could take a deep breath again. The last few weeks had been exciting and exhausting. I was annoyed at the apparent unconcern on the part of the people here, but of course I too shared their firm conviction that we should win the war. I had great confidence in the Führer and the wonder weapons.

Here we got more and more political lectures. The speakers talked about anything and everything, beginning with Frederick the Great and his laundry-women, and ending in 1942. But they never went beyond 1942; they merely assured us that victory was round the corner, and what could we do but believe them?

I got eight days' leave in Erfurt and spent my time swimming and canoeing and going to shows. Again I was struck by the great number of soldiers in Germany who had never yet heard a shot fired. I was convinced that with all these men we could hold the Rhine, at least until the wonder weapons could be put into operation.

We were re-formed into new regiments, but unfortunately we were now sent to the Eastern Front. This change was anything but pleasant. The British and Americans were more or less fair opponents who treated their prisoners relatively well. But the Russians were incredibly barbarous and had already proved beyond a doubt that they were sub-human. We had plenty of time to muse over our sorry fate on our dull journey east. Up to Krakow all seemed relatively normal. Again there were incredibly large numbers of German reserve troops having a nice peaceful time, eating cake with cream and sipping Slivovitz. Only at Lemberg did we notice that we were getting near the fighting. The trams were no longer running and the natives slunk from doorway to doorway like hunted rabbits.

We joined the second tank regiment which had just been reformed with a full complement of 80 tanks. A surprise thrust brought the Russians within 50 kilometres of Lemberg and we went forward on reconnaissance. The Russian artillery was not as heavy as we had feared and there was hardly any aircraft. We did not see a single soldier, the villages in the district were completely demolished and so the regiment followed us and we attacked the following day.

We had 40 tanks and 40 88mm guns. For the first time we had three 'Ferdinands', tanks with electric motors, which were quite noiseless and had an enormous range. We surprised a Russian artillery position and completely liquidated it, but then the Russians fought like robots. Without the least sign of perturbation they held their fire until the very last moment and then hurled everything at us including hand grenades. At about eleven o'clock we had the first losses through mines. The three electric Ferdinands had long since been bogged down, and now Russian tanks and mobile tanks and mobile guns lumbered into position and a terrific barrage was opened. It was a tricky piece of gunnery – like lobbing in tennis, they ignored the nearer vehicles and concentrated their attack on our rear so that our retreat was obstructed. Then the barrage moved forward towards the leading tanks.

We were in complete disorder. Within a few minutes the greater number of our tanks was on fire. We got a hit in the turret which smashed our commander's skull like a squashed orange. The noise was indescribable, the sense of panic like a perpetual galvanic shock. Our only thought was to get out, and we rammed in smoke grenades as fast as we could and took what refuge we could in the enveloping fog. Wounded were trying to hang on to the moving vehicles, but no one dared to open the turrets. Our directions were confused and we suddenly found ourselves on top of Russian trenches with hand grenades coming at us.

We drove on over the top of the petrified Red Army men and swung round to our proper bearing. Like blinded beetles we felt our way hesitantly through the smoke and emerged on our side of the battle area. We only stopped when we had got quite close to Lemberg. We scraped off the remainder of the commander and staggered on to terra firma. For twelve hours we had not left our tanks and we were utterly exhausted. When the regiment finally reassembled that night, only nine tanks were left.

The retreat gathered momentum. The population was friendly and gave us food and milk. Our own provisions had been wretchedly inadequate. In eight days we covered about 400 kilometres, but our vehicle stood up well to the strain.

And whilst we were thus retreating old-fashioned little biplanes dropped leaflets on us from the national committee of 'Free Germany'. This was supposed to be a group of German officers who were in Russia to fight for a 'proud and free fatherland'. But their attempts were ludicrous. 'Soldiers, don't be fools. War is senseless. Stop fighting.' There were pictures of Berliners, now Russian prisoners, with their addresses, photographed eating bread and sausage, and laughing. They were so obviously posed that no one bothered about them, and they were left lying by the thousand.

I did not really bother about anything. Somehow the fighting spirit had left me. It was not only the continuous retreating, but even more that there was never a respite, and there did not seem to be any plan or pattern which could give us hope of ever advancing again. We just kept on the move incessantly, fighting the Russians when they came too close, but always back and back. The many months that went by like this seem to me now like a shapeless and timeless nightmare, and apart from a few vivid impressions only mixed feelings of exhaustion, helplessness and anger remain.

But I still remember clearly the countless Russians camouflaged in the thick golden cornfields of Hungary, firing at us from all directions and endlessly harassing us; the roaring flames when we set light to the fields, and Russians popping up from the flames and zigzagging away like frightened hares; hordes of Hungarian troops, disorganised and shaking in their boots, allowing themselves to be disarmed by us after they had staged a futile revolt; lying on the floor of a railway truck with a bullet in my shoulder and wincing from pain at every jolt and bump. I travelled like this, with only a bare wall, cockroaches and beetles to look at, from Northern Rumania, through Slovakia to Vienna. The peaceful and clean atmosphere of the hospital in

Vienna was marred only by the sarcastic remarks made about the 'Thousand Year Reich', the New Order and the Greater German Reich by some of the Austrian doctors and nurses.

Then there were the pathetic old gentlemen and boys marching proudly through the streets of Vienna carrying banners: 'We go into training for the defence of our beloved Fatherland,' 'Do your duty! Remember your wife and children,' 'For a United Greater Germany,' etc., and the giggles and mock applause with which the onlookers greeted those who wanted to save their Fatherland; the crowds of sullen, unwilling sailors and airmen being put into army uniforms back at the base in Erfurt, and being drilled and drilled until they had no will of their own left, and were transported to the front.

And then I remember the nightmare train journey back to the front, during which we were incessantly bombed and machinegunned, so that our train had to be diverted countless times, and we reached Breslau after having crossed half Czechoslovakia, the slow advance by road forcing our way through an endless crowd of refugees with handcarts, prams and cows harnessed to broken-down cars and motor coaches; the bitter cold and deep snow and the misery of the refugees who took no notice of us, completely enveloped in their suffering and desperation, driven on only by a deadly fear of the Russians; the dying and the dead dotted about on snow along the road like bundles of rags carelessly thrown away.

And there was the sudden change of mood when our Squadron was attached to the SS, where there was still the old fighting spirit, the confidence and the will to victory which again made us certain that we Germans were inferior to none. The exhilaration when, in a daring and well-planned Panther attack, we cleared Stiegenau of Russians, and the horror of advancing into the little town laid in ruins; from a window dangled an old man on a rope; the streets were littered with bodies of soldiers and civilians with household goods and furniture; in the cellars the terrified girls and women who had been raped, and the inhabitants who were still alive, staring at us with blank eyes and only one thought in their minds, to get away; the feeling of hatred and revenge that filled me and the others, and our oath never to take any more Russian prisoners.

Of course, it was not long before we were once again in full retreat and at the beginning of April I was wounded again and taken to hospital in Prague. Everything was still quiet there, but thousands of our soldiers from Slovakia moved into Prague. The authorities no longer knew what to do, and the Czechs were becoming openly hostile.

After 3 May we could no longer go into the streets unescorted. Trams and street walls bore the inscription 'Down with Germany'. Several times we were mobbed and disarmed by Czech civilians. In the Burg district there were cases of street fighting. One of Prague's two broadcasting stations was still in our hands. Prague I continually exhorted us to hold on, for the Vlassov army was approaching. Prague II announced the Russian entry into the city for 10 May, but promised us that they would let us go free to Germany if we allowed ourselves to be disarmed.

And indeed what they said about the Vlassov army was true, only that they fought against us and not for us. This army consisted mainly of Ukrainians who had volunteered to fight against the Russians. Their latest idea evidently was to escape their punishment by coming over to the Russians at the last moment. As the Russians were simultaneously advancing on Prague we were cornered. I met an air force captain and we procured a large Mercedes which we loaded with supplies and joined a motor convoy. Although there was an infantry major, two captains and other high-ranking officers, this convoy was under the command of an SS lieutenant. We may have numbered about a hundred.

We got as far as the river Moldau and were about to cross over when we were caught by terrific Russian artillery fire. We tried to rush the bridge but halfway across we were halted by barricades and concentrated small arms fire. It was all over; Czechs advanced on us firing their guns, and there was nothing for us to do but to hold up our hands – we had run straight into their trap.

At first the Czechs were rather faint-hearted and did not really dare to come close. But, of course, resistance was out of the question. The Wehrmacht men at once ranged themselves separately from the SS, hoping to get better treatment. But the Czechs did not care for such nice differences. They soon plucked up courage, stole all our personal belongings and beat us with belts and rifle slings. As I was wearing the black tank uniform with a death's head on it they took me for an SS officer.

Together with a great number of German civilians we were taken to a town through whose streets we had to march with our hands raised above our heads. The people threw filth and stones at us, spat at us and screamed abuse at us. We were taken to a building which had a cinema on the ground floor.

The civilians were taken upstairs and we soldiers were billeted in the cinema. I heard some Czechs say that they needed a doctor for the civilians, and I saw a chance of getting better treatment and reported that I was a doctor. They took me upstairs to the civilian prisoners.

These were in an awful state. The Czechs had treated them horribly. Several women were almost naked and had huge swastikas painted on their backs. Others had had their hair shorn off and had been whipped. Many were ill with exhaustion. My duties as a doctor was not very exacting, as there was a total absence of medicine and dressings. All I had to do was to look at tongues, take pulses and look important. Later we were taken to a school, where we had to sleep on straw on the bare boards. The military prisoners had meanwhile been sent away to be handed over to the Russians, which made me more pleased at my own ruse and escape.

It was scorchingly hot and we were formed into labour battalions. There had been fighting in the town and rubble and corpses were lying about. The stench was excruciating and the work of clearing it all much too hard for most of us. The food was very bad; three times a day we got three-quarters of a litre of watery soup.

As my position as doctor entitled me to several privileges, someone who was jealous denounced me as an escaped SS officer. I had organised a civilian coat but was still wearing black breeches, so the Czechs believed this informer.

I was taken for questioning before a high-ranking officer. As I refused to admit that I was an SS officer I was badly beaten up and locked in a cellar outside the town.

It had been cut in the solid rock and had been used as an air raid shelter. It was now half filled with water. It occurred to me that, being an air-raid shelter, there must be another exit. I fumbled around for a long time in the pitch darkness and finally found a shaft up which there were iron steps. With an effort I succeeded in lifting the heavy trapdoor, and found myself in a garden outside the town. I hid till nightfall, and then walked off.

I set off in a northerly direction. On the way I found rhubarb in gardens, which I ate. When day came I lay low in some deserted outbuildings of a farm and the next night continued my journey with two turnips, the only food between me and starvation. In my exhausted state I nearly ran into a Czech patrol, but managed to fall into a ditch and lie there unnoticed. On the fourth night I reached the Elbe. There was no bridge left, and I had to swim against a fiendishly strong current. On the other side I found some clothes in a deserted village and also had a chance to wash and shave. And then at a street crossing I ran directly into a Russian lorry convoy.

I had been afraid that they would take me prisoner, but the officer merely asked me in halting German whether I knew the way to Cottbuss. I had not the faintest notion but I said 'Yes, of course,' and so they took me with them. After a few stray attempts we really did hit on the right road and just outside Cottbuss I managed to jump off the lorry and escape in the darkness. I made a wide detour round the town and during the night sheltered with a German family, who lived in a cottage on the outskirts.

I now awaited an opportunity of getting to Berlin and at length managed to hide myself on a coal train. After 24 hours we had only got as far as Grunau, but after that I had no further difficulties.

Up to now, the continual danger and nervous strain had left me hardly a minute for reflection. But now, on my return to Berlin, my mind suddenly relaxed into a black and numbing despair. Germany, our greater Germany, was beaten. The Führer dead, most of the other generals and leaders taken prisoner. The Wehrmacht had ceased to exist. Berlin was under the whip of the Bolsheviks and their Jewish commissars. It was all over. Now there was nothing but myself to consider.

When I reached our house in Steglitz, I found only a heap of rubble. The neighbours told me that my parents were still underneath. I got two men to help me and we started digging. After six days we found the unrecognisable shape of the body of an elderly woman. On the eighth day I found my father. I knew his clothes, and his spectacles were still grotesquely perched where his nose must have been. The woman may have been my mother. Anyway I buried them together in the corner of the park.

My next problem was the jewels that I had advised my parents to bury. I was terrified that looters might have got there first, but it was all right. At the appointed place I found the tin and in it the jewels quite intact. My father's gold watch, my mother's pearls and diamond earrings and a few other pieces that had been quite valuable and soon were to be more so.

At first I lived from one day to the next without bothering much about the future. My health had suffered and I had to recover my strength again. I got 2,000 cigarettes for the earrings from an American officer. I heard by chance that there was a vacant flat in Kieler Strasse, where I had lived. It had belonged to an SA commander who had escaped into the British zone. I got this flat by giving the re-housing officer 300 cigarettes. Two rooms had been half-bombed out but I soon had them restored. I had sold the greater part of my parents' jewellery and realised quite a decent sum, for the Russians were buying everything they could at enormous prices. I joined forces with three other men and we set ourselves up very comfortably. One of them, Hans, I had known in the Hitler Youth; the other two, Erich and Walter, were army chums who had also got through to Berlin. They had been back longer than I had and had already adapted themselves to the new conditions.

They taught me the only correct attitude. There is no point in mourning for our past glories. Now a good German and National Socialist has only one duty; to try to keep above water as well as he can and to harm the Allies wherever he can.

Erich had at first tackled so-called 'honest work'. That meant shovelling rubble, carrying bricks, pulling down ruins. No work for a keen young chap. There is no money in it. At a wage of 0.72 marks per hour your daily earnings are just about enough for one American cigarette!

No, we were after something better. All of us, except Hans, had been with the Wehrmacht, either as officers or as officer cadets, and we felt no responsibility for having lost the war. Our leaders should have been harder, more ruthless in waging total war and dealing with the reaction in the army. At least they could have gathered their forces in Slovakia or Austria and continued the struggle from the mountain redoubt. Again we had been stabbed in the back.

Our generation was not to be blamed, and we were not inclined to feel like poor vanquished people dependent on the victor's mercy. The war was over but the fight could go on. There were resistance groups in the French zone, wanted men who were trying to reach Spain. In the new Polish territory east of the Oder there were still whole units of SS and army stragglers. But all this was empty and rather pointless heroics. The time for that sort of thing was over for the time being anyhow. We fixed on different tactics.

The Allies here live at the expense of Germany. They pillage us, dismantle, rob and profiteer as we had never done. They keep the German people hungry in order to keep them weak. Thus it is not only our right, it is our duty to preserve ourselves. And, of course, we have to try to live at the expense of the Allies.

Hans, for example, does it with girls. This became a real working proposition only when Americans, British and French entered Berlin; for no German girl would voluntarily have anything to do with a Russian.

Hans kept what he called a 'racing stable' of young Fräuleins for the benefit of the casual Yanks on pleasure bent. He had drawn up a proper organisation and saw to it that they kept in order. Most of them were very young girls who patrolled outside the Titania Palace, the American GI Cub or the negro barracks in Lichterfelde. All Hans had to do was to see that the girls kept peace with each other, that no strangers interfered and that there was plenty of warning of raids by military police. Since he had several friends amongst the Wannsee MPs this presented no difficulty. The whole business paid very well. He got his regular cut in cigarettes and food and a lot of money besides. The negroes in Lichterfelde and from the transport column in Zehlendorf were extremely easy with their money and often paid in dollars.

Sometimes he got special commissions from Yanks who were spending only a short time in Berlin. 'Emergency' supplies always cost double. Hans knew hundreds of Yanks and he got on extremely well with his racing stable. Business began to slacken only when the military government was run more and more by civilians. The military police had become much sharper, too. The Yanks were scared stiff of VD – and, of course, most of the girls had it – it just couldn't be helped.

But this work was hardly up my street. I can't handle girls the way he does, and in that profession it really is quite an art. Chance had introduced me to two French officers working on the Repatriation Commission in Kurfürstendamm. My French is quite good and they engaged me as a driver. The work was congenial for I was only needed in the afternoon and at night, and we never drove on official business. They had their reasons for engaging me privately. Their journeys were always connected with business – buying or selling or other affairs.

This position was very lucrative. I acquired various number plates for my car and spent the morning going to Allied petrol stations. As soon as my tank was full I drew the petrol off again and sold it. At that time petrol was very scarce, and my daily earnings were anything up to 1,000 marks.

We had lots of fun at bottle parties, either at my flat or, later, at Hans's place, for he had already got a flat of his own at Lichterfelde. There were always plenty of girls and plenty to eat and drink.

Here we came into contact with another group, real youngsters they were. They were in business too, but they got the goods from the Yanks direct, and not through roundabout ways as we did. They worked mostly on the lonely American villas in Dahlem. As they always used experts, everything was done very quickly. Watches, cameras and jewellery could be sold most easily and at the best prices to the Russians and UNRRA Jews. Apart from such goods they would only consider money, food or cigarettes, provided they could be had in sufficient quantities. Owing to their excellent organisation all went smoothly for a long time. Their boss was a young *Untersturmführer*, a wonderfully smart man who kept up a rigid discipline. Unfortunately he was given away by a woman and British military police arrested him in a bar in Kurfürstendamm.

At first I knew nothing of these goings-on. I got wind of it gradually and to be quite frank, I didn't like it much at first. But then Hans put the matter right for me. It was just the same as taking loot in a war. Enemy property was loot and the Yanks were our enemies. I had to admit he was right.

Later on there was an affair which might well have ended with Hans and me parting company. It was like this. Hans went into hiding for a couple of weeks with a girl in Neukölln. I found out that they had been caught at their work at night in a lonely district in Wannsee, by a German policeman. Hans had not meant to do him serious harm, but in the excitement of the moment he had hit him a little too hard and killed him.

Hans sent the two youngest of his associates, sixteen-year-old boys, into hiding in the British zone and stayed for some weeks with the girl in Neukölln. But there again he had bad luck. The girl was denounced, and when they came to arrest her, Hans only escaped by sitting in a chest in the bedroom. Afterwards he came to me. I was not very keen to go to jug for him, and tried to get him away in the west – but he would not go. And in the end the affair blew over, but I found it wise to withdraw a little from that association. I prefer quiet transactions.

As time went on I learnt two things. It is better not to tie oneself too closely to any one group, and though one needs one or two reliable men to do one's routine work, it is wrong to keep the same men for long. An associate whom one keeps too long learns all the ropes himself and becomes difficult. I almost invariably picked my companions from amongst returned prisoners-of-war. There are always a lot of boys hanging around the Schlesische station and the Alexanderplatz who have been released and don't know what they are going to do. I take my men from amongst them – and this principle has nearly always served me well.

I need them for missions in the eastern zone. This is too strenuous for me, and also takes too much time. I can't bother my head about trifles of this kind. There were always some watches or jewellery to be had cheaply and these were sold at a good profit to the Russians who had the most money. These transactions were carried out by my men and I paid them commission at the rate of 20 per cent of the net gain. On the way back they generally picked up Russian cigarettes or meat that had been illegally slaughtered, for which I had a good clientele of Germans in Berlin.

In the meantime I had acquired a small DKW motor car for 18,000 marks, which was cheap. With this car I sometimes went into the British zone to buy cigarettes at three or four marks apiece, which could be sold in Berlin at ten marks. But I soon dropped this line. It was too hot for me, and I had no mind to be caught at the frontier.

Later on a German girl introduced me to her American boyfriend, a Mr O'Reilly who had brought large sticks of penicillin with him which he wanted to sell. I could sell it for 4,000 marks a phial and gave him 2,000, which later went down to 1,500. Of course he had no means of checking up on me, and he was only too pleased to get rid of the stuff so easily and safely. There were fairly heavy penalties for trading in penicillin.

My purchaser for this stuff was Captain Czrinczitzky, of the Polish military mission in Berlin. He took it to Warsaw where he sold it at an enormous profit. Later on he became suspicious, for there was too much fake penicillin on the market. There had been a great scandal in which a whole gang was exposed who sold glucose diluted with water as penicillin. The Yanks gave them very hard sentences. After that I kept out of the penicillin trade.

The best deals could be made with the men on the smaller military missions. The black market dealings of the Poles, Yugoslavs and Czechs are on a scale which would keep thousands and thousands of Germans fed and supplied. And even the Chinese and the rich Brazilians work the black market. If we do it they send the police after us, and yet we do it only because we must eat. These fellows do it for fun or just for greed. A nice democratic sport, to make money out of the hunger of the conquered! And they want to teach us culture!

The safest trade still is the one in cigarettes, even though it is a bit monotonous and not too profitable. The smaller fry amongst the Americans invest their earnings from it in jewellery and *objets d'art*. The really big ones have a different method. For their yield, they buy dollars on the black market and they can average 500 per cent profit this way. When there was a temporary shortage of dollars I devised another method which later on was copied by others. Today I am sorry to say many are doing it, but the original idea was mine.

I sold cigarettes and coffee for the Yanks in the ordinary way, and for the German money thus acquired I bought French occupation francs which a French officer took to Paris, exchanged into regular francs and purchased dollars with the proceeds. In this way I made a 2,000 per cent profit instead of the usual 500 per cent. The important thing in this type of work is to know a reliable Frenchman, and I think mine was. He even asked me to look after his girlfriend while he was away from Berlin.

Anyone not acquainted with Berlin and conditions here will think all this slightly fantastic. But in actual fact the greater part of the population live on this kind of trade, although on a much smaller scale. One need only be inventive and versatile and one will not have to go hungry. And one must keep up appearances. If a man gets a reputation for black market dealing he is lost. All my Yanks and Frenchies (most of the British are no use, they are too stupid for profiteering!) believe that I do it as a personal favour and only for them.

They like calling on me. I can be useful in so many ways. You want a car? I can get one for you. A yacht, carpets, penicillin or women? There you are, Sir. I don't normally do this, but I'll do it for you as a special favour. You understand! You are sympathetic – and we understand you Americans. Oh yes, we understand them.

It is an arrogant and conceited race. And stupid, like self-satisfied schoolboys. They think they are using me. They cannot see that it is I who am using them. They only see me bowing and smiling, they do not hear me laughing behind their backs. With their dollar notes, their Lucky Strikes and their cans of coffee they feel like demi-gods – and they are at bottom no better than the little bartering VNRRA Jews who stand about at railway stations and street corners.

And because of this, because they are all alike, with no other thoughts than to make as much as possible as quick as possible, no one here takes them seriously when they burble on sentimentally about the American way of life and democracy!

Once, somebody dragged me along to one of those American debating societies in Dahlem. The Yanks picked up a few young men in the street to educate and enlighten them, and I happened to be one of them. Each of us was given a bottle of Coca-Cola and a cigarette and then a couple of them began mouthing a windy rigmarole about respect for human dignity and why they had to wage war against Hitler. All of them spoke extremely good German, those gentlemen, and I suspected they hadn't been Americans very long.

Then they started talking about racial theory and the 'crimes' we had committed against the Jews. 'We Americans,' one exclaimed, 'are a living example to you. In the States men of all races and nations live peacefully side by side …'

I had had enough by then. 'Oh yes,' I interrupted, 'we've seen you doing it. Yesterday in Lichterfelde I saw three drunk GIs beat up a negro soldier because he went with a German girl. They kicked his face in with their heels to show how peacefully the races live together in your democracy.' All they could do then was to lose their tempers. So we left them to it. We'd had our enlightenment.

A few months ago I wanted to go to Munich to get some cloth for suiting. I had bought an inter-zone pass for 8,000 marks and everything went well at first; but on my return journey there was an identity check-up by American military police. They suspected my pass was not in order and arrested me. I came before the summary court and admitted at once having bought the pass off a girl who worked in an OMGUS office. I told them I was an army invalid, unfit for work, and had meant to search for relations in Munich and that there had been no way of getting a pass legally. This made them quite soft and I got away with a fortnight in jug.

It was quite comfortable in Lichterfelde. We got enough to eat and every other day I reported to the MO on account of a pain in my wound. So I didn't have to work and got half a litre of unskimmed milk and a large piece of cheese every day. Many try this on and the Yanks are usually foolish enough to fall for it. I was even visited by a padre in my cell. He asked me whether I thought of the future at times, and whether I felt any remorse. I told him I didn't feel any remorse, in fact I could not think at all, for I could only think of cigarettes. I was such a keen smoker, and when I was without anything to smoke I was ill. Then he produced a packet of Camels and also left some YMCA literature behind for me to read. But I used it for something else …

When I came out I found that the two Frenchmen had taken on another driver. I thought this was a dirty thing to do, to take advantage of my misfortune to sack me. I suppose they thought a jail-bird wasn't good enough for them. I thought I would show them something. I wrote an anonymous letter to the French Gendarmerie Militaire and told them that the Capitaine Polluud and Lieutenant Labasse-Pourchie were continually engaged in black market dealings with the Yugoslavs, and that they had a financial interest in a night club in Kurfürstendamm. It worked all right. They were arrested one night by the military police in the British sector.

At first things were not easy for me. I opened a small business with a Greek who lived in the Russian sector in Ackerstrasse. We traded in identity papers, food coupons, inter-zone passes and petrol coupons. But it was never very successful and in the end they arrested the Greek. Luckily, I had not told him my real name, or else he would surely have dragged me in as well.

Then I was robbed. Carrying 40,000 marks, I had called on an agent, also in the Russian sector, who wanted to sell me cocaine. I saw through him at once, for it was nothing but gypsum, an old trick. And I told him what I thought of him and left. I was smiling to myself at my quick-wittedness, when I noticed that my briefcase seemed lighter. It was lighter by 40,000 marks and there was absolutely nothing I could do about it.

Then followed one stroke of misfortune after another. On account of a paltry collection of 400 silk stockings I got involved in a German police raid and had to drop the lot. Then my car was stolen in broad daylight, and as I had a British number plate on it I could do nothing about that. I had to buy a motorcycle because I couldn't afford a car, and that was confiscated in a military police check-up. But finally I managed to fall on my feet again.

I am now driver and jack-of-all trades for a Yank who is working for OMGUS. I got the job by accident. A few Yanks went out sailing with their women and someone recommended me to be their boatman. This fellow Richards started questioning me about politics and so on and I gave him a nice shock by saying that I was still loyal to the Führer and a good Nazi. He said I was the first German who had been honest enough to admit it and we ought to have another talk. I saw him several times and always got the better of him in discussion. And now I hold a confidential post under him. At first he trusted me as little as all his other German employees, but I gave him my word as a German officer that he could rely on me, and from then on I have done everything for him. I sell his goods for him, find him the jewellery and pictures he wants and introduce him to a few of the healthier of Hans's old 'racing stable'. Safety first is my motto now.

4

HERMAN VOSS

Although Herman Voss was a businessman like my father, he was really more a friend of us children. This was largely due to the fact that my father disliked having anything to do with colleagues outside business hours, and Voss liked young people about the house – especially my brother Karl-Victor, my sister Nina and me. Voss played tennis with Karl-Victor, took Nina out riding most mornings before breakfast, and allowed me to sail his yacht and tinker with the engine of his motor boat.

It was not until years later, when all of us had left Germany and only my parents remained that he really became friendly with them. That was typical of Voss; outside influences never affected his personal opinions and private life.

When I went to see him in 1947 at his charming little estate near Brunswick, it was almost as if I were back in the old days tying up my dinghy at the landing-stage of his Babelsberg house. He looked almost the same as he had done eleven years ago. He was immaculately turned out and exuded the same boyish charm and easy self-confidence. There was no doubt that he had got over every post-war difficulty, as far as his personal life was concerned, as effectively as he had done in 1918.

This time he was concentrating entirely on food production, now that food rather than marks and dollars was trumps. His table and cellar were excellent, and his house ran as smoothly and efficiently as it had in Babelsberg. He was still the absolute despot, the king of the castle, and everything and everyone revolved around him.

I spent the best part of three days and nights talking to him, and when I checked on his stories in Berlin, I found that what he had told me was correct in every detail. I was not surprised, since Voss honestly believed that he had nothing to be ashamed of. In his opinion any decent businessman, whatever his nationality, would have acted in the same way as he did.

Herman Voss, born 1895

I was born in Lueneburg into the confined and depressing atmosphere of a small bourgeois home. My father was a minor official in the Lueneburg Town Council, assistant secretary of the Land Registry. We had no other sources of income, and it was only my mother's economy and good housekeeping that enabled him to keep up a style compatible with his rank as one of His Majesty the Kaiser's civil servants.

We never experienced outright need – that might have been bearable. But what seemed to me worse than that, we were forever scrimping and scraping. We had always to think twice before spending a penny; we had to go without most of the ordinary little pleasures and luxuries of life, and often we did not have quite enough to eat. I was the unwitting cause of much of this, since it was a point of honour in a civil servant that his son should go to the ancient and celebrated Lueneburg Gymnasium.

Our condition might have been much worse if my father had not been a man of remarkably frugal tastes. He neither smoked nor drank and his private life was completely absorbed in the reading of the monarchist newspaper *Kreuzzeitung* and with his club evenings. He belonged to no fewer than four clubs. First there was the military association Victors of Sedan where he could meet his regimental cronies. The patron of the association was His Imperial Highness Prince Eitel Friedrich, whose autographed portrait hung duly framed in the committee room. He also belonged to the Men's Harmony Song Circle which was under the direction of the precentor of the Lutheran Church. He was treasurer of the Society for the Study of Lueneburg Lore and was on the committee of the Union of Lutheran Christians for the Elevation of Morals in Rural Districts.

These interests filled his life, and he did not ask for more. Mother was even more modest. It was enough for her to know that father admired her cooking, and her life was spent in keeping our home and kitchen clean and darning, mending and patching our well-worn and only just respectable clothes.

The sacrifices which sent me to the Gymnasium were, to my mind, completely wasted. Why should I be stuffed up with old dry Latin and Greek? What good would Sophocles and Virgil be in modern life? I would rather have gone to the modern school where I could have learnt science and economics and things that could help me to get on in the world. For I meant to get on. I swore to myself that on no account would I become a civil servant, and rot in genteel poverty in a county town. I wanted money – a lot of money. Not for itself but for all the things money can buy. And all the things I had been denied up to then. I wanted to wear smart modern clothes, eat rich food, drink choice wines, know rich gay women and go to theatres and night clubs and cabarets. All these I wanted. But how to get them I had no idea.

When my chance did come it was at a time and in a way that I had never imagined. In 1911, quite suddenly, my father died. The State pension was wretchedly inadequate and I had immediately to leave school and start to earn my living as quickly as possible.

At that time a Lueneburg metal firm were looking for a young man to learn the trade. Although I had no references I applied for the job. The owner of the firm was a certain Samuel Marcus, a small, lively Polish Jew with a narrow and highly intelligent face. He interviewed every applicant personally.

He asked me why I wanted to start in his firm. I replied that I had no particular leanings towards the metal trade; I would just as gladly sell soap or wicker chairs. But I particularly wanted to work for a Jew; for in my opinion Jewish merchants were generally more liberal minded and also more successful than others. This got me the job, and Samuel Marcus subsequently took a great deal of interest in me.

Very early I had found out the secret of success in business. From the very first day I concentrated all my interest on the metal trade as thought nothing in the world existed beside it. I read innumerable books on metallurgy and attended evening classes in commercial subjects. In this way I very quickly surpassed my more easy-going colleagues. For their part they scorned me as an upstart climber and a would-be boss's bright boy. They were right of course, but I didn't worry. I knew I was on the right road.

Mr Marcus obviously thought I had promise and was gratified by the attention I paid him. I often had to accompany him on his business journeys to foundries and factories, and as he was a talkative man he used our long travels to initiate me into all the secrets of the business. Gradually my position in the firm changed until I was Mr Marcus's private secretary. One day he gave me a chance of sharing in a business deal on my own account. The profit was small, but as I knew that this had been against Marcus's normal practice I was very pleased. By that time I was already forming useful social connections and I had become very friendly with Marcus's only son, Mischa, who was heir to the business. He was a few years younger than I but seemed older than his age. We got on very well together. Mischa admired my business sense and energy; on the other hand I admired him for the social graces I lacked, his easy manners and conversation and his successes with girls. He was generous to the point of lavishness and lived in a style which, to my mind then, was highly luxurious.

We planned to go into a business partnership when we were older. This was our great secret which no one, not even old Marcus, knew anything about. Meanwhile, however, my career suffered an unpleasant interruption.

I was nineteen when the Emperor William II, speaking from the balcony of his Berlin palace to a rejoicing crowd below, declared that he would not sheathe his sword until Germany's last enemy lay defeated on the ground. Gripped by the universal enthusiasm, I volunteered for the colours, and was drafted into the 3rd Brandenburg Reserve Battalion. After a short training as officer cadet I went to the front early in 1915. I took part in the great battles in Flanders as the youngest lieutenant of my regiment. At the beginning of 1916 I was transferred to a machine gun unit and ended up in the great charnel house before Verdun. I was wounded in the leg at the storming of the fortress of Douaumont, and after a long time in a military hospital I was discharged.

Mischa had not been a soldier. He had nothing but contempt for the general enthusiasm, and laughed openly at my lieutenant's dagger. For many years Mr Marcus had been in close contact with the AEG [the largest electrical concern in Germany] in Berlin, whose director, Walter Rathenau, had created the Central Office of Supply called WUMBA, and there, in one of its Berlin offices, Mischa was comfortably installed in a nice 'bullet-proof' job. Mischa now organised a job for me in his own division at WUMBA. I found him a very easy-going boss and we lived together in Lützowufer where he had a very elegant and magnificently furnished flat.

Mischa had not wasted his time. He turned to his own use the innumerable connections which his work in the supply office afforded him. Through him I came to know the other side of business life: I learnt that the most important matters are not settled in the office, but in bars, restaurants and night clubs. Mischa spared no expense to impress the businessmen with whom he came in contact. He nursed these connections carefully for our future benefit, for we still planned to open a business together after the war.

The collapse of the Empire was no surprise to us. But we had no sympathy for the radical leftist elements who now threw their weight about in Germany. I had never been an ardent nationalist, but at least I knew that the Kaiser's rule had commanded the loyalties of the best and most well-meaning sections of our people and a communist Germany was unthinkable. The Weimar Republic with its multi-party system and its incompetent parliamentary government could not satisfy Germany's needs. The rancour and incompetence of the Allies had foisted upon us a political system that was foreign to our national character.

In 1919 we started, and the firm of Voss & Marcus, metal merchants, with offices in Berlin, was duly entered on the company register. But the deals we put through differed greatly from those good old Mr Marcus had made in his Lueneburg offices. Our first object was to obtain capital quickly; and now we came to realise the wisdom of having secured good social and business connections.

Our big chance was the surrender of war material ordered by the Treaty of Versailles. Trains carrying aeroplanes, guns and tanks were continually rolling west to be turned into scrap metal. Like many others we managed to secure a part of this valuable scrap. Through the agency of French buyers, whom we had met in a Cologne night club, we even contrived to have some of this material sent back to Germany as soon as it had arrived in France. At that time it was impossible to do business on any basis. A 'respectable' businessman might think this procedure corrupt; to us it merely demonstrated our 'commercial elasticity'.

The inflation which now led to the sudden and ominous depreciation of the currency, worked to our advantage. By accident we hit on a very profitable routine which we made the model for a great number of other deals. For the sum of 5,000 marks we had bought a rather large item of scrap copper which was lying in Duisberg, and which we forgot about for several months. To our great amazement we noticed one day that its value had meanwhile risen to 20,000 marks. Our next step was simple; by selling a quarter of the copper we recovered our original outlay which left us with 14,000 marks worth of copper.

The fall of the mark continued unabated. In May 1920, the dollar stood at 60 marks; in January 1922, it was worth 200. No one could fail to see that capital funds were worth nothing while non-perishable goods could be worth anything. We decided to risk everything on a really big coup.

One of our former colleagues in the supply office, called Petersen, who was still engaged on its winding-up, had told us confidentially that a cargo of copper was lying in the east port of Berlin. Its nominal value was five million marks, but through him it might be secured for three million, since this material was 'listed' for delivery to the Allies. The only difficulty was how to raise this gigantic sum, which was far beyond the capacity of our small business. To this problem, which I thought insoluble, Petersen provided the answer.

One of his friends was Dr Rudolf von Struven, a director of the Darmstadter Bank. This bank advanced a credit of 2,400,000 marks to us on the security of the cargo of copper which was not yet ours. And then with great difficulty we succeeded in raising the remaining 600,000 marks ourselves.

From then onwards we had a spell of good fortune. The credit of the Darmstadter Bank was at first repayable after three months; but Petersen knew how to get our payment postponed for another nine months. When, at length we paid it in October 1922, the dollar stood at 7,000 marks. Our copper had risen in value to 105 millions, and after the sale of about 20 per cent of it we were left with a clear profit of 80 million marks' worth of copper. It was like a fairy tale.

Then came 1923 and the occupation of the Ruhr. The mark reached dizzy heights. We no longer traded in metal alone; like everyone else we bought whatever valuables there were: landed property, jewellery, works of art and antiques. We even bought the all-powerful dollar on the black exchange; officially it was not quoted.

Our speculations were, of course, complete tight-rope walking. But we stepped with such a hypnotic sureness and such constant good luck that even to think of it today makes me dizzy. This kind of life needed the vigour and iron nerves of youth. And it needed the callousness of youth too, for we were surrounded on all sides by hunger and dire need. Old people who depended on pensions or savings found that their monthly income would buy no more than a tram ticket. For a few crusts of bread they had to sell all that they possessed. And the younger men of the working and salaried classes were little better off. Their pay was generally worthless a few hours after they had received it, and they lived from hand to mouth. Business men who didn't ride the wave soon went under, and suicides were the order of the day.

We were living in the most luxurious style. I had furnished a complete floor in a house in Hubertus Alle in the Grunewald district, which was in no way inferior to Mischa's Lützowufer flat. My servant and my driver wore cream-coloured liveries which today I consider a little ostentatious, and I drove a sixseater Mercedes, which was the most expensive car one could get.

Despite our youthful light-heartedness we saw that this kind of business could not go on flourishing indefinitely. Germany seemed to be heading irretrievably for economic disaster. The idiotic Versailles Treaty and the impossible Allied reparation demands put Germany in a desperate situation. On the strength of the palpably untrue allegations of war guilt, the enemy nations were all out for the biggest pickings from our unhappy country. They should have known better, for Europe needed

Germany, and our economic collapse would damage their economies no less than ours. But such an obvious truth was beyond their vision.

Meanwhile, the rate of inflation still increased. Between September and November 1923, the dollar rose from 320 million to 2,500 million marks. It was obvious that this state of affairs could not go on.

Our business intuition now told us to reverse our strategy. While everybody else went on buying we got rid of everything as quickly as we could, retaining only our stocks of metal. The proceeds came to a sum of astronomical dimensions whose true value could only be gauged by expressing it in terms of dollars. Everyone thought us mad to sell; but we had a plan.

Our most valuable possession was our stock of metal. We were prepared to part with that too, but only in return for foreign currency, preferably dollars or sterling. This would have been strictly illegal. But we knew quite well that deals of that kind were made every day, usually with members of allied military and trade missions. Through Petersen we got to know some smart American businessmen who, in their turn, introduced us in the bar of the Adlon Hotel to Captain Gadsby, a young Englishman whose father owned large factories in the English Midlands.

Gadsby was typical of his race: fair, slender, with a bored and hard face. He was not at all perturbed about the stringent currency restrictions; but his suspicions, the most prominent English characteristic, were at once aroused. Why should we want to sell at a time when everyone else was buying? We managed to convince him that we were in urgent need of capital in order to get a footing in a large concern. He believed us, and from that moment everything went smoothly.

At his request we had lowered the purchase price by fifteen per cent, but in return we demanded that a quarter of the price should be paid in sterling into a special account with the Bank of England. Gadsby was agreeable to that, and as this keen young businessman had the use of military telephone lines we knew that our deal would be put through promptly.

We were not a week too soon; a few days after our contract had been signed the mark was stabilised. Through Gadsby's connections the permission to ship the metal to England was easily obtained, and soon after we received payment of £300,000. This represented six million marks in the new currency; our remaining property was valued at four million.

The following period of deflation was marked by a considerable scarcity of ready money. Our ten million marks placed us in a powerful position. The time for speculations was now past, and I began looking round for some more solid investment.

At that time I made the acquaintance of Kommerzienrat von Eberstein, a leading personality in German industry, owner of steel mills, machine-tool and motor works. These had been in the possession of his family for three generations. He had been ruined by the inflation and was desperate for capital. He had to have at least three million marks on a six months' credit.

I advanced this sum to him at the rate, not then thought excessive, of one per cent per day. Then I sat back and awaited developments. After six months, as I had expected, I was asked by von Eberstein to his country house near Brandenburg. I was received by von Eberstein's daughter Traute, a fair-haired, capable-looking girl with considerable charm. She was nervous and anxious to please, and I thought perhaps she had been crying. After dinner von Eberstein confessed his inability to repay the loan which with accumulated interest, was now eight million marks. I asked him what terms he could offer.

He suggested that I should join his group of companies as an active partner. Von Eberstein's son Heinz, who was an engineer, was to run the technical side. This offer was too good to miss. But it meant that I had to sever my business relations with Mischa, which I did on the best of terms.

The time had now come when the German economy was helped to its feet by British and American loans. I have always been nauseated by the hypocrisy with which these loans were offered under the guise of charity. They cared no more for us than we did for them. It was a pure business deal. They knew that if they wanted to exploit us and extract reparations from us they had first to make us financially solvent. Their credits were virtually paid into their own pockets. Whatever their motives though, the good effects soon became noticed. The general position became easier, factories were running again. I could only welcome these developments; I was sick of the strenuous and nerve-racking life I had been leading and wanted nothing more than rest. Moreover, I felt it was time my cultural development caught up with my business development. I had started reading avidly and wanted time to study and absorb, and a place of my own where I could build up a library.

At that time I heard of an old aristocratic estate in Babelsberg being offered for sale. I went there and found a beautiful old house with a park of about 40 acres, both in a somewhat neglected condition. As the price was reasonable I bought the house and gave orders for it to be restored and furnished.

I was now well off enough to afford this. Thanks to Heinz Eberstein's efficient technical direction the Eberstein works had recovered very quickly and there was no dearth of orders. Only one thing worried old Eberstein.

We had large factories at Landshut in Bavaria, where tractors, lorries and armoured cars used to be made. But by the Treaty of Versailles the manufacture of armoured cars had been forbidden, while the German market was glutted with tractors released from army stocks. Unable to sell his machinery, Eberstein was faced with the necessity of having to shut down these factories.

At that time it came to my knowledge that tremendous orders for tractors and lorries were being placed by a Soviet purchasing commission. In a Berlin bar I met a German businessman who was already in contact with the Russians, and I was taken by him to the mysterious Soviet headquarters in Lindenstrasse.

Everything there was reminiscent of the way Russians are depicted in comic papers; there was an atmosphere of complete and unmitigated suspicion. Behind every painting one suspected an automatic camera, in every lamp a hidden microphone. The Russians argued with a dogged persistence and with some lack of the social graces. However, after much hard bargaining we concluded the deal. Shortly after we received orders for about twenty million marks' worth of goods.

I went down to Brandenburg to report my success to Eberstein. This time Traute seemed a different woman. When I had seen her before she had been expecting ruin daily. Now she greeted me with a warm smile. She was acting as her father's private secretary and I was very impressed with her grasp and knowledge of business details. Eberstein was delighted by the Russian orders and asked me to take over the direction and the expansion of the Landshut works.

Once the factories were running smoothly I decided to travel abroad. Hitherto I had had no time for travelling and, apart from what my military service had shown me of France, I knew no foreign countries. It was not merely to be a holiday; I intended to revive some of my old connections and to establish new ones. I also wanted to study conditions in the tool and motor industry in other countries.

Paris was novel and splendid and at the same time disappointing. My contacts with businessmen and industrialists showed me that the war years had not yet been forgotten. While innate good manners and natural charm never allowed those differences to come out into the open, I nevertheless noticed that the French were reserved, suspicious and even afraid. They seemed awed by the industry, swiftness and organising ability of our race. I confess I felt a little elated by their attitude. It showed that despite a lost war and a paralysed industry we were still respected and even feared. For the first time in many years we could again be proud of our country.

England – what a contrast after France! Everybody knows England from travellers' accounts or from books. Everybody knows that it is a country where people carry umbrellas, wear bowler hats, eat raw beefsteaks and play tennis. Well, England didn't quite live up to this picture, but all the same it was more English than I had expected. Immediately after my arrival Gadsby came up from Birmingham to take me under his wing. Our first evening was spent in his club where we reposed in heavy chairs, smoked pipes and spoke in whispers. Next day we went shopping in the West End, to Anderson and Sheppard's in Savile Row, bought hats at Hill's, umbrellas at Briggs', and I made the remarkable discovery that in this country all the night life stopped at midnight unless one had access to private and very expensive night clubs.

There was little for me to do in the way of business except to settle the division of Mischa's and my own English property and so, accepting an invitation from Sir Charles Gadsby senior, we went to the family seat near Birmingham. Sir Charles and Lady Gadsby received me very cordially in their old castle, and I spent some pleasant weeks with them. I visited their factories, where I found the scale of production astounding, but the production methods and factory organisation inferior to German factories. Unlike the French, Sir Charles discussed all questions of business in a sober and dispassionate manner, without any reference to politics. On the whole one can do business more easily with a British than a French businessman, which seems to support the thesis that in their whole way of life the English are akin to the Germans.

On my return I called on Eberstein at his castle in Thuringia. He showed a keen interest in doing business with Britain. But, quite evidently he was no longer in the best of health and it seemed to me that it was time for the old gentleman to take a rest. I asked Traute what she thought and found she had been anxious about her father for some time. He had been sleeping badly and had lost much of his keen grasp of business matters, and Traute had been doing more and more herself. She agreed with me completely that he ought to give up, but said that he wouldn't because it would be like handing over the family business to a stranger. An obvious solution occurred to me – and looking at Traute I saw that it had occurred to her too. It was an admirable solution and an extremely pleasant one. I knew then that Traute thought the same. A few weeks later I asked old Eberstein for the hand of his daughter in marriage.

Like many others we might have had to shut down our factories during the great depression of the thirties if our Russian orders had not kept 40 per cent of our production capacity employed. It became increasingly clear that through the system of foreign loans German industry was so tied to other countries that it responded very sensitively to the ups and downs of their economies. This only screened the German economic plight. The number of unemployed rose steadily. The Darmstadter and National Bank and the Dresdner Bank, as well as most of the smaller banking firms, had to stop payments. This resulted in general panic, widespread bankruptcy and a fresh wave of suicides. Everybody saw that this state of affairs could not go on. Everybody said 'This cannot go on,' but nobody did anything.

Our government proved itself incompetent in the face of a situation for which, apart from the short-sightedness of other nations, our own lunatic swarm of more than 30 political parties was to blame. The whole fabric of the Weimar Republic was corrupt, rotten and moribund. A people like the Germans could not be ruled in that way. We should have modelled our government to a much greater extent on the Soviet system. By this I do not mean to endorse the communist doctrine, any more than the Russians themselves do. What I mean is that a group of leaders of superior intellect and endowed with dictatorial powers was best suited to lead a country out of an unbalanced economic situation.

I probably do not go far wrong in assuming that the Allies deliberately supported the Weimar Republic because they wanted to prevent a German economic revival. Through that policy they gave indirect support to the National Socialist movement and this achieved the very thing that they had set out to avert. The attitude of a businessman or industrialist to the National Socialist movement and its programme could only be one of bewilderment. No one amongst my friends could take the Nazis seriously. The economic foundations of the Nazi programme were both vague and crude. They took no account of the complex nature of the international economic situation, and no one could trust these amateurs to repair the dislocated German economy. The nebulous, vague and hardly comprehensible tone of their speeches, slogans and propaganda might serve to stir up certain sections of the population or to inflame unstable youths; but a businessman had no time for this kind of Valhalla hysteria.

None of the leaders of that party were of recognised social standing. Apart from a few impoverished noblemen and superannuated soldiers they consisted mainly of shipwrecked middleclass people and a few young desperadoes who had nothing to lose and everything to gain. To imagine this clique in power seemed even more far-fetched than the possibility of a communist Germany. All the same I discerned certain danger signals in the situation, and thought it advisable to interest myself in politics and also to sound out my fellow industrialists on the matter. I began talking politics at my clubs; the Düsseldorf Association for Heavy Industry, whose influence on the country's economic life was enormous, and the Herrenklub in Jagerstrasse in Berlin.

The latter had a very diverse membership – land owners, artists, industrialists, lawyers and politicians. The members were held together only by a common and pronounced leaning towards the right. But the most important club I belonged to was the Unionklub in Schadowstrasse. As I had kept racing stables at Karlsborst I was eligible for this club, which was ostensibly a meeting place for those who were interested in racing, but which,.in reality, I found was far more. Membership in the first place was confined to followers of Hugenberg's right wing Deutschnational Party, and extreme right-wing army officers. The committee included Herr von Papen with whom I had two important discussions, together with Reichsbank president Schacht, concerning the participation of Germany in an international steel cartel. Papen, of whom I thought highly, convinced me that the policy of the effete and ineffective Cabinet of Herr Bruening had become intolerable; and as the communists were gaining more and more ground it was imperative to give active and financial support to the parties of the right, of whatever shade they were.

I need hardly say that I was not at all keen on being harnessed to any one party vehicle; but on the other hand there was no denying that the present policy would lead us nowhere. I must confess quite frankly that I had confidence in a man like Papen who represented the good old national school, and who was so superior to the Nazi ruffians.

In the summer of 1931 I went to Brussels for the cartel talks. I now found a noticeable improvement in our relations with other countries. The same crisis gripped us all, the same anxieties worried us all; and so our smaller differences were readily sunk in our common problems. Sir Charles Gadsby was also in Brussels. He spoke openly and apprehensively about the state of his factories. Like everyone else, he had been obliged to dismiss great numbers of his workers and his production had been switched over to small commodity goods. He was particularly perturbed about the bad market for agricultural machinery. Though the talks were not completely successful, an international price control for steel was agreed upon.

On that occasion I made the significant discovery that the industrialists of all countries, and not Germany alone, had become increasingly afraid of communists. As a natural consequence their politics had become more conservative and nationalist than before. I found nothing strange in this; but I think it should be placed on record, since we Germans are now blamed for a development that was not confined to our own country.

Our continuing business with Russia shielded the Eberstein concern from the worst effects of the depression; we had even been able to acquire some more factories, in Nuremberg, Landshut and near Brunswick. Owing to the crisis these factories were idle, and we did not put them into production until later.

Since business was relatively quiet my wife and I found time to go on more extended holidays; we visited Egypt and the near East, and on one of our journeys my old WUMBA colleague Petersen went with us. Throughout all these years I had been in more or less close contact with him, during which time he had undergone various political vacillations. He had recently joined the group around Schacht and the Unionklub, and prophesied that this connection would shortly become very important. Later I heard that he was then already a member of the NSDAP and formed the link between Papen's set and heavy industry in the Rhineland.

In the autumn of 1932 Traute and I went on a tour of the Mediterranean. After a few lovely months in Split on the Dalmatian coast we went to Corfu. There we heard, in February, that Hitler's Cabinet had assumed power in Germany. I cannot say that I was upset by this news; nor were some British businessmen who were spending their holidays there. At the same time I thought it better to return at once to Berlin. I found that several of our old employees, some of them men of more than 30 years' service, were suddenly sporting the Nazi Party badge and were tending to throw their weight about.

Early in April, 1933, Schacht asked some 20 or 30 industrialists to come to the Reichsbank for talks. Through Petersen I learned that those summoned to Berlin were all the important industrialists. I went keyed up with expectation. After we had waited for about ten minutes in the great hall of the Reichsbank building, Schacht came in accompanied by several others. 'Gentlemen, I have the honour to present you to the Reich Chancellor.' It was Hitler. He wearing a well-cut dark grey lounge suit and for a few moments seemed very shy and embarrassed. Then he began.

He pointed out that in his work of political reconstruction he depended very largely on our assistance. German economy was the crucial point for Germany's recovery. Although his party had made a strong appeal to the masses he thought that a reasonable capitalist system was the only possible one; we need have no fear of too radical reforms. Then someone assured Herr Hitler that German industry, whose representatives were here assembled, knew very well who its true enemy was, and that they welcomed the strictly anti-communist policy of the government. He then turned to us. He explained that during its hard struggle against reactionary and radical elements the NSDAP had run into grave financial difficulties and had incurred heavy debts. He was sure the industrialists would think it their duty to make a small contribution to the struggle of this 'truly national party'. He had, therefore, taken the liberty of dividing the Party's total debt into several small portions, each quite reasonable, and he would be glad if we could consider taking over these insignificant obligations.

The upshot of it all was that every one of us had to shoulder an obligation that was by no means trifling. Our own share was something over 100,000 marks. This cunning move gave us an idea of what to expect from the new regime.

In common with other industrialists I thought it was only a question of time before the Nazis fell. Personally I gave them half a year, or at most a year, after which, I was convinced, our national economy would have broken down. Furthermore, I could hardly imagine that other countries would allow Germany to be governed by a gang of sword-waving, war-happy thugs.

After the trade unions had been dissolved the NS works organisations took over their functions. Their newly appointed head for the Eberstein works, a young account-ant from our Berlin offices, came to me with a list of employees who were 'politically unacceptable'. Though I was not actually compelled to dismiss them, I though it better to yield in some of the cases. It would hardly have been wise to begin by offending the men of the new regime. I succeeded, however, in keeping those who were in important posts and who could not be easily replaced. Unfortunately, I had to act more harshly with our Jewish personnel. I had not noticed before how large a proportion of our staff, especially on the commercial side, were Jews. But most disa-greeable of all was the pressure put on me on account of our legal adviser, Justizrat Sobel. This old gentleman had served for almost 40 years with the Eberstein concern, of whose affairs he had a much closer grasp than old von Eberstein himself. I pointed out to the men of our National Socialist works organisation that I could not pos-sibly spare him at the present time. And as I had dismissed some of the other Jews the matter was tacitly, but temporarily, dropped.

Once again, Petersen, the human weathercock, became extremely useful to me. At first he had been close to Papen's cabinet, but after January 1933, he suddenly emerged in the uniform of a brigadier in the NSKK [National Socialist Motorised Corp]. At the same time in some mysterious way he had become the confidant of Reich Air Minister Goering. I had every reason to be glad of his offer to help me again – just for 'auld lang syne'. He was able to act as a go-between on our behalf with the new masters. Of course he didn't lose on the deal.

Petersen had an astounding social agility. In 1934, while I was abroad, the so-called Roehm revolt gave the Nazi leaders a pretext to rid themselves of their unwanted colleagues. I was worried that Petersen too might have fallen from his too dizzy height. But my concern was quite unfounded. With unerring instinct he had left the threatened group and already joined the circle around Himmler, who had just taken over the newly established Secret Police, and who was the coming man.

When shortly afterwards I went to England again I noticed a certain reserve in my friends over there. Not that my reception was in any way less cordial or polite; but a few of them seemed to have adopted a critical and censorious attitude towards Germany. They saw only the Nazis' forceful methods; they either did not see or did not want to see the tremendous improvements in our economic life. I told them that they were not without responsibility for the new course in Germany. It had been the idiotic and impossible reparation demands which had forced us along this road. But in any case they had to agree that the danger of a communist Germany, which might have been a menace to all Europe, was definitely past. This view of things was typical of the British: they welcomed what was useful to them, but rejected all the rest.

Up to 1935 business had gone on as usual. But now that military sovereignty had been re-established, there was a decisive change. Petersen called on me and sug-gested that the time had now come when the Eberstein concern should make its contribution to the strengthening of Germany. His proposal was that I should take a credit of 100 million marks at five per cent from the 'Bank for German Aviation'.

This terrific sum should serve to expand our small Brunswick works into a large aircraft motor factory.

At first I roundly rejected this proposal, although Heinz Eberstein, who had joined the Party in 1934, advocated this course. Petersen then brought along a number of highly placed members of the general staff, amongst whom was general of the Air Force von Mansfeld, Goering's most active lieutenant. The possibilities offered by this plan were painted to me in the most glowing colours, and at the same time it was hinted that I would incur the displeasure of high personages if I did not take my part in the new policy.

In the end I had no alternative. Our Brunswick factory was switched over to aircraft motors. This was not the end. I was pressed to take another credit of 30 millions from the Dresdner Bank, which would switch our tractor works in Landshut over to mobile artillery. Without in any way having wished it, and without wanting war or Germany's expansion, I was by 1936 deeply implicated in the rearmament programme.

In 1936 I had to get rid of our few remaining Jewish staff, including our old legal adviser, Dr Sobel. But I made sure that Sobel would be looked after. With my connections it was not difficult to arrange an emigration permit for him, and I got in touch with Gadsby who not only found him a place to live but got him a job with some business acquaintance of his. After Sobel had gone to England I was able to arrange for his wife and family to follow him. It was a sickening business having to get rid of an old and trusted employee, but the authorities were set on their anti-Jewish purge, and one just could not afford to go against them. As it was I risked severe censure by helping them as much as I had done. His place was taken by a gentleman from the Himmler clique, who had been suggested by Petersen: Botho Edler von Krieberg, holder of the order of the blood of the NSDAP and a member of the old Bavarian aristocracy. Though he proved utterly incompetent in business, he was nevertheless a useful link with the highest Party authorities.

At that time the first four-year-plan came into force. Industry was being most energetically geared up. Planning of production became tighter every day; first, certain materials were not allowed to be used, next, certain products were not allowed to be made. The aim was to create an absolute internal self-sufficiency which would mean a complete independence from imports.

The result of these efforts was an incredible widening of bureaucratic control and a tremendous amount of red tape. There was such a flood of orders and special regulations that only a specialist could make sense of them. Although I welcomed the momentary prosperity I was sure that it could not last long and that sooner or later the Nazis would have partially to retreat from the isolationist policy.

The economic structure of the modern world makes it impossible for a single country to shut itself off from the rest of the world. The German economic system now was something of a tight-rope balancing act – an act brilliantly and expertly performed by our unparalleled German organising ability – but an act which had somehow got stuck in the middle of the rope and could move neither forwards nor backwards, and which must inevitably end in a crash.

But meanwhile the profits of industry were between two and three times as high as in the best years in the twenties. And the introduction of piece-rate payments, without which these huge programmes could not have been carried out, meant that the workers' income had in many cases doubled.

In 1936 the Olympiad took place in Berlin. Official preparations for it showed that a sports event was to be made into a piece of political advertisement. Our guests were to see the new Germany in all its power and glory. Personally I had always hated the combination of sport and politics; I knew also that my British friends, for example, would not only not understand but would be embarrassed by it. But, on the other hand, I relished the prospect of taking the wind out of their sails. This would show them that our country was not quite so contemptible as they seemed to think.

My Oympiad guests were young Gadsby and his wife, my friend Lambert from Paris and his wife and about a dozen more, all of whom I accommodated in our Babelsberg house. We entertained them royally. I arranged a great firework display in my park; there were several motor cars set aside for their use. I had also hired a Havel steamer, for the whole period, and we made excursions into the Mark lakes. I saw to it that my guests had preferential treatment at all official functions, and I introduced them to the exclusive Wannsee golf club. And, indeed, they were delighted with their entertainment and full of enthusiasm, but whether their enthusiasm could change their real views about Germany I could not tell.

While morning rides in the Grunswald or balls in the club were the chief interest of the ladies, I arranged for the men to gain an idea of our economic development. I arranged several works inspections. We went together to my Spandau factory, to the Brunswick factories and we even went as far afield as Nuremberg and Landshut. Whatever they thought of the Olympiad our visitors were deeply impressed with our organisation and our production methods.

As soon as my friends had left, an unpleasant incident occurred. In October, the *Schwarze Korps* and the *Angriff* (organs of the SS and SA respectively) published several attacks on me, accusing me of employing recalcitrants and reactionaries, in particular the manager of the Landshut works who had been an active member of the Catholic Zentrum party. I was also accused of having ignored the workers' recreational organisation, 'Strength through Joy,' and the national drive to make factories more beautiful, 'Beauty of Labour'.

I had perhaps been a little careless in some ways, but some of these charges could easily be disposed of. We built sports grounds, a convalescent home for the workers of our Brunswick works and their families, and we sent some especially deserving workers on a 'Strength through Joy' cruise to Madeira.

Botho Edler von Krieberg stressed that the Führer and the SS would be pleased if I made a donation to 'Lebensborn', which was an eccentric kind of institute for racial experiments. It was necessary to pander to the whims of the high-ups if one wished to be left in peace, and so I had to pay quite a large sum. Then, after I had admitted several virulent Nazis into our organisation, it was conveyed to me that Hans Schwarz von Berg, the all-powerful editor of the *Schwarze Korps*, would refrain from any future attacks. Having thus put myself well into the Party's good books I felt a little safer about helping friends and acquaintances who had got on the wrong side of the authorities. I arranged exit permits for several friends, and I was able to help two Jewish ex-employees to sell some of their property to enable them to pay the dues demanded from emigrants, and smuggle a little money abroad. By selling for them I got them a much better price than they could get themselves. And these too I put in touch with Gadsby. Wollny was in a different case. He was one of my works managers, a staunch Catholic who had refused to adapt himself to changing conditions. He was arrested one day for making seditious statements, and put in a concentration camp. He was a good manager and there was no real harm in him, and so I used my influence to get him released and posted bail myself for his good behaviour. But the KZ had given him a good shaking up and although his opinion of the regime was obviously unchanged he behaved with much more tact and refrained from speaking about it.

The next important political events were the Anschluss and the march into Czechoslovakia. I simply could not see how other countries could passively watch these developments. The Nazis' hazardous politics could easily plunge Europe into the abyss. Unprejudiced foreign observers admitted that there could be no effective internal influence on German politics. By their inaction the other European countries were directly responsible for what subsequently happened.

However incredible it may sound today, at that time I was still firmly convinced that Germany had no intention of making war – certainly not for many years. Despite our thorough rearmament the German general staff had again and again warned and restrained our leaders. And I did not overestimate the scale of our rearmament. France was still the strongest military power on the continent. Before Hitler's invasion of Czechoslovakia I had not believed that he would dare to provoke this powerful neighbour through hasty military actions.

But Hitler's Prague speech changed my mind. It was now clear that our great war machine would one day be set in motion, and that the day was not very far distant. My fears were justified by the increasing tension of 1939, and all hopes of peace were finally destroyed through Hitler's Saarbrücken speech and the repeal of the naval agreement with Britain. [In the speech – actually October 9 1938 – Hitler railed against the conservative 'warmongers' Churchill and Eden: 'We Germans will no longer endure such governessy interference. Britain should mind her own business.'] There seemed to be no country left in Europe who dared call a halt to the perilous course steered by the Nazis. In vain I and likeminded people gave warnings against a continuation of the present political course; no business man wants war. But I had done all I could.

When it came, neither I nor my friends were surprised. The so-called manoeuvres on our eastern frontier were no more than a massing of forces against Poland. And the swift defeat of the little Polish republic was inevitable. But Hitler had to puff it up into a dazzling victory to offset the loss of face his government had suffered after the pact with Soviet Russia. Everybody saw the strategic and political expediency of this re-hash of Bismarck's eastern politics; but nevertheless the betrayal of all previous ideological principles had been unfavourable to the government.

Whatever else one might say it was undeniable that Hitler showed a certain cleverness in foreign politics. This man possessed to a very high degree the ability of choosing the right moment to strike. And that was impressive. No one had imagined that after years of venomous anti-Bolshevik propaganda an understanding between us and Russia was still possible. Despite some ideological doubts, I was impressed by the clever and determined way in which our government had solved this problem.

On the outbreak of war I was appointed *Wehrwirtschaftsführer* [Armament Leader] in the *Kriegswirtschaftsrat* [War Economic Council] which had been created under the chairmanship of Goering. I was not at all keen on this position, which harnessed me wholly to the service of the war industry. But this was not the first time I had had to sacrifice my own feelings. In 1938 I had had to take over 'aryanised' businesses. At that time I had still been able to help some of my Jewish friends to emigrate before I had to incorporate their firms in the Eberstein concern. I need hardly feel a sense of guilt about these events. If I had not done it someone else would; and would have done it in a less considerate and less polite way. Moreover, these businesses were excellently taken care of by me; and there was always the possibility that I could return them one day to their rightful owners.

Even after the Polish campaign I had still not given up all hope of a compromise with the Allies. The strength of French armaments had been overestimated; the bad condition of the French divisions on our western frontier made it appear improbable that the Allies would take the initiative. And it appeared even more improbable that Hitler would insist on frontal assault on the Maginot Line. I thought it to be my duty to express these doubts – though with all necessary caution – at the meetings of the War Economic Council. Most of the influential industrialists agreed with me. Only the more inveterate Nazis bandied about such slogans as 'The German soldier knows only one way of fighting: to attack!'

At first the French campaign seemed like a miracle to me. But when the dimension of our neighbour's defeat had emerged clearly I realised the magnitude of French corruption. Those of us who had been in the First World War simply could not imagine such a thing as a surrender of the fortress of Verdun without a fight. Then there was the utter defeat of the British Expeditionary Force. The only explanation that offered itself to my mind was treason or large-scale bribery. How right Hitler had been when he warned us again and again not to overestimate the democratic countries!

I do not know whether it was lack of information or political expediency that was responsible for our propaganda to minimise the extent of the British defeat. The British may have saved four-fifths of their men from Dunkirk, but it was palpable that they had been completely beaten. Perhaps it was typical of us that we were impressed by the way in which Britain took this defeat. British prestige emerged strengthened from this affair. But this only offset the damage to British reputation after the invasion of Norway. The inability of Britain's mighty navy to prevent the amateurish occupation of Norway with a few dozen old merchant ships had severely shaken my belief in British naval predominance.

We all thought the heavy bombing raids on England in the summer of 1940 were the prelude to an invasion. When invasion did not come many of us, despite the prevailing high spirits, began to ask how this war would ever be finished. It stood to reason that we could not remain at war with Britain till the end of all time; and any attempt at invasion would surely have drawn the United States into the war. This seemed to be a deadlock.

The German government had undoubtedly counted on a peaceful settlement after the French campaign was over. The Reich Control Office for Industry issued directives to lower production in certain sections of the war industry, including the construction of heavy tanks. The switch-over for peacetime production was being prepared. It was confidently expected in high quarters that Britain would now sue for peace.

It was difficult for us to survey the political situation properly. Apart from occasional broadcasts from London we were completely dependent on the German press. This received directions from the Ministry of Propaganda, and as all newspapers brought the same 'approved' news, no reliance could now be placed on them.

The few Swiss papers that one managed to get seemed to be terrified of offending either side and long before the United States entered the war American papers had been unobtainable. Thus it came that even highly placed personalities were groping in the dark. The crudest misjudgements were only too natural; we all believed Britain was defeated.

Instead of that, the leadership of Britain now passed to a really able and vigorous man, and we slowly began to realise that far from being defeated Britain was even now preparing to defend herself to the last drop of blood. And all the daring adventures which Hitler now brought off – such as the invasion of Yugoslavia and Greece, and the opening of the North African front – were merely confessions of his inability to defeat Britain by direct attack.

I was aware that frontier 'incidents' on the German-Russian demarcation line in Poland were on the increase. Yet it came as a heavy blow to me and all other thinking persons to hear of the German invasion of Russia in June 1941. This should have been prevented at all costs. I could not believe that it would end well. Our leaders were aware of the superiority of Russian tanks and it was believed that the Russian strength was something like 200 divisions. As we had to occupy Scandinavia, France and the Balkans and at the same time fight in North Africa, our prospects were not too rosy.

After the twin battle of Vyasma and Briansk, Hitler announced that the greater part of the Red Army had been defeated, and that the remaining Russian troops were retreating towards the east. At that time a meeting of armament leaders was called in Berlin at which we were allotted certain functions in the occupied eastern territories. I was chosen to take over large motor and tool factories in the district of Stalino. Despite our quick advances this carving-up seemed to me a little premature, and putting forward various excuses I succeeded in evading these eastern duties for some time. I had been getting steadily more and more fed up with my numerous official duties. I found the working of bureaucracy cramping and dispiriting. I decided that my mind needed a holiday – a busman's holiday – and I arranged a journey to France. Although in September 1941, it would have been possible to describe the purpose of this journey officially as 'information', I preferred to have an endorsement from the Reichsgruppe Industrie. This endorsement stated that I was enquiring on behalf of the section into the state of the French automobile industry. Of course this was only a pretext.

The real reason for my trip was twofold; firstly I felt a very strong urge to get away from Germany – from the bureaucracy, the goose step and, strange as it may sound, from the Germans themselves. They had become unbearably self-satisfied and boisterously pleased with themselves – it seemed that my countrymen showed up at their worst when victorious.

The second reason was simply one of business or, rather foresight in business. Little as I was interested to take over, or have anything to do with the industries of the East, at this stage of the war, France, Belgium and Holland was quite another kettle of fish. It had always appealed to me to be an international industrialist, linking the economic of many nations, building up cartels and international groups; there was no limit to the possibilities for anyone with enough foresight and initiative. But the opportunity had to be taken now, as later the German bureaucratic machine would step in and incorporate the Western European industries into those of the German Reich and the New Order.

Besides, whilst France was still in a state of chaos there were plenty of pickings and deals to be made, and there was a chance to contravene the currency regulations of the Finance Act. I felt it a useful precaution to deposit a nest-egg in Switzerland or South America. It was not really that I was foreseeing defeat, but somehow I never had real confidence in the Nazis' ability to run the economy of Germany, and far less the whole of Europe. I was by no means the only one who felt and acted like this and there was a general rush amongst the people who could afford it to get at least something deposited abroad. The leaders of the Party were no exception.

I stayed at the Claridge in Paris. Anyone who was connected with industry stayed there; the Ritz was the headquarters of the Gestapo and the SD [security branch of the Gestapo, a special formation of the SS]. The Marignan housed the big bosses of the Labour Front and Todt Slave Labour Organisation, who seemed to play quite an important part here. The first man to meet me in the foyer there was Petersen; he had come on behalf of 'Continental', the tyre people, but in reality for the same business reason as I and lots of others who stayed at Hôtel Claridge.

The next day I called on Lambert who had lived in relatively modest conditions in Rue des Sts Pères but who now occupied a luxurious apartment in the Bois de Boulogne. Lambert was an Alsatian and so, before the First World War, he had been a German subject. At Heidelberg he had belonged to the exclusive student association of the Saxo-Borussians; later on he served with the equally exclusive Halberstadt Cuirassier Regiment. After the war he found it profitable to remember that Alsace was now French. He was conveniently free from prejudices and commanded first-class information and connections. Immediately after the arrival of our troops he had been able to make the most of the situation. In that one year he had already made huge profits, and was on very good terms with our authorities. In short, he was the very man I needed.

I told him that I would stay for some time and that I needed an apartment. I learnt that persons in my position could acquire accommodation only through the so-called 'Organisation Rosenberg', which looked after the homes of fugitives and Jews. One could not do this officially; it had to be done with cigars and cognac. Lambert confirmed my expectation; our authorities and the French collaborators were equally corrupt and everything was possible with money and connections.

At about nine o'clock we drove in his car to the Monseigneur. This bar was well known to me from previous visits; it was celebrated for its cuisine and its gipsy band. As in all good restaurants no ration card was needed, but then a dinner together with all that goes with it cost at least 1,000 francs, and often considerably more. At first sight the clientele proved to have changed; there were German officers and a number of Frenchmen with their ladies who would not normally have gone there. I noticed a Frenchman at the next table who, like the lady with him, seemed to have drunk too much. They were making fun quite openly of a number of Labour Front Bigwigs.

'Isn't that Dubois, the big armaments man?' I asked Lambert. He nodded.

'He should be more careful,' he added in an undertone. 'He seems to rely on the Germans here knowing very little French, but if one of them should understand him even his high position will be of no use to help him.'

'He is working for the Germans then?'

'For the Germans, amongst others,' Lambert replied in even softer tones.

But nothing happened to the world-famous armament king. A young captain, holder of the Ritterkreuz, who was a little tipsy, went over to start trouble. But then the two turned out to be known to each other and Dubois made him join his table. Champagne was brought, the young hero quickly made friends and, fifteen minutes later a terrific drinking bout was in progress in their corner.

Most of my former business friends were now retired and living on their estates. Almost all the important industrialists had been eliminated and replaced by Germans; or, if they apparently held their posts, our men occupied all the key positions. One only met the parvenus, who had grown fat under the occupation. It was the heyday of sharks and scoundrels.

Informers were flourishing in Paris. One of Lambert's friends, a Dr Hellwig, was a German with quiet, unobtrusive manners and some insignificant commission in Paris. At home he was a lecturer in jurisprudence at Munich. His commission was only a pretext. In actual fact he had to keep an eye on the high SS and Gestapo officers in Paris and make weekly reports to the *Reichssicherheitshauptamt* [Reich Security Office]. He was neither a Party member nor an SS man; today he lives peacefully on his estate in South Germany.

At that time the Maquis were not yet important. In Paris they became noticeable only in the autumn of 1943. But even now the division between collaborators and patriots was very pronounced. Everybody spied on everybody else, French and Germans alike. The strange part of it all was that only the SS, the Labour Front and Todt Organisation men were genuine Nazis. The high army officers were all 'anti'. Everybody else had come to France to get as much as they could, and no one can say they were slow at it.

Today one is inclined to rate too high what the common soldiers sent home from France in the way of clothes, food and other things. The tankers who took their wine in the Moulin Rouge and Folies Bergère were not the real exploiters of France. The real culprits were those who had been sent by the Party or Rosenberg Organisation on official missions.

Of course the French population suffered, but her industry profited from Wehrmacht orders. These were mostly for fortifications, chiefly along the north coast. The workmen engaged on these orders were placed under the Todt organisation and from then onwards were 'live freight', which could be sent to Germany, Norway, Poland or elsewhere as required. Thousands of workers who became redundant after the construction of the western wall went into the great IG Farben factories in Auschwitz.

My business travels were interspersed with pleasure trips in the neighbourhood of Paris, to Versailles, Saint Cloud, Sèvres and Fontainebleau, in the course of which I got to know the rural population. Here, one would often meet with hatred and contempt, an attitude carefully nursed by the fanatical clergy. The French directed their hatred mainly against collaborators. Germans who were known not to be Nazis even entered society here and there. Thus I succeeded in establishing friendly relations with several families.

Lambert, who had bought the palace of Bredole near Meaux, did everything possible to make social contact with the surrounding country nobility, but was completely ignored. For the festivities in his palace he generally had to bring his friends from Paris. Hardly ever in my life have I seen so brilliant a concourse of profiteers, cutthroats, parvenus and bought women as at Lambert's parties. Amongst them were medium-rank German officers and those Todt and German Labour Front men who were seen wherever dubious people met for dubious purposes. One of Lambert's special friends was SS Brigadier Koblenk, an intimate of all the black market dealers who met at Maxim's, and a noted and insatiate roué. I would not normally have gone to these parties if they had not been so useful to me for business purposes. Here one met the connections one needed – not only amongst the Germans but amongst the collaborators. These gentry were leading triple lives – they had to keep in with the Vichy authorities, the unofficial German trade delegations and the Maquis. The last they bribed with 'protection' money. They kept double accounts; an official one for the Germans and Vichy and a second one for the Maquis who demanded a considerable proportion of their profits.

Since America's entry into the war the whole situation had undergone a profound change, and after this first disastrous Russian winter our campaign began to look as though it might stretch out to the crack of doom. My projected journey into the eastern territories could not be postponed beyond the summer of 1942. I was still expected to take over a number of factories in the Stalino district. The Reich commissar of that district now pointed out in unmistakable terms that the time had come for me to look after these factories.

My experiences with Russian industries bore out what I had already been told by a number of friends. Before retreating, the Russians had blown up the greater part of their factory buildings after having dismantled and removed the machinery. They had also evacuated the majority of their skilled workers and specialists. And those workers who happened to have been left behind would only return to the factories under compulsion.

This had not been so at first. The Russian workers had then shown themselves quite willing to work for us, as the Bolshevik regime was not particularly popular. But the crazy policies which the Party had decreed for the East destroyed all hope of collaborating with the Russians. The political aim, elaborated by Rosenberg, was to keep the entire population of these territories at the lowest possible level of civilisation. It was thought unnecessary for the Russians to bother with such black arts as reading or writing. Schools and colleges were quite superfluous. If we had taken advantage of the very pronounced nationalist tendencies of the various Russian peoples by establishing independent states with autonomous administrations, we might have gained millions of valuable workers. As it was we were masters of a gigantic flock of underfed and sullen helots.

The Ministry of Economic Affairs had several times suggested that we should acquire Russian factories and installations from them on very favourable terms. Nevertheless, only the largest concerns, such as IG Farben or Krupps, were prepared to take over Russian factories; and even then not on their own account but only as governing trustees. I followed the same line. I declared that at the present time I could not undertake to develop the Eberstein concern in these territories. In any case I now had large-scale obligations in France. After spending a short time in Berlin I returned to Paris in February 1943.

I arrived in Paris a few days after the remainder of the Germans in Stalingrad had capitulated. Only a fool could have shut his eyes then to the ultimate outcome of the struggle. The German armies in North Africa were in full retreat. The occupied Balkan territories were in continual upheaval. After the Allied landings in North Africa the German rulers expected an invasion of Southern France. The increased activities of the Maquis in the region between Marseilles, Toulon and Lyons suggested that even the French counted on that possibility.

In Paris the resistance carried out more and more acts of sabotage. They followed a very ingenious plan. There were no large-scale bomb outrages or similar plots, but all the same the Maquis succeeded in putting entire works, such as the Renault factories, out of action. The electricity supply was continually cut. No sooner was a brand-new cable laid than it was cut and the machines were idle once more. This, together with the repeated interruptions of work due to air-raid alarms, meant that a regular flow of production was no longer possible.

As time went on the atmosphere amongst the Germans and collaborators in Paris became more and more strained. Then came the Allied landings in Italy; and here the British raid in Dieppe was not regarded as the ridiculous affair that the German press tried to make of it. The collaborators began to realise that their time would soon be over. Some tried still to make as much money as possible; others doubled their contributions to the Maquis and prepared for their flight to Switzerland. They all pinned their hopes on their Swiss bank accounts.

By now it had become a little risky for a German to go out alone into the streets, especially at night. Incidents in the working class districts had become more frequent. The trains, where special coaches were set aside for Germans, were under military guard and could be regarded as safe. But if one motored on the high roads one knew what to expect.

My friend Lambert's spirits showed signs of hysteria. The parties in the palace became wilder. There was an air of forced and convulsive frivolity under a black cloud of inevitable and impending doom. These people all knew what they had to expect once the Germans had gone. But they dared not think of it. They had to drug themselves with laughter and gaiety and wine. Once, after the tipsy concourse had been gloating over a nude cabaret show of an incredible blatancy and lewdness, a time bomb was discovered under the stage which would have been sufficient to blow the whole chateau sky high. But the feasting went on.

During these eighteen months I more or less commuted between Germany and France. Somehow I felt a morbid fascination in watching events shaping towards the final catastrophe. But I did not want to watch them from Germany. There the tension under the continuous air raids and the atmosphere of distrust and hatred under the savage rule of the SS was quite unbearable. Besides, the more time one spent in Germany the bigger the chance of being drawn deeper into the Nazi war machine and Party organisation. That was the one thing I wanted to avoid at all costs. So I spent as much time as I could manage in France.

I was in Paris on 6 June when the long-expected Allied invasion broke into Normandy, and in the evening the emblem of the Maquis, the sun with the Gallic cockerel, was chalked for the first time on the wall of Lambert's house. In more than one sense this was the writing on the wall.

Lambert proposed going to Switzerland. Dr Kruger, the watchdog of the SS, had already organised things in Geneva. He could also help us. He had only to give in our names at one of the Franco-Swiss frontier stations and he assured us that we should have no difficulty in crossing the border. Lambert persuaded me to join him. A fool could have seen that Germany was doomed. I was sure that the German armies would capitulate the moment the first Allied soldier set foot on German soil. When that happened I intended either to go back to Berlin or to arrange for my family to join me in Switzerland.

Our plans for escape were still not ready when the farcical officers' revolt took place. This was a model of amateurish dilettantism. On 20 July the not very numerous SS and Gestapo in Paris were arrested by heavily armed groups of officers and shep-

herded, jittering with fear, to a shelter in the Place de la Concorde. The female staff of
the Gestapo and the SS Maidens were also dragged from their beds to an hotel near
the Place de la Concorde. The city was now firmly in the hands of the officers and
reliable troops. The German Commandant of Paris was amongst the rebels. The Allied
front was within a few kilometres. So all conditions for success were ensured. Then
came the news of the failure of the attempt on Hitler's life which was the whole crux
of the plot.

The revolution collapsed like a pricked balloon. The gentlemen rebels slunk back
to their barracks and a little while later allowed themselves to be arrested by the SS.
The German Commandant drove out of the city, ordered his driver to wait while he
went into a wood and shot himself with his service revolver. Even this was muffed
and he merely blinded himself. He was seized by the SS, taken to Germany and there
more expertly shot through the neck. All this pitiful pantomime had taken a bare 24
hours. At that time Patton's and Bradley's tank formations were already in Avranches
and under favourable wind conditions the gunfire could clearly be heard in Paris.

Then the general dissolution set in. Day and night transports of wounded men
rolled through Paris. The bombers zoomed incessantly above the city; one alarm
followed another. Every morning streets and houses were covered with the sign of
the Maquis. Next to them were the names and addresses of collaborators who were
wanted and those whose last hour had struck. All German civilians, all the agents
and profiteers and most of the collaborators had gradually left Paris. Everybody was
feverishly trying to reach the Swiss frontier, or to cross the Rhine with the retreating
German armies.

The scramble that now ensued was a fantastic comedy. There were not many ave-
nues of retreat. The trains were terribly overcrowded and terribly dangerous. Railway
lines were under continuous bombing or machine-gun attacks from American,
British and Canadian aircraft. Nor were the high roads any better. Those who escaped
the bombers were caught by the Maquis, who were entrenched in woods and ravines
and covered the roads with accurate fire.

We had obtained all the necessary documents. The roads and bridges were still
under the control of the German field gendarmerie and the SS. To pass them we
needed German military passports, but we also had French identity papers, Vichy
papers and others.

There were four of us; Lambert, his wife, a lady friend of hers and myself. At first we
went back to his chateau in Bredole. It was completely deserted and no one took any
notice of us. We packed everything we could find in the way of jewellery, diamonds,
gold and valuables, and then set off north-east for St Quentin, where Lambert had
kept some cash in one of his smaller factories. We found that everyone had left it. The
manager had absconded with the cash, and everything was in a state of chaos.

The decay was absolute. The retreat of the German armies had turned into a rout,
and over wide areas Germans were fair game. The villages were congested. Columns
of cars, transports of wounded, tanks, guns and civilian cars blocked up every road.
Some SS divisions who had remained intact gathered behind the German lines trying

in vain to stem the general retreat. Above this witches' cauldron was the unceasing roar of Allied bombers and fighters. The days were parching hot. No water could be had; there was nowhere anything to eat.

We now turned south, towards Rheims. We ran a certain risk in that our projected route ran across the line of retreat of the German armies, but that was unavoidable. Facing tremendous difficulties, sleeping in barns and forests, in danger sometimes from this side, sometimes from that, we went to Toul via Châlons and Bar-le-Duc. Behind Toul, in the woods of the Lorraine which lie in front of the Moselle, the Maquis were encamped. We managed to get through towards Belfort. As the retreat of the Wehrmacht had come to a temporary halt behind the Moselle it became more and more difficult to evade the numerous controls. The Gestapo were out in force combing the villages near the frontier.

But by great good fortune we got through, and we almost cried with relief when we reached the Swiss frontier station of Delle. The Swiss made no difficulties; those whose names had been put on the list could cross the border directly, and all formalities would be seen to later. But those whose names were not on the list had either to turn back or to try to cross the Rhine with the German armies. To our consternation and fury it appeared that Dr Kruger had either made a mistake in having sent our names to the wrong frontier station or else – and this seemed more likely – he had taken our money and left us in the lurch. Anyway, there we were and something had to be done.

We were told of a man who could take us across the border illegally. In these little places Maquis and German soldiers were sitting opposite each other in a state of armed neutrality. At first all four of us were regarded as French, and we put our hopes in the Maquis who maintained a regular illegal border traffic. But the man who was supposed to take us across was ill. And Lambert had to go back to Belfort because his driver, who had taken us to Delle, had been arrested and jailed by the Germans. He got him out after some trouble, but on his return the Maquis took his car away. He came back only after several days.

Our situation had become more precarious as time went on. It was soon apparent that we were trusted by neither side. It was a dreadful situation. At one time I was burning some of our private papers in the lavatory of the hotel while Lambert's wife was having wine downstairs with the Maquis, and her friend was drinking with German military police next door. Finally, the Gestapo arrived and thoroughly searched the whole place. So far we had been French; now we thought it better to produce our German passports.

The Gestapo man with whom I spoke gave us another 24 hours in which to clear out. Shortly after we were told that the Maquis believed we were spies and would shoot us down if we attempted to cross the border. We had no choice, and at dawn with our headlights screened we headed towards Germany. Behind us came the last stragglers: SS, secret military police and Gestapo. The French chapter was closed.

Once across the border I soon had to part company with Lambert, who joined a group of Vichy officials who were setting up headquarters somewhere in Thuringia.

I went back to Berlin to wait for the imminent collapse. But the American armoured spearheads were halted on the Moselle and severe fighting broke out round Aachen. People began to make bets about the date of the Allied entry into Berlin. I suggested to my wife that we should go to Bavaria, for I expected a new Russian offensive. But she was against this, so we stayed on in Babelsberg.

The year 1945 began dark and ill-omened. Hitler had thrown the last unscathed German tank divisions into a hopeless offensive in the Ardennes. I hoped that this act of folly would entail the collapse of the Western Front and enable the Western Allies to advance into the interior of Germany. Instead the Russians staged a gigantic offensive from the Vistula and within a few days had overrun all Eastern Germany as far as the Oder. Our feeble-minded High Command, not realising the danger until it was too late, hastily withdrew troops from the west. By then the Allies had secured the Remagen bridgehead, while Patton's tanks rushed into Bavaria and central Germany towards the Czech frontier. It was possible with fair accuracy to name the day on which Germany would be cut in two, and now I made a last attempt to reach Bavaria.

Before this plan could mature I was called up for the Volkssturm. Even in my position I could not avoid this – and I must confess it was not altogether unexpected. I was given the command of a company and spent three very unfortunate weeks supervising the building of fortifications round Zossen, where Hitler's headquarters lay. Then fate took a hand and I saw an opportunity of getting out again.

Although the Americans were by now in Saxony, and the Canadians outside Oldenburg, it was decided that all ministerial offices and departments should be evacuated to Bavaria and Schleswig-Holstein. A completely harebrained scheme. Nevertheless I managed to get my own indispensable position in the Reichsgruppe Industrie recognised, was relieved of my Volkssturm duties and was allotted a place on the transport for myself and my family.

The transport consisted of three motor-coaches. The leader of the convoy was an ardent young ministry official who planned to take us first to Saalfeld, and then to the Bavarian Alps, where, he said, several SS divisions were making a last-ditch stand. Apart from him no one was very enthusiastic about any lastditch stand. And three of us – myself, another Riechsgruppe Industrie man and an army staff courier – organised the complete breakdown of two of the motor-coaches just before we reached Saalfeld. Then, while the convoy leader rushed about like an hysterical hen looking for spare parts, we sat in the local inn and toasted ourselves in schnapps. But we had gone a bit too far, and when a motorised artillery section came through the village on their way to the capital the mad young zealot ordered the whole company back to Berlin. Thus I reached Babelsberg again just two days before the big Russian offensive.

During the next few days I thought it expedient to lie somewhat low. The Russian attack started with an incredible inferno of artillery fire, and three swiftly moving wedges were driven in the city. There were innumerable rumours to the effect that the Americans were over the Elbe and approaching fast – the rumours brought them swiftly nearer and nearer – Magdeburg, Brandenburg, Potsdam – at the gates of Berlin. I believed the rumours – not because I thought them at all likely, but because like everyone else I fervently hoped that they might be true. They were, in fact, unmitigated nonsense. According to a prearranged plan the Sherman tanks stopped on the Elbe while the Russian forces completely encircled Berlin. The advance troops were probing quickly forward. They were through Potsdam and any moment we might expect them in Babelsberg.

Everybody urged me to hide my wines or smash the bottles. Otherwise they said the Russians would get drunk and smash the place up. But I thought this was going rather too far. For many years I had collected the best vintages and I was justifiably proud of my cellar.

I welcomed the first Russian arrivals at the door, in one hand a bottle of Burgundy, in the other a cordial Medoc. My conscience was quite clear, and I had nothing to fear from the Russians. I knew them; I had done business with them. That evening I was entertaining some half dozen Russian officers, few of whom could stand, and I managed to take the opportunity of arranging for a young and very charming general and his staff to be billeted in my house. They were admirably behaved and although there were undoubtedly excesses during the first few days, not a single person of my house was molested, nor was any damage done to my home.

My political past was unobjectionable as I had always kept away from actual Nazi circles. As far as the armament programme is concerned, I had only done the absolute minimum of what was required of me. I found the Russians sympathetic and helpful and was even given facilities to visit two of my factories. Peaceful collaboration with them seemed quite possible. But in the summer of 1945 the Russians suddenly changed their policy. They arrested the majority of the leading industrialists, Nazis and non-Nazis alike. They were brutally dragged away in the middle of the night and have not been heard of since. This unprovoked and ruthless attack on businessmen and civilians disgusted and disillusioned me. To try to work with or under such barbarians was out of the question. So, in the autumn of 1945, I moved to one of my estates in the British zone of occupation, where I now live in complete retirement, awaiting events.

5

WERNER HARZ

Werner was a fair, lanky, neatly dressed boy of fifteen when he first started coming to our house. He was five years older than me and was really my brother's friend to begin with, but after 1933 when Karl-Victor had left Germany, he and I became very intimate.

Werner's background could not have been more different from ours. Whereas my parents allowed their children to run wild and encouraged them to solve their own problems and develop their own tastes, he had had a strict and conventional upbringing in a bourgeois home. Our free and easy life, where no topics were frowned on and where everyone said and did what they liked, was a revelation to Werner, and from 1926 onwards he became very much 'one of the family'.

Then, when the Nazis had come to power, and we had become social outcasts, our friendship with Werner grew closer than ever. And as things went from bad to worse it was he, I think, more than anyone else who helped me retain my faith in human nature. His decency and normality, his sane rejection of everything Nazi and his ability to remain true to himself enabled me to see things in proportion. He was a constant reminder that some people, at least, had not gone mad.

In 1946, when I found him again a bit taller and thinner but hardly changed at all, it never occurred to me that we should not be able to pick up our relations where we had left off. But soon after the first excitement of meeting had simmered down again I found that Werner was uneasy. He was quite unable to take the resumption of our friendship for granted. Too much had happened in between. He said he felt that as a German he had no right to be my friend after what I had suffered at Germany's hands, and it took me a long time to persuade him to accept the fact that nothing had changed between us. This diffidence of Werner's seemed to me to be the most conclusive proof, if proof were needed, that he was as fine a character as ever. He, and a few others like him, who had nothing to reproach themselves with, were the only Germans I met who suffered from a feeling of guilt and shame. In other words, they alone had managed to retain their conscience.

Werner Harz, born 1911

My father was a teacher in a high school in one of the most respectable suburbs of Berlin, and a man of strong national convictions. He had four children and he brought us up in an atmosphere of stolid respectability and narrow academic conservatism.

We learnt at an early age that of all the countries in the world Germany was first, and that the Jews – particularly at the end of the First World War – were up to no good as far as the Fatherland was concerned. Till 1926 I grew up unquestioning and contented in our close-knit family circle. Then, through mixing with school companions and older friends, I came across books which completely contradicted all that my father had taught me.

I remember that this was a significant, exciting time for me. And, as well as I could, I cut myself off from my family and retired to an attic in our apartment house where I began to read. An unsuspected world sprang inside me. I felt at the same time happy and rebellious. I had found on my birthday table only books of German heroes, formal classics or idealised history books. But now I suddenly saw the world in an entirely new, and an entirely different light.

Perhaps I was too young to read authors like Kafka, Thomas Mann, Heinrich Mann and Werfel: at that time I could only understand a very limited part of them. But I swallowed everything with tremendous zest. Occasionally my father visited me in my retreat. He was displeased when he saw what books I was collecting from the libraries. He warned me frequently, and finally, after a bitter quarrel, forbade me once and for all to have anything more to do with such things.

But these ideas had by now become unexpectedly valuable to me. I had to work in secret. It was the same with many of my friends, and we exchanged the forbidden books amongst ourselves. We went to theatres without the knowledge of our parents. And since we had so little money we made a game of it, and pledged ourselves to get in free to all the important Berlin productions.

We saw Max Reinhardt's famous productions; we spent evenings in the 'Gods' watching Elizabeth Bergner beginning her rise to world fame; and we delighted in the contemporary political plays which in those days could be seen in many of the *avant-garde* theatres.

Almost in a spirit of reverence we visited the Romanisches Café and the other cafes and restaurants where so much of the intellectual life of Berlin was found. And all the time we went to concerts – quite free, after the first interval – and heard a tremendous amount of music and understood a tremendous little. But we did all these things in complete peace and in complete happiness because they were different, because they were new, and because they were the direct opposite of everything we were used to at home.

In these years we didn't take politics too seriously. We felt ourselves very superior when we saw the innumerable and tawdry political processions and demonstrations. But my casual disregard of politics did sustain one tremendous shock. Early one morning I awoke and heard someone screaming in the street. Leaping to the window

I saw in the grey morning light three men in SA uniform who hacked with their jackboots at the prone body of a man, and then ran off.

For the last phase of the pre-1933 political struggle I was no longer in Germany. My father had remembered one of his sisters who had married years earlier and had gone to live in England. He was worried by the way I was developing and hoped that the influence of life in England would, as he put it, 'make me all right again'.

Thus in August 1931, I was sent to my aunt in Edinburgh. My father thought that a year and a half would be sufficient completely to free me from the 'degenerate intellectual atmosphere' into which I had so regrettably fallen.

In the first weeks I was very unhappy, although I found much to interest me. But my aunt's household was only slightly less nationalistic and only slightly less academically conservative than my own home. Here, too, security was the basis of every thought and action. Nothing was questioned or discussed. Here, as at home, respectability was God.

But it was not long before I came into contact with other people – students, art pupils, architects and musicians. And there I found the same things from which my father was trying to save me. Yet it was different; for the thought, discussions and writings had not the same extreme radicalism as in Germany. The voices I heard here did not scream so stridently for revolution. Here everything had more solidity. And the main difference was that here thought did not always get mixed up with politics. Here politics was a thing apart, and did not obtrude into every sphere of life as in Germany.

Amongst the people I met in these two entirely separate groups there was no one who had any idea of the danger of our political situation in Germany. And questions – very infrequently asked – showed only a brazen ignorance. The people here had no real interest in politics – either in Germany or in their own country.

And yet at the same time they showed a wide knowledge and interest in the German theatre and German literature. The same people who knew all about Hindemith, the newest book of Thomas Mann or the last success of Elizabeth Bergner, knew next to nothing of the political forces which in this very year were in process of tearing Germany apart.

When I returned home in March 1933, the struggle was already decided and I found that the political power was now in the hands of those my father liked so much and I so little. I turned my attention to the more important matter of my own life.

My father, as a teacher himself, thought I should become a teacher. But, although I agreed, I was not so sure. I hoped, sooner or later, to make my living if not in literature, then at least in journalism.

The University of Koenigsberg had been decided on for me. My father thought that here I should lose the remainder of my 'unhealthy tendencies'. Koenigsberg University had an old, strongly national tradition. The National Socialists too, soon called it the 'Reich University' and gave it thereby a strongly political bias.

Most of the students were delighted supporters of the new political development. And not only supporters but ardent proselytes too. They wanted everyone to join the Nazi Studentenbund. They wanted everyone to join the SA, the SS or the Hitler

Jugend. They wanted everyone to join the new burning ideology of the people. They knew also that Party members would get the best jobs afterwards.

Nevertheless, there was one small group of friends, bound together only by the single aim – to do always the opposite of what was expected. We continued to read the books which now suddenly had become notorious and dangerous. And while political activities kept most of students away from classes, we attended all the lectures and discussed them amongst ourselves afterwards.

In the midst of a world delighting in organisation and mass thought, we led egoistic and individual lives. We just could not understand the others, and all we could do was to laugh at them. They ignored that freedom which till now had been the main pleasure and prerogative of German students. They scorned privacy – lived together like sheep – and tried to ape the life of soldiers. They moved iron beds into their rooms and bared them of all ornaments except their Nazi banners, and of all furniture except trestle tables. When we reached the University refreshed by a good night's sleep, they were already there dog-tired, sweating and filthy in their inevitable uniforms.

Some of the East Prussian students particularly intrigued us, because not only did they wear riding-boots the whole time, but they were complete with spurs, although there was no horse within miles. When we went off to the Baltic on Sundays, our brown-shirted colleagues set off at the crack of dawn with hard-set faces and ruck-sacks filled with heavy stones to practise forced marching. They returned at nightfall, staggering and exhausted.

While we went off to dances, or met together to talk in our tiny furnished rooms, they were off in their uniforms to evening classes where they not only studied the so-called philosophy of National Socialism, and the administrative organisation of the Party, but also (as we were in East Prussia and the dangerous Poles were perilously near) they absorbed wide-eyed the principles of military strategy.

There were certain professors of whom we were careful. These had swung themselves energetically into the new order and after 1933 adapted their original lectures to the official ideology. There were others who successfully withstood the change and refused to move a step from the truth. In the first years this was still possible, but thereafter it became increasingly difficult.

We kept aloof from the political fever, partly amused, partly anxious. And our continued refusal to be persuaded into any form of Party membership naturally aroused suspicion. By Christmas, 1935, our position was so difficult that I had decided to tell my father that in these conditions I could not be a teacher. I could not imagine how a grown man could teach children from the newly published history books without laughing.

In them one learned that Germany was the centre of the world, that Europe could be divided arbitrarily into race groups, and the kings and generals whose characters I had found so differently portrayed in other books, were now posed heroically on comic and precarious pedestals. Frederick the Great, for example, suddenly emerged as a generous, noble and heroic character – a founder of the freedom of the German people. How could I teach children this 'truth' when from so many authorities I knew the exact opposite to be the truth?

I loved the painting of Paul Klee or Kokoschka or Hofer. How could anyone expect me to keep a straight face when I had to show children the myriad reproductions and postcards of the masterpieces of 'Aryan art?' There was the tight-lipped face of the Führer rising from a suit of medieval armour on horseback, a waving swastika flag in the background and the whole thing daubed with a bovine realism. Or that other picture of Hitler which showed him as a sower, with a dream-look in his eyes, scattering the seed on the true German soil. Or the pictures, which lovers of pornography took such pleasure in, of the women, painted as if in syrup, so over-rich in their nakedness that they almost looked dressed.

And what could one say in school about the 'poets' who now found themselves hurled into an undreamt-of popularity and whose literary value was less than nothing? Every poem was a marching song. Interminably they sang the Führer's praises in every stanza, every line, every foot. With sickly lumps in their sickly throats they bleated the words 'Homeland, Fatherland, Germany, Race, Generosity, Blood, Soil, Honour, Mother Earth, Sorrow, Breeding, Sacrifice, Reproductive Force, Earthlove, Flags, Standards, Faith in Ancestry, Faith in Kindred, Faith in the Führer, Faith in Fate' – which just about composed their complete vocabulary.

It was quite impossible. As things were, I would not be a teacher. And as I went off for the Christmas holidays, I had made up my mind to break this to my father. I was prepared for his bitterest recriminations, but I resolved not to budge from my decision.

I was amazed to find that my father had undergone an unexpected change. The impossibility of the new faith had not worried him seriously in literature or in history, but his strong feeling of right and honour had been deeply shocked by the Nuremberg Anti-Jew Laws and by the general spreading of an anti-Christian immorality. I found my father completely agreeing with me. We resolved that I should end my studies as quickly as possible and then try to get a job in one of the still independent newspapers.

I went back to the University. In the next few weeks it became apparent that the noose was being drawn tighter. One of our professors was a Quaker, who taught the history of English literature. This man was our particular hero because he held rigorously to his own personal beliefs and refused to move an inch from the truth. This month he was dismissed from the University on an apparently trumpery pretext.

He was replaced by a Nazi professor who explained English literature to us only by discussing whether or not it dealt with heroic themes. He was greatly dissatisfied with the latest developments, seeing signs of degeneracy during the last 50 years, and proving sadly that our brother people – so near to us racially – were now on the downward path. I refused to study English literature any longer under this system, and moved over to German literature, which was taught by a famous Catholic.

It was soon clear that his work was going to be made difficult for him. Brown-shirted students of medicine, agriculture or law were officially sent to his lectures by the Nazi Studentenbund to test him and to cause trouble. And it soon came. The professor was asked to give a lecture on Dietrich Eckart – a newspaper rhymester, an intimate friend of Hitler and a pioneer of the movement – only in the widest sense to be called a poet at all. He refused, and then the storm broke.

The next day the lecture room was full of blustering brownshirts, and our professor could not make himself heard. They began to shout and to demand that he officially rehabilitate Dietrich Eckhart, the greatest contemporary German poet. In chorus they shouted in the lecture room the poem 'Sturm, Sturm, lautet die Glocken von Turm zu Turm'.

Storm, tempest, thunder-shower
Ring the bells from tower to tower.

Meanwhile some of them, the particularly stalwart partisans of the new literary theses, started a rough-house and tried to throw the professor's few supporters out of the room. And although morally we could hardly approve of these new educational methods, I am afraid we took great pleasure now in using them against their supporters, and we were soon giving them more than a taste of their own 'battle honours'.

Retaliation came quickly. Leaflets were stuck on all the blackboards and passages with our pictures and names and we were branded as 'Traitors to the National Socialist Fellowship'. Our professor immediately resigned his post. And we were slung out of Koenigsberg University.

I made an attempt to continue my studies at Berlin University, but after my first interview with the professor I found this inadvisable. They knew what had happened at Koenigsberg – and the shame with which I was surrounded.

It was time I started to organise my own life and I turned to my plan of joining a newspaper. I found that I should have to attend a school and undergo an intensive examination about my knowledge of the Nazi Party and my understanding of all branches of the official teaching. So that was out too. But I tried writing freelance and slowly began to sell short stories, essays and literary articles to the newspapers. Soon I obtained similar work on the radio and was even invited to give critical talks on films and literature.

Inevitably I ran into trouble. In one of my broadcasts I mentioned a book, the hero of which was the owner of a German aircraft factory, and which was nothing but blatant propaganda for the Luftwaffe. But I went too far. The author brought a legal action against me, complaining that I had insulted his patriotism and had tried to bring him, an officer of the war, into public ridicule. Strangely enough I was not heavily punished, as I had expected. Fate had left an old liberal-minded judge on the bench, who quoted from the Weimar Constitution the right of any citizen publicly to criticise a published work and released me.

Nevertheless I was not long a critic, for in 1937 Dr Goebbels published his orders against criticism. The ideology of the new art was granted official validity and protection: only praise was allowed; no work of art should be analysed – only described and explained. I retired to belles lettres, wrote short light essays and carefully avoided any mention or taint of politics.

My life at this time was one long struggle between my conscience and my belly. I had to earn a living, and at every turn I had to use all my skill and diplomacy to avoid propagating and supporting the ideas I hated. If asked to do a broadcast that would have to have a political leaning, I dared not refuse outright. I had to temporise, to misunderstand my instructions, or plead ill health or a suddenly remembered engagement.

In 1938 I was again invited to my aunt in England. I was picked up at the station by my cousin. No sooner had we begun to talk in the taxi than I automatically leaned forward and closed the glass window between us and the driver. This typically German reflex amused my cousin tremendously.

I noticed that I had caught something of the anti-Jew bacillus – in spite of the fact that I despised the discrimination against the Jews, and that in Germany I had a whole crowd of Jewish and half-Jewish friends. In London I instinctively noticed Jews that I passed in the street – they seemed to stand out from the others. In spite of my complete moral and intellectual disapproval, I had been infected by the sheer insistent drumming of propaganda.

Amongst my English friends I noticed even greater changes. Political affairs were now much more talked about. Even my aunt's smug and self-satisfied circle were now awakened. I was asked continually about what happened in Germany. And from outside I could see more exactly where the whole thing was moving. The Czech crisis was just over and I saw how England was slowly beginning to realise the consequences. And as I said goodbye to my friends and relations at the end of the three weeks, we knew that if we ever saw each other again, it would be after the war.

As I returned home for Christmas 1938, I felt that I was going back to a prison. One of my best friends, Max Friedrich, had started an *avant-garde* cabaret with a political flavour before 1933. In 1935 he had spent six months in a concentration camp and his anti-Nazi jokes had earned him the surveillance of the angry and suspicious Propaganda Ministry. A few days after my return he was again banned. And by chance we learned that the Gestapo intended to arrest him again.

We had only just managed to slip him out of the back door when the front bell rang and two men appeared who took me for my friend and wanted to arrest me immediately. I found this rather funny as every child in Berlin knew Max and every other person had passed on the destructive jokes which he had made, or was said to have made. Only the two policemen didn't know him by sight. And realising how badly informed were these two of the lowest of Himmler's creatures it amused me to play with them a little. I told them that Max had quarrelled with his wife, and, since he was as unreliable morally as he was politically, I had no idea when he might be coming back. I offered them both seats, but they were more accustomed to waiting in the street. And in the street they waited for hours – and later, relieved from all other duties, for days in front of the house for Max's return. In the meantime he was staying with one of the most famous German actresses and, with suitable care, I was able to visit him there.

War broke quietly and as if under a cloud. There were no frenzied people in the streets such as we had read about in 1914. No flags, no processions. No cheering and marching troops and flowers. The streets of Berlin seemed empty and there were no troops to be seen. There was only a particularly dull sense of waiting, which gradually faded and then, with the finish of the 'siege' of Poland, completely changed to a wild excitement.

Dreadful as it was, the outbreak of hostilities seemed to us almost like a relief. We had known for some time that there was no possibility of opposition to the regime from inside. Now at last the people outside seemed to be in earnest. We knew that Hitler was now going surely to his doom, and I remember each day I invited about ten friends home and we celebrated with the best of food and a great deal of schnapps the end of the Thousand Year Reich.

The quick, and for the Nazis joyful, end of the war in Poland was a hard shock for us. But, we argued, there would soon be a decision in the West. Instead came those dreadful months of waiting before the war really began. And then the break through the Maginot Line was another bitter blow. But even then I firmly and steadfastly believed that the Allies would soon succeed in ending the war. I believed it right up to Dunkirk.

The Nazis, even the most sceptical, now broke into loud jubilations, their war frenzy finally fulfilled. Now nothing could go wrong. The Führer was right. Europe would be German. Even the strongest anti-fascists began to doubt. I remember clearly how I felt all hope of an Allied victory, and all hope in the triumph of right in the world, to be completely lost. For the first time in my life, hopelessness and bitter doubt brought me near suicide. I experienced this deep depression in the politically neutral atmosphere of the barracks.

In 1940 I was called up to the Artillery Replacement 172 in Frankfurt. A gruesome, and yet strangely interesting experience. At long last we were freed from politics. Once the barracks gate had closed behind us, the incessant weekly, daily, hourly flood of Nazi propaganda suddenly stopped as if turned off by a tap. We read no newspapers and heard only the most fragmentary news. Most of us were too tired from our arduous and novel duties, and so completely occupied, that we had no time, energy or inclination for politics. But strangely enough it was in this political vacuum that I first realised that the army was Germany's last chance.

The army proper was united in a common hatred of their particular form of Nazism as civilians could never be. Nazis in the army were to be found almost entirely in the SS. All the officers I knew hated the SS from the bottom of their hearts, and this hatred spread down to the lowest ranks. They were hated above all because they were always given the best equipment, and the best food and the easiest treatment. And because officers and soldiers trained on the real Prussian tradition had nothing but scorn for their military bearing and appearance. Most of the army officers, even to the highest ranks, were completely non-Nazi and despised the politicians in power for the plebeian uncivilised clods they were. They did go so far as to hinder the SS in the worst of their excesses – and the soldiers were so completely drilled and regimented that they would have followed to the letter any order to attack the SS and the Nazi Party. If only one general had ordered his troops against the regime, I was and am still convinced that they would have succeeded.

This was why at the beginning of the war I gladly and firmly believed the growing flock of rumours. Rumours that Hitler had already been arrested by the General Staff and would shortly be declared mentally deranged; rumours that an army was marching on Berlin from the West to hurl the Nazis from power and to make peace. I believed everything implicitly, and waited for the day. But I waited in vain. The army let one opportunity after another go by.

Again I withdrew my preoccupation with outside events and concentrated on my own position. As a writer I managed to get into the company office – and there I was cock of the roost. I could make out leave passes and share them amongst all the soldiers I liked. I went home myself at least three times a week. I arranged interviews with officers for comrades I liked who were easily able to bribe my superiors (almost without exception Reserve officers with very humble backgrounds) with meat, chocolate and dress material for their wives. All the officers were in the racket, and I was given a free hand with my 'duties'.

Right at the beginning I had made a particular observation: the only men who were decent, straight and uninfluenced by propaganda were the simple manual workers. I spent my evenings almost entirely with soldiers who had been peasants or labourers or, as we were a motorised unit, lorry and transport drivers. With them one could talk. They had retained a healthy scepticism. They knew war instinctively for what it was – the greatest misfortune. Their staple argument was 'even the best war is a bad war.' But those people from whom one had a right to expect more – teachers, small-time solicitors, minor officials and shopkeepers – disappointed and silenced me. They all talked in the same way, with muddled phrases regurgitating the official propaganda. They were untruthful, unreliable, unstable and unbearable.

In these early days I formulated my own personal war objectives. I decided that this was a useless and hopeless conflict, and that at all costs I would keep myself out of the front line. Moreover, I decided by hook or by crook to have my war in my own home.

Nevertheless, it took me two years, two bitter and depressing years in this soldier-crammed town stinking of sweat, latrines and leather, before accomplished my escape to Berlin. And then I could only do it by deception, since my commanding officer opposed every application that I made to get me out of the regiment.

On Sunday morning he appeared in the office in a state of drunkenness. This was my chance, and I put a letter in front of him for signature. He little knew that he was giving his permission for my transfer to the Army Film Unit in Berlin. When fourteen days later my papers came through all hell was let loose. But drunk or sober, a signature was a signature, and I was free.

A distant relative had recommended me to the Army Film Unit, as director and scriptwriter for military training films. I had never seen a camera near to in my life, and had never had a film script in my hand. But that didn't really matter at first, since most of my colleagues seemed to be in a similar position. They were nearly all ordinary soldiers like me, who were trying to organise as free and comfortable a life as possible during the next few years. We lived at home and went to work like office employees.

Immediately after the fall of France a branch of our department had been opened in Paris. We travelled there frequently, officially to work on the film, actually to buy things and sell them at a profit in Berlin. At times the entire black market of Berlin was supported by our efforts. In the Paris–Berlin special train were always two mysterious compartments reserved for the film unit. In Paris a taxi brought boxes and cases of film to the station. In Berlin they were fetched from the train. When the boxes, carefully marked 'film negative' were opened, no foot of celluloid was ever found inside but only coffee, chocolate and tea.

This went on until a public scandal put an end to it. A higher military authority got to know of the racket and threatened to arrest the commanding officer of the film unit, who had already made a fortune. He made a clumsy suicide attempt and lost an eye in the process. However, he came through the war safely and now holds a high position.

The best thing about the film unit was that the actual work we were doing couldn't very well be inspected. I was commissioned to write the script for a military film on 'Gas Defence'. And as no one in the film unit knew enough about films to say how long such a commission should take, I was able to spin it out indefinitely. It was summer, and I made numerous journeys to the Army Gas Defence School near Celle, where I studied the official teaching and training and visited friends in the district. I returned to Berlin after three happy weeks, and slowly began work on the script, having in the meantime been shown roughly how to do it. To write a film script I had to have absolute quiet. Because of this I said I had to wear civilian clothes, and that it was essential that I should do the whole of my work at home. Only twice a week I had to get into my uniform and show myself at the film unit – otherwise I was a free man.

The form, which I had learnt from my friend, was as follows: after a fitting period of time one prepared a rough outline of the script and at the same time clarified it. Then complicated and important military material had to be over-simplified for the troops. Because of this at least one more, and possibly a third, script would have to be drawn up.

So I drafted out my Gas Defence film in three tremendous parts. I treated not only the defence of people, but also of horses, message dogs and ration stores, and from the outset made sure that this would be a film that would take at least eighteen months to finish, even if one hurried.

And one didn't hurry. I began this film in the summer of 1942 and wanted at all costs to make it last for the duration. For although I did not feel as hopeless as I had felt at the time of Dunkirk, my pessimism had not completely disappeared. But event followed event and then, after the surprise attack on Russia, I was strengthened in my deep inner conviction – for Germany the war was already lost.

And so I whiled away my life in the film unit, writing my gas film – or more often, not writing it. And it would have been even peaceful if a great new trouble had not now happened.

Until now I have spoken little about my family. My two sisters had had little place in my life. They had married early and left Berlin. We seldom met. My brother

Gerhardt was born in 1922. He was eleven years younger than I, the youngest of the family. And this difference in ages, and also our completely different interests, had prevented our ever being really intimate.

Gerhardt was the only one of our family with a marked technical ability. He went to the modern school but left after one year and spent a few more terms at the Gauss School, one of the Berlin technical institutes. He went straight from there as draughtsman in the Borsig works, and soon became a designer.

This position saved him from being called up. The Borsig works was a famous equipment factory and the technicians were consequently reserved. Gerhardt could have gone through the whole war without any trouble or discomfort, but his youthful impetuosity organised things otherwise for him.

In this factory a so-called Opposition Group had been formed in which were anti-Nazis, foreign slave workers and particularly a number of older workers secretly pro-communist. Gerhardt joined this group. Serious opposition to the regime was by that time quite impossible, and their activities consisted mostly in listening to foreign radio stations, particularly to the very well-informed 'Atlantic Sender'. The news they spread amongst their friends. They also had a tiny laboratory in a house in Hallischen Ufer where they photocopied RAF leaflets and sent them to soldiers through the Field Post Office.

That is what they called 'opposition'. But at the same time they did do something really positive. They hid in their houses and fed a number of Jews and political fugitives. So far everything had gone well and safely, but they suddenly got the blood-and-thunder notion of collecting a small arsenal of pistols and ammunition. I think they had been reading too much about the anarchists of the early Russian revolutions and it had gone to their heads.

As time went on they become careless. My brother would announce on a Monday what the Army News was going to say the following Friday. And then finally it happened. He and his friends were arrested and taken to the *Reichssicherheitshauptamt* [State Security Head Office] in Prinz Albrecht Street.

A friend telephoned the news to me in the Army Film Unit and I was very angry about it. I found the whole thing so utterly unnecessary, as at this time such 'opposition' was worse than useless. Such tiny groups could do nothing against the organised terror regime of the Nazis. But there was nothing more to be done. Gerhardt was sitting in Prinz Albrecht Street, and as things stood the outcome looked pretty obvious: People's Court trial for high treason, prison, condemned cell, guillotine.

It was not easy to find a defending counsel for him. Finally, a lawyer took the case over who was an official defence counsel and who relieved us of a matter of some 2,000 marks. And then he could do nothing as the Gestapo refused to allow him to interview Gerhardt.

I knew that the worst thing about prison life was hunger, and I took a small packet of sandwiches and food along to Prinz Albrecht Street. To my astonishment they took it from me and sent it immediately to Gerhardt. Thenceforward I brought him a packet of food weekly to the prison.

He stayed there over a year, without anything happening, and without one being able to find anything out about how the affair stood with him. I was beginning to hope that they had forgotten him when on 20 July 1944, the attempt was made on Hitler's life. At a stroke the situation was altered. The Prinz Albert Street prisons were emptied and the prisoners sent outside Berlin. The cells were needed for Witzleben and his confederate officers.

Gerhardt was taken to Hanover where the prison was nicknamed by the experts 'The Bug Palace'. From here he went to Bremen. In the meantime November had come. Naturally the perspicacious Gestapo had linked up Gerhardt's valorous Opposition Group with the July rising, and in Hanover and Bremen Gerhardt was confronted with a great crowd of people who belonged to Witzleben's circle. Naturally he knew none of them.

Finally the Gestapo realised that he was only a very tiny fish and he was sent back to the Moabit Investigation Prison in Berlin. He was given the privilege of joining a labour gang. They had the task of preparing air defences in the prison grounds. And Gerhardt made a quite stupid, hopeless and badly prepared attempt to escape. He was caught before he reached the street. The result of this was that he was sent to a small closely guarded working party in the Spandau factory. Here the food was quite insufficient and the work consisted of carrying and stacking heavy sacks of cement.

One day I received a postcard from one of the workers in this factory and called on him. He had a letter from Gerhardt to me. From this time I was able to send him an occasional parcel which was a great relief to him as he was suffering dreadfully from hunger.

It was only after the war that I discovered why he had not been convicted. The People's Court in Bellevuestrasse had been bombed and many documents destroyed, amongst them the records of my brothers' case. Officially, he was forgotten. And then another ridiculous attempt at escape brought him back to the Moabit Prison, where he was treated with particular brutality. Shackled and unable to move, he was lodged in a cell high under the roof while the bombing attacks became increasingly fiercer, At last in April 1945 the Red Army liberated him from his desperate plight.

But I have run on ahead. In spite of this private sorrow my work with the film unit continued. As the year 1944 came I realised that the end of the war could not be far off. At all costs I must not be in uniform when that happened. In April the film unit was dissolved as a military organisation and transformed into a private firm. I was sent back to my regiment with the request that I should be granted leave to continue work on my Gas Defence film which was still far from completion.

This leave was granted and I never returned to my regiment. When my leave expired everything was in a state of chaos. I arranged to get hold of all my military papers. Back at the regiment they were waiting for my return. I got some friends to spirit away my records and so from March 1944, I was to all intents and purposes a free man.

In fact too free. For I had no kind of pass to protect me from the continual police and military surveillance. In every restaurant and cafe soldiers and civilians were in danger of being questioned and having their papers inspected. This was my continual worry. Every morning they were waiting by the underground when I went to the film offices, and it was only a question of time before I should be stopped either there or on the street. I was consequently overjoyed when we received permits from the firm and from the army to travel to France to complete part of the film.

First we had to find a suitable location. This was rather difficult. We spent four weeks searching between Paris and the Spanish frontier without finding anywhere suitable. Then we returned to Paris and finally decided on a place by the Loire. It was an unforgettable summer. We wandered through the town in civilian clothes and were overwhelmed with the beauty of it, which we were seeing for the first time. But soon we were experiencing tremendous air attacks. The whole railway system was being systematically plastered. For weeks we waited for our film equipment, which was shuttled three times backwards and forwards from Berlin, and was finally engulfed in the complete breakdown of all transport and never reached us.

What did reach us, however, was one of the anti-invasion units of 6 June 1944, who, as we were here obviously as civilians, wanted us to join an army unit and take part in the defence against the invasion. We managed to escape this duty and, taking advantage of the general disorder, chartered an omnibus, and during these June days we travelled right across France. Although from time to time we were warned not to proceed without a guard, we noticed no sign whatever of any defence preparations. It was like a Cook's tour through the most beautiful part of Europe.

It was obvious that with the invasion the war had entered its last phase. And I was almost delighted by the amount of stupidity which made even officers bolster their morale with theories like this: 'The Führer's only doing it to get the maximum number of English and Americans into France and then he'll slam the door shut!'

I was terrified now that the changed conditions in Berlin would close down our obviously inefficient and superfluous film company. Here a huge staff of healthy men were working on a film that would not be ready for months, while the enemy had already overrun the impregnable Atlantic wall. But my fears were groundless. On the contrary, our production schedule was actually increased.

I now arranged for a part of the film to be shot in Pomerania. This meant that the whole script would have to be rewritten and that all that we had shot so far would have to be done again. This ensured me at least another month's breathing space. I went to Pomerania and wrote a new part of the script, and then returned to Berlin. When I prepared to go back on location I found it was too late – the Russians were now 'on location' in Pomerania.

Now it was decided to shoot part of the film near Bayreuth, which was absolutely safe, but the other part, which needed a Russian setting, I intended to do in the neighbourhood of Berlin because it was in Berlin that I made up my mind I should finish both the film and the war. The officers who were working as producers on the film had gone on ahead, and now telegraphed me to get the unit together and take them down to Bayreuth. They expected to be there about twelve weeks. I shook my head sadly, as I had just heard the BBC news and knew how far the Americans had advanced. I let a couple of days go by and then on the Friday evening as I started slowly to assemble my equipment I got the news I had been waiting for: Bayreuth was in American hands.

Now there was no-one who would miss me in the film company. And it seemed silly to go on pretending that I was working. The one thing I had to be careful of now was the Volkssturm. I simply had to get out of that one. The Party block leader at my flat had been deeply suspicious of me now for more than a year. But he was never quite sure whether I was in the army, or whether he was supposed to report me for conscription into the Volkssturm.

Berliners in those days spent their lives, case in hand, between cellar and workplace. But even at this stage people were still scared to say what they thought of the war. They were either sunk in complete apathy and automatically did what they were told; or they bolstered themselves up with the inane catchwords and arguments which had been drummed into them.

It was quite impossible to stay in our air-raid shelter even in the fiercest raids. There was a woman there, a hideous and rampant lesbian who belonged to the inner circle of the *Reichsfrauenführung* [Reich Women Leaders] who preached incessantly on the glories of Nazism. She wore trousers, smoked a pipe and hated Jews worse than death. But lately we had had some peace, as she was conscripted into the *Frauensturm* in Spandau where she threw hand grenades and learned how to attack tanks. But at nights in the shelter she was still lively enough to expound her theories at great length: we must all trust the Führer absolutely. He was all wise and all powerful. He was only holding back until the very last moment, and would then suddenly astound the world with a miraculous new weapon and at a blow would sweep the enemy hordes out of Germany. The present situation was permitted by him especially to test people – to find out who would desert the Party and who would stick it to the bitter end.

After the event, the description of this figure sounds completely grotesque, and probably she was. But then, one such character held the lives of all those surrounding her in her hands. If I had dared to oppose her a little more strongly she might have destroyed my already suspicious position simply by ringing her party HQ. There were plenty of examples of this sort of thing. The papers were full of announcements of the shooting out of hand of saboteurs and defeatists. At almost every corner were placards with the names of such victims. One after another one would read the names of soldiers or Volkssturm men who had deserted from their units and had paid with their lives.

Lieut. Schmiedemann, 126 Res. Inf. Regt. was absent from his unit without leave. He was shot …

But finally this disgusting female caught me after all. I passed her window after one air raid. Shortly before I had been listening to the English news and I was quite unconsciously whistling the 'Siegfried Line'. She flew like a fury to the window, which she didn't need to open as the glass had just been blown out, denounced me for whistling

Hitler speaks to a small crowd at the first NSDAP rally.

German Communist Party members take to the streets.

Ernst Roehm, leader of the SA.

An SA unit parades through the streets.

University students vote while an SA trooper looks on.

Hermann Goering delivers a speech at the District Party Day rally in Weimar in April 1931. Hitler stands beside the car.

Propaganda minister Joseph Goebbels, known to SA men as 'club-foot'.

Adolf Hitler and Heinrich Himmler review SS troops during Reich Party Day ceremonies in September 1938.

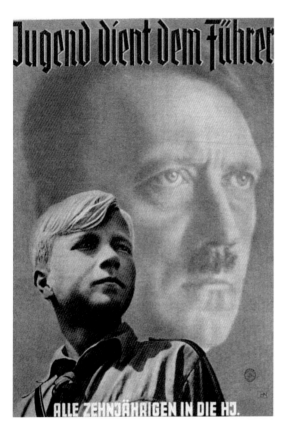

'The Youth Works for the Führer.'
A poster encourages all ten-year-olds
to join the Hitler Youth.

Bund Deutscher Mädel girls salute at
a rally.

German troops march across the Rhine to reclaim the zone demilitarised by the Treaty of Versailles, 7 March 1936. (ANY)

A German soldier is welcomed by jubilant crowds after the Austrian Anchluss.

SS Standard bearers on parade.

Hitler reviews an SS unit.

A Tiger tank straight off the production line is loaded onto a railway car.

A Ju 87 fighter bomber prepares for takeoff.

A banner at a rally which reads 'the Jews are our misfortune!'

Order Police harass an elderly Jewish man.

Cleaning up the broken glass in front of a Jewish-owned business on Berlin's
Potsdamerstrasse the morning after the Kristallnacht pogrom of 9 November 1938.

A synagogue burns.

Women and children who have been selected for death walk toward the gas chambers at Auschwitz-Birkenau as part of the Final Solution, May 1944.

Members of the US Army embarking for the invasion on D-Day.

Black US troops in England preparing to cross the Channel.

A German soldier lies dead beside his rifle where he fell during the German retreat in Normandy.

A dead SS man on Nijmegen bridge.

Soviet troops achieve a river crossing.

Soviet troops asleep in an American lend-lease Jeep, a captured German MG 34 on the bonnet, 9 May 1945.

German civilians fleeing the advancing Russian Army.

Captured Wehrmacht troops are led out of Berlin as Russian tanks advance into the city.

An ex-Nazi Party member hands in his papers as part of the US denazification process.
Berlin, March 1946.

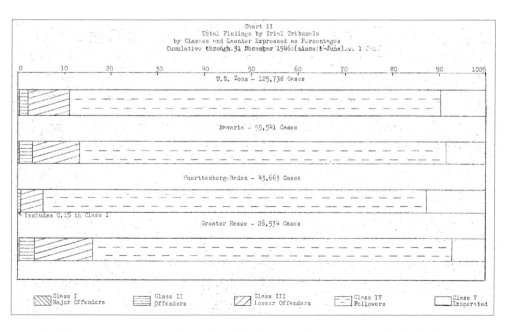

Chart II
Total Findings by Trial Tribunals
by Classes and Laender Expressed as Percentages
Cumulative through 31 December 1946 (since 1 June) . . . 1 . . .

U.S. Zone - 125,738 Cases

Bavaria - 55,541 Cases

Wuerttemberg-Baden - 43,663 Cases

Includes 0.1% in Class I

Greater Hesse - 26,534 Cases

Class I
Major Offenders

Class II
Offenders

Class III
Lesser Offenders

Class IV
Followers

Class V
Exonerated

US military government graphs on denazification rates show most cases as being in the
'Follower' category.

Two views of the ruins of Berlin after the war.

enemy tunes and warned me that she would report me to the block leader in the morning for sitting at home like a coward instead of taking up arms for the Führer. I suppose I shouldn't have told her that I had already done my day's quota of fighting by having destroyed a couple of Russian tanks before breakfast and I was only prepared to continue my good work the next day. A few moments later I did not feel so good. I knew she would be as good as her word and that the result for me might be extremely dangerous. And the very next morning I received a call-up notice for the Volkssturm. I had to report to the 43rd Battalion in Bülowstrasse.

I did think of hiding with friends outside Berlin. An old schoolmaster of mine had even offered me his cellar, but I could not feel justified in putting his life in jeopardy in order to save my own. In any case I had a strange masochistic desire to take an active part in the impending death throes. As a writer, the experience would be more valuable than cowering in a cellar. I could not remember who he was but I agreed with the poet who said 'If this is Armageddon one had better be in it'. So with a mixture of fear and curiosity I reported dutifully for service with the 43rd Battalion, and found there a motley collection of grey-beards and cripples with a few spotty youths and, as far as I could see, only two other men of my own age – these were Albrecht Quappe and Peter Weiss. We gravitated together and during the ensuing weeks became firm friends. Quappe was a gentle, soft-spoken Bavarian who had made his home in Sumatra. He had returned to Germany for a holiday in 1939 and had been unable to get back. Weiss was a baker whose family had come originally from Luebeck. He had lost a leg in a street accident and walked with some difficulty. We were all packed off to Rupenhorn where we were put eight men to a room in a large villa. Next day we drew our uniform from the Reich Athletic Ground. The clothes were thrown at us anyhow and nothing seemed to fit anybody. It was only after we had complained fully and bitterly about the bad fitting and condition of the clothes that we realised we were clad in worn-out fire brigade uniforms. Next we received our armament – French single-shot rifles made in 1886 and five cartridges per man. We marched out sullenly and ashamed.

We started work on a large tank barrier in the Heerstrasse, and after five days a formidable construction was ready. We were drawn up in three lines while an officious Wehrmacht general, accompanied by a buzzing horde of Volkssturm functionaries, inspected first us and then the barrier. What he thought of us I can only surmise; the barrier failed to come up to textbook standards and he ordered its demolition. This took another five days and I was beginning to think that my own experience of the 'purple testament of bleeding war' was going to be something uninspiring.

However, the following Sunday afternoon wild rumours were flying round the barracks to the effect that we were going into action, and at two o'clock in the morning there was a general alarm and we assembled with our full panoply of war – five cartridges per man and our toothbrushes – and marched to an assembly centre where we waited expectantly until the following afternoon. The only sign of action was that our officers were now resplendent in real army uniforms which had apparently been looted from a bombed supply depot.

Finally, however, the lorries arrived and we were carted off to Grunheide. Here we were only five kilometres from the front, and were told we had to march that distance. It was a gruelling trek, not helped by the absence of any maps or clear instructions. Twice the whole company was completely lost and scattered in thick woods, and crossing a damaged bridge twenty men fell into the water when a buttress suddenly collapsed. They were fished out minus their guns and five cartridges. When we reached what the officers decided was our intended positions, we dug ourselves in very thoroughly and went to sleep until the morning.

There was heavy artillery fire behind us in the night and we awoke to find that three men had been captured by Russians and that we were in a completely wrong position. The orders now were to retreat to Grunheide; but when we reached it the damaged bridge was completely gone and we straggled off along the river bank in what was considered to be the direction of Grunheide. It started to rain very heavily, and we were soon soaked through. About four kilometres farther on military police were shepherding stragglers into an assembly point. That afternoon, when there were a few hundred of us, soaking, tired out and hungry, we were told that we were completely surrounded by Russians and that we should have to break out.

We were formed into a tatterdemalion column and marched south through the woods. After half an hour, violent machinegun fire from the front sent us stumbling off to the right. More machine-gun fire from this direction sent us back to the opposite flank, and then a burst of firing from the direction we had just come from speeded our flight through the woods. Emerging into relative calm, we could see the lowland of the Spree stretching for miles below us. There was a group of farm buildings a little down the slope and we had only just started moving towards them for shelter when we saw a series of white puffs, and mortar shells were falling and exploding between us and the buildings. We rushed back into cover. When our officers had finally been coaxed out of the undergrowth, a council of war came to the unhappy conclusion that as the Russians were on all sides of us and we had to move one way, the best plan would be to storm the occupied farm buildings, as the country looked clear beyond them. At that moment the remnant of an infantry battalion joined forces with us and the officer in charge of them started to make a big show of activity. He ordered us to advance on the buildings, while his men covered us from the woods. Of course we flatly refused. The situation became very acrimonious and tempers were beginning to get frayed. But as the commanding officer was a captain and the Wehrmacht officer was only a lieutenant he couldn't very well insist. We compromised by digging ourselves in in the woods. I was stuck in a pit with two of the infantry men. They were old hard-bitten fighters from the Russian front who looked nameless things at my fire brigade uniform and answered all my conversation with grunts. They did, however, unbend enough to smoke most of my cigarettes.

The next day we were all so hungry that we insisted on going on to the attack. Someone had found a discarded machine gun and some ammunition, and this was set up to cover the farm buildings. We were split into three groups – the first to attack to the left of the buildings, the second to the right and the third with the machine gun to go straight in from the centre. We went off to our positions ten minutes before zero hour. Weiss and Quappe came with me, and we got ourselves so well hidden in the undergrowth that we thought we might as well stay there and watch events. But one of my veteran companions of the night before stumbled on our hideout and we decided it would be more politic to join the attack. 'This was it,' I told myself and felt a mounting excitement, yet outwardly I remained perfectly calm. The seconds ticked on – two minutes to go, one, thirty seconds, ten … then screaming at the top of our voices and firing as we ran, we rushed into the attack. After the second shot my gun jammed and I slung it away, still running. Out of the corner of my eye I noticed that I had tossed it under the feet of the suspicious veteran, who sustained a very nasty fall. But I couldn't stop – I was caught up with the excitement of the charge and the intoxication of the noise of the rifles and the stuttering machine gun. There seemed little opposition from the buildings and we were swarming inside without apparently having lost a single man – except the one I had tripped up with my rifle. Every building was occupied now by our men and everyone was asking where the Russians were – had they been slaughtered or taken prisoners? Our officer was shrieking: 'Take them alive – for information – don't kill them – that is an order.' But when the excitement had died down we realised that there wasn't a single Russian in the place. We had been storming a completely deserted position. The Wehrmacht officer blamed us for having said there were Russians there. We blamed the Wehrmacht for having been too cowardly to make the attack the day before. So dishonours seemed to be about even.

The trek continued – a dreary anticlimax after the preceding heroics. After a couple of hours we came across a village where military police were assembling stragglers into companies. We were put into two partially bombed houses and immediately fell into an exhausted sleep. We were awakened by the sound of a violent explosion that had made a huge rent in one wall and hurled four of our comrades through it. There was a fearful panic and everyone was rushing to get into the open. I looked at Weiss and Quappe and they looked at me; we stayed where we were and went back to sleep.

When we awoke everything was strangely quiet. We were by now extremely hungry, and set off to forage. There was a woman in the courtyard who told us that the Russians were already in the village. With one accord Weiss and Quappe tossed their rifles into the bushes, watched curiously by two Russians from the window of the house opposite. But they made no move and we rather tremulously set off up the main street. All was quiet but at the other end of the village a Volkssturm major grabbed us and told us to get rifles and man the trenches. We said we had strict orders to join the 43rd Battalion in Schulzendorf, and we thanked him for the rifles and shouldered them until we were out of sight, when we dumped them in a ditch.

When we reached the Schulzendorf road there was a certain amount of transport going in our direction, but nothing would stop to give us a lift. At a bridge we were stopped by a lieutenant of the military police who asked where we were going. I said we were rejoining our battalion. He said nobody was allowed past that spot and we would have to stay and fight there. I explained that we had been in action for three days without food or sleep and had gone almost mad with hunger. He relented and directed us to a soup kitchen on the far side of the bridge. We thanked him profusely, carefully avoided the field kitchen and continued on our way to Schulzendorf. In the villages curious civilians were asking us how the fighting was going. We made up wonderful stories of the Russians being thrown back by gigantic counter attacks and varied them with warnings that the Mongol hordes were hot on our heels. As we approached Schulzendorf, we took to the woods and, finding a pool of water, decided to shave and refresh ourselves. Clean and rested, smoking in turn one of our last cigarettes, we gazed down on Schulzendorf. To the north-west we could see the forest of Grunau with huge columns of smoke rising behind it. West were the chimneys of Neuköln. The gunfire from the direction of Schmoeckwitz seemed nearer and had grown in intensity. From the north we could hear the ceaseless rumbling of besieged Berlin with the multiple whine, made ghostly by the distance, of the Russian rocket-firers which we called 'Stalin's organs'. As we smoked and watched, two men suddenly appeared out of the trees. They seemed as surprised as we and as suspicious. But when we asked about the Nazis in the town they realised we were all on the same side and offered to shelter us in their homes.

We were lodged in a roomy rabbit hutch at the end of a small garden. We had clean straw to sleep on and a rich soup of turnip and horsemeat to satisfy our hunger. We were awakened in the middle of the night by the tramp of a marching column and shouted commands in Russian. We lay motionless in the dark. Footsteps and voices could be heard approaching us and the door was flung open. Luckily we were almost covered in straw and the two Russian soldiers who came in flashed their torches at the rabbits without noticing us. In the morning our host told us that the Russians had occupied the village and had searched everywhere for hidden arms and soldiers.

We lay there for three days and then decided that we must not jeopardise our host's life any longer. We borrowed shabby civilian clothes and set off, Weiss towards Kuestrin, Quappe and I towards Berlin. There were many people on the roads travelling as we were and the Russians everywhere allowed us to pass. Russian columns passed us at tremendous speed and in front all the time one could hear the thunder of the artillery barrage which we learned had by now completely surrounded Berlin. Many refugees were streaming south loaded with bundles, with handcarts and with bicycles.

Suddenly there was a burst of rifle fire and a panicked rush of women who cried that the Russians were shooting all the men refugees. A squad of Cossacks came into sight herding all the people off the road into a large farm. We were caught up with the crowd but I noticed a large black Russian car with an important looking woman in uniform covered with decorations. I took a chance and rushed up to this car hailing the female Commissar as an old acquaintance from Paris.

She was intrigued and we carried on a lengthy and inconsequential conversation in French, to the astonishment of the Russian guards, who left us well alone while continuing to drive the rest of the people into the farm. I introduced Quappe as my batman, kissed her hand with a flourish and walked off to freedom leaving the rest of the unfortunate rabble to their fate.

As darkness fell we reached a bridge over the Niepitz guarded by a Russian sentry. He made us understand that we must not stay out after dark and directed us to the local commandant. The village was crowded with tipsy Russians and I approached the commandant's house rather nervously. About twenty Russians were staggering and roaring in the courtyard and they surrounded me and demanded my papers which I gave them. They read them instantly from all angles, passed them round, and then started snatching them from each other. They called a young Ukrainian over who had a smattering of German and asked him to read my passport. My profession had been given as film producer and this he translated as film actor, which produced a tremendous change in my treatment. I was given a box to sit on, patted on the back, shaken effusively by the hand, given all my papers back, including some more that weren't mine at all, and Quappe and I were marched with honour to a local farmhouse and lodged in the best and warmest barn.

Next day I parted company with Quappe and continued alone. I was nearing some thick woods near Luckenwalde when suddenly an SS officer in camouflage uniform stepped silently from behind a willow and halted me with his machine pistol. He asked me whether I was German – I said I was and he asked me for food. All I had was an old crust of bread, but I gave him this and he gnawed it like a ravenous dog, telling me that there were several thousand of them hidden in the woods and had had nothing to eat for days. He finished his crust and brusquely told me to go with him. When I asked why, he said 'To fight,' and there was such a fanatical light in his sunken eyes that I dared not begin to point out that it was now too late for fighting. Luckily a group of Dutchmen came suddenly into sight, and he leaped back to the woods and disappeared amongst the foliage. I joined this party. At the next village we were halted by a Russian patrol, asked our nationality and searched. I said I was German, and my interrogator looked surprised and said I could go. The others, some of whom were Dutch, some Belgians, were given an exhaustive search.

As I got nearer to Berlin, the signs of fighting and destruction became more apparent. Gross Sieten I found almost completely devastated and occupied by more than usually savage-looking Russians. A long column of military and civil prisoners were just coming from the north. I stopped to watch and was promptly arrested and put into the column slogging steadily back east – the way I had come. My fellow marchers seemed resigned and despairing. I thought quickly. Something had to be done. Then I noticed a Russian officer standing on the pavement searching for a light for his cigarette. I promptly fell out, struck a match for him, and started talking volubly and disarmingly. His utter astonishment changed mechanically to laughter when I guffawed heartily at the end of a particularly salacious joke that I had told him. I started reciting Faust, putting in a chuckle every now and then, which never failed to get an amused response, until the whole long column had passed. Then I shook him breezily by the hand, nodded affably, and strolled casually but firmly in the opposite direction.

Soon I was nearing the shattered capital. There was a smell of mortality – rubble strewed the streets, dust hung choking in the air, the smoke and rumbling evoked the sensations of a hellish nightmare. There was no transport; everyone was walking.

I tramped on and in the evening came to my own street. There was rubble every-where. Houses were gone that had been standing when I left, but I noticed – almost with surprise – that my house still stood. As if in a dream I continued up to the door, up the stairs and into my flat. Voices I heard and faces I saw swimming in front of me, but my mind could contain one thought only – sleep.

When I had slept out my sleep I began to look around. About 40 Russians were billeted in my two rooms. The house had been badly knocked about in the fighting but seemed to be standing by a miracle. The inhabitants squatted most of the time in the cellar, as fighting was going on. Salvoes of artillery were being loosed off from near the Tiergarten and flew over our heads into the distance. In our neighbour's garden two women had been killed the day before.

For days we had had no water, and most of the neighbours were in a state of per-manent drunkenness. They had found casks of wine in a nearby army depot and had broached them with axes. An old man, a plate-washer at Aschinger's Restaurant, sat on a heap of coal and bellowed the Internationale. Others, whose National Socialist sense of honour I had never doubted, now spent their time cringing up to Russian soldiers begging for food and cigarettes. Others made surveys of empty houses in the neighbourhood and helped themselves to objects of value and the most amazing kind of loot. A painter, for instance, who lived in our house, went from house to house taking all the pictures off the walls, destroying the canvas and only taking the frame.

In order to be able to cook something we had first of all to get over our perennial wine sousing. So I opened the great rusty boiler of the central-heating plant and for a few days we had water of a kind. It was like living in a shipwreck.

Two of us went out and from motives of unalloyed piety began to salvage the bodies of the neighbouring bombed ladies. We were still under gunfire and we had only just got the battered, torn and dreadful looking bodies to the surface when the shooting from the direction of the Chancellery began to get dangerously close and the Russian multiple pom-poms screeched over our heads towards the nearby Tiergarten. We decided that discretion was the better part of piety too, and got under cover. Things in the house itself now began to get unpleasant. Something we had never believed and had·always thought of as some of Goebbels' filthy propaganda suddenly appeared to be true. Namely that the Russians made war on women. We were warned by our neighbour to keep everything female in the attics – because the Russians couldn't usually be bothered to climb upstairs first.

The same evening new troops kept on dropping in to ask for women or girls. This started an ever-recurring pantomime performance which I repeated as often as nec-essary during the next few days. Every time I was asked for women I blew my nose, sobbed, waved my arms about and led the bewildered soldiers into the garden. Then with a tragic gesture I threw back the blanket from my two grisly corpses and burst into uncontrolled weeping and moaning. The soldiers would pull off their caps, cross themselves, pat me sympathetically on the shoulder, and often start crying themselves. They understood perfectly, the same things had happened to them. Then they would surreptitiously hand me some bread or cigarettes, show me pictures of their wives and families, beg me to bear up and have faith, and tip-toe quietly and sadly away. But their grief and sympathy usually disappeared before they were more than a few houses away and they started as keenly as ever on the grand hunt.

The atmosphere during the next few days was incredibly complicated and perplexing. We could scarcely realise our joy that the war was over because we had perpetually to be on the watch. The Russians were celebrating everywhere: in our house, in the streets, in the gardens, their victory celebrations lasting night and day for weeks. Unluckily a huge store of wine and spirits had been found just down the road, and an unending stream of keen-eyed soldiers flowed up the street, while on the other side a rolling flood of paralytic conquerors staggered back.

They were mostly from Eastern Russia, with Mongolian faces, Chinese-looking beards and earrings. There were little undersized men from Turkestan and sturdy-looking Siberians. But one thing they all had in common – an absorbing and childish fascination in domestic gadgets and machinery.

My electric radiogram really intrigued them. But having no electric current I found it rather difficult to explain and as the machine obviously wouldn't work they showed me their displeasure in no uncertain terms-by smashing it. They were also fascinated by the water-closet which again, in spite of my rather undignified pantomime, they completely failed to understand. They searched steadily through my library looking for pictures. They sought continually after watches although we had already paid off our share of the reparations with every watch and clock in the place. They played with two cameras and broke them immediately. With deathly calm they took a lovely antique grandfather clock to pieces, and no one has since been able to reassemble it.

The street in front of our house looked like a fairground. Dirt, rubbish, pieces of cars and tanks were strewn everywhere and amidst everything dozens of Russians were riding bicycles – obviously trying this new type of transport for the first time in their lives. They fell to left and right but clambered back again like armless little apes. Some, just able to stay on, began immediately to try acrobatics; others stared proudly at their rows of watches, usually extending up both forearms. Then, when they were tired of it, they let the machines lie where they fell and walked away.

We had to watch like lynxes to prevent our inquiring visitors taking too much away that interested them. And my room was full of interest. I found it a matter of some delicacy to persuade a chummy Uzbeker not to demonstrate his prowess with the pistol by shooting the Iphigenia of Tauris illustration out of my Goethe first edition.

One national trait puzzled us. This was the habit of nearly every Russian who came to visit us of relieving nature in various, and to us strange and unusual places. We discovered these faecal visiting cards in every corner, on tables, beds, carpets and one, strangest and most ambitious of all, on the top of a particularly high stove. My own theory that this was the remains of an old superstition which implied than an object be possessed if the owner had stooled on it, did not obtain any general currency. But I still think it a possibility in the absence if any more valid theory.

It was all incredibly tiring. One had to be on one's toes the minute a soldier came near, and dozens of them came near all the time. Each one had to be conducted through the whole house and couldn't be trusted alone for a moment. As long as one watched them, kept talking, and treated them as guests, they could be dissuaded from taking away what they wanted, and breaking up what they didn't. But they were always inspired with awe when they saw my row of books and the pictures on the walls.

The demand for women continued unabated and the unfortunate girls had to stay hidden under the roof for a whole week. We had nothing but admiration for the physical endurance which made the Russians capable of this exercise at all hours of the day or night. Fortunately I had a pornographic book in my library with which I managed to divert them from their more practical excursions in this sphere.

Since the exercise of hospitality took up the major part of our day it was a continual worry to find things to eat and drink. During the early days it was quite simple. Dozens of dead horses were lying in the streets and all one needed was a bucket and a sharp knife. Or it was merely a question of following the looters and joining in the free-for-all fights that were always in progress in the many grocer's shops and food depots.

Two young men from our household had gone to the Chancellery and brought back a handcart of coffee beans. They said they had waded in coffee up to their knees and that the place was full of tinned milk and conserves. Unfortunately, they had a particular passion for coffee and had left the other things behind.

But in these days it was harder to get water than coffee. Very few hand pumps were still working. Three times a day we made up a small caravan and tramped about a mile away to the nearest pump, where queues of hundreds were patiently awaiting their turn.

The getting of food became more difficult day by day. And after the horses were no longer usable, meat was entirely a thing of the past. We organised a safari to the nearby zoo but only came back with two minuscule tropical birds. All that remained was one small elephant, lonely and melancholy, who seemed himself on the verge of starvation.

All this time the whole town lay under clouds of thick smoke coming from still burning houses. Why they were still burning no one knew. There were rumours that the werewolves were setting fire to them and were to take advantage of the confusion to organise a rising: other rumours that the Russians were setting fire to houses where they had found weapons or uniforms.

The reek of corpses and dead animals and excrement hung interminably and horribly in the air. We were plagued by enormous fat green flies which couldn't be driven away. And now and again the scattered sound of shots, and the screams of women, and always and everywhere the strange, alarming hoarse Russian voices.

A few houses away from us some more artistic Russians had requisitioned a gramophone and one record, and now made the day hideous with the continuous repetition of the same Christmas carol. It was all utterly mad – and what made it worse was that we could never become sober. Jolly conqueror after jolly conqueror seemed to be handing us toothmugs of schnapps or rum or something else they'd found which we had to drain at a gulp, or they would be deeply insulted.

Thus we spent those first days in a perpetual state of intoxication and were unable to consider anything seriously. For hours I would be engaged with a companionable Russian who had brought a crate of Jamaica rum. We had to drink, sing, dance, embrace until finally his soul ran over. Then he began to weep and show by elaborate gestures what a wicked man he was, and pressing his pistol into my hand begged me to shoot him then and there. But he was still sober enough to show me exactly how the mechanism of the pistol worked. Then with a Dostoyevsky face he turned to the wall and waited for the shot that would release him.

A dreadful moment, when I had almost given myself up for lost. All it needed was for another Russian to look through the window and I should have been released. But now my melancholy friend had another change of soul and rushed at me and snatched the pistol from my hand. My last hour really had come. But he merely staggered out of the room, slammed the door and a moment later I heard a shot.

This was even worse. If a dead Russian were found here the whole household would be shot. I peered tremulously out and discovered the Russian being violently sick. The shot had gone through a mirror.

The behaviour of the Nazis was at this time almost laughable – so completely did they appear to be lacking in character. They were convinced that the end of the war would be the signal for a general rising against them on the part of those they had trampled on for so long. The loyal warriors of the Führer hid trembling in bolt holes. When nothing happened they started to emerge, at first sheepishly, and then, gaining confidence, denied that they had ever believed in Nazism or in the possibility of German victory, and looked round for Jews or anti-fascists with whom they could claim acquaintance. Suddenly I had friends on all sides and they all tried to make me into a little Führer. The habit of obedience dies hard and they all came to me to ask for orders, and whether I knew the official directives, and whether they could put their names down for a new pro-Russian communist party.

Actually some of them did take advantage of the general confusion to form themselves into two groups which immediately started requisitioning houses, cars, food and furniture for their own personal use. It was a time of complete lawlessness – looting, pilfering and stealing going on all the time under the specious guise of requisitioning for anti-fascist purposes. Most of them were quite unashamed and open about it. A small coal merchant I knew told me one day that he simply had to get to the west end of Berlin because he'd set his heart on a house there and if he didn't hurry they'd all be taken.

Amongst the slowly re-emerging Nazis came the Nazi priestess of the air-raid shelter. But how changed. Gone were the man's trousers, the pipe smoking, the military step. She rode demurely on a new bicycle dressed as a charitable nursing sister in blue and white stripes with a Red Cross armband.

I was surprised to find how little my thought turned on revenge. For years one had nursed the idea that once it was all over one would get one's own back. But whether the opportunity had gone, or whether it had suddenly become unimportant, i don't know. But the Nazis' sudden change of face was so utter and contemptible that one couldn't really be bothered to rake up the past.

As far as our Nazi priestess was concerned I felt less philosophical. I was never one to make a scene, but the moment I saw her I seemed to boil up inside. I rushed downstairs shouting at her madly. I gave her no chance to answer. I told her just what her tyrannical behaviour had done to the people in the house, how she had terrified and tormented them all and how she had made the shelter life hell on earth with her interminable parrot cries and how finally she had put my life in danger.

But as I was shouting at her I noticed out of the corner of my eye that two 'Mischlings 2nd Grade' were quarrelling over her bicycle, each claiming that he had suffered more under her than the other had. To finish the argument I confiscated the bicycle and declared it to be for the common use of the whole household.

Something very strange seemed to have happened to her memory – as it happened to most of them at this time. She was by now in tears. I was misjudging her – she only joined the Party in 1933 and her simple heart and credulity had been imposed upon. She was really a victim of the system herself. And in addition she had had nothing whatever to do with the *Reichsfrauenführung*.

My fury somehow suddenly faded, however, and I was left with the painful problem – what was to be done with such a person? Whether she worked for the werewolves or the antifascists her attitude was bound to be intolerant and tyrannical. She was, in fact, a public danger – particularly just now. There was no police and no law courts, and so I was very happy to see a NKVD officer whom I informed about our returned traveller. He sat with her in the garden for two hours and then took her away with him.

The next morning a strange figure appeared with a shaven head, a filthy old coat and striped prison trousers, and rags wrapped round his feet in place of boots. When he saw me on the balcony he beamed with joy and winked at me. Suddenly I recognised my brother Gerhardt, whom I had not heard of for over two months. He looked dreadful, was ingrained with dirt and alive with fleas but in a better mood and happier and livelier than any of us were.

His story was short. I have already told how he had spent the last weeks of the war in a top-floor cell. As the Red Army got nearer, the warders had got fewer until finally the whole prison was guarded by only a dozen men. Since the prisoners were never sure how far the Russians were advancing they thought it safer to stay in prison. But as the shots and shouting came steadily nearer they started to get out, first singly and then in small groups and then in one great rush.

But the Russians were quite friendly. Their prison clothes were better than passports. As the street fighting seemed to be moving backwards and forwards, Gerhardt thought it better to lie low with some friends in case the rumours about a new German resistance were true. But before this much talked of secret army was ever seen the victory was completely won by the Russians, and the Germans had capitulated.

The friends with whom Gerhardt was staying lived near the Alexander Platz, one of Berlin's most crowded working-class districts. There, the political atmosphere had quickly declared itself. Power was in the hands of the communists, or those who called themselves communists. In a very short time the original communist cells and groups were reorganised, and the entire local government of this district was in the hands of the KPD [*Kommunistische Partei Deutschlands*].

Shortly after the arrival of the Russians a certain Binderich had requisitioned a hotel in Dirksenstrasse and had nailed a board on the door with 'Burgomaster's Office' on it. This man was the manager of a night club and had never been burgomaster except in his own imagination. But he went off to the Russians and came back with a quite illegible document in Russian script covered in signatures and rubber stamps. He then started to govern the district. His first civic duty was to stamp out looting. Not Russian looting which was legal, but German looting which was the only means by which the population could obtain food.

Binderich collected a dozen ham-fisted labourers together, dressed them up in red armbands and posted them in front of the town market where most of the looting was taking place. The red armbands still showed the marks where the swastikas had been hastily unpicked. And after a couple of pitched battles out of which the Praetorian Guard emerged triumphant, looting was abolished.

Soon after, the ersatz burgomaster received his first directive from the Russians. The Commandant wanted to issue ration cards and ordered Binderich to make a census of all inhabitants. Everyone said it was impossible. But inside 24 hours Binderich had registered each of the 40,000 inhabitants of the cellars, sheds and ruins of the district. But this was only possible with the assistance of the KPD group who had agents and representatives in every street.

But the distribution of the cards was different. For some reason or other the people had to collect their own cards, and now thousands of people surged the whole day against the one door of the ration office which was in a public house. There was an unbelievable thronging and pushing and screaming. Inside sat a completely bewildered Binderich with his bodyguard and a dozen typists, all terrified of being lynched by the hungry crowd. Binderich, so keen and energetic to start with, now realised that he had bitten off more than he could chew. And when everything seemed about to break, and the crowd about to storm the ration office, the figure of the filthy shaven headed prisoner, which I had mentioned before, broke into the office waving another illegible Russian document with even more signatures and rubber stamps which gave Comrade Gerhardt Harz control of all local government departments by the order of the Head Commandant of Inselstrasse, which orders must be obeyed without fail.

It happened thus. In prison Gerhardt had been converted by his fellow prisoners to communism. He was too young to understand Marxist doctrines from his own experience, too young ever to have understood Marx or Lenin, but still he held on to and absorbed all he was told with the burning faith of a religion. This psychological twist was rather like a conversion to Christianity – and happened frequently during long periods of imprisonment. The inner meaning of his new doctrine which he clasped like a lifebelt was of no importance. Faith of one kind or another he had to have, and communism happened to come first.

Immediately he was released he had put himself at the disposal of the Russian Commandant. And some commissar or other felt a liking for this young man, who alleged that he had been imprisoned for his communist convictions. And as chaos reigned in the district they thought they couldn't do better than send this energetic young man of barely 23 to deal with it. To help him to enforce order he was given a lieutenant and a few soldiers.

He was an immediate success. He cowed the turbulent citizens with his armed military force and sent them all back home. Then, using the KPD organisation, he distributed the ration cards to their houses within a few hours. His second municipal act was to requisition an even larger house and to start business in great style. He got hold of secretaries and office personnel, organised a few dozen typewriters, a band of Russian interpreters and a bodyguard to keep order and to do odd jobs whenever needed.

Apart from the ration office he opened a food office, a housing office, a labour office and any other office he could think of. Then, finding that his office staff were all half-starved anyway, he sent out a raiding party who managed to bring back an assortment of food, bread, cheese and coffee – from heaven knows where.

And subsequently Gerhardt managed to satisfy all the Russians' not always easy commands. Frequently, by day or night, the Russians would demand a few hundred men to unload food or other supplies and Gerhardt somehow would manage to find them. Food had to be brought into Berlin from outside; the bakeries had to be started again and needed coal and flour; rubble and corpses had to be cleared from the street; pumps had to be organised so that the people could draw themselves drinking water; and finally an emergency patrol had to be organised to inform the military police of looting raids by Russians or by foreign slave workers. All this had to be done and all this was done, but Gerhardt and his whole organisation had to work day and night in order to get it done. For as much as three days at a stretch he never slept a moment or even got out of his clothes. After a few weeks the worst had been coped with.

When I saw him he had already helped himself to a car which was waiting for him at the corner. Our greeting was very short; he said merely that he needed me urgently and that I had to come with him. That was all right for me. I had had enough of passively watching the suffering, the troubles and cares of those last days without being able to do anything positive about them, and I thought it was time I did something to help to get the life in Berlin going again. On the way he told me of the new difficulties and what we had to do. And as soon as we reached his office in Dirkenstrasse we started work.

The trouble was that while Gerhardt had been occupied with his burgomaster duties – with the official approval and support of the Russians – a new rival organisation had opened in the new Schonhauserstrasse. This naturally further complicated the existing chaos. A group of extremely radical young men between seventeen and twenty-five years old had requisitioned a couple of houses and decorated them from roof to cellar with blood-red flags and monster pictures of Stalin and collected an assortment of typewriters, handcuffs, chains, rubber truncheons and similar paraphernalia from the Gestapo offices in Burgstrasse. These worthies now turned themselves into a self-styled political police.

And although the Russians were particularly touchy in these matters, these chaps did not seem to worry them. They made arrests, interrogations, sent for those suspected of having been Nazis and threw them into prison, and in fact did exactly as they liked. And who were they – these young men with their sickle and hammer badges and red flags? The leader was a man called Bergdorf; he was the eldest, about 30. On his coat he wore a most impressive looking giant red star which, however, if one looked more closely, was seen to be a Turkish good conduct medal from the First World War. Herr Bergdorf could sign his name to anything, since nobody knew what he was. He could have been a coiner, a body-snatcher or a postman and was in fact a typical Jacobin. His most energetic henchmen were Gustrow and Meyer. Gustrow, very young, a student and an idealist, was a little out of place here. Meyer was a small-time crook and a middle-weight boxing champion. These two got themselves a magnificent office with soundproof doors in which they could bellow to their heart's content. Schultze liked long-drawn interrogations during which he put his feet up on his desk and toyed idly with his rubber truncheon. His particular delight was to reduce his victim to tears. In the same office were a couple of trim sixteen-year-old beauties with bright-red scarves on their heads and permanent cigarettes between their bright red lips.

We only got rid of this set-up, which was by no means the only one in our neighbourhood, after we had a pitched battle which, thanks to our sturdy guards, ended in our favour and in the course of which Burgomaster Gerhardt got a black eye. It was a Pyrrhic victory and we had to compromise – finally they agreed to move a few streets farther away, out of our district, and to set themselves up in the former police headquarters. This crowd was the foundation of the new East Berlin police.

My spell of duty in the government offices was short. I soon realised that it was difficult to work under the orders of a younger brother – eleven years one's junior – however sympathetic he might be. And I was heartily sick of what I saw of the new democratic government. Power was in the hands of crooks, gangsters and fanatical youths who in their intolerance and brutality were giving a fair imitation of the Nazis they were replacing. I took the earliest opportunity of getting out.

But I think I should briefly continue my brother's story because he was at that time completely typical of two things. Firstly he showed that incredible lengths of chicanery were possible in Berlin at that time, and how careers and reputations could be made with nothing but push and a loud mouth; secondly because he is a typical representative of his generation – immature youths without responsibilities and without experience thrown into this incredible and unparalleled chaos.

His mistakes were that he over-estimated his own abilities and didn't get out in time. For with incredible swiftness the whole business of local government was investigated and consolidated. Bergdorf and his tribe of Jacobins and young revolutionaries disappeared overnight, and soon it was not even to be thought of that a young inexperienced man should occupy the position of burgomaster. Even the KPD thought the risk was too great, for if he failed this would reflect on the party.

By the end of June 1945, Gerhardt was getting hints and suggestions on all sides about the advisability of his getting out. He did the opposite. He took on a particularly arrogant tone with the authorities and for a short time managed to intimidate and frighten them. But one day things did blow up and Gerhardt was out.

But he had an undeserved stroke of luck. Fate offered him another big chance in the shape of a Dr Liebert with whom he had come in contact during his municipal duties. Dr Liebert had been promoted to the new office of Municipal Treasurer and had charge of all the public finance of Berlin. He offered Gerhardt a job as his secretary and right-hand man. He was a pleasant man and in a few years Gerhardt would have … would have, if he weren't Gerhardt. But no longer was he dealing with thousands of people a day, travelling by car, morning in Charlottenberg, midday in Grunau and evening in Spandau; no longer the servile workers, listening cap in hand to the wonderful young man's words. Now for ten hours a day, day in, day out, Gerhardt sat in a tiny office and studied documents, figures and registrations; passing from records of the banking situation to reports of the municipal properties and to a study of blocked banking accounts. No longer personal interviews, but interminable sitting and writing.

That wasn't Gerhardt's idea of a life. And he soon brought matters to a head. And now comes one of the black marks in his career. Instead of merely telling Dr Liebert that he had other plans, he had to leave a notice on his desk one morning reading: 'My dear Mr Liebert, my conscience will no longer allow me to work with anyone as completely Fascist as you are. As a respectable communist I know what to do.'

This respectable communist went to the police, and said he wanted to denounce a leading government official as a fascist. But instead Gerhardt himself was immediately arrested. However, 24 hours later he was leader of the Investigation Department.

The Investigation Department was one of the most important departments of the police. They made out warrants for arrest, had charge of all enquiries and examinations, organised raids throughout Berlin and kept observation of all stations, public houses, clubs and above all the general black market. Gerhardt had about 200 officials working under him.

In the meantime the Western Allies had reached Berlin and the English and Americans were energetically reforming the whole police system. They formed police schools, and examinations had to be taken by all, whilst police activity was suspended and every single individual was carefully vetted in respect of his knowledge and ability. Gerhardt, who had already reached the rank of commissioner, had to start at the bottom again.

And, of course, Gerhardt didn't like it and so he got out. But just as before his pretext was of a political nature. He said he intended to spend his time entirely in the service of the Party, and did so. He sank lower and lower. When he joined the Party administration it was already much too late and all the soft armchairs were occupied. He started as secretary of a small ward – and never got further. The work was unbelievably tawdry – vote canvassing, sticking bills, organising meetings of a few hundred people where he himself perhaps talked for five minutes. It was petty work, boring, tiring and unbearable. The salary less than the average typist's. A dismal fate.

And at last Gerhardt began to think about his ruined chances. But still he couldn't blame himself. It was all due to his idealism. He could have been anything, but had sacrificed himself for his political opinions. He gritted his teeth, blinked back unshed tears and thought himself no end of a hero.

But it didn't help. And slowly he began to realise that this was not the way to get on. At last he began to study the works of Marx and other approved Party writings and attended the Party school. He came back from his courses full of new wisdom, inflated with Party catchwords which he handed out to everyone he met. He visited American discussion groups to show off his new learning and apparently to 'gather material'. Someone noticed how he stole a silly worthless OMGUS information leaflet during a visit to an American. As a true servant of the Party, information must be gleaned, even from the wicked enemy. But nothing availed; whatever he did he could not get on. He burrowed deeper and deeper into the communist ideal, became more and more intolerant and his pronouncements got steadily more impossible for anyone with a liberal mind. And still it all came to nothing. Success still avoided him.

I don't know in detail what happened then, but he left his job. Naturally he said he had had a political difference with his superior, whom he denounced as a secret Trotskyite. In any case he sat in his bare room in the middle of winter without a job. I did try to persuade him to a more 'bourgeois' way of thinking, but it was no use. For hours he would relate what wonderful offers had been made him, from the communist *Berliner Zeitung*, from the communist youth organisation and so on. He had another tremendous offer as editor of a communist paper – a terrific job, of the greatest importance, starting at 1,000 marks. Finally he got a real job in the publicity offices of the Party, where everything went magnificently for four weeks. Then he got tired of it. And then, of course, he decided that the publicity office was a rather reactionary outfit – he'd like to stay there, but one has to sacrifice for one's ideals. Nothing is as important as the purity of the communist ideal.

I have purposely gone far ahead with my brother's story and now I shall return to those early weeks soon after the capitulation. I had just finished my short and rather unsuccessful period in the municipal offices and once again sat in my own room firmly resolved at last to do something worthwhile.

This time was quite indescribable and I can never remember having worked so much, so happily and so uselessly. A highly excited film producer had appeared at my door gasping out that I must begin work the next day on the film the German people had been waiting for for twelve years. He had brought a second author with him who hadn't even had time to put his shoes on before setting out to visit me.

Hour by hour and day by day we poured out into our unfortunate and useless film script all that we had been holding in for ten years. It was an incredibly brash and anti-Nazi tract. And while we discussed the script at great length we never failed to get an exciting shock from the new freedom which allowed us to do what a few days before had been a capital crime.

The work lasted day and night. While we were writing, the producer went out and formed a new company; he rushed around all over the city and persuaded an incredible number of official departments to give him an incredible number of licences and permits, and hurried off to a banker and persuaded him to put aside the money for the film. And then he disappeared. We learnt that the Russians had deported him for reasons they never explained, we never saw him again. Today the manuscript seems to me like an old-fashioned and touching silent film.

The film work wasn't the only thing in those days. There were also people who insisted on starting – and it had to be the very same day – a new, good, free newspaper. In one of the myriad mushroom political clubs I met a man who told me long and moving stories of how much he had suffered under the regime as a communist. He told me he was an old newspaperman and insisted that we two should get control of the new Berlin press.

There were no trams in those days. And one dared not go by bicycle, for even when one was actually sitting on it there was great danger of its being grabbed by the playful Russian comrades. So we dragged ourselves all over the city on foot, trying to find newspaper offices and printing machines that were even half intact. My guide had a very forceful way of requisitioning entire buildings. He roundly abused the poor owners for having worked for the Nazis and told them that a new epoch had dawned. With great foresight he carried always a rubber stamp which he used on a home-made requisitioning form. He took over scores of businesses and buildings and usually forgot where most of them were. Never once did any of the owners raise a sound of protest and they often dared not return to their houses or businesses for weeks.

Finally my enthusiastic colleague was recognised as an old Nazi Party member, and another soap bubble had burst.

Then some old friends broke in with a most enticing scheme. In the western suburbs they had taken possession of a turreted villa where they wanted to start a new school which would be completely different from what had happened before. Boys and girls would be brought up together from infancy and the main accent would be on art. Above all, the children would play, sing, dance, paint and draw and only incidentally would they come to pure knowledge. I would have a post as teacher to bring the children to an understanding of all the works of art which up to now had been forbidden in Germany. But after a few days the villa was requisitioned by the Commandant and this scheme fell through.

All this happened while the city still lay under the thick smoke clouds, and the stench of the corpses filtered evilly through her streets.

The rumours about the date of arrival of the English, the Americans and the French were many and various. But that they would come soon was obvious – and most people, deeply disappointed with the Russians, said that they simply had to come. The preparations became daily more hectic. The streets were cleaned. Every house was ordered to prepare four giant flags of exactly the same size. Suddenly the streets were clean, and the flags were waving and Berlin gave at least the impression of having made order out of chaos.

But there was no order or security for the individual and the slightest and silliest things could have the most serious consequences. For example, shortly before the Americans took over I was walking along a street when I heard screams and sobbing coming from a house I knew. I rushed there and found a Russian soldier engaged in loading the furniture on to a lorry.

The standing order now was that all private looting and requisitioning was completely forbidden. And we had been told to report any breaking of this order to the nearest Kommandatura. Consequently I ran off and made a complaint to the nearest Russian Commandant, who sent an officer with me to the scene of the crime. He started a long and interminable argument with the soldier, which naturally I could not understand, except that every now and then I got the words SS and fascist. The soldier kept on pointing at me, and then I found myself arrested and thrown into the cellar of the local guardhouse.

For two days I had no idea what would happen to me and only ate once through the kind and accidental offices of a German employee. No one asked after me, and at the end of two days I was brought up and told I was a fascist. I said I wasn't and was promptly released. I was lucky because the Russians were giving up this establishment to the Americans and their lorries stood already loaded outside.

The Americans came in to find the town completely cleaned up but alive in apparently only one respect. Anything that could be remotely classed under the heading of 'culture' was pursuing a feverish and dubious activity. In almost every street a cabaret had opened, some of which were even trying to reach a literary standard. Others were of extremely dubious artistic value but for the first time in seven years one could dance in public, drink any amount of very strong and very expensive beer, and get anything to eat one wanted at tremendous prices.

The fighting was still in progress when the famous Deutsches Theater in Schumannstrasse was reopened. And now all the other theatres received immediate permission and support from the Russians to open as soon as possible. Even the State Opera put on a concert shortly after the end of the war and, soon after, their first full-scale production.

An entirely new artistic organisation was built up under the direction of Paul Wegener, an old and respected actor who supervised and issued licences for theatres, films and books. And this was the scene of the first fight of the new political culture.

It was all quite different from what I had expected. The new art did not grow up from below, from the people; it was not in the hands of those who could bring to it something new, or whose talents had something new in them. Instead it was officially directed from above. And most writers and actors and other artists thought only how good it was to be able to work at all.

Days were wasted by private intrigues between artists. The most grotesque machinations occurred between famous theatre directors and producers, who fought like wild cats over the tiniest buildings which might be turned into theatres. One of the fiercest protagonists was a former opera singer and director, who sat in control of the State Opera like a tin god and who was later denounced as a Nazi and thrown out again.

The Russians gave this new organisation complete freedom, and it was a magnificent opportunity to build up something valuable and worthwhile. But the Berlin magistrates, entirely under the control of the German communists, and often themselves returned refugees from Moscow, put every obstacle in the way. They were terrified that something might grow out of this which was not under the complete control of the Communist Party. A group of men who apparently were free to hold and express their own ideas was incredibly dangerous. The *Kammer der Kunstschaffenden* [Chamber of Artists] as it was called, came increasingly under the fire of the crusading communists until, finally, it was held to be undermining the State and was dissolved.

We had greeted the Germans who had taken refuge in Moscow with the greatest pleasure and hope. We did all we could to get into the quickest and closest contact with them, with disappointing results. The only really human part about them was their obvious pleasure at returning home and their desire to stay in Germany, but they never spoke of their life during the last twelve years. Whenever we asked for personal details, their answers were shrouded behind an impenetrable veil. Any intimate contact or any frankness with them was impossible.

But with the Russian officers and men we had during the first few months a completely friendly relationship – as far as we could with the language difficulties. They frequently visited us in our homes and, knowing that we were hard up for food, brought always generous gifts of meat, bread, flour and sugar. They sat and argued with us, mainly about art. They were naturally convinced that in Russia the most advanced books were written, and the best pictures were painted, and the greatest contemporary music was composed. But some of them had a surprising knowledge of foreign art and literature.

However, closer questioning revealed that they only knew about authors who were politically on the left. The only American and English authors they knew were people like Priestley, Shaw, Spender, Wells and Hemingway. They knew nothing of Charles Morgan, T.S. Eliot, Lawrence or any other American and British authors. And we learnt from this that the further left an author stood politically the better chance he had of being known in Russia. For them art was only a branch of politics.

With the Russians we could establish human contact, and friendly exchange of ideas. But our great pleasure at meeting English and Americans was often turned to bitter disappointment. I heard that an English friend of mine, who had stayed with me in Berlin and with whom I had frequently stayed in England, had arrived in Berlin. I went immediately to see him. For three days, armed with a handful of forms, I waited on the pleasure of an English sergeant who looked on us all as from a great height, and treated us without exception as criminals. Like most of the English at this time he made no distinction whatever between Nazis and anti-fascists – the possibility that there might be a distinction probably hadn't even crossed his mind. To him the whole German race was obnoxious, and he didn't mind showing it. It was dangerous to approach him nearer than three paces, or one would be sent home again. He worked only through an interpreter, even when his victim spoke better English than the interpreter, as I did. When I spoke to him he shuddered, deeply hurt by my lack of tact, and said to his interpreter: 'This man is talking to me. Send him away.' Which didn't prevent my coming back the next day.

The Americans whom we met treated us with rather more interest. They immediately organised tourist parties amongst the ruins and treated us as some of the more interesting exhibits. They were delightfully frank, usually asked me if I was a Nazi and when I said not, immediately lost interest. Having seen Berlin and the Chancellery and the ruins, all they needed to complete the picture was a real Nazi. They threw us cigarettes now and then, tried interminably to buy Nazi souvenirs and books, had not the slightest interest in us as individuals and tore off in their jeeps amid clouds of dust.

And now politics began slowly to revive in Berlin. It was the epoch of the birth of the newspapers. Every day a new one, and they could only exist by screaming a new idea, a new tendency, a new faith. And having until now been united in a common anti-fascist trend, they were soon at each other's throats. They pounced on suspicious expressions in their rivals' publications, denounced each other and got each other banned – or 'shot down' as they called it. German journalists brought their whole trade into disrepute by their unbridled extremism on behalf of their patrons. The journals licensed by the Russians supported Lenin even more fiercely than Lenin himself, and those licensed by the Western Allies were louder in their praises than were the Western Allies. The whole thing became ridiculous. After a year men who had suffered in the same concentration camp had become bitter enemies and would not even speak to each other.

But however much this and other developments disappointed me, my whole life was overshadowed by a turn of events in my private life which meant more to me than anything else. A friend got permission from the English to start a daily paper and he asked me to work with him. What I had wanted during my whole life now happened. At last I could write about contemporary events critically and controversially. No one now 'controlled' or 'limited' or 'directed' my work. For the first time in my life I could write and express exactly what I thought, and this gave me unlimited pleasure.

6

TASSILO VON BOGENHARDT

My sister Nina, who was a keen and expert horsewoman, had a number of 'horsy' friends – amongst them the young Baron von Bogenhardt. Like most young brothers I was inclined to be prejudiced against my sister's men friends, especially when they were as spectacular-looking as Tassilo. My first impression of him was that he was far too handsome and correct to be nice. But he was so charming and modest and pleasant that it was not long before I changed my mind and we soon became friends.

Besides riding in tournaments and horse shows with Nina, he was usually a guest at her parties, and one met him around Potsdam at tennis parties and dances. Like the majority of the Potsdam aristocracy, Tassilo behaved as if the Nazis did not exist. Whatever the Party said about the Jews made no difference to his friendship and admiration for Nina, and after she had left Germany he always went out of his way to be pleasant and courteous to my parents whenever he met them in Potsdam.

My meeting with him in 1947 was pure coincidence. I was staying with some relations of mine at their Schloss near Hanover and we happened to motor over to Schwanebeck. There I found Tassilo, but so changed that I would never have recognised him. It was impossible to believe that he was still only 33; he looked like 53. His mutilated body was shrunken and bent, his hair was grey and his face was yellow and lined; nothing remained of the tall blond young superman. It was all the more surprising when I discovered that his spirit was anything but broken.

To begin with I thought his poise and self-possession were simply the result of inborn Prussian discipline. But as he told me his story, I began to see that they were a genuine expression of his state of mind. Unlike most of the Germans I met, Tassilo was not in the least resentful, and was quite prepared to take things as they came. I think this was largely due to his own strength of character and the fact that during the last two years he had had time to do a great deal of thinking. In spite of all his sufferings he had managed to achieve peace of mind and a clear perspective on life with the result that he was now able to bear his troubles without bitterness.

Tassilo von Bogenhardt, born 1914

I was born in January 1914, in Potsdam, but as my father retired to his estate when the Imperial Army was liquidated after the Great War, my earliest recollections are all of Falkenwalde. This tiny village of about 400 inhabitants belonged to our 600-acre estate and was built around the Schloss.

The nearest town was Morin on the Oder. Our estate with its Schloss and village was typical, and there were dozens like it lying in the Naumarkt bordered by the Oder, the Polish frontier and Pomerania. Our family, whose members had been the Prussian army, farmers and public servants for generations, was typical too. There was an extremely close and deep-rooted relationship between them and the villagers; the village had belonged to the family and the family had belonged to the village for longer than anyone could remember. Nobody questioned the traditional leadership of the Schlossherr, my father the Graf von Bogenhardt, and everyone led a happy self-sufficient life in which the outside world played very little part. In fact, for us there was no outside world beyond Morin and the neighbouring estates, which lived and worked in exactly same way.

Apart from the vicar, the schoolmaster, the cobbler, the baker and the innkeeper, almost all the men in the village worked on the estate. So did most of the unmar-ried women. The married ones only liked working on special occasions, as when my mother invited them up for an evening's cherry stoning, followed by coffee and cakes, or during the harvest. Then, every man, woman and child lent a hand, because the harvest was everyone's responsibility. In the same way the harvest festival with the brass band from Morin, the triumphal march, the formal speeches and recitations, the crowning of the Schlossherr and the all-night drinking and dancing, was the high-spot of the year for the whole village.

All our domestic staff were local except the cook who had been with us since before I was born. The menservants and the maids were hand-picked by my mother who, if a child was especially bright and pleasant, would often reserve him while he was still at the village school. The inside jobs at the Schloss were very much coveted; I never heard of anyone not wanting to come. The men-servants usually remained for life, but the maids came and went all the time. They invariably left because they were going to have a baby. Getting pregnant was a kind of traditional blackmail which the village girls used on my Father. There was a chronic housing shortage in Falkenwalde, and if a girl waited to get married until a cottage fell vacant, she was liable to die an old maid. On the other hand if she 'got into trouble' and came weeping to father, he would immediately see to it that her seducer made an honest woman of her so that the child could be born in wedlock. That meant he was bound to find somewhere for the couple to live.

Although he ruled his little kingdom like a benevolent feudal despot, Father was not a rich man. In fact he was always complaining how broke he was – as were most of the other landowners in the Neumarkt. But although our brokenness meant that we couldn't dress at Drecoll's and my father couldn't have his suits made in England, it made very little difference to our comfortable home life.

The estate produced everything we needed in the way of food and fuel; our cellar was as well stocked as any other and my parents, who were both very hospitable, could entertain to their hearts' content. There was always something going on, if not at Falkenwalde, then at one of the neighbouring houses. There were tennis parties and birthday parties and christening parties and hunting parties and, most important of all, there were the shoots. These were terrific affairs, beginning with a colossal sit-down breakfast in the early morning and ending with a fulldress dinner that finished somewhere around midnight. A shoot was always an excuse for my mother to ask her friends down from town; she loved having them and they loved coming.

I think we children probably had more fun than anybody. There were four of us; Utz, who was two years older than I, Gertrude who was eighteen months younger, and Spatz, our baby brother, born in 1920. Apart from Mother's old nanny, who looked after Spatz, mended our clothes and dosed me with castor oil from time to time, there was nobody really in charge of us, and we were allowed to run wild with the rest of the village children. They were the only playmates we had any use for.

We were bored stiff on the rare occasions when we were sent over to any of the neighbouring Schlosses to play with our social equals, or any of them came to Falkenwalde. That meant having to behave ourselves and wash and dress up; worse still, it meant having to let them ride our ponies and mess about with our rabbits. Luckily we weren't required to be social very often; most of the time was spent playing soldiers in the village.

As soon as we were six years old we were packed off to the village school. Then, when we were nine, we moved on to the high school at Morin. Several of the more ambitious village children did the same, including our bailiff's son and daughter. The only way to get into Morin, unless you wanted to bicycle, was to go in the milk cart that left at six every morning loaded with produce from the estate. It was fun rattling along, sitting on the churns while old Emil the driver heard our lessons.

When Utz was thirteen he went to the Internat [boarding school] near Lueneburg, and two years later, 1927, I followed him there, while Gertrude went off to the Augustastift [girls' Internat with Prussian traditions for daughters of officers and landed gentry] in Potsdam. As soon at Utz had taken his Abitur he began working on the farm belonging to a friend of my father's in East Prussia. As heir to an estate, Utz had to know how to run one, and in East Prussia they saw to it that he started right at the bottom and worked like a galley slave into the bargain.

Following the family tradition that the second son should be a soldier, I was going into the army, and in the autumn of 1932 I went up for my interview at the Reichswehr Institute at Potsdam. Judging by the number of applicants, it looked as though every other boy of my age wanted to become an officer. Owing to the limitations imposed by the Treaty of Versailles, the chances were about ten to one against one's getting in, even though they were inducting about three times as many cadets as were officially allowed.

I went back to school quite convinced that I hadn't an earthly, and when I heard I had passed I could hardly believe it. It was only then that I really allowed myself to think about how much I had always wanted to be a soldier. The chief reason for this was my terrific admiration for mother's brother Manfred von Strahlwitz. He was my godfather and my hero and my one aim and object was to be as like him as possible.

Uncle Manfred was every inch a soldier, tall, slim and impeccably dressed, with a clipped, precise way of talking, correctness of bearing and ease of manner that I never ceased to marvel at. Although he had had a pretty tough time since he had been forcibly retired at the end of the war, there was nothing bitter or defeatist about him. On the contrary he was a born optimist with a passionate belief in the future of his Fatherland.

The one thing he could not stand was weakness and disloyalty, and that was why he never tired of cursing the November criminals, the Bolsheviks, the Pacifists and the Weimar Republic. Like most ex-regular officers, he was a member of the Stahlhelm. ['Steel helmet', one of several paramilitary organisations that arose after the Great War. By 1930 there were something like 500,000 members.]

It was one of Uncle Manfred's axioms that the true Prussian spirit could not be quenched any more than the old Imperial Army could have been conquered in the field. And one only had to hear him tell of the old days before the Imperial Army was stabbed in the back by the November criminals to know that he was right. But as far as I was concerned he was right about everything.

Because it was Uncle Manfred's custom to spend Christmas at Falkenwalde, I always enjoyed the Christmas holidays best. It was then that we used to play our games of which he was the moving spirit. Once the present-giving and carol singing were over, the great hall would be cleared and the entire floor space covered with hundreds and hundreds of toy soldiers, guns, tents, vehicles, trees and so on to reproduce the complete layout of a battlefield. The battles raged from morning till night right through the holidays, with Uncle Manfred advising each side in turn, and presiding over the post-mortems.

When he wasn't helping his young nephews to work out a system of movement and fire, the chances were that he was talking politics. For the most part when the grown-ups talked politics – and they never seemed to talk about anything else in those days – I never listened. But I did listen to Uncle Manfred; whenever he expressed an opinion it was worth hearing. It was he who made me realise the horrible mess that the Reds and Bolsheviks had made of Germany and the uselessness of men like Bruening, Stresemann, and even Hindenburg, with his love of big business and industrialists. Like my father and most of our friends and neighbours, Uncle Manfred belonged to the Deutsche National Partei. They stood for rearmament, the rebirth of the old spirit and government by the traditional officer corps, with the possible restoration of the monarchy. They also advocated an end of party politics and so-called democracy.

It was the National Socialists' emphasis on rearmament discipline and the national spirit that made Uncle Manfred more tolerant of the Nazis than he would otherwise have been. 'A pack of boisterous hooligans led by a loud-mouthed vulgarian' was how he frequently described them. Then he would screw in his monocle and add:

'The trouble is, they're the wrong people wanting to do the right thing in the wrong way. And we may have to join forces with them for a bit.'

He would go on to explain in his clear, concise manner that nowadays one simply had to be realistic and look facts, however unpleasant, in the face. And the depths to which the German masses had sunk was a very important fact. In their present degenerate state, they were more likely to respond to the crude tub-thumping of the Nazis than other more subtle and refined forms of propaganda. Hitler and his gang spoke, or rather shouted, in a language that even the dullest and most apathetic could understand. There could be no harm in letting the Nazis unite the people and clear out the Reds once and for all. They could rely on the blessing of the Deutsche National Partei for that part of their programme.

The great thing was to let the Nazis use up their enthusiasm on the dirty work; after that their ardour, if they had any left, would need damping a little. For instance, all their grandiose plans for land reform and those exaggerated racial laws – to say nothing of the SA and the SS – would have to be stopped. But that would be quite a simple matter once the Reichswehr was built up again. The experienced leaders of the Deutsche National Partei, backed by a powerful army, would be quite capable of keeping a bunch of political novices in their place. But it was more than likely that the Nazis – if it really became necessary to let them come into power – would become as bourgeois and mealy-mouthed as the Reds had turned out to be when they got in after the war.

When Hitler was finally appointed Chancellor by Hindenburg, I was so busy swatting for my Abitur in my final term at school that I hardly remember anything about it. Anyway my school with its strong Prussian tradition paid very little attention to political ups and downs. By the time I was through my exams and ready to begin my military training, Hitler was firmly established and had already begun on his policy of rearmament.

This was his one saving grace, according to Uncle Manfred and his cronies, who never tired of deploring the Reich Chancellor's lack of tradition, breeding and scruples. The Nazis were not to be trusted any more than the Reds; even Hugenberg, the leader of the Deutsche National Partei, was the pawn of big business … The one hope for the country was the Reichswehr, which was the only honourable and stable organisation in Germany. Staying with Uncle Manfred in Potsdam, waiting to hear if I had been accepted for the 4th Cavalry Regiment (in which both he and Father had served during the war), I listened to this kind of conversation day after day.

I felt better and better about being a soldier. I was a bit worried that I mightn't get into the 4th Cavalry, it was such a terribly crack and exclusive regiment, but Uncle Manfred said that I had nothing to fear, as he was great friends with the CO and he'd made a point of going with me when I called to present my letter of introduction from Father. It was up to me now, said Uncle Manfred, to make the most of the next few weeks and get to know the right people.

'Invitations are a short cut to promotion,' he told me. 'But one must not only know people, one must be popular. And to be popular one must have polish and social graces.'

And so he packed me off to the best dancing school in Potsdam, which was run by an ex-cavalry officer, Captain van Loewenstein, in his house in the Grosse Weinmeistrasse.

The dancing classes took the form of *thé dansants*. While mastering the foxtrot and the waltz, one also got the knack of manipulating cakes and cups of tea and learned how to make suitable conversation. The male pupils were either officers and cadets sent along by their regiments or local young men of good family having the corners knocked off, while meeting the right sort of girls, many of whom came from the Augusta-Stift [a strict boarding school for the aristocracy in Potsdam].

It was very funny meeting Gertrude there and waltzing her politely round the floor. I was surprised to find that she was really quite an asset, as she had grown very pretty in the last few months and everyone admired her tremendously. But it was Gertie's friend Chrystal von Kleist who fascinated me. Chrystal was the daughter of a naval officer who had been killed in the war. She lived with her rather flighty widowed mother in Potsdam and was a year younger than Gertie. She was graceful and slender with wonderful soft brown hair, a small pale face and enormous grey eyes. She had the most beautiful legs I had ever seen and besides her all the other girls looked large and lumpy and pink. Although she danced with me occasionally to please Gertie, it was obvious that she had no time for anyone who wasn't in uniform. All I could do was to pray that I should meet her again when I could compete with the young officers of Potsdam on their own ground.

One could also learn bridge at Loewenstein's; his bridge club was patronised by half the old Potsdam Excellencies and their wives. On Uncle Manfred's advice I joined. 'An officer who plays a decent game of bridge gets his majority twice as quickly,' he said. 'And besides you'll get plenty of invitations like that.' There was no doubt that Uncle Manfred knew the ropes. I soon found myself going out to tennis, sailing, dances, the theatre and the opera. The first time I danced on the Eden roof I knew I was really grown up.

But I think what I enjoyed most during those weeks was riding at Colonel Mayer Hussel's stables at Bornstedt. I probably liked the riding best because I showed up better on a horse than on a dance floor or at a bridge table. I did pretty well in the gymkhanas and jumping competitions and this pleased Uncle Manfred a lot, but what I found more fun was the musical riding on Saturday evenings and hacking along the sandy lake side tracks lined with lilac and apple and cherry blossom.

It took the 4th Cavalry Regiment about eight weeks to make up their minds about me, and I never knew time to pass so quickly. After the gay, easy life I had been lead-ing, the cold musty-smelling old-fashioned barracks with its stone floors and endless gloomy corridors felt like a prison. It was hard to see any connection between this grim establishment and Uncle Manfred's maxims about dancing and bridge. In spite of what the CO said in his speech of welcome, about every cadet being a member of the elite on whom a great honour had been conferred, it was quite obvious that here we were starting right from the bottom and there were going to be no short cuts.

We slept about 20 to a dormitory with a corporal in charge. Ours was a slow-witted disgruntled old sweat called Grobauer; he was a paragon of spit and polish and knew his job inside out. We had to call him 'Herr Obergefreiter,' and his resentful, piggy eye was on us from five in the morning when he bawled us out of bed till lights out at night.

After fifteen minutes of early morning running and PT with Grobauer, most of us had headaches which lasted for the rest of the day. It was he who cursed us as we shivered under the cold shower, chivvied us into our clothes and through a hastily swallowed breakfast, pounced on the slightest fault in our bed making and hustled us on to parade.

Here the officer and the Feldwebel had their innings. Nothing escaped them. A button undone or a little loose was slashed off on the spot; if the upper of the boots was not as shiny as the toecap, or if a hair had been missed while shaving, we found several hours fatigue waiting for us after dinner. Every minute fault, which only a highly trained eye could detect, was pounced upon. But even when we had passed muster on parade, Grobauer was always with us to see that there was no respite. You had only to loosen your suffocatingly tight collar for a moment when crawling on your stomach, marching, running, goose-stepping or drilling to call forth a flood of abuse and a lot more fatigues.

Hauptmann von Strube, the officer in charge, was our other bogey; he seemed to be everywhere at once, meting out withering sarcasm and extra drill in the evenings for anyone who happened to catch his eye.

Everything had to be learned by heart – our NCO instructors had no time for reasoning or logic. We soon discovered that it was better to give the wrong answer than our own reasoned version of the right one. The only thing to do was to stop thinking altogether and try to turn yourself into a mechanical parrot. I found this very hard indeed.

For the first two weeks of our training, we were drilled for the oath-taking parade. Once this was over and we had been sworn in as members of the Reichswehr, we had another two weeks intensive drilling to teach us how to behave as such, before setting foot again in the outside world.

To begin with, I did not really enjoy my time off; I was usually far too tired and harassed to relax properly. I was always haunted by the thought of the fatigues that were waiting for me when I got back. At the start of our training we seemed to be eternally polishing shoes, buttons, arms and floors, peeling potatoes and cleaning latrines.

As time went on fatigues slowly gave place to longer and faster route marches ending up with 45 miles in 48 hours with full pack. There were daily exercises in elementary tactics, and range-finding with all kinds of arms came more and more into the foreground. Towards the end of our six months we went for three days on manoeuvres. The umpire took notes on our individual performances, and when we got back we took a written exam.

On passing out, we were promoted to the rank of *Gefreiter* [corporal] and transferred for two months to ordinary Reichswehr units. Here each of us found ourselves in charge of a dormitory full of old sweats who had to call us 'Herr Gefreiter'. They hated our guts for being promoted after only six months, and did everything they could to show up our lack of experience. They disobeyed orders whenever they got half a chance, and messed up our equipment or sewed up our sleeves to make us late for parade. Winning their respect was the toughest job we had had so far; it needed endless tact and patience and firmness and made us realise how much we still had to learn. Just before Christmas 1933, I was promoted Fahnenjunker Unteroffizier [loosely, officer candidate] and given two weeks' leave before reporting to the military school at Dresden.

Everything at home was the same on the surface, but my parents seemed rather preoccupied and depressed. Father could not stand the way the Nazis were interfering with the running of the country estates. Nowadays, he told me, he and his friends were being spied on by a lot of jumped-up ignorant little officials who were there for no better reason than to stir up discontent amongst the peasants and farm workers and teach them to strut about and denounce each other in the name of Adolf Hitler. Father had been outraged when the Stahlhelm was incorporated in the SA and had resigned immediately. Both he and mother were disgusted by the Jewish boycotts and the interference by Reichsbischof Mueller with the Church. And then, the old amicable political discussions, which had been so much a part of our home life, seemed to have gone for good. Father and his friends had lost their former humorous tolerance of other people's opinions; tempers were short, there were scenes and recriminations and people stopped inviting one another. The countryside was divided into opposing camps – Utz, who was home for Christmas, said that it was just the same or worse in East Prussia and Schleswig Holstein.

It was interesting to compare my parents' growing pessimism (or perhaps distaste would be a better word) at political developments, with Uncle Manfred's obvious optimism. Apart from an occasional afternoon's riding at Colonel Mayer Hussel's and a few outings with Gertie which were just an excuse to ask her about Chrystal von Kleist, I had spent nearly all my free time with him during the past six months. Of course he too had been furious and had resigned at once when the Stahlhelm was taken over by the SA in the spring, and the sight of an SA uniform – especially if worn by a former Stahlhelm comrade – was enough to make him wish Hitler and his gang in hell. That was where he and his friends usually did wish the Nazis; but, nevertheless, Uncle Manfred was the first to admit that these thugs, however rough and ready their methods, had to be credited with saving the country from a revolution of the left. They had finally done away with the Bolshevik menace and had also managed to knock those half-baked ideas of democracy out of the people's heads. That was definitely a step in the right direction. It did not matter so much how Hitler had achieved national unity, so long as he had achieved it. National unity meant rearmament and rearmament would pave the way to a military dictatorship and a quick despatch of the Nazis. Therein lay the salvation of Germany.

Apart from the army, who else was in a position to get rid of the Nazis now that they had served their initial purpose? asked Uncle Manfred. You had only to look at what had happened to the rest of the political parties to see how spineless they were. Even Hugenberg, the leader of the Deutsche National Partei, had let himself be tricked into leaving the Cabinet without a fight; while the social democrats, trades unions and even the communists had knuckled under without so much as a protest. The Reichswehr alone remained uncompromised, uncorrupted and unintimidated. It forbade Nazi propaganda, its non-Aryan officers were protected, and within its ranks a man could still speak his mind without fear of denunciation and retribution. Uncle Manfred prophesied that as the Reichswehr expanded and consolidated its position, the power-drunk Nazis would continue to discredit themselves. The worse they behaved, the quicker it would force the issue, in his opinion. And in this way he regarded the burning of the Reichstag and other crude stunts as something which might be turned to the Reichswehr's advantage. One day the Nazis would over-reach themselves and then the people would turn again to their hereditary leaders. By that time these leaders would be ready for them.

On my way back to Dresden, I stopped at Potsdam to collect my kit. I found my uncle wearing his Colonel's uniform and as excited as a schoolboy. He was back in the army after fifteen years' enforced retirement, and had been given a job in the garrison administration office. Whatever he thought of the Nazis, they at least had given him back his old job and made him the happiest man in Germany.

The military school at Dresden was a nice change from the dreary barracks at Potsdam. Surrounded by trees and flowerbeds, the comfortable living quarters, lecture halls, stables and tennis courts covered a wide area.

The whole atmosphere at Dresden was very free. It was much more like a university than a military academy, and it was definitely considered bad form to look as if one were working too hard. It was a point of honour with most of us to wear our hair as long as possible. And anyone who did not want to appear a prig, did everything he could to make his uniform look different from the design laid down in orders. But, of course, in reality we found the training tremendously interesting and were all eager to get on and learn everything we possibly could.

This was a bumper year; the cadets who came from all sorts of regiments and outfits were packed in like sardines. Apart from the ordinary infantry, cavalry and artillery cadets, there were a number of doctors who were taking commissions in the Sanitätskorps, men who had had flying experience in the Lufthansa and were now going to be officers in the 'black' Luftwaffe, and Panzer cadets who had been trained by the Red Army in Russia. They and the fliers kept very quiet about their previous training, which was supposed to be strictly secret. Many of these men were much older than I was but whatever our age or regiment we followed the same syllabus.

The subject to which we devoted the most time and attention was tactics. Our instructor was a Major von Hasenklebel from Bavaria, who was the author of several important theses including *War of Movement, Self Sufficiency and Mobility of Panzer Divisions in Attack*, and *The Panzer Division as a Weapon of Opposition*. He was a gentle, unassuming man, more like a scientist than a soldier, with a natural gift for teaching and infinite patience and helpfulness. In the camp he would discuss tactics for hours at a time, using large-scale sand models. Then, he would bundle us into buses and take us out into the country for the practical part of the lesson. His detailed system of movement and fire could be applied to any sized unit. And, as every man was made to know the other man's tasks as well as his own, we were soon able to apply the system to any situation whether it be attack or defence. But what endeared the Major to us most of all was his theory of camouflage and use of natural cover. This saved us hours of polishing and did away with anything shiny in our uniforms or weapons.

Besides topography, signalling, transport and supply, driving and riding school and all the other regular military subjects, three times a week we assembled in the lecture hall for Heereswesen [literally, 'army nature']. Everyone liked these lectures which were given by an elderly lieutenant, Baron von Broadersheim. The Baron wore a monocle, an embarrassingly tight coat and a pair of fantastically wide breeches. He was always accompanied by an Irish red setter, and in every way was a walking example of the good breeding which it was his duty to instil into us.

To begin with he dealt with the intricacies of card-leaving and the art of paying calls. Each type of call, and there were dozens, had its corresponding dress. The Baron would fire questions at us, in his high staccato voice, that went something like this:

'You are calling for the first time on the wife of your CO. What time would you call? What would you wear? Would you take flowers? How long would you stay? What would you do with your hat and gloves? The Frau Oberleutnant has one son, one married and three unmarried daughters ... How many cards would you leave?'

Practical demonstrations in etiquette required a good deal of play-acting and charades, and there were always plenty of volunteers to play the part of the Frau Oberleutnant. We learned how to introduce her, how to kiss her hand, help her into her coat, present her with flowers, open the door for her, and ask her permission to take her daughter out. But although learning how to pay our addresses to this estimable lady was great fun, there was one subject that we enjoyed even more. This was 'the personal honour of an officer,' when the Baron dealt with the vexed questions of insults.

'You come back from manoeuvres and find your wife in bed with another officer of the regiment ... What do you do?'

The obvious answer was 'Bash his face in.' But this would have horrified the Baron, since it was beneath the dignity of an officer to stoop to any kind of violence. Nor could you challenge your wife's lover to a duel, now that Hitler had forbidden duelling in the army. The correct procedure was to put on your dress uniform, call on your CO, name the officer who had cuckolded you, and demand a Court of Honour. Both interested parties would then be confined to their quarters until the Court's findings were made known. Whatever the Court decided was final; there could be no appeal.

The methods prescribed by the Baron for dealing with insults were not unlike Major von Hasenklebel's tactics: a spontaneous reaction was never the answer. First came the appreciation of the situation, secondly the decision on a course of action, thirdly the putting of that decision into practice. The charades performed to illustrate situations of this kind were frequently the excuse for some terrible overacting and horseplay and invariably gave rise to a great deal of giggling.

To implement the Baron's teaching, we were sent to dancing classes, which were very much like those I had been to in Potsdam. Here we met eligible young ladies from Dresden and the surrounding countryside. They were sent in search of husbands by their hopeful parents, and they continued to attend year after year, only dropping out if and when they managed to get engaged. Each time a fresh course arrived at the military school, hopes ran high and then gradually subsided again. What these young ladies did not realise was that there was an unwritten card-index on them and their parents which had been handed down from generation to generation of cadets. Before I had had my first dancing lesson, I knew exactly whom to avoid and whom to flirt with, which mothers were dangerous (and liable to lay traps for the unwary or resort to blackmail) and which could offer the best shooting, tennis and horses – with the least risk.

The whole social life of Dresden really revolved round the military school, and all the local families vied with each other to entertain us. Apart from the fact that we had to be moderately discreet and watch our step a bit as everything we did was gossiped about, we had a wonderful time and could not have enjoyed ourselves more. The only people in the town who disliked us were the members of the SA and the SS. They disliked us and we despised them. As they were allowed to carry arms and had had some kind of makeshift training from the Reichswehr, they regarded themselves as our equals. Their officers felt that they had a right to be accepted by our instructors and saluted by us, while the swaggering rank and file were jealous of our obvious popularity with the better class local inhabitants.

Finally, in June, the tension that had always existed between us blew up into a first-class crisis. The first thing I knew was when an order was issued confining us to barracks. Soon after this a state of emergency was declared. No explanation was given, but wireless communiqués began to be issued telling us of an impending SA revolt. We naturally assumed that we were being mobilised and everyone from the CO down to the cook was spoiling for a fight. Here at last was our chance to have a smack at the SS; it was about time that somebody showed these upstarts which was the official armed force of Germany.

Arms and live ammunition were issued and a defence system was organised. Some of us were sent to reinforce the Dresden garrison and help them man the machine guns and strong points at the main junctions throughout the town. I stayed behind at the school, where we were fully prepared to repulse any attack. Bulletins continued to be issued and it was given out that Roehm and a number of the SA leaders had been shot. The revolt had been squashed in its infancy and Hitler, with the help of the SS, was credited with having won a great victory.

This was a terrible disappointment after the excitement of the past 24 hours. Everyone felt that the Reichswehr had been cheated out of a great opportunity. Given half a chance we could have liquidated every National Socialist military organisation, including the SS, but instead of this the SS had gained a lot of prestige while we could not even take the credit for having smashed the SA.

A month or so later, President Hindenburg died and Hitler appointed himself Führer and Reichskanzler. Now we were called upon to swear allegiance to him personally, and the oath taking ceremony was combined with our last respects to the old president. This took place on a boiling hot day.

The whole military school, the entire Dresden garrison and all the troops in the district marched to the stadium. The band played 'Ich hatt einen Kameraden' and flags were dipped as we stood to attention with the heat becoming more and more unbearable. I remember cursing my steel helmet and tight collar and wondering if I was going to faint; people kept going down like ninepins. After a short speech about the 'Grand Old Man,' the General conducting the ceremony pronounced the new oath to the Führer and, like a Greek chorus, we repeated it. I was too hot to bother much at the time, but later when I got my collar undone, I thought how strange it was that all this should be in honour of Corporal Hitler.

In the autumn of 1934, I passed my first exam and was promoted to the rank of Fahnrich. Then, just before Christmas, I took my final and passed out as Oberfahnrich. After fourteen days at home and three months at the riding school at Hanover, which was my idea of heaven, I reported back to Potsdam at the beginning of April. I got some more leave and went home again. On Hitler's birthday the following telegram arrived at Falkenwalde:

> Oberfahnrich Tassilo von Bogenhardt promoted Lieutenant April 20th. Effective as from April 1st. Congratulations. CO. Regiment.

Visualising myself as a dashing cavalry officer, I returned to Potsdam only to find that my regiment was to be mechanised. Rearmament was a secret no longer, conscription had been reintroduced in March and the Wehrmacht's programme for wholesale mechanisation and motorisation was now in full swing. Although I realised how necessary this was, the idea of trundling about in a moving coffin was so prosaic and unromantic that I had a wild idea of transferring to the Luftwaffe. But after talking it over with Uncle Manfred, I decided to stay with the old crowd, as most of the staff of the 4th Cavalry were being taken over to form the cadre of the 6th Motorised Regiment.

The regiment was stationed at Wunsdorf, but before I joined it I was sent on a two months' course to an experimental panzer development unit in the neighbourhood. Everything about this unit was terribly secret; the grounds were surrounded by barbed wire and patrolled by guards, and there was an atmosphere of adventure about the place which was very infectious. In spite of this, there were a number of diehard cavalry officers on the course who were quite determined not to be converted to mechanisation. But the lecturers and instructors (who had been trained by the Red Army, which was streets ahead of anyone else in mobile warfare) were very persuasive. They pointed out that panzer and mechanised divisions were going to be the most powerful weapon we possessed. With them we should be able to wage a war of movement and prevent a repetition of the war of position which had largely contributed to the outcome of the Great War. Mechanisation would enable us to cross our own frontiers at a moment's notice and, by sheer weight and speed, break through the enemy's defences and drive a steel wedge deep into his territory. The lecturers also explained the unlimited possibilities of the panzer arm when used in conjunction with the Luftwaffe, until even the horsiest and most conservative officers were won over to the idea of mobile warfare.

After a thorough study of the theory of mechanisation maintenance, convoy technique and workshop organisation, we learned to handle the Panzer I. This was nothing to write home about as a weapon; just an armour-plated hull built on to the largest agricultural caterpillar, fitted with a machine gun and sight. But the Panzer II with its heavier armour, diesel engine and greater speed and manoeuvrability was quite another proposition, although of course one realised all the time that this was only a beginning.

Back at the regiment, too, everything was still very much in its infancy. New vehicles arrived every day and the NCOs and men had to be trained for their new jobs. I enjoyed this kind of work and liked the idea of starting from scratch and watching the regiment grow into an effective fighting machine. Oberst von Bergdorf, our CO, was a delightful man. We had ridden against each other in several tournaments before I joined the regiment, and I had always found him very friendly and kind. The 6th was one of the first regiments to be fully mechanised and the Oberst had surrounded himself with a bunch of really go-ahead officers. He kept us on our toes by allowing us complete freedom of action and encouraging us to put forward new ideas about training and organisation.

Everything was made as pleasant as possible for us at Wunsdorf, and the only snag as far as I was concerned was the fact that I was always chronically short of money, as were most of the junior officers. Keeping up with my social obligations was a terrible strain on my finances although my parents and Uncle Manfred did everything they could to help, as they realised that this was a necessary part of my life. We were expected to entertain our brother officers both in the mess and at the local casino. There were drinking parties which took a bit of getting used to, several times a week. You were more or less obliged to attend if you wanted to get on, and the more you drank the better you were liked by your comrades.

We were able, and even encouraged, to have a good time outside the barracks as well. My father had given me a motorbicycle for my twenty-first birthday and, as Wunsdorf was less than an hour's run from Potsdam, I spent at least two evenings a week there. I found that the two months I had spent enjoying myself before I joined up now stood me in very good stead. I was invited all over the place and, what was far more important to me, I was able to renew my acquaintance with Chrystal. She had left the Augusta-Stift the year before and was now studying art at the Academy at Berlin. She was lovelier than ever now and terribly cool and self-possessed, but she consented to come and see me ride in tournaments from time to time and allowed me to take her to the theatre and the garrison dances at the Potsdam casino.

I was terribly happy nowadays; my private life was ticking over just the way I wanted it, and I was madly keen on my job. We did not seem to have much time to think about politics in the regiment but, whenever we did, we were more or less agreed that things seemed to be going pretty well. Apart from our resentment at having to salute the SA and the SS, it had to be admitted that we in the Reichswehr

had very little to complain of. We could speak our minds when we pleased and criticise everything and everyone to our heart's content. The Nazis had too much sense
to try to coerce us in any way, although they did their level best to woo us by making
a great fuss of us and inviting us to all their big political and diplomatic functions. We
continued to drink their champagne while remaining a law unto ourselves.

In the meantime, the country's economic position was improving by leaps and
bounds and our prestige with the outside world was increasing every day. In the
spring of 1936, some of the senior officers thought Hitler was taking too big a risk
in reoccupying the Rhineland. They thought that France might use this move as an
excuse to come in and put a stop to Germany's rearmament, and as yet we were in
no position to prevent them. Later, these officers had to admit, rather grudgingly, that
they had been wrong and Hitler had been right.

But even so, there were one or two sceptics in our mess who believed that we
were heading straight for war. They argued that there would come a time when the
other countries would no longer stand for Hitler's aggressive tactics, and anyway, they
could not see how the country could afford to go on building up and maintaining
an immense war machine without making it justify its existence. To most of us this
seemed an unnecessarily gloomy view. As we saw it a powerful Reichswehr was the
best insurance for peace; I was especially sure of this as I knew from Uncle Manfred
and several of his high-up friends that another bloody slaughter was the last thing
the High Command wanted. Germany could only defend her frontiers and prevent
encirclement by the communists if she was really strong, and when the Spanish War
began, it seemed a god-sent opportunity to show the Russians and British and French
Marxists just what they might have to contend with.

We were delighted but not particularly surprised when we heard that our ME 109s,
Ack-Ack artillery and other new equipment had proved far superior to anything the
Reds had managed to produce. A lot of my comrades volunteered to go to Spain
and so did I. We looked upon it as rather a spree besides being a chance to get valuable experience, and the pay they offered was terrific. Being an instructor I was not
accepted, but the others went off to Hamburg in civilian suits and boarded a 'Strength
through Joy' ship which was going on a holiday cruise to Italy and which put them
ashore in Spain. I was greatly disappointed, but at least it meant that the regiment
could not spare me and I could go on seeing Chrystal once a week.

After our autumn manoeuvres, I got a fortnight's leave and she and her mother
came down to Falkenwalde. We had a marvellous time, but father was terribly irritable
and depressed about the way the *Bezirkszellenobmänner* [political county supervisors
for farming districts] were interfering with everything. He felt that he was no longer
master of his own estate now that he was told whom to employ and whom to sack,
what wages to pay, what to plant and where to buy his seed. Some individual had
been appointed supervisor of the political organisation and education of the farm
workers, and there were constant bickerings and denouncings in the village. Some of
our neighbours had even been arrested and imprisoned for voicing their disapproval,
and father was fully prepared for this to happen to him.

'It's time you fellows got going before they start messing about with the Reichswehr,' he said. And when a few months later our chief of staff, General Fritsch, was suddenly accused of the most revolting immorality, I wondered if Uncle Manfred and his friends had not been a bit over-confident about the immunity of the Reichswehr and that perhaps father was right after all. [Fritsch, on occasion openly critical of Hitler, was accused of homosexual activity and forced to resign in January 1938. He was recalled just before the outbreak of war.]

Fritsch was an ideal officer and no one who knew his record or had ever seen him could believe that there was any truth in these charges which had obviously been manufactured by the SS. He was retired and thirteen generals resigned at the same time. We felt that this concerned each one of us; our honour had been jeopardised and now at last the time had come for the Reichswehr to take action. We waited impatiently for our superiors to give the word, but they seemed to be waiting too. Time went on, and nothing happened except that Adolf Hitler said he was looking into the matter.

If this had happened earlier, there is no doubt that the Fritsch affair would not have been allowed to fizzle out as it did. But just then the Austrian crisis began to blow up and it became absolutely necessary for the country to present a united front to the increasingly hostile outside world. Germany was in danger and this was no time for internal quarrels and strife.

At the beginning of March our regiment was sent on manoeuvres to Grafenwoehr in the Oberfals. Our armour went by rail as far as Freilassing and from there we went by road. At first it was just like any other manoeuvre but it soon became evident that we were there for a very good reason. The news from Austria showed that the situation was deteriorating rapidly; Schuschnigg was on his way to see the Führer, and we were liable to be called in to help at any time. Austrians came over to discuss the best ways for us to cross the frontier. They told us that some of the workers were well organised but that the whole border region was 100 per cent Nazi and it was unlikely that we should meet any trouble.

Then, one evening, we got orders to move the next morning. We moved off at dawn and from then on the whole thing was like a triumphal march. At the frontier our Wachtmeister and the Austrian Zollbeamte removed the barrier while everyone stood to attention and the first German flag was hoisted on Austrian soil. We advanced towards Salzburg with crowds cheering and waving us on all the way. Austria seemed to have gone mad with joy; swastika flags appeared everywhere and girls jumped onto our vehicles and hugged us. In Salzburg, the singing and drinking and dancing in the streets went on all night. Next day we moved on towards Vienna and there were rejoicings and celebrations wherever we broke our journey. In Vienna, we had a large parade and there were more festivities. After less than three weeks in Austria, we loaded our armoured vehicles on the trains and returned to Wunsdorf. On 20 April we took part in a tremendous parade to celebrate the union between Germany and Austria. Austrian troops from the Hoch and Deutschmeister regiment marched with us.

That summer I was promoted full lieutenant and became brigade adjutant. On the strength of this, I summoned up all my courage and asked Chrystal to marry me. I made great capital out of the fact that we might be at war with Czechoslovakia at any moment, the way things were going in the Sudetenland, and that I had to get things straightened out between us before I went off on manoeuvres. I could not believe it when she seemed to see the logic of my argument and said yes. But she managed to convince me by choosing a terribly expensive ring at Friedlands in the Unter den Linden. I had to sell my motor-bicycle and borrow the rest from a friend in the regiment to pay for it.

Our manoeuvres that year on the Lüneburg Heath were the largest and most realistic I had ever experienced. It was obvious from the word go that this was a dress rehearsal and a very full one at that. Concrete bunkers were built and enemy positions protected with barbed wire were attacked by shock troops carrying live ammunition. The Luftwaffe and the latest flak units were there, and we even had conscript civilian lorries with their drivers. After a fortnight we were suddenly ordered back to Wunsdorf; by the time I got there ammunition was being handed out and the first reservists had already arrived to bring the squadrons up to strength.

The political poker game with Czechoslovakia, Britain and France continued, while the situation for the Sudeten Germans became more and more unpleasant and dangerous. After a few days I and several officers from various other units were ordered to get ourselves some civilian clothes. We then set off in private and disguised army cars to reconnoitre on the Czech border. The whole frontier region was crawling with people who looked as if they were on their way to a fancy dress party. Any child could have spotted the regular officers under those ill-fitting suits and old-fashioned shooting outfits. It was terribly funny to see a junior officer meet one of his superiors in the village street; he would stand rigidly to attention and his arm would go up smartly in the beginnings of a salute which turned into a rather self-conscious doffing of the hat. And then we could never get used to calling each other 'Herr'. In the evenings, when a call came through from Headquarters and the innkeeper shouted that 'Herr so-and-so' was wanted on the telephone, nobody moved; then, the penny would drop and someone would scramble to his feet. As everyone was giving a shockingly bad performance and forgetting his part every five minutes, we were all in the same boat and the whole thing was tremendous fun. I managed to map out what seemed to be a very satisfactory route, with the help of several Sudeten Germans who went to and fro across the frontier all the time and gave me all the advice and information I needed. After a week I returned to Wunsdorf and we loaded our tanks and vehicles on to the train, unloaded them at Oppeln and made our way to the Czech border where we waited.

Finally, France and Britain compromised; the Munich agreement was worked out and we got our orders to move in. In spite of the fact that a peaceful settlement had been arrived at, we were fully prepared for the Czechs to resist. But everything went as smoothly as our entry into Austria. When we crossed the frontier area and saw the super-modern defences, we were glad that we had not had to fight our way through them. Not that we had any doubts as to how we should have made out, but it would have been tough going and have meant a lot of bloodshed on both sides. I could not help feeling terribly sorry for the Czech officer whose duty it was to hand over and guide us through the Sudetenland to the new frontier; he was exceedingly correct but obviously very depressed, and I did my best to be friendly and polite to him. The Sudeten Germans were delirious and after three weeks we returned to Wunsdorf.

The next thing that happened was that the Czechs and Slovaks started squabbling. And although President Hacha asked the Führer's help to prevent civil war, I was not altogether convinced that we should have moved into Czechoslovakia. It seemed to me rather a dirty trick after signing that non-aggression pact. Nevertheless, it had to be admitted that this was the best way of settling Russia's hash, as from now on she could no longer menace our flank.

Then the trouble began with Poland. The papers were suddenly full of terrible stories of the German minorities being beaten up, sent to concentration camps and massacred in the Blomberg blood bath. Many of us were sceptical of these tales. After all, it was only yesterday that the papers had been plugging our non-aggression pact with Poland and recounting Goering's hunting exploits on his Polish estate, to say nothing of the Polish art exhibitions and ballet companies that had been on view in every German town. Our interest in Danzig and the corridor was more understandable; there was no doubt that the Poles' refusal to build an autobahn through the corridor was most unreasonable. But one could hardly believe that that was sufficient reason for our two countries to go to war.

From then on, events moved so quickly that it is very hard to remember their exact sequence. The papers became increasingly vitriolic. The British Mission to Moscow failed, which was a tremendous defeat for Britain. Our pact with Russia was signed which came as a complete surprise to everyone. It was hailed as the Führer's greatest triumph, in view of Cripps's and Strange's failure, and the thought that our eastern frontier was safe was a great relief to everyone.

The ordering of general mobilisation came almost on top of Britain's and France's guarantee to Poland; reservists were called up, vehicles and troops mobilised and ammunition distributed. We loaded our tanks and trucks on to the train and travelled for three days in Paprad in Slovakia, where we waited about ten miles from the Polish border. Several of us went up to the frontier to reconnoitre, and after the third day we got orders to move up during the night. At dawn we crossed into Poland.

The whole thing was so like an occupation or a manoeuvre that we could hardly believe this was really war; it all seemed too well-ordered and familiar. There was virtually no resistance, and for days on end we advanced towards the Polish Ukraine. There were rumours of sharpshooters and partisans but I never saw or heard anything of them, except for the occasional sound of a shot in the distance. There was a certain amount of sporadic fighting when we got to the river barriers, but the Luftwaffe had already cleared the way for us. Their Stuka dive bombers were deadly accurate and as there was no opposition they had it all their own way. The roads and fields were swarming with unhappy peasants who had fled in panic from their villages when the bombing began, and we passed hundreds and hundreds of Polish troops walking dejectedly towards Slovakia. The Poles seemed to be completely apathetic, and there were so many prisoners that nobody bothered to guard them or even tell them where to go.

The most unpleasant thing that occurred while I was in Poland, happened after we had been advancing for about a week. My staff car was stopped by an excited SS Corporal who said that he was the sole survivor of a company which had been captured by the Poles and then brutally murdered. He went on to relate how his comrades' throats had been cut and how they had been dismembered and disembowelled. I was not convinced by this story; it struck me as altogether too lurid to be true, and I decided to keep him and question him again next morning when he had cooled down a bit. But there were one or two people who did believe him and who took good care to spread what he had told me round the whole brigade. Our troops, who had shown no sign of brutality up to now, lost their tempers, and during the night shot every Polish prisoner they could lay their hands on. As soon as I heard what had happened, I managed to stop any further slaughter by taking stern disciplinary action, but, of course, by then the damage was done.

After cross-examining the SS Corporal again and really putting him through it, it became quite clear that he had never seen the Poles committing anything remotely resembling an atrocity. Ignoring orders, he and his company had obviously taken it upon themselves to advance far beyond the rest of the German Army and had simply run into the Polish lines where they had been taken prisoner. No one had laid a hand on them, and they had been liberated when our mechanised troops overtook the slow-foot slogging Polish companies. In the excitement the Corporal had become separated from his comrades and, because his superiors had told him that the Poles were atrocity-mongers and no better than beasts, he had thought they might quite easily have massacred the rest of his company; even if they hadn't, there was no harm in saying so. When I told him that he was a half-wit and a liar and that he was probably responsible for the death of several hundred Poles, he merely clicked his heels and said 'Yes, Herr Oberleutnant'.

I sent him back to the SS unit under escort with the request that he should be severely punished, and I enclosed a copy of a long report I had made. But I never heard another word about it. As far as I know there was not even a court-martial. The whole affair probably went the same way as everything else that required cooperation between the army and the political units: it was simply dropped.

A few days after we reached the Ukraine, it was given out that the Russians had started advancing into Poland, and the day after that we sighted some tanks and opened fire. They returned our fire, doing no damage at all, and it was only after we had shot up two of them that we realised they were Russians. Our meeting was on the chilly side; just a few desultory handshakes and some mutual photographing. There was something rather phoney about our soldiers with their swastikas posing self-consciously beside the Russians with their hammers and sickles. But the papers at home made a tremendous splash about it and ran stories of the friendship that was springing up between the two armies. Nobody seemed to know exactly where the new Russian frontier was supposed to be. First we moved back and the Russians followed up, then we got orders to move forward and the Russians had to go back again.

In between the two armies the Ukrainians were like frightened cattle. Their frantic efforts to get behind our lines were hindered a good deal by the SS, who were busy rounding up all the Jews and herding them over to the Russian side. It was here that I realised for the first time the tremendous difference between us and the Jews. I had known Jewish people before and never noticed that they were any different from anyone else; but some I met now looked like illustrations from *Der Stürmer* [weekly Nazi newspaper published from 1923 to 1945]. In spite of their rather unappetising appearance, our troops got on with them much better than with the Poles. All these Jews could speak some sort of German and our men patronised their shops, chatted with them and gave them lifts in their trucks. It was only after the political occupation began and the SD took over that they were driven from their homes. I hated having to stand by and watch this going on, but there was nothing anyone could do about it as the orders were that Poland was to be freed of Jews as quickly as possible.

After a week or so we were sent back to Wunsdorf. I received the EK II [Iron Cross, 2nd Class] which made my comrades in the regiment rather jealous but pleased my parents and Uncle Manfred a lot. Chrystal was so delighted about it that she agreed to our getting married then and there. I was very surprised because I knew she had wanted a really slap-up wedding with full regimentals, but now she was content with quite a small affair with just our families and most intimate friends. We borrowed a car and motored down to the Tegernsee for our honeymoon. When we came back, Chrys moved into a flat in Berlin which we had taken from one of her cousins who had gone into the Navy, and I came over from Wunsdorf as often as I could.

In March our whole unit was transferred to Coblenz. From there we went on small manoeuvres and exercises, keeping on our toes all the time. No one was in the least worried nowadays as to the outcome of the war. Of course we knew that the fighting was bound to flare up any day and that this time we were facing millions of well-trained French troops and the British armies as well. Then there were the formidable defences of the Maginot Line to be dealt with. All this was going to make it a much tougher proposition than anything we had encountered before, but this did not worry us or shake our confidence in any way.

On 8 May we suddenly got orders to start moving towards the French frontier near Abbeville. I remember the funny feeling of excitement mixed with uncertainty that I had when I knew this was 'it' at last. But that was just where I was wrong; this was not 'it' any more than our entrance into Poland had been. We advanced on and on into France, meeting hardly any resistance at all. After we had passed through the defeated areas we began to overtake vast columns of fleeing civilians. These people were completely bemused; they did not even seem to realise that France was in the process of suffering a total defeat. They could not take it in because there had been no fighting; you couldn't very well have a defeat without a battle they said. They never stopped talking about the German arms and equipment; the most fantastic rumours were circulating about the secret weapons and inventions we were supposed to have used to blast through the Maginot Line. One Frenchman whose car had run out of petrol came up and asked me for a 'tablet'. When I asked him what he meant he said:

'One of those tablets you put in your petrol tanks that turn water into petrol.' He then went on to discuss the collapse, blaming it half on the British and half on the French communists who had refused to fight.

Apart from the volubility and general incoherence, most of the French people I met during our advance were very polite and helpful. Wherever we went and whatever we asked for the villagers did their best to get us what we wanted. And I was impressed by the way they seemed to be making the best of things. We finally halted just north of Lyons where we waited for further orders. The French campaign had finished; it had turned out to be just another pushover.

The French Army seemed to have been utterly degenerate and corrupt. Apart from a very few isolated instances, which I personally never experienced, our armies had met with no resistance at all. I wanted to find out why this was, and I questioned as many French soldiers about it as I could. The Poilus all began by cursing their officers, who, they said, had calmly driven off in their big cars and left them to get on as best they could. In comparison with our men, the French had been abominably fed and equipped and what was more, they had not the least desire to fight the Germans. They were all violently anti-British and made great play with the way the Tommies had repeatedly 'let them down'. In view of the fact that the BEF was known to be the first and only adversary which, in spite of its out-of-date equipment, had stood up and given us a proper fight, I was pretty sceptical about that part of the story. I was inclined to think that the French found in their traditional enemy a useful scapegoat for their own sins of omission. If they hadn't had the British they might have had to blame themselves. Even more than the British, they hated the Italians: 'We would rather have three Germans here than one Italian' was something that was repeatedly said to us. Of course, Italy's triumphant entry into the war after it was over, to all intents and purposes, was our biggest joke to date. Nevertheless, it was generally agreed that it was better to be able to laugh at them than to have to fight them, as we fully expected to do. All the plans for the occupation of North Italy had been prepared and the maps had even been issued when, in the words of the song:

Musso went to Nice one day
To pick himself a large bouquet

and saved us the trouble.

We really did feel that the war was over now. It looked as if we should not even have to land in England. With our U-boats blocking the sea routes, it seemed as if the British hadn't a dog's chance of getting help from the Empire or America. This meant that eventually they would simply have to throw in the sponge; all we had to do was to send in the Luftwaffe to help them make up their minds.

In the meantime I wanted to get to Paris as quickly as possible. And when Colonel von Burgdorf offered me a job on the Armistice Commission which was just being set up in Paris, I jumped at it. I knew Paris would be marvellous, but it managed to surpass my wildest imaginings. This conquered city was so much gayer, so much more leisurely and luxurious and peaceful than victorious Berlin. There was nothing to suggest that these people had just lost a war; everyone seemed light-hearted, the women were chic and attractive and everything one could possibly wish for was there for the asking.

There was more food than we had seen for years and years in Germany, and the shops were full of exquisite clothes and perfumes and jewellery and *objets d'art*. The shopkeepers were obliging and courteous, and I let myself go in an orgy of present-buying. I bought perfume and lingerie and shoes and silk stockings for Chrys, gloves and a handbag and bonbons for mother, more perfume and stockings for Gertie; I sent Father a dozen Cognac and a case of Burgundy and Uncle Manfred a dozen Champagne Nature.

Paris was not only paradise, it was a complete education as well. Eating Caneton at the Tour d'Argent. Homard au Champagne at Pruniers and Sole de ma Tante Marie at La Perouse, made me realise how ignorant I had been, gastronomically speaking. And the first time I drank a Nuits St George 1921 at Maxim's, I determined to get to know everything I could about the French chateaux and vintages. This was my idea of really civilised living and I wanted to learn everything I could from it.

Of course, we all plunged feet first into the night life; everyone from the generals downwards. It was rather disappointing to find that there was no dancing in Paris, but the other entertainments more than made up for it. We went to the Folies, the Moulin Rouge and the Tabarin; the girls there were really lovely and one could meet them later at the Florence Bar. We went to maisons closes, where the filles de joie proved successfully that French love-making is all it is made out to be. We went to cabarets where the girls danced stark naked, and to clubs where the women made love to each other. We went to intimate sophisticated places like the Scheherezade which was exquisitely decorated like a Russian palace and where they sang really witty French songs, and to low dives like the Monaco and places in back alleys where they showed pornographic films after which you were supposed to go off with one of the girls to the hotel next door. I had not really expected to enjoy the sordid places, but oddly enough I did. They were so much part of Paris, and Paris was so strange and wonderful and exciting, I felt I could take anything she had to offer.

Although there was a very strict eleven o'clock curfew for our men, which meant that they could not go to the night clubs and late bars, they managed to have a pretty good time too. They had their own restaurants, went to early cabaret performances and seemed to have plenty of girls to go out with as long as their money lasted. I found that they liked Paris quite as much as we did, and were determined to stay there for as long as they possibly could.

I felt it was terribly important that the troops should make the best possible impression on the French, and I made a point of seeing that the men under my command were always smartly dressed and reserved and courteous in their behaviour. It was very satisfactory to know that the German Army was considered to be much better behaved and far more orderly than the British and the Poles, who had lived in Paris in much the same way as we did.

After the first few weeks of riotous spending and hectic pleasure, I found I was flat broke. My pay as a full lieutenant came to about 2,000 francs a month in occupation chits. In spite of the fact that I was able to wangle a few extra hundreds from time to time out of my paymaster, and Chrys occasionally managed to send me chits – which were valid in France – bought from men on leave in Poland, I found I was spending far more than I could afford. All my allowances for living and uniforms had gone the same way as my pay, and I realised that I should have to take a pull at myself and go a bit easy on the gay life.

My parents had written telling me to look up some friends of theirs, the St Aubyns, and I also had the address of a cousin of my mother-in-law's in St Cloud. In the heat of the moment I had rather forgotten about these people but now I decided to go and see them. My mother-in-law's cousin had gone to live in Brittany, but I found the Comte and Comtesse de St Aubyn in their lovely old house which had once been a shooting lodge at Boulogne-sur-Seine. They were very courteous and charming and seemed to be genuinely glad to have news of my parents, but I noticed a certain restraint in their behaviour, and I had an idea that the presence of a German in their house made them feel rather uncomfortable. I did my best to explain to them that we in the army had no animosity towards France and that we did not want to be identi-fied in any way with the Nazi Party. But I do not think the St Aubyns understood. They were typical of the small minority in France who saw no difference between the army and the Nazis. As far as they were concerned, we were just Germans – the Boche in other words – who had conquered and overrun their country. I was sorry about the St Aubyns as I should have very much liked to make friends with them. All I could do was to hope that they would get over their prejudices as time went on. When I thought it over, I decided that it was probably a bit too early, in any case, to make contact with this type of highly conservative family.

Far more approachable were the French people with whom I came into con-tact through my work in the Armistice Commission. Apart from those we employed, I had to deal with quite a number of others and there was one in particular, a M. Raimon, an ex-officer, whom I got on with very well. He was in charge of the transfer of surplus French Army stock to Germany, and he frequently invited me to his very pleasant flat where his wife and two daughters made me feel really welcome. I think Madame Raimon was grateful to me for having seen to it that their flat was not requisitioned. Anyway, she, Germaine and Mireille always went out of their way to be charming to me.

I found Raimon and his friends very interesting to·talk to. They all welcomed the Armistice and were hoping for an early peace treaty with Germany. They were convinced that it would not be long before Britain broke under our air attacks (I sus-pected that the fortitude and stoicism of the British in the face of our bombing rather annoyed them) and then there would be peace again in Europe. These Frenchmen admired and respected Marshal Pétain as much as they detested the communists and

Blum's Front Populaire which – along with the spineless younger generation – they blamed for their country's collapse. In their opinion, it was a good thing that we had come and rid France of that pigsty of corruption and intrigue once and for all. Now, Germany would bring back order to France and France would benefit Germany with her culture.

Unlike the St Aubyns, Raimon and his friends fully appreciated the difference between the Nazis and the Germans like myself, and they realised that General von Stülpnagel's military government was sympathetically inclined towards them. [Carl-Heinrich von Stülpnagel was military commander of German-occupied France from March 1942. Guilty of war crimes on the Eastern Front, he was a member of the July 20 plot to assassinate Hitler.]

And it was just the fact that the French were prepared to respond and cooperate, provided they were treated in a civilised manner, that made us in the army so resentful of interference by the SS Gestapo and the German Embassy. Of course, more and more SS and political personnel were coming to Paris every day. With their noisy, overbearing manners and their unspeakable ignorance and vulgarity, they were as incapable of dealing with the Parisians as they were of appreciating a rare claret or burgundy. Caret and burgundy were just 'red wine' to them, and the French were just another conquered people to be bullied and pushed around. One heard constantly of hostages being taken and sometimes even shot, of the Gestapo rounding up French Jews, of secret deportations and the setting up of concentration camps. Everything we in the army had done to try to give Germany a good name and bring about a genuine understanding between the two countries was in vain, once these swaggering louts took over; it made one bitterly ashamed.

The presence of these smart-Alecs was the one fly in the ointment as far as I was concerned. My job in the Armistice Commission became cushier and cushier as time went on, and in April 1941 I managed to wangle a trip to Paris for Chrys. She adored my flat on the Isle of St Louis, and I was able to explore the city all over again as an excuse for showing her round. In May we went down to Nice for my leave. It was even lovelier than we expected and I fell completely in love with the Mediterranean. The local French people were thoroughly pleasant and friendly, but the Italians, who were there in full force, strutting about as though they had won the war single-handed, were revolting. We could quite understand why the French hated and despised them so much.

In June Chrystal found that she was going to have a baby. She was a bit annoyed at first but, of course, I was terribly thrilled. We decided to call it Louis Manfred if it was a boy and Héloïse if it was a girl. Louis, because we had lived on the Isle St Louis and Héloïse because she had lived there when she fell in love with Abélard in the twelfth century. In July Chrys went home, as it was too hot for her in Paris, and once she had gone I began to think it was time I got on with my career. Work in the Commission was more or less a civilian job nowadays, and although quite a few of the officers were doing their best to spin things out in the hope of spending the rest of the war in Paris, I could not help feeling that while there was a war on I ought to be in it. I explained to my chief when I applied for my transfer, that what I needed was experience and promotion; sitting in Paris having a wonderful time was not going to help me very much. He was quite nice about it, and I finally arrived back in Wunsdorf in December.

My Christmas leave that year was just like one of our old family parties. Besides Chrys and her mother and my parents, Utz and Spatz had managed to get home by an amazing piece of luck, the one from the artillery and the other from the Luftwaffe. Gertie was there with her new husband, whom she had married while I was in Paris. He was a young diplomat and they were leaving in a few weeks for Madrid. Last, but not least, there was Uncle Manfred.

Besides the foie gras and wine I had brought from France, Spatz contributed vodka and caviar, while Utz provided oranges and lemons, olives, raisins, almonds and the most luscious selection of candied fruit. With these trimmings to add to our solid country fare, we launched into a glorious orgy of overeating.

Everything was exactly like the old days, except that now it was Utz and Spatz and I who held forth and told battle stories while Uncle Manfred and Father listened. As the only professional soldier in the younger generation, I was usually given the floor and expected to do most of the talking. But in point of fact, Spatz was now the most seasoned warrior of the three of us; when I heard about some of his experiences in Russia, I felt quite ashamed of my EK I and EK II. Of course, I had heard rumours about things in Russia being pretty tough and it was common knowledge in the army that there had been large-scale retreating, but, according to Spatz, the whole Eastern Front was in chaos. The situation sounded very nasty indeed; it looked to me as if some very drastic reorganisation would have to take place in the Eastern command before we finally righted ourselves.

Chrys was rather upset by Spatz's stories and said I was a fool to have left Paris. She made up her mind that I was going to be sent east and killed immediately, probably before Louis/ Héloïse was born. It was only after I had gone back to Wunsdorf, and had begun to be issued with tropical kit, that she calmed down again. She did not seem to mind the idea of my not being there when the baby arrived; she said it would all be so horrid that she would rather get over it by herself. It was awful leaving her, but apart from that, I was delighted with the thought of going to Africa. Not only because I should be joining a crack fighting force and have a real job to do, but because I should see the Mediterranean again and Egypt and the desert. Also, I was almost as relieved as Chrys that I was not going to Russia, although of course I did not tell her so. About ten days after we said goodbye, I was in Reggio waiting for transportation to Africa.

There was only one topic of conversation here; that was how much everyone hated the Italians. One heard endless macaroni jokes and Musso jokes and stories about the King and Umberto and the Pope, all of whom ware said to be working against each other like mad. There was so little to do while we were waiting about that I began to explore the waterside cafes and pubs. I thought it might be amusing to find out what the Italians themselves were talking about for a change. The sailors and airmen I spoke to seemed to be more or less in agreement with us on the subject of their country, their government and their service chiefs. They ran them down incessantly but were full of praise for our Panzers and Luftwaffe which, they declared, were marvellous. Where they differed from us completely was in their attitude towards the British, whom they really loathed. There was a great deal of outraged talk about how Britain had let them down in the last war, which was obviously an attempt to cover up the humiliating fact that the Tommies had knocked hell out of them in this one. The more I saw and heard of the Italians, the more farcical their slogan 'Credere, Combattere, Obbedire' (which was plastered in huge letters on every available wall) appeared to be. A more distrustful, cowardly, disobedient people it would be hard to imagine. I began to realise that there was a good deal of truth in the saying 'It's cheaper to fight against them than with them' and I had had quite enough of Italy by the time we left for North Africa.

We flew on a lovely clear day. The African continent appeared out of the dark silky-blue of the Mediterranean like a gold band, and before long we were circling over the beautiful harbour of Tripoli. Landing was like walking into a picture postcard. Everything was there; the white buildings, the highly coloured gardens and the palm trees lining the long promenade against a background of exaggerated sea and sky.

Our group stayed at the staging camp 'Five Kilometres' while we waited for orders to join our respective units. Listening to the seasoned fighters, I soon found that the main topic of conversation out here was Rommel. He was the hero of every anecdote and story. There was the tale of his personally capturing a British supply dump when food was short and then sitting down with the ordinary rankers to his favourite meal of corned beef fried in sardines with lots of onions. There were a dozen different accounts of his amazing ability to find his way anywhere in the desert. The 'Afrikaners' told how he would climb into his British armoured car 'Mortiz' and set out on an all-night search for lost men with his headlights blazing, never once missing his way and never covering the same ground twice. I heard an amazing story of his sneaking through the enemy lines with two paratroopers to visit our wounded in a British hospital. And only a few weeks back his 'Rommel Panzer' had saved us from a crushing defeat near El Agheila. The 'Rommel Panzers' were his own invention; they consisted of Volkswagens with chains, sacks and tins trailing behind which made a tremendous clatter and churned up clouds of dust. These had been driven behind our few remaining real Panzers and the British who had been hard on our heels for some time, with a vast superiority in men and material, were fooled by the apparent strength of our armour into giving up the chase.

It did not take me long to find out that it was Rommel who made the Afrika Korps tick, that he personally planned every single move, down to the smallest detail, and that he knew more than anyone under his command. Everyone trusted him implicitly because he never asked his men to do anything he did not do himself. He was obviously an ideal commander; worshipped by the soldiers and feared and respected by the officers.

I got orders to join a Panzer squadron which was operating on the front somewhere between Benghazi and Tobruk, about 600 kilometres east of Tripoli. Like everyone else I hitchhiked my way from staging camp to staging camp up the dusty Via Balbia. Transport seemed to consist almost entirely of thoroughly solid and reliable British vehicles, all fitted with a fourwheel drive which meant that, unlike ours, they did not get stuck in the sand. These, and the provisions we carried, were the fruits of earlier victories.

For the past few weeks, the front had been established just west of Tobruk, and that was where I found my unit. I also found a telegram waiting for me: 'Louis-Manfred arrived safely weighing three kilograms, both well, take care of yourself, love, Chrys.' I was so relieved and happy I hardly knew what to do.

The next two or three months were spent waiting for reinforcements to pile up. This gave me a good chance to get to know my men. They were obviously first-class material; as good as any officer could have asked for. The relationship between officer and man out here was something entirely new to me. Discipline as such, was practically non-existent; the whole unit lived, ate and slept together quite irrespective of rank. There was no formality of any kind and everyone swapped opinions and confidences as if they were members of one family. Back in Dresden if anyone had told me that this would work the way it did, I should probably have told him he was crazy.

There were several reasons why the barriers of rank could be dispensed with out here. Firstly, we had a leader who had our interests at heart, and each man knew it. Then, we were a completely self-contained army, fighting our own self-contained war in which each of us was equally involved. And, lastly, the resolution of the Afrika Korps needed no bolstering up; its morale was sufficiently high.

I wrote a long letter to Uncle Manfred about this, pointing out that it exploded a number of well-established theories and opened up certain possibilities for psychological training. Something which was also completely different here, but about which for obvious reasons I could not write to Uncle Manfred, was the complete absence of any political interference. There were no SS Gestapo or PGs [*Partei Genossen* (Party members)] swanning about making speeches and trying to run the show, and, within reason, anyone could say what he liked. Because of this there was a clean military atmosphere which was thoroughly refreshing in spite of the heat and the dust and the sand flies. I for one would not have changed places with any officer on any front, and I think most people felt the same.

At the end of May, our preparations were completed. We had brand new Mark IV tanks, which were vastly superior in armour and firing power to anything that Tommy could muster. These, together with the best men the German Army had ever turned out, were a formidable combination. When we finally began to advance on 28 May, it seemed as though nothing could hold us back.

Tobruk fell according to plan, and it was here that we took our first coloured prisoners. It was impossible to imagine anything more different than the Indian and Negro soldiers. The Indians were so uncommunicative that it was a sheer waste of time to question them. When you put them to work or ordered them about, they obeyed silently without the slightest sign of emotion. Our soldiers nicknamed them the 'Turbaned Stones'. The Negros, on the other hand, jabbered away in their

Afrikaans German, answering any questions you put to them and adding that what they needed was a Führer of their own to deliver them from the British oppressors.

As we advanced, we passed along columns of prisoners being marched back under Italian guard. Up to now, the Italians at the front had been used only as ammunition carriers, drivers and general handymen, and in these jobs they had proved themselves quite useful. But now that they had to guard the large number of prisoners who were coming in, a serious problem arose. The day after the fall of Tobruk, one of my corporals knocked down two Italians on the spot when he saw them using their rifle butts on some exhausted prisoners, and a few days later I was hailed by a British officer who complained that he had had nothing to drink all day. When I questioned the guard, he just grinned and said 'Inglesi nix aqua'. In this particular case, I was able to give the officer some water and deal with the Italian as he deserved, but it was horrible to think of the hundreds of others who were ill-treating the prisoners to their hearts' content. Until now I had never really taken the Italians seriously, but now I detested them. I could sympathise only too well with the anxiety of the British about whose prisoners they were going to be. I did what I could to protect the Tommies that I captured, but it made my blood boil to think what might happen to them later. The thought was particularly revolting because I admired the soldierly spirit of the prisoners I took. I thoroughly enjoyed talking to them, in spite of the fact that I could never get them to give any real information away; they were always so confident and cheerful. I once showed a major one of our 88mm guns and he burst out laughing when he saw it. 'You've no damn business to be using a gun as powerful as that,' he said. 'It's most unsporting, shooting at armour as light as ours.' I told him I thought any weapon was justified if it helped us to catch up with an enemy who ran as fast as the Tommy, and we parted the best of friends.

We continued to advance farther and farther into Egypt, outmanoeuvring and outgunning the enemy whenever we managed to catch him. There was practically no resistance at all, apart from the increasingly severe air attacks which were annoying but made no difference to our progress. But what hindered us all the time and eventually halted us altogether within a mere 100 kilometres of Alex was lack of fuel. There we sat, knowing that petrol for one division would have enabled us to go straight through to the Suez Canal. It was maddening but there was nothing we could do but wait.

My position was just north of El Alamein on a narrow strip of desert between the sea and the Qattara depression. There was not much to do except see to the proper placing of guards and supervise the servicing and camouflage of my panzers, as we had to be very careful to see that nothing gave away our position. The air attacks were getting to be a real nuisance and the British had complete mastery of the air, although our planes and pilots were quite as good as theirs. The trouble with ours was that they were never there when we wanted them, there were simply not enough to go round.

Every bit as efficient and annoying as the RAF was the British field artillery, their 25-pounder which we called the 'Ratschbumm'. It was this gun that I admired most, accurate, powerful and, what was far more important, highly manoeuvrable. As soon as we had located one and laid the aim, it would start firing from a new position. The 'Ratschbumm' governed our whole lives; it woke us at five in the morning, gave us a short rest during the hottest part of the day between 10.00 and 15.00 hours and then signed off about 18.00 hours. This gave us plenty of time for talking, cards and swimming in the lovely Mediterranean, but we could never relax completely as the Tommies were always up to tricks.

They were past masters at surprise attacks, and neatly executed raids behind our lines. They would creep in at night wearing rubber-soled shoes, cut the throats of our guards, play havoc with our positions and disappear as silently as they had come, taking a prisoner or two along with them. Sometimes they even wore our uniforms and carried our identity papers and pay books. I rather admired these raiders; they had plenty of guts and initiative, and in spite of their ferocity there was no personal animosity against them throughout the Afrika Korps.

The Tommy was looked upon as a clean fighter and an enemy to be respected. A good example of British decency was the way in which they frequently used to send us a message when they had captured one of our patrols, so that we should know that our men were not lost in the desert.

We often talked about the idiocy of having to fight these people who in many ways were so like ourselves. We were the same racially and we had so many interests in common. Britain was the sea power, Germany the land power; together we could have formed an invincible combination. We thought it a thousand pities that the British were so short-sighted and so intent on their own destruction, but since they had made up their minds to fight us that was that.

At the end of August I was called to Headquarters and awarded the German Cross of Gold for outstanding leadership during the recent advance. At the same time I was informed that I had been promoted to the rank of Captain. I was terribly pleased with my 'fried egg', as awards and promotion in the Afrika Korps were well worth having.

Back at the front we got down to celebrating my good luck with corned beef and tinned fruit washed down with English gin and whisky. The whole squadron was in on the party, and we had just begun to drink the toasts when an order came through that all COs were to report to Headquarters immediately. It took me a minute to realise that now I was a Captain, this meant me.

Rommel presided over the conference and, in his clipped precise way, he told us that the Afrika Korps could not remain stationary indefinitely. He said that we must attack and attack quickly, as the enemy was regrouping and being reinforced all the time. Up to now we had been waiting for petrol, but a message had come through to say that of the three tankers despatched from Italy had been sunk by enemy naval forces and the third was now burning in Tobruk harbour. As at least five days' petrol was needed to get to the Canal, and as only one and a half days' supply was available at present, the rest would have to be provided by the enemy. Intelligence had been received that there was a large British fuel dump about fifteen kilometres east of our lines. This was to be captured immediately and at all costs. After refuelling we were to push straight on to Alex. Opposition was to be expected.

Rommel was certainly right about the opposition. From the moment we set out on this 'September Rommel', flares lit up the whole desert and the 'Ratschbumms' pounded us without mercy. But we battled on; there was no alternative; we simply had to get that petrol. The nearer we got the worse the artillery fire became. It was as if every single gun was concentrated on the area immediately in front of the dump. And so they were. Nor did the dump, which we eventually reached with very heavy losses, contain a single drop of petrol. We had fallen, or rather fought our way into, a diabolically clever trap. However furious and frustrated one felt one had to hand it to the Tommy; he certainly knew what he was doing.

All we could do now was to start waiting again for another God knew how many weeks in that blistering dusty desert, at the same time providing a sitting target for the RAF and British artillery. Rommel had been right, too, about their reinforcements. After a day or two we got orders to withdraw to our more favourable original positions. From now on, petrol and stores were flown up to the front in old 'Aunt Jus' [Junkers Ju 52]. But we never had enough to stage a fresh all-out attack, thanks to the RAF, which was playing havoc behind our lines. It was quite obvious to me that unless we got air cover we should be stuck here for months and months. In the meantime the enemy would continue to amass guns and armour. In fact, the situation looked pretty sticky. But the men were as confident as ever; they even talked about an 'October Rommel'. So I kept my pessimism to myself.

My fears were fulfilled on 23 October, when the British opened up with a devastating artillery preparation. I had never experienced anything as intense as this before; until the barrage lifted, we could do nothing but crouch in the dugouts and hope for the best. Then, they attacked with their new American tanks – which we soon found were a match for our Mark IVs – supported by an overpowering weight of artillery and a withering naval bombardment.

We began to roll back step by step before this relentless tidal wave of steel. I had serious casualties in my squadron and lost nearly half my panzers in the first few days. Then the order came to disengage and withdraw – which was obviously our only hope of survival. But this was immediately superseded by another which came directly from the Führer: 'Troops will defend the positions they hold at the moment.' This was sheer lunacy; any child could have seen that the order might just as well have read: 'Troops will commit suicide immediately.' It was absolutely typical of those ignorant Nazi advisers with whom the Führer surrounded himself; civilians who thought it no end of a lark to dabble in military matters.

Thirty hours later the order was withdrawn, but by then the damage was done. Tommy had broken through on both my flanks and was knocking hell out of my squadron, which was almost surrounded. I gave orders to blast our way out and make a dash for it; there was really nothing else I could do, it was every panzer for itself now. How mine got clear I shall never know. It was as near a miracle as makes no odds. Only two other panzers escaped besides mine; so that was pretty well the end of my squadron.

All the fight seemed to have gone out of the men; they were gloomy, dejected, fed up and bitterly resentful of the meddling Brass Hats back in Germany who knew

nothing about desert warfare and who had got the Afrika Korps into this mess. All
the soldiers wanted now was to get back to Europe as soon as possible. In the circumstances no one could blame them.

We were carpet bombed, dive bombed and machine-gunned from the air. Nor
were we ever free from the danger of being outflanked and surrounded. Weariness,
fear and the nerve-racking sensation of being relentlessly pursued filled my days and
nights. Looking back on that week following the British breakthrough, I have the
impression of a long, blurred nightmare; terrifying but without any particular details.
The last thing I remember clearly is blowing up my panzer when the petrol had run
out, and watching the flames slowly envelop it. It was then that I knew without the
slightest shadow of doubt that this was the end of our Afrika Korps. I was far too tired
to feel any regret; I just accepted it as a fact. I remember wondering why the British
advanced so cautiously … if they only knew. I almost wished they did know.

It must have been a day or so after this that I was wounded in the head while we
were being machine-gunned by low flying aircraft. I remember nothing about it, and
only found out what had happened when I came to in an overcrowded hospital in
Derna. All I was conscious of was a blinding headache and the awful feeling that my
brains would spill out on the pillow if anyone removed my bandages. I have a vague
recollection of someone bending over me and telling me I had been wounded and
that I was going to be flown back to Italy.

About two months later I was more or less composed again. A general came
and pinned a Ritter Kreutz to my pyjamas for the part I had played in the Grand
Finale of the Afrika Korps. The total defeat of our armies in Egypt did not really
surprise me. But the news that the Americans had landed in French North Africa
was a horrible shock. I had reckoned without the Americans, fondly imagining
that our U-boat blockade in the Atlantic would take care of them. And in any case
I had never really believed that the United States would send troops to fight against
Germany. Our news bulletins had always stressed the fact that the Americans had
more than enough to do defending their own interests in the Pacific. But it was
not so much their soldiers that we had to fear – they were a nation of pacifists
with no military tradition, and one knew more or less what to expect from their
men after the poor showing that they had made in the First World War – it was the
thought of their material that worried me; the quality and above all the quantity.
The worst blow of all came early in February when Field Marshal von Paulus's
army was obliterated before Stalingrad. Suddenly, the outcome of the war began
to be something about which I dared not think; but as nobody else seemed to be
particularly disturbed or pessimistic, I told myself that it was probably just my headaches making me morbid and depressed.

Eventually, the doctors decided to send me back to Germany for a brain operation. They said this would probably relieve the pain quite a bit. I arrived at the brain
hospital in Buch in the outskirts of Berlin at the beginning of March, and after they
had taken my head to bits and put it together again, I woke up one day without a
headache to find Chrys sitting by my bed with a large bunch of daffodils in her hand.

Now that I had her to come and see me, it was easier to keep my mind off the military situation, but something that rather upset me was the discovery that she had come back to Berlin and taken a job. I had imagined that she had come up from Falkenwalde to see me, but I now found that she had left LouisManfred with my parents, and had been working at the KddK [the Nazi Organisation for Foreign Arts and Artists] for the past five months. The actual job sounded exceedingly vague; as far as I could make out Chrys did practically nothing apart from helping to arrange an occasional reception for some visiting foreign artist. The rest of her time seemed to be taken up in making a good impression on the people who came to call on *Reichs Bühnen Bildner* [official chief of the Stage Décor Artists], Bruno von Klagen, who, she informed me, was working night and day on the décor for the victory celebrations.

That was the only part of the story that made me laugh; I took a rather poor view of the rest of it. It was quite obvious to me that they were paying Chrys that handsome salary simply because she was Gräfin von Bogenhardt and very pretty in the bargain. That was bad enough; but what I disliked far more was the idea of my wife having anything to do with an out-andout Nazi like von Klagen. It was no use telling me that the job was purely social and had nothing to do with politics, or that the 'Reibübi' [abbreviation for *Reichs Bühnen Bildner*] was perfectly sweet and such a fine artist. I hated this Party and did not much like the sound of him either. In any case, I could not make out what had possessed Chrys to want to leave home and the baby.

She explained that she had been terribly bored; Falkenwalde had become so dreary and depressing, she had felt that she must get away. Although she had wanted to bring Louis-Manfred with her my parents had begged her not to in case of air raids; so here she was on her own. But she flatly refused to argue with me about the job or anything else until I was better.

Finally, towards the end of June, I arrived home on three months' sick leave before reporting to a medical board. Meeting my son was a strange experience; I had an awful desire to cry and my head began to throb violently. But luckily no one noticed as Louis-Manfred was raising hell at being put into the arms of strange man, instead of being allowed to hug his mother.

Chrys had been right about the atmosphere at Falkenwalde and the fact that it was all looking lovelier than ever made it rather worse. The first thing I discovered when I arrived was that Spatz had been killed in Russia at Christmas, but they had thought it better not to tell me while I was in hospital. Mother was like a ghost; just as sweet and charming as ever, but all the life seemed to have gone out of her. She no longer did things, she just went through the movements. I knew it was not only Spatz's death that made her like this but the conviction that it was only a matter of time before she lost Utz and me as well.

Whereas Mother was resigned, Father was bitter. His troubles on the estate had become almost an obsession; so much so that he had more or less lost interest in the war. I tried to change his thoughts by telling him that we should be very lucky if we managed to get through at all; that there might not be any Germany left, much less any estate, by the time it was all over. But he had such blind faith in the Wehrmacht's ability to win the war that he dismissed anything I said as neurotic depression brought on by my wound, and went back to his brooding and grousing, after telling me that I should soon feel better.

But instead of feeling better, I began to feel worse. The combination of Father's perpetual grumbling about relatively unimportant things and Mother's looking at me as if I were already dead made me terribly irritable – for the first time in my life – and my headaches began to come back. Chrystal and I started bickering; mostly about her job. I got absolutely furious when she talked about 'Reibübi' and all the amusing 'arty' people she had made friends with at the KddK and the wonderful parties they had had. I did my best not to be unreasonable, but I had taken such a hatred for stay-at-home Party members, I found it very hard to control myself.

There were quite a few of these characters living in the country; talking and behaving as if they personally were winning the war. I could never make up my mind which annoyed me most, their over-elaborate uniforms or their over-patronising manner.

The whole thing came to a head after I had been home about six weeks. Father and I met the local Kreisleiter in Morin and I lost my temper when he slapped me on the back and asked me jovially what the young Hauptman had done to deserve a Ritter Kreutz and a 'Fried Egg'. I replied that I had not done much but that was a damn sight more than the Kreisleiter and his friends in the Party had done or were ever likely to do. Trembling with rage, the Kreisleiter took his leave saying darkly that I would hear more of this later. [A Kreisleiter was the leader of the largest subdivision of a Gau, so a powerful figure.]

Chrystal was furious with me and said I was a fool, and Mother was terribly upset. But Father was really cheerful for the first time since I had come back. He seemed prouder of my having told the Kreisleiter where he got off than of Spatz having died for the Fatherland.

'Hearing more' consisted of a farcical interview with the Gestapo, who summoned me to their parlour about a week later and informed me that they had been 'looking into' my record. They accused me of 'Demoralisation of the War Machine'. I could not help thinking that if by the war machine they meant the Kreisleiter the sooner he was demoralised the better. The Gestapo advised me to go back to the front where I belonged before I got into any more trouble on the home front, and before they decided what course to take. I could, of course, have shown them my doctor's certificate, but I was damned if I was going to bandy words with them. Anyway, it suddenly struck me they were right; I did belong to the front, among the hardship and bullets. There, at least, was comradeship and decency and mutual respect.

I packed up as soon as I could and returned to Wunsdorf. Chrys came with me as far as Berlin; there was nothing now to prevent her returning to her precious 'Reibübi' and his arty Party friends. I had to do a bit of wangling with the MO at Wunsdorf to get myself posted, but it was not too difficult and before long I was on my way east to the Russian front.

I had no idea which sector or what unit I was going to. The express went straight through from Berlin to Krakow and from there I changed into a front leave train going to Lemberg. Here I was told to take the train for Tarnopol. The moment we set off from Lemberg, I began to feel the queer awe-inspiring atmosphere of the Russian front. I noticed how everyone piled into the back of the train, and my fellow travellers explained that trains were mined and ambushed by partisans every day. That was why the locomotives always pushed two empty carriages in front and guards kept constant watch at the windows. No train was allowed to go faster than 25 kilometres an hour, and during the journey, which lasted several days, we kept stopping for hours at a time. Each time this happened the rumour would go round that the train in front had been blown up.

It was amazing how completely resigned and philosophical the seasoned fighters on the Russian front were. They took all these interruptions as a matter of course and did not seem to be in the least disturbed or frightened at the idea of going back to the front. They were apparently so used to this life that they had almost forgotten that they hated it.

I was both disturbed and frightened. I had the same sinking feeling that comes to a patient before an operation. I think this was caused by the knowledge that the Russian front was going to be utterly different from anything I had experienced before, and as the train rattled eastwards through the flat monotonous countryside, a vague jumble of all the terrible stories I had heard about Russia jolted in and out of my mind.

We arrived in Tarnopol, and from there I walked and hitchhiked my way towards Kiev, which was the nearest big town to the village where my unit was situated. It was only after I had joined my squadron that I realized how lucky I had been to get through with so little trouble. There were reports and rumours every day of large supply units being ambushed, and bridges, railways, aerodromes and ammunition dumps being blown up. From this point of view the front was the better place to be, as the partisans preferred to work well behind the lines where they could dislocate our supply route to their hearts' content.

I was very conscious of being a stranger at first. There was a family atmosphere here which I realised had been brought about by common suffering. Officers and men were as close as they had been in the Afrika Korps, but for different reasons. There, it had been a matter of choice; here it was sheer necessity. Conditions were too primitive and the struggle too grim to allow for anything so relatively unimportant as rank. Everyone slept where there was a little shelter.

Things were pretty quiet just now and had been for some time. Reinforcements were on the way and everyone was busy making preparations for the winter; collecting warm clothes, boots and anything that might come in useful. But no one had any illusions about the inevitable Russian offensive that would engulf them with the coming of winter.

During this autumn breathing space, I spent a good deal of the time finding out all I could about my new enemy. My comrades made it quite clear that both individually and collectively the Russian was stronger, more dangerous and more unpleasant to fight than anyone else. Not being a European, his mind and emotions worked quite differently from ours. He was a fatalist, and whatever position he was told to defend or attack, he would defend it or attack it with his dying breath. To die was unimportant to a Russian; what was supremely important was to kill Germans.

The Russian equipment had improved tremendously in the last year or two. They now had the T34 tank, which was equal to our Tiger, and seemingly unlimited artillery. Whereas they had formerly suffered from lack of transport, they now had the latest and best American trucks. Their small arms were in many ways better than ours; they were much simpler and stood up much better to the wet and the dirt and the cold. Almost everyone in my unit had equipped themselves with Russian light machine guns, rifles and small anti-tank guns.

The Russian Army of today could not be compared with the rabble the Reichswehr had encountered in 1941 and 1942. The High Command had learned everything they could from blitzkrieg and all the other German methods, and in many respects could now be said to be beating us at our own game. The soldiers that faced us now had had a first-class training, incorporating all the lessons learned during the first hurried retreat. An unlimited supply of trained infantry was the Russian trump card. When the infantry attacked and could not get through, it attacked again and again, sometimes in as many as 30 waves, and kept on until our numbers were so reduced that we could no longer hold on. It was this feeling of being up against such vast masses and weight that made fighting on this front so depressing.

And yet, I was amazed how high our men's morale was. Each German soldier considered himself vastly superior to any single Russian, even though their numbers were so overpowering. The idea that they would eventually enter Germany did not really worry any of us because by the time that happened, if it happened, we should all be dead. Everyone took the idea of being killed completely for granted. It was either kill or be killed. There was not a single man who did not feel that it was better to be dead than to be taken prisoner. To be captured by the Russians was unthinkable. We knew how they treated their own soldiers and that was quite enough. Civilised standards and the value of human life simply did not exist for them, and it was the knowledge of this fact that conditioned all our feelings. Each officer whether he was a regular, a Nazi or a conscript, felt exactly the same.

In the late autumn, Ivan began to attack. After a preliminary artillery preparation, wave after wave of infantry surged towards our lines. But our positions were so well prepared and each man so well trained that we managed to move back in an orderly way, shortening our lines step by step. Our companies became thinner and thinner until after a few weeks only 40 or 50 men remained where 200 should have been. But the enemy never actually managed to break through, and their losses must have been ten times as many as ours.

This slow, orderly retreat did not depress us too much. We felt we were holding our own and we looked forward confidently to getting reinforcements. Then the rain started and the whole country turned into a morass. Soaked to the skin and chilled to the bone, we fell back on one waterlogged position after another. How long we continued to retreat I do not know. All the days were the same falling back, being mortared, mowing down Russians, falling back again and always knee deep in clammy stinking mud, always cold, always damp. One day reinforcements arrived, and we were able to advance again. Our squadron got six new Tigers and we attacked for four days, regaining much of our lost ground. Then, for no reason, we were told to halt and dig in. This was hell, because we had blown up and burned everything that could possibly be used as cover when we retreated. We lay in these positions shivering and dejected until Christmas Eve when, just as we were opening the cases of food and champagne that had arrived from France to cheer us up, terrific artillery fire started. The barrage continued for four days and after that the all-out Russian attack started.

They broke through and encircled us, and we fought our way out losing half our panzers. Then, when we thought we were safe at last, we found that they had pushed through on both our flanks and encircled us again. In the break-out we lost more panzers. It went on like that month after month. Our squadron lost its last panzer, picked up reinforcements, lost them again and again and again. But in order to get out and go back we had to fight our way inch by inch through country infested with partisans, while the relentless T34s rumbled perpetually at our heels.

Up till the beginning of July, I seemed to have led a charmed life. Then, during the heavy fighting for Minsk, I finally 'bought' the wound that had been so long overdue.

It happened quite undramatically; our panzer got stuck in a shell crater and while we were trying to get it out again we got a broadside from a Stalin's Organ and a splinter shattered my right knee. I fainted and came to in an auxiliary hospital somewhere behind our lines. The relief of hearing German voices again was so great that it almost made up for the pain in my leg and I must have fallen into a sort of doze.

The next thing I remember is being awakened by someone suddenly flinging open the door and shouting 'Ivan's on his way, get the hell out of here!' The two medical orderlies, who had been bending over the man on the next palliasse to mine, dropped their bandages and tweezers and bolted. Someone lying near the door began to scream and my two neighbours rolled themselves painfully off their palliasses and began crawling towards the door, carrying their uniforms in their teeth, while those who were still able to walk staggered out into the corridor.

Remembering the gruesome stories I had heard of bayonetings, blindings and castrations, I had a sudden moment of panic and made a desperate effort to wriggle off my palliasse. But the pain in my leg held me there and I lay listening to the engines revving up in the yard and the cries of the wounded begging not to be left behind.

Now that I knew that I could not get away my mind cleared and I felt comparatively calm. The first thing I had to do was to remove the epaulettes from my uniform, as I remembered being told that the Russians massacred all officers out of hand. It was a painful job, but I managed it somehow, mostly with my teeth, and eventually stuffed the incriminating gold braid under my palliasse. I was so exhausted after this that I more or less passed out again. I was terribly hot and thirsty, and my old head wound began throbbing so that sometimes I imagined I was back in Italy. I only remember three things distinctly about that night; one man who wept like a girl for hours on end, another who made interminable communist speeches and an old major opposite me who reached for his pistol, loaded it very deliberately, put the barrel into his mouth (so that I wondered in a dazed sort of way if he was thinking of spraying his throat) and fired.

It was daylight when I was awakened by the sound of trucks rattling into the yard. The door was flung open and four Russian tank men burst in brandishing machine pistols. They dashed through the room tearing the blankets off one or two men as they passed, shouted something in Russian and were gone again. There was more noise and running about outside but no one came near us again throughout that day or the following night. Everybody suffered terribly; our dressings had not been changed and we were tortured with thirst. By the next morning four severe casualties had died.

At noon a Russian officer came in with three or four privates and several unwounded German prisoners who looked terribly scared. The officer went round the room glancing at each wounded man, presumably to see whether he was fit enough for transport. I asked one of the Germans in a whisper whether I ought to mention that I was an officer. He gave me a resentful look and muttered 'Not half! You blokes get better grub and they don't make you work.'

A Russian soldier shouted at us and the officer came over to me and said:

'Du Fascist?' I shook my head.

'Du Offizer?' I nodded and answered, 'Ja, Hauptmann.'

One of the Germans translated 'Eto Kapitan.' The officer acknowledged this with a bored nod and began pointing out those who were to be taken away. The prisoners lifted us on to stretchers and carried us outside into the yard, where we could still hear the cries of the hopeless cases who had been left to die.

The jolting of the stretcher was so painful that I passed out again. I came to lying on the ground in what appeared to be a shot-up railway station. It was getting dark and I looked for my watch only to find that it had gone. I then discovered that I had been relieved of my wedding ring and penknife as well. My neighbour grinned. 'Ivan's a great one for souvenirs,' he added.

It was now that we got the first medical attention we had had for over 48 hours. A very young and boisterous Russian woman doctor, her blouse blazing with decorations, arrived accompanied by some German prisoners carrying medical equipment. The doctor spoke a little German and barked peremptory orders at her assistants and wounded alike. She dressed our wounds, using paper bandages which immediately became saturated with blood, and gave injections in a matter of fact way. After this, we were given a drink and we each got a loaf of bread which we were told would have to last us for three days. We were put into goods wagons which had a thin layer of straw on the floor and a trellis work of barbed wire covering the sides.

Our journey was agonisingly slow. The woman doctor was in charge of the transport and there were a few Russian guards besides the German medical staff. On the third day we were given a little bread, and after that we got something to eat every day but at very irregular intervals, sometimes in the morning, at other times late at night. Eventually we were unloaded on an open field where thousands of prisoners were waiting. These prisoners had to carry us on the trek that now began.

The Russians were so afraid that typhoid might break out that they drove our columns along at an impossible speed, using clubs from time to time if they noticed any
slackening of the pace. Everyone suffered terribly from the heat. There was nothing
to drink, and whoever dropped out was shot. We had been divided into sections of
1,000 men each. In my section alone, 30 died on the way, three committed suicide
by jumping off a bridge and two went out of their minds. After two days' continuous
marching, we arrived at a camp. It was just an enormous field surrounded by barbed
wire with several dozen huts and some ruined buildings in the far distance.

As soon as we arrived, we were registered and examined. The camp had quarters
for light casualties and a 'hospital' in the huts to which I was sent, for the severe cases.
Here, there were a few benches covered with straw but most of the sick and wounded
lay on the floor. As soon as the German doctors saw my leg, they said it would have to
come off and after getting permission from one of the young women in charge, they
amputated it. There were practically no dressings, medicaments or narcotics here, and
there was barely enough ether for the operation. But they took a lot of trouble over
me and thanks to my strong constitution I began to recover.

The hospital, which became more and more crowded as time went on, was exceedingly unpleasant in every way. There was a chronic water shortage, and only the very
severe cases were allowed to wash once a day. As a result, we were infested first with
lice and then bugs. But far worse than the vermin were the Russian nurses. There
were about two dozen of them and they went out of their way to be unpleasant. They
liked to show us how much they despised us and how much our filthy condition
revolted them: 'Deutshes nix Kultura' they said with grim satisfaction as they picked
their way among the bodies on the floor. The chief of the hospital was a Russian
doctor, a god-like figure who floated in and out from time to time and paid no attention to anything. The women doctors were a good deal better; they took their job
seriously and were comparatively decent and friendly. But all the real work was done
by the German doctors whose one aim and object was to appear as busy as possible in
order to avoid being sent back to the general camp, where the food was even worse
and where they would have lost the few privileges that they had here.

The camp consisted of two sections, one for the officers and one for the men. The
men's section was divided into five groups. Groups one and two were made up of
those who were strong and healthy; they drew the best rations (600g of bread and 40g
of barley or gruel a day) and went outside the camp to work. These prisoners had to
do clearance work, cut peat and build roads and aerodromes. They were sent out in
brigades and each brigade was given a target which it had to reach on pain of having
its rations cut. Added to this, they were driven on by relentless male and female civilian
overseers who got a bonus every time the brigade exceeded its target. Group three
consisted of the older and weaker men who worked inside the camp, building cook-
houses, huts and latrines. They drew a smaller ration. Group four consisted of all the
prisoners under eighteen, of whom there were several thousand. They worked inside
the camp but they got the same rations as group one. Group five contained convales-
cents who did no work at all but they drew a slightly better ration than group three.

I eventually arrived in the officers camp after several months in bed, or rather on the floor. Unlike the ranks, we were not allowed to work, which did not seem a privilege. Complete inaction was far more soul destroying and degrading than the heaviest work, and apart from the fact that we got an allowance of ten cigarettes a month, we were, if anything, worse off than the men.

During the German occupation, there had been a training school for army messenger dogs on the site of the camp. The living quarters had been burnt out, but the kennels were still standing and each kennel now housed two officers. The shadow of our canine predecessors fell also across our food, as the Russians had captured the training school's store of dog biscuits which they assumed in all innocence to be some foreign form of wholemeal bread. For weeks on end we were served with 'Biscuits soup' until nearly every inmate of the kennels had gone down with dysentery. Dropsy, hunger, oedema and dysentery, from which people died like flies, were endemic in the camp owing to the complete lack of vitamins in our diet. Food was the worst part of our life; not so much the lack of it, as the deadly monotony. We got three warm meals and a half a kilo of bread a day, but it was always the same, month in, month out, just gruel without a trace of meat or fat.

Our mortality rate stood at 25 per cent during the first six months or so and rose steadily as time went on. But although typhus and dysentery were the chief causes of this fantastically high proportion of deaths, morale, or rather lack of morale, had a good deal to do with it. Everyone suffered terribly from the feeling of being lost, cut off and forgotten. There was no means of writing home or letting our people know we were alive; we could not communicate with the outside world and the outside world could not communicate with us. The Russians said blandly that it was nothing to do with them. It was the fault of our own armies which had destroyed all the railways and roads in their retreat. Whatever the causes, the effects gave rise to chronic anxiety, depression and even melancholia, which produced a daily crop of suicides and a general weakening of the will to live. The total absence of any kind of mental or spiritual activity was another reason for the steady decline of morale. There were no books or anything else to take our minds off our present circumstances, apart from an occasional political training lecture.

These were given by commissioned and non-commissioned officers who wore the black and white and red armband and were known as 'agitators' or 'instructors'. They had all been through a special course of Marxism, and many of them had been recruited from the 'Free Germany' movement. Others were turncoat Party members and HJ boys and a few of them were emigrants, many of whom had been in Russia since 1933. The Free Germany agitators and former Party members ranted constantly about German guilt, as did the ex-HJ boys; this impressed nobody. The emigrants held forth on conditions in Germany about which they obviously knew nothing; this was even less impressive. None of them seemed to have anything constructive to say. Even their motives for becoming agitators in the first place were suspect, when one saw the good food and clothing they got and the way in which they bossed the working parties around in their spare time. We neither liked them nor trusted them,

and we thought their lectures were rotten. But we all took part in the political training because it was something to think about, something to disagree with, above all,
something to do.

Although the 'agitators' were there to spread the Marxist doctrine, no one compelled us to listen to them, least of all the Russians. They left our internal affairs
entirely to us and, apart from smiling on any display of nationalism, provided it was
not fascist, they did not seem to be interested in our political pasts or opinions. Even
when a particularly pompous agitator annoyed some of the younger prisoners so
much that they rioted, shouted 'Heil Hitler' and sang the Horst Wessel song, the
Russians took no notice. There had never been any general screening of the prisoners, and even the SS, provided they removed their badges and kept quiet, were treated
the same as everyone else.

Only a very few high SS officers and NS leadership officers, who had been caught
red-handed in their full glory, were kept under guard in a 'political' hut. This also
housed one or two people suspected of war crimes, members of the Vlassov Army and
some unfortunate Russian civilians who had tried to escape to the West.

Whereas the Russians were pretty consistent in their political attitude towards us,
their personal behaviour varied enormously. Some of them were really brutal and
seemed to enjoy using their clubs and rifle-butts on the prisoners, while others were
friendly and quite humane. It was obviously impossible to hold them responsible for
our appalling living conditions, as their own were hardly any better. They lived in
ramshackle hovels and mud huts and their food and clothing were almost as poor as
ours. The only big difference between us was that they had never known anything
better than this and so they could take their hard lot more or less for granted.

But, according to the prisoners who worked outside the camp, the Russians were
very far from taking their regime for granted. Most of them made no secret of their
loathing for it. It was patriotism and patriotism alone that united them, and the
stupendous efforts of the Red Army were due solely to the determination that no
enemy should remain on the sacred soil of Mother Russia. Communism had nothing
to do with it.

The Russian guards and camp personnel, including 35 officers and MOs totalled
about 80. But only four of them were communists. These four always kept together,
and we got the impression that they were feared and disliked by the rest. The fact
that communists were very much the exception, even in Russia, was probably the
reason why the Russians never believed a German when he said he was a communist. If a prisoner tried to convince them by saying that he and his wife had lived
in a two-room apartment at home, he was immediately marked down as a capitalist.
Almost every trade and occupation was classified as capitalistic, with one exception:
for reasons best known to the Russians, if you had been an accountant you were
definitely considered to be proletarian. The one thing nobody admitted was having
been a skilled worker. Everyone was terrified of the transports that went east from
time to time, taking engineers and metal workers to the factories in the Donetz basin.
The only hope of ultimate release was to appear as useless as possible and trust that

the Russians would one day get fed up with us and send us home. But even this was a very faint hope. One was far more likely to die and simply vanish into oblivion, for the Russians kept no records of the prisoners who died.

The non-stop 'Freie Deutschland' propaganda that blared out of the camp loud-speakers made it very hard to know what to believe. The camp was alive with rumours. There was a new crop every day; they would start in the morning and peter out the same night. Whatever the loudspeakers said, the rumours said exactly the opposite. The best example of this was the story that America, England and Japan had declared war on Russia. This was the main topic of conversation in the camp about three days before we heard that the war was over. Not that we really believed the interpreter when he came in one morning at the beginning of May and said 'Hitler Kaput. War finished. Comrade Ruski Berlin … You all home.' I suppose the reason I couldn't believe it at first was because I did not want to. I kept telling myself that this was probably the interpreter's idea of a joke and that what the loudspeakers were saying was just the usual propaganda. But when the guards started careering tipsily round the camp, shouting and singing and offering vodka to every prisoner they met, I knew it was no use pretending any longer.

Apart from the fact that no new prisoners arrived after this and that for days on end the guards continued to ply us with drink, everything went on very much as before. The possibility of our release was the sole topic of conversation and the one theme of every rumour. Group Five were the only ones with any immediate hope, and even we had to wait till the autumn before we were transferred to a so-called release camp.

The formalities here were interminable. The Russians were determined not to release any officers unless they were desperately ill or so badly wounded as to be virtually helpless. It was another three months before I finally got my papers and climbed on to the transport a 'certified wreck'.

Those last three months at the release camp were pretty nerve-racking, but, compared to the weeks that followed on the transport, they were positively pleasant. That transport was the worst experience of my life.

We were packed together in uncovered goods wagons and only fed every second or third day when our guard threw us a few loaves. The filth and stench were indescribable. There was no means of washing and no medical care at all, with the result that a number of prisoners died every day. The Russian system of single-track lines made the whole journey agonisingly slow, and we were for ever being shunted into sidings where we sometimes remained for days on end. This meant that we had to rely on the local population for our food, which would have been all right if the Russian peasants had had any food to give us. They were friendly enough, but they had precious little to eat themselves, and whenever they got a chance, they would swarm into our wagons and try to persuade us to swap what little bread we had for tobacco.

As soon as we crossed into Poland, the people were openly hostile. They cursed us and threw stones, and the Poles who had replaced our Russian guards made no attempt to protect us. A rabble boarded the train, stripped us of our few remaining possessions and worst of all tore up our release papers. This was certainly hitting where it hurt; back we had to go to another clearance camp and there we sat for another six weeks in a tangle of red tape waiting for our new papers. As this camp was in what had formerly been German territory, some of the more able-bodied prisoners decided to make a dash for it. Almost all of them were captured before they had gone 30 kilometres. After being thoroughly beaten up they arrived back at the camp. They all told terrible stories of the devastated countryside; of ruined towns and villages where weeds grew as tall as a man, where corpses still rotted in the streets and where the only living creatures were the wolves. The would-be escapees were rather chastened after this and decided to wait along with the rest of us.

Eventually, we piled into a train and set off along the same old track via Thorn and Lansberg-am-Warte to Frankfurt-ander-Oder. Here, the red tape was unbelievable; but it was nothing to the political propaganda! Every poster exhorted us to join the KPD, and also before we were out of the train we were showered with pamphlets extolling the tremendous contributions the Party was making towards the rebirth of Germany. This was hardly the moment to make converts; all we wanted now was to get home as quickly as possible. In our innocence, we had imagined that the authorities would appreciate this and give us a helping hand once we were finally through the formalities. But what we got, once we had filled up the last form, was a speech from a communist official who admonished us at great length not to forget the splendid and wonderful things we had seen in Soviet Russia. When he had said his piece, he gave each of us three marks and told us that every prisoner was entitled to a slice of bread which could be obtained at the distribution centre.

And so, having strengthened and sustained us to the tune of three marks, a piece of dry bread and an eloquent speech, this representative of the new democratic Germany washed his hands of us and left us to make our way home as best we could.

We set out for the station. On the way I tried to telephone, but I was told that it was out of the question; such lines as were working were reserved for the Russians. I was still wondering whether I ought not to try to get back to Falkenwalde direct. It seemed very unlikely that the family would still be there, but of course I couldn't be sure. If half we had heard, even in the short time we had arrived, was true, they would almost certainly have moved out before the Russians reached the Oder. At least, I hoped that was what they had done.

I had suddenly begun to worry frantically about Chrys and Louis-Manfred and Mother and Father. All the time I had been in prison, I had somehow always thought of them as being quite all right and perfectly safe. I had had awful depressions about their thinking I was dead and I had longed for them till it hurt, but I had always comforted myself by thinking that this was happening to me and not to them. In my thoughts, they had had no background or connection with events; they had simply represented security and happiness and love and all the things that I had to get back to. It was because of them that I had had to hang on and stay alive. Now that I was almost within reach of them again, I suddenly realised that this had probably been all wishful thinking. Just because I had survived by a miracle, it did not necessarily follow that they had. The chances were they were all dead or worse. It was probably just as well that I could not get through to Falkenwalde; I had an awful feeling that perhaps it would have been better if I had been killed in Russia after all. We arrived at the station and came face to face with a poster which said:

RETURNEES!
By order of the
KOMMANDATURA

You are forbidden to wear military uniforms. Get yourselves civilian outfits *immediately*. Anyone caught wearing uniforms will be liable to severe punishment.

What the posters omitted to tell us was where and how we were supposed to get ourselves civilian outfits. Probably the Kommandatura's guess was as good as ours. Someone suggested the town hall, pointing out that in any case we needed some money and food for our journey. At the town hall we had to show our release papers and answer innumerable questions about our pasts and political backgrounds. After that we left to cool our heels for a couple of hours. Finally, an official came in and told us that nothing could be done about clothes or provisions, and as regards our fares, we had better apply to the Welfare Office. He could not guarantee that they would help us, but they might.

The Welfare Office was shut by the time we got there. The porter told us to come back in the morning between eleven and one. When we asked him if he knew of anywhere we could sleep, he shrugged his shoulders and slammed the door. It soon became obvious that the entire population of Frankfurt shared the porter's opinion of returning POWs. Some of them questioned us, especially the women, who thought their husbands might still be in Russia, but apart from that they were openly hostile.

Four of us had made friends on the transport and we decided to stick together. One of the others was minus a leg like me. He and I waited while the other two went from door to door trying to persuade someone to take us in for the night. Most people made some sort of excuse, but one man did not even bother to do that. He said quite openly that he wasn't going to risk letting people with lice and God knew what diseases into his house; quite apart from that, we were probably thieves. We eventually spent the night in a derelict hut on a sports field.

When we presented ourselves at the Welfare Office next morning, our conversation with the official began something like this: 'What the hell do you think you're doing in those uniforms? You ought to be in civvies.'

'And where the hell are we supposed to get them?'

'That's none of my business. But I have strict orders from the Russians not to deal with anyone in uniform.'

And so the argument went on. The official admitted that even if we had had civvies he would not have been able to help us. 'There's no room for anyone in Frankfurt,' he said, 'and even if there were, we've no food or money. The sooner you get out of here the better.' Berlin was the best place for us to go to, he said, things were better there, and he wrote out a chit for us to give to the railway company.

I now saw that my idea of trying to get to Falkenwalde was hopeless. A cross-country journey through this hostile territory that called itself the Russian Zone (even supposing there were any trains) was obviously out of the question. With the wrong clothes, one leg, no money and no food I could not begin to attempt it. As it was, it was all we could do to persuade them to give us our tickets at the station; we spent over an hour arguing the toss. By the time the booking office had made up its mind, the Berlin train had gone and we were faced with a nine hours' wait until the next one.

By this time I was in a pretty bad way. The effort of hopping round Frankfurt for the past 24 hours had brought on a severe pain in my groin and I felt faint from stomach cramp and sickness that always came on when I was hungry. Gottfried, my one-legged friend, was completely done too. He and I huddled together for warmth on the platform while our two able-bodied comrades went off in search of food. One of them came back after an hour or two with a hunk of bread, a couple of turnips and an onion, but we never saw the other again. He probably had better luck and decided not to share it.

The train was packed; passengers overflowed on to the roof, the running-board and the buffers. Most of them were laden with sacks of potatoes and everything else they had managed to scrounge.

Nobody seemed particularly interested in us. Some of them showed a little superficial curiosity and asked a few senseless routine questions, while one or two, like the people in Frankfurt, wanted to know if we had come across their husbands, brothers, cousins and nephews. We spent most of the journey getting more and more depressed as we listened to our fellow travellers. It was not difficult to see why people had no time for us and our plight; they had far too many troubles of their own to worry about anyone else. There was a despondent, but mostly bitter note in everything they said, and the longer I listened to them, the lower my spirits became. It was on this train that I first heard of the large-scale dismantling of industry and the disastrous effects of the communist land reform.

The train stopped at Erkner, a suburb of Berlin, and from there the passengers had to get on as best they could. My best was none too good, especially as it was pitch dark and there was no underground or any other kind of conveyance. Everyone made for the main road in the hopes of getting a lift; and I hobbled after them. A few lorries went by, but none of them stopped, and one by one the people from the train set out on foot. Those of us who could not walk were still sitting by the roadside when it got light. I finally got a lift in a Russian military car which put me down outside what was left of the Stettiner Bahnhof.

I wanted to get to Potsdam. Even if Uncle Manfred and my mother-in-law were not there, I was sure I could find some of my friends or their friends who would help me. But at the moment I was so exhausted and weak that I decided to try to find somewhere in Berlin for one night at least. My first thought was Chrys's cousin's flat. Whoever was there now would be bound to know something of the family; and they might even give me a bed for a few hours. With my remaining pfennigs, I took the tram to Charlottenburg.

Where the block of flats had stood, there was an imposing pile of rubble; it was hard to believe that Chrys and I had once lived there. After that I tried an address in Olympische Strasse where some friends of mother's had lived. A strange woman who said she had never heard of the Beneckendorfs answered the door and gave me a look which reminded me of the hausfraus in Frankfurt-am-Oder.

I could only remember one other address within hobbling distance of Olympische Strasse. This was a house belonging to some people called von Hahn who had formerly lived in Potsdam. Their son Stefan had been to Loewensteins' dancing classes at the same time as I, and he had been one of Gertie's admirers. During the war I had run into him once or twice in Paris. I knew that if the von Hahns were not there I was more or less done for; I had no money left and the pain in my groin was coming on again. I wondered who (if anyone) would pick me up if I collapsed in the street and where they would put me.

Only half the house was standing; it had no roof and no windows, but Doctor von Hahn and his wife were there. They received me with open arms, fed me and put me to bed. Better still, they had news of my parents, and although they were not sure where Chrys was, they knew that she and Louis were all right. That was all I wanted to know and I promptly fell asleep for the best part of 24 hours.

When I woke up Frau von Hahn sat on the bed and told me all she knew. She could not tell me much about Chrys, except that some Potsdam friends had said that she and my mother-in-law were in Freiburg; probably Louis-Manfred was with them. Falkenwalde had been 'land reformed,' which meant that my parents had had everything confiscated; even the furniture and mother's jewellery had been taken. Mother and Father had joined a refugee train coming west and had arrived more dead than alive in Berlin, after a nightmare trek. It was then that the von Hahns had seen them. Father had told the Doctor that however terrible the Russians had been during the invasion and occupation at Falkenwalde, the German communists had been infinitely worse. He and mother were now living with some cousins of hers at Schwanebeck near Hanover and Uncle Manfred was there too.

The Hahns were amazingly kind; they fitted me out with some of Stefan's old clothes, 'lent' me money and insisted on my staying with them while I was in Berlin. My first idea was to try to get to Freiburg, but the friends who had told the Hahns about Chrys had left Potsdam and no one else seemed to know her address. So I decided to go first to Schwanebeck where at least I was sure of a roof and something to eat. Officially, no interzonal passes were being granted, but here again the Hahns were able help. They were friends with a British official who promised to arrange things for me; after several weeks of filling in forms and hobbling from office to office, I boarded the train for Hanover.

In the old days, the journey had taken four to five hours; now it took three days, two of which were spent in a siding on the Russian side of the zonal frontier. From Hanover I was able to send a wire, after which I set out to hitchhike the remaining 40 kilometres to Schwanebeck. As I came out of the post office an RAF truck pulled up to ask the way to Buckeburg. When the driver found I could speak English, he began chatting, and in a few minutes we were swapping North African experiences. Two hours later, I was standing outside the gates of my cousin's Schloss reading a notice which declared in English and German that by order of the military authorities this property had been declared an historic monument; anyone damaging it, looting from it or entering it if not authorised to do so would be subject to severe punishment. If only Falkenwalde had been in the British zone!

Returning from the dead to those one loves is a heart wrenching experience. The truck had got me to Schwanebeck ahead of my telegram and Mother was completely unprepared for the shock. I had not realised how much of a shock it would be until I saw the mingled bewilderment and pain in her eyes as it slowly dawned on her that this unrecognisable scarecrow with one leg was her son. Mother's look was like a mirror. In it I saw my own reflection, and for the first time, I realised how much the last two and a half years had changed me. Then Father came in and Mother began to cry and it was all right. Father was wonderful; he had aged terribly – he now looked like a very old eagle – but he refused to talk about his own troubles. I found that, unlike Mother, he had always believed that I would come back. Mother's questions came tumbling out so fast that it was quite a time before I could ask about Chrys and Louis-Manfred. The moment the words were out I knew that something was wrong. Mother began to cry again and Father took a letter from the bureau and handed it to me. The date was about two months old. It was in my mother-in-law's writing from an address in Freiburg.

> …Chrystal and Louischen crossed into Switzerland yesterday … hoping to join them in Ascona as soon as our friend can arrange it … surely we must know in our heart of hearts that there can be no more hope for poor dear T … even if by some miracle he *were* to return what sort of a life would it be for Chrystal and Louischen … Germany is *no* place to bring up a child … such a *wonderful* chance to make a fresh start … not sure what their permanent address will be. Hope *eventually* to get to America … Louischen picked up quite a lot of English … talking with an American accent … *Everyone* has been so kind … never want to see Germany again.

So that was that. There was nothing really to be said any more than there was anything to be done. I comforted Mother and pointed out that it was probably better for Louis-Manfred that way.

The Schloss was like a rabbit warren. Besides my parents and Uncle Manfred, there were about 40 other refugee relations living there. Most of them had come from Silesia, East Prussia and Pomerania, where they had either been driven from their estates by the Poles or subjected to the land reforms as was the case with Falkenwalde. What made life at Schwanebeck so strange was the fact that there was absolutely nothing to do. For every job on the estate there were about ten people to do it. This was due to each refugee relation having arrived with a number of employees who had not wanted to stay behind. Every out-building and hayloft was crawling with farmhands, while the kitchens and attics overflowed with their wives and children.

I was filled with admiration for my parents and my other relations of their generation. They had lost everything they possessed and were entirely dependent on charity, but they hardly ever grumbled and did everything they could to keep cheerful and at least make a show of being busy. Father, for instance, had made himself responsible for cutting the hedges in the park, while Mother fed and looked after the ducks in the moat and Uncle Manfred wound and repaired the clocks throughout the Schloss – much to the butler's annoyance. Uncle Manfred did have one grievance, however, and that was the ban on firearms which meant that no one could go shooting for the pot. The only way to fill the larder with game was to invite some British officers over for a day's shooting which was something, in spite of his liking for the English, that my uncle found very difficult to stomach.

There were several other ex-prisoners here besides myself, and although they did odd jobs on the estate whenever there were odd jobs to do, I was very surprised to find that none of them had any plans for the future. Several of them were drinking pretty heavily, and beyond prophesying that the Western powers would be bound to need seasoned professional soldiers when the inevitable war with Russia broke out, they had not the least idea what they were going to do.

The idea of marking time until the next war started struck me as thoroughly unhealthy; even if I had been able-bodied I should have disagreed with it. Of course, it was wonderful to be able to sit back in comfort and relax, to sleep and eat and talk again like a civilised human being. But I had no intention of sitting back and relaxing for the rest of my life, even though I had no profession outside soldiering and my wound was going to debar me from most jobs. As soon as I was rested and feeling a bit stronger I got Father to take me to see a specialist in Hanover. After examining me he said that all things considered I might have been in much worse shape. He diagnosed a duodenal ulcer, which accounted for the sickness and stomach cramps I had suffered from when I was hungry, but he pronounced my amputation quite successful and said that everything had healed the way it should. What was not so encouraging was the seemingly hopeless prospect of my ever getting an artificial leg. This was something, the doctor said, that could not even be bought on the black market. Still, you never knew, he said, something might turn up; it was no use getting depressed about it. In the meantime I must try and put on some of the twenty odd kilos I had lost in Russia and get all the rest I could.

I am determined to earn my living as soon as I possibly can. And, although I have not yet discussed it with my parents or my next-warmongering cousins; I have a plan. I want to learn a trade like watch making, or I might even become an optician. But whatever happens I am not going to spend the rest of my life as a schnapps-drinking cripple, with nothing to think about but the past.

7

HILDEGARD TRUTZ (NEE KOCH)

When Hildegard was a young girl, she used to come to Potsdam to visit her Aunt Minna, who was our cook.

I cannot remember what Hildegard talked about but I do remember her pretty face, her beautiful golden hair and her exceedingly well developed figure. I was two years older than she was and was just beginning to notice these things.

· I also saw her quite often when we went to Stielke's bakery in Berlin to buy Baumkuchen and Mohrenköpfe, which were her father's speciality. Hildegard used to help behind the counter after school, and when we were not in a hurry, she would take us downstairs to the bakery where her father showed us round and allowed us to taste the things. She was very proud of her father and he was even prouder of her.

Later, I remember Minna telling us that her brother-in-law had bought the bakery, and when we asked her why Hildegard never came to see her nowadays, she shook her head sadly and said: 'She has no time for me now – her mother and I are too old-fashioned, she is much too busy with the BDM [Bund Deutscher Mädchen, the female equivalent to the Hitler Youth].

Much later, after the war had begun, Herr Koch refused to sell bread to my parents.

When I returned to Germany for the first time in 1946 one of the first people I looked up was Minna. She told me that Hildegard was still living in her old flat in the former SS Siedlung, and that her husband was interned by the British because he had been in the SS. Minna suggested tentatively that perhaps I might help them? That was the last thing I intended to do, but I went to see Hildegard all the same.

She was obviously not expecting visitors when I called; her straggly bleached hair was screwed up into a knot, her face was sallow and unhealthy looking and her teeth were terrible. She looked the perfect picture of a slut, with her grimy bare feet and filthy ragged dress. She did not recognise me at first. When she did her emotions were a mixture of exaggerated pleasure and genuine embarrassment at being caught with her hair down. She nattered: 'How wonderful to see you back. I often wondered what had happened to you all, and how are your dear father and mother? I was so happy when I heard they had escaped in 1940. You must excuse my get-up but I was just doing the washing.' She refused to let me in 'with the place in such a mess,' but I promised to call again the next afternoon. When I did, she was painted up to the nines and her peroxided hair was combed into what was supposed to be an American bob. She began by inquiring after my family but as soon as I mentioned that some of them had been gassed by the Nazis, she changed the subject at once and began to talk about her own troubles. When she found that she had a sympathetic listener she really got down to it. I had to listen to the same tale of woe each time I saw her.

But it needed a certain amount of strategy to get her to stop resenting the present and talk about the past. I had to take her out in the car away from her immediate surroundings, coax and flatter her before she loosened up and began to talk. Once she had begun there was no stopping her; everything she had absorbed during the Nazi years of triumph came out parrot fashion and completely intact. And as Hildegard recaptured the 'good old days' she became again the Nordic Beauty with the 'childbearing pelvis' who queened it over her less fortunate sisters and had everything just the way she wanted it.

Hildegard Trutz, born 1918

In 1933 we lived in Schloss Strasse in Steglitz. I went to the Hildegard Lyzeum, although Father couldn't really afford the high school fees. He had even sold our small allotment at Siesdorf so that I could carry on at school; Father was like that.

He worked in a large bakery at Steglitz. The name of the boss was Stielke; he was very rich and employed lots of people. Father didn't like Stielke much, and he hated being an employee on weekly wages on which he couldn't make ends meet anyway.

Mother was six years older than Father. She had had childbed fever when I was born and had been more or less an invalid ever since. Actually, our doctor's bills weren't as bad as they might have been. Dr Dobriner, funnily enough, never pressed for payment, in spite of his being a Jew. But then he did not look like one either; he was not fat and greasy and he did not gesticulate. If he hadn't been a Jew one might have thought him nice. Father said he was exceptional, too, seeing that he had been an officer in the Reserve and won the Iron Cross First Class at the front. That was why Father allowed him to attend Mother. He had a great respect for anyone who had been at the front. Father himself was in the Stahlhelm. It was the only thing that he really enjoyed. He said the Stahlhelm still carried on the great tradition of the Prussian Army. He was mad on Frederick the Great, Moltke and so on, and he collected regimental histories. He said his military service was the best time of his life.

Father's best friend was Gustav Motze. During the Great War they had been in the same regiment, the Magdeburg Artillery; at that time Father was a sergeant-major while Motze was only a lance-corporal. In the depression Motze had had bad luck and Father had helped him while he was unemployed. Father used to cheer him up by talking about the old front-line spirit, and saying that Flemish clay cemented a friendship stronger than fire and brimstone.

Gustav Motze joined the SA early. This was the one subject on which he and Father disagreed. Motze said that the Stahlhelm contained too many out-of-date old officers and lacked a real leader, while on the other hand the SA was Adolf Hitler's Brown Guard, and he was a man who knew what he wanted.

Before long Father came to see that Motze was right and in 1933 he went over to the SA along with his whole section. By this time Motze was a Sturmführer. Father enjoyed the SA. He liked clearing out the communists, the Reichsbanner and the Jews.

I myself was mad about Adolf Hitler and our new better Germany. I remember our school being taken to see 'Hitler Junge Quex'. It was a film about a boy who comes from a communist family and secretly joins the Hitler Youth. He pays for his loyalty to the Führer with his life and is murdered by Red thugs. When we came out of the cinema I made up my mind to join the brown columns as soon as possible and fight for the future of Germany.

A new branch of the BDM opened in Steglitz and I remember Motze saying to Father: 'Your Hilde is a real Hitler girl, blonde and strong – just the type we need.' And then he said: 'Don't let her come under the degenerate influence of the Jews, make her join the BDM.'

I was glad of his support as at that time the BDM was still something special and many parents would not let their daughters join. Father, of course, said 'Yes' but Mother was against it. This was my first big row with her.

It began when I brought home some school friends who were already in the BDM and Mother didn't like them. She even had a down on their excursions and hikes and games and folkdancing and sport and community singing. She was terribly old-fashioned and full of Christianity and all that sort of thing and she would keep asking them what they thought about it in the BDM. When the girls said quite truthfully – for a German girl never lies – that religion was Jewish and unsuitable for the Germanic soul, Mother flew into a rage and said that I couldn't get into the BDM.

Of course I went all the same; Father's consent was enough. There would probably have been a lot more trouble with Mother, but luckily the affair with Stielke gave her something else to think about.

Stielke owned the bakery where Father worked and Father said that he was a democrat, or maybe something worse, he might even have been a secret communist. He was always making rude remarks about the SA, saying they were a pack of ruffians and too lazy to work. He even insulted the Führer. Father once heard him say quite distinctly that no self-respecting baker would have any truck with an upstart housepainter. It was then that Father warned him, but Stielke merely laughed. Things came to a head soon after that. In 1934 all Jewish businesses were boycotted. Father was very keen on this and saw to it that an SA man kept watch in front of every Jewish shop in our neighbourhood. Then Stielke got abusive and said that he would rather have ten Jews working for him than one man like Father. Of course that finished it. I can still remember the evening when Father told Sturmführer Motze about it. They suddenly dropped into a whisper and I was sent out of the room. When Motze left I heard him say: 'Don't worry, Wilhelm, I will settle him. He's had this shop long enough.'

Next day the SA took Stielke to the Columbia-Keller which meant that he was a traitor to the Fatherland. When he was questioned he confessed to all sorts of horrible things. This meant that Father had to work even harder than before because now he had to carry on the business by himself.

Then Frau Stielke heard that her husband was in a re-education camp to make him a good German. If Father had wanted to, now was his chance to show who was master, but he was much too decent for them. He even allowed her to live on in two rooms above the shop. Later, when her husband did come back, Father helped her by offering her a very fair price for the shop. He borrowed the money from Motze and another comrade in the SA and in the end Frau Stielke agreed, although she could have kept the business if only she had consented to divorce her husband. But she was stupid and so Father got it, although I don't even know if he was especially keen to have it.

It was still quite unusual to be in the BDM and I was very happy. We could still wear our lovely Dress of Honour at school, though later this was not allowed. The other girls envied us our smart brown leather jackets, although of course there were a few silly idiots who looked down their noses at us because they wanted to appear grown up, but they were only snooty in secret. They didn't dare to do it openly because they knew we wouldn't stand for it. 'A German girl stands no nonsense,' our Group Leader used to say.

It was in the BDM I learned how tremendously valuable we young people were to Germany. 'You are the guarantee of the future, the Nation's most precious asset,' the Reich Leader told us, and we all felt this was something worth living up to.

We were given rooms in Steglitz. They were in the barracks, which had belonged to a Protestant Kindergarten which had been requisitioned by the Party. Led by our Group Leader we marched there in close formation to take possession of it. A flag was hoisted and we raised our hands in the Hitler salute and sang the Hitler Youth song:

> Our flag flutters ahead of us
> Into the future we march, every man,
> For Hitler we march through night and death
> With the flag of youth for freedom and bread.
> Our flag flutters ahead of us,
> Our flag is the new age,
> Our flag leads us to eternity,
> Yes, the flag is more than death.'

A crowd had gathered round us to watch us. I held the pennon of the Mädelschaft and could have wept with pride and happiness.

We had to work for weeks to clean out the barracks. The nuns had left it in a filthy mess and any self-respecting German girl would have been sick rather than sit down there. Then we decorated it; one of the girls painted beautifully and she covered the walls with pictures. On one wall she had an SA man guarding the Reichstag which had been set on fire by the communist murderers, on the other wall there were BDM girls and Hitler youth marching with flying colours through a beautiful landscape. Above the door was our motto: 'Be good and noble, German girl!'

Every week we had our meetings there. We sang songs or did needlework, some-times we recited or one of our leaders spoke to us, mostly about Germany's heroic struggle in the Great War, but there were other topics as well, like the stories of the brave German women of the past. I liked the stories of 'Black Huntsman Johanna' best. She was a girl who disguised herself as a soldier and fought against Napoleon.

Of course, we had speakers from the Reich Youth Office, and from the Party, who lectured about important problems. Now I began to realise for the first time the terrible sufferings of our German brethren abroad. The speakers told us how they were oppressed and degraded by other nations, about England's perfidy which started the Great War in order to snatch our colonies; about the terrible role of the Jews, Freemasons and Marxists who wanted to ambush honest Germans; about the Roman Catholic Church which with its Jewish doctrines corrupted the Germanic sense of honour. All these and lots of other things were clearly explained to us and made us hate all the enemies of the Fatherland more and more.

Besides serious work there was of course lots of fun and games. I shall never forget our first outing when we went camping in Storkow in the Mark with knapsacks, pen-nons and all our camping equipment. A group of Hitler youths marched with us and that night chorus and our voices echoed through the wood. It was simply thrilling:

'… We shall march on
When everything lies in ruins!
For today Germany is ours,
And tomorrow the whole world!'

Gosh! Those were lovely days! On the last morning we had military exercises against the boys and we won, which meant we took their pennon, and weren't we proud of it!

As time went on more and more girls joined the BDM, which gave us a great advantage at school. The mistresses were mostly pretty old and stuffy. They wanted us to do scripture and, of course, we refused. Our leaders had told us that no one could be forced to listen to a lot of immoral stories about Jews, and so we made a row and behaved so badly during scripture classes that the teacher was glad in the end to let us out.

Of course, this meant another big row with Mother – she was pretty ill at that time and had to stay in bed and she was getting more and more pious and mad about the Bible and all that sort of thing. I had a terrible time with her.

After all, we were the new youth; the old people just had to learn to think in the new way and it was our job to make them see the ideals of the new nationalised Germany. When I told her about the camp with the Hitler Youth she was shocked. Well, suppose a young German youth and a German girl did come together and the girl gave a child to the Fatherland – what was so very wrong in that? When I tried to explain that to her she wanted to stop me going on in the BDM – as if it was her business! Duty to the Fatherland was more important to me and, of course, I took no notice. But the real row with Mother came when we BDM girls refused to sit on the same bench as the Jewish girls at school.

Like Father I could never stick Jews. Long before our classes in race theory I thought they were simply disgusting. They are so fat, they all have flat feet and they can never look you straight in the eye. I could not explain my dislike for them until my leaders told me that it was my sound Germanic instinct revolting against this alien element.

The two Jewish girls in our form were racially typical. One was saucy and forward and always knew best about everything. She was ambitious and pushing and had a real Jewish cheek. The other was quiet, cowardly and smarmy and dishonest; she was the other type of Jew, the sly sort. We knew we were right to have nothing to do with either of them.

In the end we got what we wanted. We began by chalking 'Jews out!' or 'Jews perish, Germany awake!' on the blackboard before class. Later we openly boycotted them. Of course, they blubbered in their cowardly Jewish way and tried to get sympathy for themselves, but we weren't having any. In the end three other girls and I went to the Headmaster and told him that our Leader would report the matter to the Party authorities unless he removed this stain from the school. The next day the two girls stayed away, which made me very proud of what we had done.

At home things were pretty awful. Mother just lay about being terribly tearful and sentimental. Father came back late from work, now that he had the whole business on his shoulders. Luckily for me there was always plenty of official work to do so I didn't have much time to sit at home and get depressed.

I was the Sports Group Organiser in our Section. I was the best at sports, especially at athletics and swimming. I got the Reich Sports Badge and the Swimming Certificate and came out first in both of them and got a lot of praise from our Leader. Altogether she was pretty pleased with me. When we had any street collections my box was always full first and I worked on the other girls to buck up so that our group always made a good impression wherever we went. In the summer we went to the great Reich Youth meeting. Thousands of boys and girls marched in close formation past the Reich Youth Leader, Baldur von Schirach. He and his staff stood on a dais and gave the salute; the trumpets blew, the Landsknecht drums rolled – it was a terrific moment.

At this parade I was right-hand Flügelmann, as always. The Gau Leader herself had picked me from amongst hundreds of girls. I was half a head taller than the tallest of them and had wonderful long blonde hair and bright blue eyes. I had to step out in front of the others and the Gau Leader pointed to me and said: 'That is what a Germanic girl should look like; we need young people like that.'

Once I was photographed and my picture appeared on the tide page of the BDM journal *Das Deutsche Mädel*. Father was delighted and my comrades were terribly jealous.

Our Gau Leader gave me several talks on the duties of the German woman, whose chief aim in life should be to produce healthy stock. She spoke quite openly. Again I was pointed out as a perfect example of the Nordic woman, for besides my long legs and my long trunk, I had the broad hips and pelvis built for childbearing which are essential for producing a large family. Mother couldn't understand this at all. She thought talking about such things was disgusting and could not understand the ideals of the BDM at all.

In 1936 I was made Group Leader, but I was not able to spend as much time as I wanted on my duties as at Easter I took my Abitur [matriculation]. I was a bit frightened of the exam as I had not thought much about my school work, but everything went off much better than I expected. We were set a very nice subject for the essay: 'The educational value of the Reich Labour Force.' This was my cup of tea because it dealt with the problems of our own time, unlike some of the old-fashioned literary stuff, and I got very high marks for it. In the orals I did better still. The examiner was a true National Socialist who picked me out and praised me in front of the whole commission because I was the only one of my year who had grasp of the most recent German history.

I had to tell a few things about the life of the Führer, his hard apprenticeship in Jew-infested Vienna, and his terrible struggle for recognition. Then there was a question about our national hero Albert Leo Schlageter, who had been shot by the French oppressors. [Schlageter was caught by the French sabotaging railway lines in the Ruhr and shot in 1923.] Last came German literature and I was the only one who could name the most typical German woman of our classical literature. Of course it was the heroic wife of Stauffacher in Schiller's *Tell* – 'To leap from this bridge will make me free.' I really came out very well and because of my good performance they winked at my rather shaky science and mathematics, and the examiner comforted me by saying that the analytical spirit of mathematics was in opposition to the synthetic way of thinking proper to the Nordic type. Mathematics, he said, and physics were essentially Jewish, at any rate non-Nordic, sciences; anyway, I passed the exam.

After the Abitur I reported at once to the Reich Labour Force. I was sent to a camp near Goldenberg, near Oels in Silesia. It was quite a small camp, just 200 girls, mostly from Berlin, although some came from the Rhineland and a few from Bavaria. We did not get on too well with them. Our Camp Leader was only 23, not much older than we were, but she was wonderfully smart and mad on cleanliness and military order. Our life was hard but I enjoyed it all right. It was shameful to see how badly the girls from the so-called better classes, mostly those who had taken the Abitur, turned out. They were stupid and clumsy at indoor duties like cleaning and washing and were always being sick.

Our main job was helping on the land at the surrounding estates. This, of course, was quite new to me. I had never done anything like it before, but I tried hard and being tall and strong I was soon quite good at it.

We had a pretty uniform which suited me very well. I already knew the importance of cleanliness and neatness from the BDM and our Camp Leader took a liking to me from the beginning. After a couple of months she made me assistant to the Leader in charge of the kitchen and washhouse. From then on I had various privileges, including not having to go out to work in all weathers. Many of my comrades were jealous, but it was not as if I had tried to get the post; it was simply that they considered me the right person for it.

Then I had the first great disappointment of my life. I got to know Helmuth von Trotha. He was in a cavalry establishment near our camp, but I first saw him on his parents' estate where we worked. We were strictly forbidden to have anything to do with men and on our off-days we had to go out in groups. But we managed to meet sometimes on Sunday afternoons and in my case the Leader winked at it because she had the fullest confidence in me.

Helmuth was a tall, slim boy with dark blond hair. He had lively dark eyes and looked frightfully smart in his cavalry uniform. He had the narrowest hips I have ever seen. I am sure he was in love with me, but he was so awfully reserved and was a bit too keen on his rank and family. And then, of course, he was not a National Socialist. The whole district was full of aristocratic families whose sons were either officers or diplomats, but they were all of them very Catholic and pretty stuck up into the bargain. They definitely thought themselves better than the rest. I tried and tried to make him understand our ideal of a greater Germany but he just couldn't or wouldn't see it in my way. Germany, yes; the Führer, no. He never called him the Führer but always said Hitler or the Reich Chancellor. I am afraid he despised the Party simply because he thought our leaders were not high-class enough.

This made me absolutely miserable. I was really fond of Helmuth. He was so refined and quiet and clever and different from all the noisy boys I had known up to then. Although he was only 21 he was quite grown up. But it was no good, we just couldn't agree. I could not possibly have married a man who wasn't prepared to swear absolute allegiance to our Führer and truly confess himself a fanatical National Socialist. The whole thing was obviously hopeless. I hated doing it but I had to tell him, and so we parted.

Perhaps if I had married him I would have been happy after all, but it would not have been for long for the Poles are there now, which means that all those rich families have lost their estates, although, of course, he was very rich and I believe his family had houses in Berlin and Munich. But I didn't marry him, so that's that.

My Camp Leader tried to persuade me to stay with the Labour Force, which was nice. She wanted me to become a Leader myself. A Leader in the Labour Force has a very good life. She wears a nice uniform, is waited on by the girls and has the satisfaction of knowing that she is an indispensable part of National Socialism. So I wrote to Father telling him that I wanted to stay on. But he wouldn't hear of it. He said he hadn't paid those school fees for all those years just for that. His daughter was going to be a cut above those Labour Corps girls. The trouble was that Father was too proud of me.

One day I got a wire saying that Mother was very ill. By the time I got to Berlin it was too late. She had died the day before, so I didn't see her again. I think on the whole it was the best thing, because she had suffered terribly for several years. Anyway, as the Camp Leader said when I got back, poor old Mother never understood our new age, and she herself was no longer any good to the State. She was simply a burden on the community.

In the autumn I had to return to Berlin. The question was now, what was to become of me? Father said I ought to study, though he didn't really know what. I wasn't especially keen; I had had enough of book learning – the way I saw it, a German woman had more important things to do. I talked to a BDM Leader about it and she said: 'I don't know what you are worrying about. If you don't know what to do why not give the Führer a child? What Germany needs more than anything is racially valuable stock.' Then she told me about the home of the SS foundation 'Lebensborn' where everything was arranged. It sounded wonderful. Of course, I had to get round Father and the family so I told them I was going on a National Socialist Frauenschaft course.

The home which the BDM Leader had told me about was in an old castle in the loveliest part of Bavaria near Tegernsee. There were almost 40 girls all about my own age. No one knew anyone else's name, no one knew where we came from. All you needed to be accepted there was a certificate of Aryan ancestry as far back at least as your great grandparents. This was not difficult for me. I had one that went back to the sixteenth century, nor had there ever been a smell of a Jew in our family.

The home was most luxurious. Each one of us had a beautiful room to herself with lovely pictures, flowers and nice furniture. There were all sorts of common rooms for sports and games, there were a library and music room and a little cinema; in fact everything we could possibly want. Nearby was a large lake on which we could row and sail and swim and there were horses for those who wanted to ride.

The food was the best I have ever tasted; we didn't have to work and there were masses of servants. The whole place was in the charge of a professor, a high-up SS doctor who examined each of us very thoroughly as soon as we arrived. We had to make a statutory declaration that there had never been any cases of hereditary diseases, dipsomania or imbecility in our family.

Then the woman in charge of the home – she was also a member of the SS – spoke about what was expected of me. She said that Reich Leader SS Heinrich Himmler had been charged by the Führer with the task of coupling a small elite of German women (who had to be purely Nordic and over five foot five tall) with SS men of equally good racial stock in order to lay the foundation of a pure racial breed. To help in the Nordification of the nation was an honourable duty and each one of us should be proud of it. We had to sign an undertaking renouncing all claims to the children we would have there, as they would be needed by the State and would be taken to special houses and settlements for inter-marriage.

During the next few days we were introduced to the SS men who had been picked for the job. They were all very tall and strong with blue eyes and blond hair. We spent pleasant days with them, played games together, went to the pictures and had social evenings. We were given about a week to pick the man we liked and we were told to see to it that his hair and eyes corresponded exactly to ours. We were not told the names of any of the men. When we had made our choice we had to wait till the tenth day after the beginning of the last period, when we were again medically examined and given permission to receive the SS men in our rooms at night.

As both the father of my child and I believed completely in the importance of what we were doing, we had no shame or inhibitions of any kind. He was a sweet boy, although he hurt me a little, and I think he was actually a little stupid, but he had smashing looks. He slept with me for three evenings in one week. The other nights he had to do his duty with another girl.

I stayed in the house until I was pregnant, which didn't take long. I was very proud that my maternal functions worked so quickly. Some of the other girls took ages; with one girl, who must have been racially inferior, it didn't work at all.

I was given the choice of either returning to Berlin until two months before my time or else moving straight into a maternity home in Bavaria. I opted for the maternity home, which meant I would not have to work and could just sit back and enjoy myself until the baby came.

The home was very nice, but rather dull. As our pregnancy progressed we had to be more and more careful not to overstrain ourselves. The unwritten law not to ask whether one was married or not was the same here. We were all called 'Frau' because the descendants that we were giving to the nation were considered more important than the accident of marriage.

My confinement came neither too soon nor too late. It was a boy and I suckled him for the first fortnight, and then he was removed. It was not an easy birth, for no good German woman would think of having any artificial aids such as injections to deaden the pain, like they had in degenerate Western democracies.

When I left the chief surgeon thanked me and told me he hoped I would come back to the Lebensborn in a year's time. The more children I had the better, he said, and I had a good mind to do it, but things turned out differently. When I got back to Berlin I applied for a post in the foreign organisation of the NSDAP and got it on the recommendation of our BDM Gau Leader. The office was in Tiergarten Strasse, a very nice district, and I enjoyed the work very much. We kept the dossiers of all Germans living abroad. My chief, Dr Kramer, was very nice to me. After two months he put me in charge of a special division which dealt with Germans in Honduras and Guatemala.

It was good to know how well our compatriots out there clung to their German ways and ran their own schools and clubs and flew the swastika on our national holidays. Only a very few among them were dishonourable enough to take foreign nationality or become citizens of the US, which is the most Jew-infested country in the world. The ones who did had a special register of their own, in which the Gestapo were very interested.

The Gestapo had a permanent liaison officer with our Department – a young SS Scharführer whose name was Ernst Trutz. He was six foot four and awfully good-looking with lovely blue eyes. He was evidently very young but he was terrifically manly, with precise, military manners.

I soon began to notice that he stayed longer in my room than was really necessary, but it was ages before we spoke about anything not connected with work. I remember that one time when one of our secretaries asked him how he was going to spend his leave, he replied curtly: 'I do not speak about private affairs on duty.' This impressed me a lot. I liked this sort of behaviour as it was much more military than Helmuth's, which I had always found a bit blasé and stuck up. It would certainly have taken us much longer to get friendly if there had not been a muddle about two important files.

Someone had to go to the Gestapo Office in the Kaiser Wilhelm Strasse to clear this up, and Dr Kramer sent me, so I went with Ernst to his office.

On the way he asked me about my family and my father. When I told him that Father was with No. 5 SS Sturm he said: 'Isn't that the Horst Wessel Sturm? Your father must be a good old National Socialist. I should like to meet him.'

We agreed that he should come to see us next Sunday. When we said goodbye he added: 'But I can only accept your invitation if you will come to one of the social evenings of our Sturm. They are always very enjoyable. I belong to the Kurt van Ahé in Charlottenberg.' Then he looked me in the eyes and said: 'I shall introduce you as my fiancée.'

From then onwards I went out with him a lot and he came to see us a good deal. Father liked him very much. What pleased him particularly was that on Ernst's first visit he saluted him in military style and addressed him as 'Untersturmführer'. Later on that evening they drank 'brotherhood' with each other.

Ernst had a canoe out in Schmöckwitz where we sometimes went at weekends. We always had to return at night because he was usually on duty with his Sturm on Sunday mornings, but I thought that it was a good sign that he put his duties before his private pleasures. Ernst and I understood each other from the first. He used to tell me his ideas about women. He said that there was nothing wrong with a girl working until her marriage, but that a woman's true task was, of course, a home and procreation. He often used to look at me admiringly, saying that I was a model of purebred Nordic Germanic woman. One evening he asked me to marry him. He said didn't I think we suited each other, and didn't I think it a splendid and sacred duty to give the Führer as many fine children as possible?

I knew that I wanted a home and a real German family more than anything and I was so pleased I couldn't say a word, but Ernst knew I meant 'yes'.

Father was delighted and very proud of me. For one thing, he was glad that I should not have to go to the office any more. He had never liked that and always said that the job was not good enough for me. And then, although an SA man would never admit it, Father did realise that the SS was the elite of the new Germany and the fact that his only daughter was to marry an SS man sent up his stock in the SA.

There was a lot of fuss and red tape about our marriage, because we had to get permission. As the children of the SS men were going to be the new ruling class of Germany they had to be very careful that the women were not racially objectionable and had the right sort of physique to produce plenty of children. The marriage permit was only granted after an investigation by the Reich Ancestry Office and a medical examination by SS doctors. I also had to complete my certificate of ancestry. This was great fun and we wrote to all the parishes in the districts from which my parents came. Father's family came from Zwickau and Mother's from a village on the Weser. Of course, getting the documents took some time as extracts had to be made from the old parish registers. In the end we got it all together. We found that my ancestors with hardly an exception had all been peasants on their own soil, as far back as 1674.

This document had to be submitted to the office for the investigation of ancestry and they then sent me my *Ahnenpass* [passport of pure ancestry]. This was a nicely bound leather book embossed with the rune of life. Then I was examined in the police hospital. They were even more thorough than at Lebensborn. All my measurements were taken and put on to a card index and again I had to make a statutory declaration about hereditary dipsomania and imbecility in the family. The SS doctor gave us a talk on planned breeding. He said the ideal German mother should have five children to ensure the necessary number for the nation. On no account should there be long intervals between the births; the number of children should be complete before she reached the age of 35. The children born after that age were liable to be weak and unsuited to their calling as the elite of Germany.

Of course, I had told Ernst long ago about my Lebensborn child. I was rather surprise to find that he was not as pleased about it as he might have been. Of course, he couldn't very well say anything against it, seeing that I had been doing my duty to the Führer, but he didn't like it mentioned. I expect he was jealous; men are like that. Ernst was very much in love with me then.

We began to look for a flat. We didn't want to marry until we found one, but in those days it was very hard to find anything in Berlin. We meant to live in a suburb, because you can't rear healthy children on the smell of asphalt and petrol. At that time the *Kameradschaftssiedlung der SS* [Comradeship Estate of the SS] was being built at Zehlendorff in the west of Berlin. It consisted of very beautiful modern buildings close to the woods of the Krumme Lanke Lake. Ernst, who had just been promoted, made an application to live there and his superior officer, who thought the world of him, and who had already promised him a marriage loan, undertook to get him a flat.

As soon as we got our permit for the three-roomed flat, I had quite a time to persuade Ernst to let Father pay for the furniture and other household things. Ernst was terribly particular about our not having cheap modern American stuff; he insisted on simple chairs and tables in the true style of the Third Reich. There were to be no trashy chandeliers and so on, just simple Germanic candelabras made of wrought iron.

When everything was delivered the flat looked lovely. Our living room had a carpet of hand-woven Frisian wool; light unstained rustic furniture and carved wood plates and painted earthenware jugs stood on the sideboard. Over the door was a carved motto, 'Obedience and dutifulness are the foundation stones of the nation.' Above the wireless in a broad oak frame was the Führer's portrait in genuine oil and portraits of Reich Leader SS Himmler and the Reich Woman Leader Frau Scholtz-Klink.

All our rooms were like that. In the bedroom we had a lovely carved wooden cradle and I had my dressing table. Ernst was a bit sticky about this at first. He said that a German woman had no need of such things, which were immoral and fit only for degenerate negroid French women. But I had always dreamed of a dressing table with three mirrors and a glass plate for the skin cream and so on. In the end Ernst gave in, but I had to hide most of my face stuff. He didn't like me to use powder or lipstick, and I agreed with him that they don't really suit a German woman or a German mother. But sometimes, when I went out alone, I put on just a little because there's no getting away from it, it is smart.

We got married early in 1939. All our relations were invited, including Ernst's uncle, who was an Obersturmführer in the NSKK and a holder of the blood order of the Party. Of course, all the men were in uniform. I wore a very pretty frock of light blue silk and at the actual consecration I wore a myrtle wreath. Father and one of Ernst's brothers were witnesses at the Registry Office but the consecration took place at home in our flat. The living room was decorated with garlands and swastika flags. Ernst wore a myrtle twig in his buttonhole and we stood under the Führer's portrait which had been crowned with garlands. A small choir of BDM girls and Hitler Youth sang:

> You now enter the holy league
> For the Führer and the nation.

Then Ernst's superior SS Hauptsturmführer gave the address of initiation and pronounced the Germanic blood blessing:

> Under the rune of life
> Fight the eternal fight.

There was more singing by the choir and a small Hitler Youth boy handed us our wedding rings in a wooden bowl. The ceremony ended with three 'Sieg Heils' to the Führer and the singing of the national anthem. Then the party began.

Father sprang a special surprise on us; he had made a huge cake which was carried in by three men and could hardly be got through the door. It was over four feet high and had a huge swastika and rune of life made of icing on top of it and was wreathed round with laurels. We had some lovely presents. Ernst's superior, for example, gave him a magnificent dagger of honour with a silver handle. The party went on very late and we were very merry and laughed a lot. One of Ernst's brothers was too funny for words; he dressed up as a parson and conducted a cod church wedding complete with sermon and hymns. He really was a scream.

It didn't take me long to find out that the spirit among the women in the settlement was very bad. As only SS families lived there, one would have expected them to set an example of community spirit, but not a bit of it. They were horribly snobbish about rank and I was never allowed to forget that I was only a Scharführer's wife and that Ernst was not a commissioned officer.

The officers' wives kept themselves to themselves and hardly deigned to look at the rest of us, and even the women whose husbands were in the Gestapo or the mounted SS thought themselves superior and turned their noses up at us, which just shows how common they were. We knew jolly well that many of them had not even been able to afford butter on their bread before they were married, and now they carried on like generals' daughters.

The men were a bit better, and anyway there had to be some difference between officers and other ranks. You get nowhere without discipline and order so I had no fault to find with them, but the women were frightful. There wasn't one of the wives who was half as pretty as me. I was taller than anyone and had far the best hair. Some of them even had to have their hair peroxided to make them more Germanic. And yet they gossiped about me in their stuck-up way and said my skirts were too short. That's typical of people whose own legs were like tree trunks!

Not long after our marriage the festival of National Labour took place in the Führer Square of the settlement. Afterwards there was a social at the nearby Sturmlokal and it was there that I met the wife of Hauptsturmführer Reisinger, who was to become my best friend. She lived almost next door to us in a charming little house and her husband worked for the Gestapo in the Reich Central Security Office in Prinz Albrecht Strasse. She had three children and was expecting a fourth. She was about ten years older than me and, of course, not half as good looking, but she was a nice person and I liked her at once because, although she was an officer's wife, she treated me almost as an equal.

Through her I was introduced into the officers' set. They were all a bit stand-offish at first, but I was always quiet and modest and as pleasant as I could be and soon the women became quite friendly. Some even came to our flat and when they did they always admired our attractive fittings. Sometimes they asked me to go swimming with them or to the pictures and before long I realised why they had been so exclusive. There were so many common women among the wives of the non-commissioned officers, and as the wives of the leaders they just had to keep their distance. Frau Reisinger advised me to do everything I could to get Ernst to try for a commission. Although he took his work very seriously he didn't seem to have the knack of impressing his superiors. He lacked push or something. Inge Reisinger told me how to get Ernst exactly where I wanted him. I can't explain that here but what she told me was quite true. She told me that my whole future depended on Ernst's promotion and it was up to me to see that he got it.

In the meantime he had been transferred to another department connected with Jewish property. I don't know what he did exactly as he never spoke about his work, and I was not especially interested anyway. He often went out in the evening and stayed away the whole night. When he got home he seemed very tired and, of course, I never asked him where he had been. Next he was transferred to a courier's job and travelled between Berlin and Prague. At the same time he was made Oberscharführer with a prospect of rapid promotion to Untersturmführer. Those women who had envied me on account of my friendship with Frau Reisinger were even more jealous now, and we were even able to start saving up for a Volkswagen.

The outbreak of war was rather worrying as I was now pregnant, much to Ernst's delight. He explained that international Jewry had incited Germany's enemies to declare war and that Jew-infested Poland was the warmongers' tool, but he was sure that it would be over by Christmas as nobody could stand up for long against our Wehrmacht and the strategy of the Führer.

Ernst didn't have to join the combatant SS but remained as a courier for his department as this was more essential. Only very few SS men from our settlement were sent on active service. Most of them were in the Gestapo or the Death's Head units where they were irreplaceable.

Soon after war broke out I gave birth to a·boy. We called him Norfried. Ernst was given three days' leave and we invited all our relatives and friends. It was a lovely celebration party. In the living room we hung a rune of life flag – white on a light blue ground, and the guests stood in a circle. Ernst carried the child in on an old Teutonic shield which he had made himself out of cardboard covered with a blanket. The blanket was of undyed wool with a long red fringe and it was embroidered with oak leaves, runes and swastikas. Then Ernst opened our son's book of life and wrote his name and birth date on the first page, with the following verse:

Child, this is the best
That need can teach thee;
To make thy hands firm
And thine eyes large
Cold heart and hard bread
Leave off thy questioning!
One day thou wilt understand
Thoroughly all thy need!

Then we both placed our hands on the boy and said 'Your name shall be Norfried Ruediger'.
Afterwards we all sang a song.

Ernst had to return to duty almost at once. Nowadays he went to Warsaw and Krakow as well as Prague, which meant that I got some very nice presents. That, of course, was an excuse for the gossips to say that I had more than anyone else just because I had several pairs of shoes from Prague, two furs from Poland and some silk stockings. All that nonsense about getting rings and necklaces and watches was just a malicious lie. Anyway, it was only right that we should make a bit out of the war; after all we neither wanted it nor started it and if our men made up a little for the privations and dangers they had to undergo they were entitled to it. What really disgusted me though was the way some of those common women strutted about in the finery their husbands had sent them quite regardless of taste. Some of them were so ignorant they didn't even know the name of the material their new dresses were made of.

From the summer of 1940 Ernst hardly got home at all. He now had to travel not only to the Eastern territories but to Denmark, Holland, Belgium, and France as well. I used not to see him for weeks at a time. All this dashing about was terribly strenuous but he never complained, he was not the type, and of course his work was very interesting as well. He didn't belong to the troops and he sometimes had to go about in mufti. He never told me what he did, though I knew that he was not just a plain courier any longer. He always seemed to have an especially good time in France, a little too good I thought sometimes, but I thought that I could trust him, in spite of what the gossips said. It was obvious that their husbands behaved very differently out there from Ernst, not that they hadn't good reason!

When war broke out against Russia, Ernst was rather worried at first, but when the Führer announced that the greater part of the Red Army had been wiped out and that the Ukraine was in our hands everyone felt much happier and I was sure that the war would soon be over.

By 1942 Berlin had already had several rather heavy air raids. Those cowardly brutes took no notice of the fact that it was an open city and that women and children were their chief victims – they probably rather enjoyed it. I made a point of not going down to the shelters at night. It was much too boring and stuffy. The best way to get through a raid was to open a bottle of Ernst's cognac, and I found that smoking helped too. It was then that I started, and so did most of the women, but of course we never told our husbands about it. I was pregnant again and I was rather worried about it. At Christmas a girl was born and we called her Elke. This time Ernst wasn't able to get back from Holland and so we were not able to celebrate her name day. But he sent me some wonderful things instead. He had finally been promoted Untersturmführer and had also been awarded the Cross for Meritorious War Service!

At last I was an officer's wife! If anyone did any patronising from now on it was going to be me, and that was a wonderful thought. For Ernst, too, it meant lots of new privileges and a nice fat rise in salary.

At the beginning of August 1943, refugees from Hamburg began pouring in with the most frightful tales of what the British had done to them. Then Dr Goebbels made a proclamation to the citizens of Berlin (especially to the old people, women and children) asking them to go to the country.

A few days before this general proclamation all the SS and Gestapo families had been notified separately so that we should not be swamped in the general rush. There were to be special motor-coaches and trains for us to travel in and we were told that accommodation in the country would be provided. As Ernst's brother Wilhelm had invited me to take the children to his farm I decided to go there instead of to one of the SS homes in Bavaria or Franconia.

Wilhelm had been discharged from the army on account of his varicose veins. He was the local *Kreisbauernführer* [District Peasant Leader] and *Kreisbeauftrager* of the *Reichsnahrstand* [District representative of the Food Ministry] and, of course, an old Party member. His farm was an Erbhof [inalienable land tenure] in a very beautiful district. There was still everything you could possibly want to eat and it would have all been fine if it had not been for Kaete, my sister-in-law.

Kaete did practically no work herself. She just gave orders to the two Polish maids and stayed in bed till ten each morning. She smoked too, like a chimney, which is hardly what one would have expected from a farmer's wife, and she never stopped carping at me; if it wasn't one thing it was another.

I began by trying to laugh it off. Then I got fed up and told her to mind her own business. Of course, the trouble was that she was jealous. She was small and dark and rather Slav in type and she saw the effect I had on Wilhelm. She even tried to make mischief with Ernst when he was on leave, Until he went to Wilhelm about it. That settled her hash once and for all.

In September 1944, I had another little girl, Heidrun. I had a very hard time with her birth, unlike the others, and felt I had had enough children to be going on with. This damned war had gone on long enough and certainly children didn't make it any easier.

It was about this time that I heard from Father that he had joined the Volkssturm. He had been longing to join up ever since the beginning and now at last he had got his wish. As he had been a Sturmführer in the SA, he started with the rank of captain. He was responsible for the training of his men and this made him terribly proud. He could hardly wait to get into action. I wrote back jokingly saying that his chances looked pretty poor just now, the way things were going in the Ardennes. The papers were full of our victory just then.

Then suddenly the Russians broke through the Eastern Front and we were faced with the prospect of an evacuation to the west. Of course, our leaders ought to have foreseen it and got us away before. But as it was we had to make all our own arrangements to move out in the intense January cold at a few hours' notice.

Wilhelm had been called up some time before into the Volkssturm and was now fighting somewhere between Birnhaum and Posen. We had not heard from him for weeks. When it came to the point Kaete refused to budge from the farm. I reminded her what the wireless had said about the Russians, but it had no effect and so I joined the trek alone. It really was disgraceful that nothing was done for the SS families. We were even supposed to pig it along with the rest. I couldn't understand Kaete. Surely anything was better than falling into the hands of those sub-human Slavs, who raped every woman and child as a matter of course. The wireless had warned us that any especially pretty blondes were always picked by the Jewish commissars for their army brothels, and whenever I felt like turning back I reminded myself of this.

Our first idea was to get on to a train and we packed as many of our things as we could on to carts, but the snow was so deep that the horses simply sank in and we hardly got on at all. Some Wehrmacht columns overtook us and requisitioned our horses. And to think that those swine were Germans! Then the peasant women tried harnessing cows to the carts, but most of them slipped on the icy road and broke their legs. They were a bigger wash-out even than the horses.

Suddenly, for no reason at all, they all started cursing and swearing at me. They cursed the SS and even the Führer, they went completely crazy and said that none of this would have happened if it had not been for people like us; like me ... I really thought at one time that they were going to beat me up, but I was not going to let them see I was afraid – I wasn't anyway, a German woman is never afraid. I simply told them that if they didn't stop this nonsense I would report all of them at the next Wehrmacht station we came to, and that frightened them so much they shut up.

The roads were blocked practically solid with cars, refugees and destroyed tanks and guns. Before long it became impossible to use the road and we had to take to the fields, although they were waist-deep in snow in places, to get out of the way of the Wehrmacht tanks and lorries which overran everything in their path. I hung on to a peasant family from East Prussia who still had two good horses. We stumbled along through the blizzard, guided by the shrieks of a woman in the cart in front. We could hear her half a mile away, which helped a lot as we couldn't see half a yard in front of our faces. She was in labour which lasted for two days, and she finally died somewhere near Lansberg-on-Warthe and they just dumped her and the dead baby by the side of the road. That was all they could do with people who died, as there was no time to bury them.

Children were dying all the time and I was terrified about mine, especially Heidrun who was only four months old. I had her strapped to my bare skin the way the peasant women showed me, and was managing to keep her fairly warm, but my milk suddenly dried up and I had a terrible time feeding her. She cried all the time, but I managed to keep her going somehow until we got to the Frankfurt-am-Oder road beyond Lansberg. Then on a particularly wretched icy day one of the wheels came off our cart and I had put her inside with the other children while we worked to get it on again. When I took her out to strap her to my breast, she was very quiet which frightened me, but I couldn't do anything much about it as I had to keep walking to keep up with the others. She felt quite warm against me but her eyes were wide open and staring in a strange way. I tried rubbing her with handfuls of snow but she didn't seem to feel it. At last I called to a peasant woman and asked her to look at Heidrun. She said she was dead. I dared not stop even now, or I should have lost sight of the cart and that would have been the end of me. All I could do was to wrap Heidrun in a blanket and lay her down a little distance from the road, where I hoped she would not be run over. I wondered how I was ever going to tell Ernst. Then I suddenly got furious thinking of him sitting smugly in a nice warm office while his wife and children were dying of cold and hunger by the roadside. A fine husband and father he was, sitting on his fat bottom miles and miles away when his family needed him most.

We finally managed to get on a goods train going to Lubbenau. That was when I parted company with the peasant family. They had decided to carry on in their cart as one of their children, a boy of eleven, had pneumonia and in their cart he could at least rest in the straw. By this time young Norfried was so tired and weak I had to carry him myself most of the time as well as Elke. This meant I had to leave everything behind and arrived at Lubbenau without so much as a suitcase, not that I cared much. I was too exhausted to mind about anything.

At Lubbenau the National Socialist People's Welfare took charge of us and found us billets in a private house. The people of the house made it quite clear that they didn't want refugees and went out of their way to be rude and unhelpful. It was only when I pointed out that they were likely to be refugees themselves any day now that they came to their senses and got us something to eat. That was the first hot meal I had had for a fortnight.

I wired to Ernst who came at once, and when our hosts saw his SS uniform they suddenly couldn't do enough for me. They even pressed me to stay on, saying that they thought it would be better for the children. To my amazement, Ernst agreed. I couldn't make out what had happened to him. He seemed to have changed completely. He scarcely mentioned Heidrun except to say that there was plenty of time to have more children, once the Fatherland was free of the Russians. Fighting the Russians was all he could talk about until I got him alone. Then he sat on the bed and buried his face in his hands and told me the war was lost. He explained that he was not working in his office anymore, he was now with the combatant SS who had been detailed to defend Berlin. His job was to form a group of Werewolves and continue the struggle behind the enemy lines. He said the Werewolf personnel were hardly more than a crowd of inexperienced Hitler Youth boys and as far as he was concerned the whole thing was pointless, but, of course, he had got his orders and would carry them out. I asked him about the Volkssturm and he said they were worse than useless. The men had no guts and they weren't even National Socialists. But what the hell, it would all be over soon, and we had better get used to the idea. He thought the best thing I could do would be to stay on in Lubbenau for the present and then try and escape to the West when it got a bit warmer. He said I must be sure to make for a part that was occupied by the British or Americans, because they would not harm women or children.

I felt I wanted to kill him! Sitting there telling me what to do and what not to do after he had got back to Berlin, thinking he could wash his hands of his wife and children and go back to play soldiers! As though I cared for his silly Werewolves! I told him that what was wrong with him was that he hadn't the guts to look after us himself. All he could do was to give us good advice and then get out and leave us to get on with it.

He got terribly upset and said did I want him to desert and get shot. Then I reminded him that all the high-ranking SS officers had cleared out long ago and taken their families to Bavaria. Only the small fry were left to face the enemy and be cold-shouldered by the population who hated us. I told Ernst if he had not been such a blockhead and content to plod along in a small job he would have been in a position to look after me now and take me away in a car like the other high officers' wives. It was I who was having to suffer for his lack of ambition … I really let him have it.

He got in an awful state and kept saying how much he loved me and all that sort of thing, but I said I was not going to sleep with a man who thought more of his blessed Werewolves than his family. I was not going to risk having another child on my hands; it was a pity the others hadn't died along with Heidrun.

Ernst went back the next day. I didn't even bother to go to the station with him. He kept on wiring me twice a week but I was too fed up to answer. He let me down and ruined my life and I had finished with him. The sooner he realised it the better.

The Wehrmacht were keeping pretty quiet but there were still a few tanks and soldiers about. If you spoke with them they still talked very big about the Russians. And then one day they were gone. There might never have been a soldier in the place. They didn't care a hoot what happened to us women and children; all they thought about was saving their own skins. Then the Russians arrived. The first thing those charming townspeople did was to tell the Russians that I was an SS woman, but they soon stopped when the Russians weren't interested.

My God! What a fuss I made with the first one! I can't help laughing when I think of it now. I held Elke in my arms and pushed Norfried in front of me, hoping that perhaps that would soften his heart. But he simply pushed Norfried aside and threw me on the ground. I cried and hung on to Elke, but the Russian just went ahead until I had to let go of her. He was quite quick about it and the whole thing didn't take more than five minutes. Then he went away.

I soon found that it was much better not to resist at all, it was all over much quicker if you didn't. I found the best thing to do was to help them a bit, otherwise they simply tore your clothes and I had so few left I couldn't afford that. After all, once you got used to the idea the thing itself wasn't so very terrible. The only time it was awful was when they were drunk. When a Russian is drunk he just can't stop. He is quite likely to go on till he kills you. And then they're so dirty! I was lucky, I didn't catch anything, but lots of the women did. Of course, I generally had the higher officers. They picked me out because of my looks.

Towards the end of May I decided to try and get back to Berlin. I hadn't heard a word from Ernst and there were no trains running, but there was a Russian captain who said he might be able to take me. I had to be especially nice to him as he was a bit scared of getting into trouble, but he did it in the end and we set out in a lorry. I was able to take quite a bit of food as some of the Russians were very decent about getting things for me from the peasants. I had a couple of suitcases full of ham, sausages, butter, eggs, cheese and vegetables which came in very handy during the first weeks after I got back.

Coming into Berlin from the east I got more and more depressed. The nearer we got to the centre the worse the damage was. All the bridges were down and every other street was impassable. It took us nearly three hours to get across to Zehlendorff. I had quite made up my mind that I had come on a fool's errand and that all I should find was rubble where our flat had been. When we finally got to Krumme Lanke I could hardly believe my eyes. The settlement was practically undamaged. It was too good to be true.

What wasn't so good was that some people had moved into our flat and that most of the SS families had been driven out of their homes. The place was crawling with KZ [concentration camp] people who had been put there. These jailbirds were swanking about as though they owned the place. I wasn't standing for that for a moment so I dumped the children with a friend and went straight round to the local housing office where I found a former Party member in charge. I had known him quite well in the old days and he always seemed a decent sort of man. When I reminded him that we had known each other before he flew into a terrible rage, called me a liar and threatened to call the Russians.

I realised that I had put my foot in it and said I was terribly sorry, and of course I had made a mistake, and would he mind making out an order for the return of my flat. But he just went on shouting at me and telling me to get out. Then I tried tears, but even that didn't work. He said as far as he was concerned my children and I could go to hell. He was a real swine about it, and this was a fellow German!

I went out and sat down in the street. I must have looked pretty miserable because a young Russian came up and asked me what was the matter. He could speak little German and I told him what had happened. Of course, I didn't mention I was married to an SS man – they hated the SS because they were such good fighters. The Russian went and got one of his comrades, a little dark man with slit eyes called Nicolai. He smelt terribly of garlic but he was very kind. The three of us went along to the flat and threw the people out, and then Nicolai took me back to the Housing Office and got the order fixed up.

After that Nicolai looked after me pretty well. He was really a nice little thing, very common and uneducated, but his German wasn't bad and he was always kind and helpful. For instance, I had noticed that the people who had been in our flat had a lot of preserves which, of course, they had taken with them. They were now living in one of the neighbouring houses. I told Nicolai about the preserves so he went and got them for me. He was very good like that. And he was wonderful with the children, looked after them like a mother. He told me the Germans had shot his little son, and, of course, I pretended to be very sorry though I knew very well that it couldn't possibly be true. Germans don't shoot children. Poor old Nicolai, he must have been listening to some silly Russian propaganda.

Food got more and more difficult as time went on and I don't know that I should have done without him. He got me anything I wanted and I only had to hint that someone in the settlement had something that I specially fancied and he would go straight round and get it. He was like a well-trained retriever dog. After all, everyone had been beastly to me and this was a chance to get a bit of my own back.

The only news I had of Ernst was from one of the neighbours. She said that he had stayed in Berlin right up to the end and had fought very bravely. More fool him when he knew that it was no use anyway! The last anyone heard of him was that he had gone to Nauen to try to get over into British-occupied territory. Everyone said that the British were much the more decent of the Allies. They didn't do anything to SS men.

One day Nicolai told me he was going. He said the British and Americans were on their way to share in the occupation of Berlin. I pretended to be very sad, but, of course, I was really very glad to be rid of him. He was such a smelly little thing. When he came to say goodbye he cried – Russians are terribly sentimental – and he gave me a very pretty gold watch, which was nice.

When the others arrived everything was fine. The British were very quiet and reserved but the Americans were wonderful. They were all so young and friendly and their uniforms were even smarter than the German ones, except for their funny tight trousers. And goodness! The stuff they brought with them! What a country America must be! At the beginning they were terribly generous and I got all the food and cigarettes I wanted. I had always been good at English at school which made everything much easier, and I soon got a boyfriend to myself. He was a parachute sergeant with masses of decorations, only 23 and terribly good looking. He always brought me lots of things besides the coffee and cigarettes I asked for, but apart from that he was a great disappointment because he was no gentleman and behaved abominably.

The trouble was that he used to get drunk all the time. Nicolai had got tight on and off but it had only made him sad and even soppier than usual. All you had to do was to comfort him when he said he was wicked, and he had been as gentle as a lamb, but Earl, my Yank, always started swearing and shouting like a maniac – not that I could understand what he said with that terrible Arizona accent of his – and he always wanted to show how strong and 'manly' he was and that meant smashing everything he could get his hands on, plates, chairs and even windows. But his great way of showing what a tough guy he was was beating me up. Once he made such a mess of me I had to go and hide with the neighbours. Tough and manly indeed! He was like a half-witted child in bed. He didn't know the first thing about it and half the time all he could do was to be sick over me. I sometimes think the reason the Yanks talk so much about it and act so 'wolfish' is to cover up the fact that they're not much good.

When Earl was sober he was all right. He used to call me 'Blondy' and promised to send me things from America when he went back. I had told him my husband was a prisoner in Russia. He said that meant he would never come back, and how would I like to be a GI bride? Silly dope, thinking I would fall for that sort of talk! I knew his sort. But of course I always pretended to believe everything he said.

Then I had to listen to him shooting off his mouth about his war exploits, how he won his different decorations and what he and his buddies had done in Italy, as if I cared! But it was better than being beaten. I can't say I was sorry when he left. He didn't even bother to say goodbye. One day he went and just didn't come back. Later I heard that his unit had been moved to Frankfurt.

For a time after Earl left I didn't have a steady boyfriend. By then Yanks were quite hard to get, every girl was after them as though her life depended on it and there just weren't enough to go round. Of course, there were always the British, but they were not really worth it with only 90 cigarettes a week and a little food. With hair like mine you could always get Yanks, so I was better off than most people, but it was a terrible strain always looking for new one and all that chopping and changing was bad for the children. It's much better for them if you go steady. They had been really fond of Nicolai and they got used to Earl, although they were scared when he had one of his fits.

On top of all that I had Father to cope with. That was the last straw. There he was with nowhere to go and nothing to do, so of course I had to take him in. He had been in the fighting right up to the end defending the Spree bridges. Then when his unit gave up he got into civvies and went back to his shop which was still standing. As soon as the collapse came he began baking again. He would have been quite all right if he had not lost his temper at the sight of all the Jews and foreign riff-raff strutting about like lords. He was so furious that he put a notice in the window 'Jews and foreigners will get no preferential treatment here.' This caused a terrible row and Father was thrown out of the shop and the flat and told he couldn't get work until he got himself de-nazified. So now I had him on my hands.

At first he was full of outraged dignity, saying he would rather see me dead at his feet than consorting with Americans. No true German woman would defile herself, and so on and so on. But I soon taught him different. Where did he think his or our next meal was coming from? I told him he could choose between his fine theories and an empty stomach, and if he wanted to stay with me he could shut up. After all, this was my flat.

Before long he became quite reasonable and even stayed out at night to make things easier for me. He did odd jobs about the house; chopped wood and so on. He was still as crazy as ever politically, but I threatened to throw him out if I had any trouble over him. I had had just about enough as it was without him lending a hand.

Then, thank goodness, I got a steady Yank again. His name was Bill and he came from Louisiana. It was a bit embarrassing at first and he took a bit of getting used to because he was a negro. Not that he was very black, just a deep coffee colour. Naturally, the neighbours talked their silly heads off, but I knew it was only because they were jealous, and took no notice.

Bill was a giant. I don't think I ever saw anyone so strong. He didn't have to keep proving it either, like that half-baked Earl. There was no doubt about his being a man, and he was a perfect gentleman besides. He knew how to behave towards a lady. He could have taught the white men a lot where manners were concerned.

He looked after me wonderfully, better than all the Russians and white Yanks put together. I didn't even have to go out with him, which might have been rather embarrassing. He was too much afraid of what the white Yanks would do if they saw him with a white woman. So he always came to the flat and he never came empty-handed, he even remembered to bring cigars for father.

We had a lot of fun together. Bill had a lovely voice and a banjo which he played very nicely, and he used to sing his songs by the hour. He was so modest and straightforward and didn't try to impress me like the others had with their tales of automobiles and ranches and businesses and God knows what. Bill never talked that way. He admitted that he was a simple farm labourer and was not ashamed of it. He was the only one I ever really liked. It's hard to say why, but I think he was the only one I really respected. I didn't feel he was just making use of me like the others. He was good and gentle and really kind. The Russians were animals and the white Yanks were a lot of common schoolboys. I was really sad when he left, and so were the children and Father.

In October 1945, I got a postcard from Ernst. He was in a British internment camp at Neuengamme near Hamburg. This was a former concentration camp where all the SS men were now interned. The Tommies seemed to be looking after him quite well, he said they were sending him to a convalescent home because he was underweight. Next I got a packet of chocolate from him – part of his fattening diet he said! After that I heard from him quite regularly. Mostly he asked a lot of silly questions that were none of his business. What was I living on? Was I working? And so on. He seemed to forget that all my troubles were his fault. Then he asked for parcels, clothes, books, tobacco. As if I had anything to spare!

On the whole I thought the best thing would be to get a divorce and try to struggle through on my own. Ernst had been with the Gestapo and there was no getting away from that. It would always be a millstone round my neck. Then it would give the children a better chance if I was rid of him. Lots of women were marrying Yanks and getting a fresh start, and I didn't see why I shouldn't too. But when I asked about the possibilities of divorce the damned fools said it was out of the question as long as my husband was interned. As though that had anything to do with it! This was just another example of my having to suffer from Ernst's mistakes.

I had another Yank for a bit after that. He came from Michigan and his name was Tom or Joe or something like that. He was dull and mean and always sat by the wireless. He had red hair and I didn't like him.

My next boyfriend was better. His name was Ed and he came from California. He was only a boy really, not more than twenty. He said he was a film director, but I found out he was just a motor mechanic. But it didn't matter; he was quite nice, only he couldn't stick Father. I always had to send him out when Ed came.

By the middle of the winter things were terrible. We had no coal and no firewood and I hadn't got a boyfriend. It was almost impossible to get a Yank, and I had a hell of a time getting my cigarettes even! I had to go almost every night to Lichterfeld near the US Barracks or to the Military Police barracks at Wannsee. The MPs are pretty good really. They look awfully stern on duty but they do more black market than all the rest put together.

I had to sell my furs and jewellery and everything else I had saved to buy coal. It was sickening how little I got for my things, but the trouble was that everybody else was selling and prices were terribly low. The cigarette situation was dreadful too. I just couldn't give up smoking and when I couldn't get a Yank I was forced to sell some of the children's rations, butter or milk or something. I didn't dare sell my last decent frock. If I had I should never have got a man. The Yanks aren't like the Russians; they are terribly fussy about that kind of thing. I had a shot at the black market, but it was no good. You have to be a Jew for that game. I am too much of a real German, and so I was always the loser.

Father was no help at all. He was completely down and just sat in a corner and mumbled a lot of nonsense. I even had to go and steal firewood myself and if he came with me he was more trouble than he was worth.

Then the Americans disbanded a small prisoner-of-war camp in Berlin and I got to know one of the prisoners. He wanted somewhere to live so I took him home with me. He was from the Rhineland and he had not heard from his family for years. He was quite a help to me. He brought back tree trunks from the forest, repaired the flat and went out organising potatoes. He was no trouble at all, really, and did what I told him. I suppose the taste of home life made him homesick, for one day he wanted to go. I tried to keep him at least for the rest of the winter but it was no use. He suggested that I should have a comrade of his from East Prussia who wanted to stay in Berlin, so the one moved in when the other moved out. The new one was quite useful, but he was a terrible ladies' man and spent all his time gadding about with other women. Then one day he cleared out and that was that.

Things were pretty awful then. I had begun to look older, two of my front teeth had broken and I couldn't afford to get new ones. My hair was coming out badly too.

My figure was still as good as ever, but you have to have everything for these damned Yanks. And then the competition is always so fierce, a decent woman doesn't stand a chance against some of these shameless little schoolgirls.

The last straw was Father's denazification. Of course, I was a witness and God knows we all did our best. Our main hope was Dr Dobriner, the Jew who had looked after Mother. We were terribly pleased when we heard that he had come·back all right from Theresienstadt because he would be able to say that Father had always been kind to him.

Father was called first. He explained that he had joined the Party in order not to lose his job; then how he had been forced to join the SA because the whole Stahlhelm had been taken over by them, and how he had always tried to remain in the background. He said he had done his best to avoid service in the Volkssturm and in the end had deserted from it, which amounted almost to resistance against the Nazi regime.

But naturally our enemies weren't going to let a chance like this go by. First came Frau Stielke who said that poor Father had denounced her husband which resulted in his being sent to a concentration camp. She said Father had forced her to sell him the bakery. Ungrateful bitch, considering how decent Father had always been to her, paying her a fair price and allowing her to have two rooms in the house! Just because her husband was a careless fool and got sent to Sachsenhausen and died there … and all this was supposed to be Father's fault.

Next came some Jews who had lived underground during the Nazi time. They said they had always been afraid of Father, because he had denounced a number of people. Then some more Jews said that he never would sell them anything although he was the only baker in the district and there was only one hour during the day when they were allowed to do their shopping. As if that was anything to do with Father! After all, he was only obeying regulations. If he hadn't he might have been punished himself.

Then some men from the Bakers' Guild said that Father had been known in trade circles as a virulent Nazi. I wouldn't have minded betting that they were jealous because he won the *Reichsberufswettkampf*! [Reich Trade Competition.]

But the worst of the lot was Dr Dobriner. Once a Jew always a Jew. And how! He had the effrontery and ingratitude to stand up and say that when he found out about Father's politics he had only continued to attend Mother because she was a fine woman – better than all the rest of us put together. He said that during the depression he had never sent Father a bill and that afterwards when he had, Father had never paid his fees regularly and later hadn't paid them at all. Before he was sent to the concentration camp Father had given him half a loaf on five occasions only. During the latter period he hadn't dared to enter our shop.

Of course, all these lies put the lid on it and Father's application was refused. No one believes a decent German nowadays, but anything those dirty Jews say goes for gospel. Now I have got Father on my hands for keeps, unless they send him to prison, which is quite likely as they are going to accuse him of 'crimes against humanity', because he is supposed to have sent Stielke to the concentration camp. I told him that perhaps prison is the best place for him now he has got himself in such a mess. I certainly don't want him here if he is going to cause trouble and be calling attention to all of us, especially now that things are better and I have got a steady boyfriend again.

Yes, things are looking up at last. He may be a Polish Jew from the UNRRA camp but he really loves me and has got pots of money. He deals in gold and diamonds and he knows how to get food and all the things I need. His name is Amschel Hirschblut. He is small and fat and nearly as old as Father. But he is very well behaved and kind and thoughtful and if I don't want him in bed he just goes next door on the sofa like a good boy. Naturally, I wouldn't have chosen a Jew but one has to have someone these days or starve. Quite a few of the SS women have UNRRA DPs now. They make very good boyfriends because they are rich and you can just do what you like with them. They are so shy and timid and grateful you are nice to them.

I hope Ernst won't come back yet. I shouldn't know what to do with him if he did. Even if I could feed him we should probably have to leave because of his having been in the Gestapo. I hope they keep him there for a bit. After that he will probably get a couple of years in a labour camp, and it won't do him any harm either. He's as arrogant as ever, judging from his letters. Some people will never learn …

In the meantime I'm hanging on to Amschel for just as long as I can. Maybe one of these days I'll get that divorce. I'm still hoping, anyway. Amschel would marry me like a shot. Jews, like gentlemen, prefer blondes.

8

CLAUS FUHRMANN

I had seen a great deal of Claus Fuhrmann when we were children; first at our private school and later at the Potsdam High School. He had been a rather grave, sensitive, spindly little boy, and although he was almost two years younger than I, he had usually been top of the class, whereas I had invariably been the dunce.

We had struck up a sort of mutual aid society, right at the beginning of our acquaintance. This had suited us both admirably and had lasted until I left school in 1933. Claus had helped me with my lessons, and I had seen to it that the tough eggs of the school left him in peace. We had been more or less indispensable to each other. Apart from acting as his bodyguard, I had always been Claus's best audience; I had sat goggle-eyed by the hour while he dilated upon the numerous subjects that interested him, and propounded his pet theories.

At the beginning of 1934, I was put in a concentration camp for being rude about the Führer on a postcard. Claus's father who, in spite of his Party membership, was a great friend of my parents, managed to get me released after six weeks.

A few months later, the Fuhrmann family left Potsdam for Celle near Hanover. I only found out later that this was the result of Judge Fuhrmann's intervention on my behalf.

After that, Claus came several times from Celle to stay with us. I continued to envy him his keen flexible brain and his ability to talk like a grown up about philosophy and religion. I remember his being more and more preoccupied with these things each time I saw him. I don't think my parents ever saw him again after I left Germany, although they heard occasionally from his father up to the time of his death.

I doubt very much if I should have recognised Claus in 1946. He had always been thin, but now he looked like an advertisement for 'Save Europe Now'; hollow-eyed, cadaverous, with a terribly ashen colour, while his dark hair hung nearly to his shoulders. His teeth too, were in a terrible shape, as were those of Bunny, his wife.

But it was not only Claus's appearance that had changed beyond recognition; the quiet, rather judicial manner that had always made him seem so grown up had given way to a feverish, almost hysterical intensity and animation. At first I put this down to his obvious pleasure at seeing me again, but as I saw more of him, I realised that the old Claus, with his objective approach, was gone for good. It was as if he were hag-ridden by some inner fury which would not let him rest. It needed no tactful probing on my part to bring things to the surface; all I had to do was listen. Poor Claus; suffering has stripped him of everything except a passionate absorption in himself and what he believes to be his rights. He has become his own worst enemy and fifty per cent of his present unhappiness is of his own making.

Claus Fuhrmann, born 1919

It was not until 1934 that my life became interesting. Then two things occurred which brought about far-reaching changes for my family and for me.

The start of it was that my father, who was a judge in Potsdam, was transferred to another town as a punishment. He had been a member of the NSDAP and a Hauptsturmführer in the Storm Troops since 1932. I have never really been able to understand what made him stay with the Nazis, because though he was a Nationalist he was no extremist. But he was an idealist and believed this the only way out of Germany's difficulties. All excesses would automatically disappear once the revolution was accomplished. A man with his solid middle-class way of life would have been more at home in Hugenbert's Deutsche National Partei or in the Stalhelm.

I was never very close to my father, but I had the greatest respect and admiration for him. I have met no other man with such a pronounced sense of justice. He was not a judge by accident, but because of a deep feeling of vocation. He had an innate hatred of injustice and coercion. That is how he came to be involved in the affair of Louis Hagen.

The Hagens were a Jewish family of bankers in Potsdam and we had been friendly with them for years. Louis Hagen and I were in the same form in the Potsdam Gymnasium. One day Louis was arrested and brought to the Camp Torgau, after he had been questioned in the usual Nazi style in the Columbia House in Berlin. The reason for his arrest was said to have been certain political remarks which were described as 'hostile to the State'. But nobody who knew Louis could believe this, because with his sixteen years he was still quite a child and without the slightest interest in politics.

Father was very indignant when he heard of this. He was convinced that this was a case of an arbitrary action taken by some subordinate official without knowledge of the proper legal authorities. Old Mr Hagen was in despair and my father promised to spare no effort to put the matter right.

This, however, proved to be most difficult. For weeks he went about with tight lips while he wrote, telephoned and interviewed all possible sorts of people, legal authorities, Party functionaries and high government officials. The best answer he could get was a regretful shaking of the head. His oldest friend, an undersecretary of state in the Ministry, refused point blank to deal with the matter; he received the same answer from the Kreisleiter of the NSDAP. The SA Standartenführer, Dr Gellert, who was a very influential man, advised him strongly to leave the matter alone. He suggested that it was not a good thing for a German judge to stand up for Jews and enemies of the State.

But Father would not give in. When several weeks had passed he sat down and wrote a long letter addressed to Hitler personally who – he felt sure – knew nothing of such crying injustice. He described in strong terms how a young man, still almost a child, had been arrested, ill-treated and imprisoned without a proper warrant for his arrest, without a proper trial and in reality without any adequate reason.

Needless to say, Hitler never got this letter. The report was put in the files, and the only result was that official interest began to be taken in this rather troublesome Judge Fuhrmann.

But this was still 1934 and the Nazis were still treading carefully. The end of it all was that Father succeeded in getting Louis Hagen released and himself went to Torgau to fetch him.

I never knew what Louis told him about his treatment in the camp. But it completely shook all Father's fundamental convictions. He had always believed that decency, respect for justice and honesty were the predominant characteristics of the German people. What he came to know now was such a depth of baseness, brutality and cynicism that he broke down completely. Then Father sat down once more at his typewriter and composed an energetic protest against the treatment of the prisoners in Torgau concentration camp.

He did not have to wait long for the result: he was transferred as a punishment to the unimportant dusty district court of Celle in Hanover; compared with Potsdam this was the dullest provincial backwater. I believe it was only because of Mother and me that he did not resign altogether.

One evening Father took me aside. He told me the time had come to disclose something of great importance to me. I would hear about it one day in any case and under the present conditions in Germany it was better if I could get used to the idea in good time.

After this gloomy introduction he told me that Mother was not really my mother, but that I was the child of a previous marriage. My mother had been a Jewess, who died before I was two years old.

I cannot say that this made a particularly deep impression on me. I was all the more grateful to my stepmother who had never let me feel that I was not her child. It was not till more than a year later that I began to understand what it meant to be a 'Mischling' in Germany, that was when the Nuremberg Laws for the protection of the 'German Blood and the German Honour' were proclaimed at the Party Congress.

It is hardly likely that anybody who was not affected by the Laws has taken the trouble to memorise the difference between 'Juden', 'Mischling', 'Mischling 2nd Grade' and 'Geltungsjuden' – 'Full Jews', 'Half Jews', 'Quarter Jews' and 'Virtual Jews' – nor will he have studied the vast number of regulations, decrees and prohibitions for each of these groups. However, I was forced to take an interest in these things. But even I would hardly have thought it possible then, in 1935, that one day a man's life would depend on whether he was a 'Mischling I' or a 'Geltungsjude'.

Although the transfer to Celle was a hard blow for my father, I had every reason to be happy about it. As there was no suitable school in Celle, my father sent me to a boarding school, the 'School Community at the Manor of Marienau' near Lüneburg. It was surprising that such an island of peace could continue to exist despite the Nazi school policy. The headmaster was a Jew called Dr Bondy and he had continued to use all modern advanced methods. There was self-administration of the pupils, co-education, study groups, instruction in art and crafts, work in the fields and garden, a great deal of sport – in other words the very opposite of the military ideal of the Nazi school.

When I say that the years in Marienau were the happiest of my life, this is only speaking relatively, for I was not happy in Marienau, and I can speak of happiness only in comparison with that which came afterwards. To be quite honest I was desperately unhappy.

It was not as though I had any reason to complain, because unlike most schools the influence of the Hitler Youth affected Marienau very little. But I suffered because I could never be alone, because there were infinitely more games and athletics than I cared for, and because I was not allowed to occupy myself with literature as much as I felt inclined to. I felt repelled by my fellow pupils because they were brutal and uncouth. I was just at the age when one likes being unhappy, and so I wallowed in my unhappiness and felt like Shelley in his college days.

I cannot remember what made me first take an interest in Catholicism. My family and, of course, I too, had been baptised as Lutherans, and we only went to church on the occasion of weddings, births and deaths. But in Marienau I studied Catholic literature very seriously. For all that, I was not then really deeply religious any more than I am now. I did not really have a faith, per se, but I had to look for something to find a way out of the mental and spiritual chaos of modem life. It was not only with my mind that I was seeking the answer. It was more than that.

I was not hard enough. I was too soft and defenceless for the life of a Mischling in Nazi Germany. To see a dog beaten or hear a child cry was a form of torture to me. For weeks and months I was haunted by a brief paragraph in the paper stating that at the annual floods of the Yangtse River several hundred thousand Chinese had been drowned. I once saw a begging drunkard staggering about in the harbour district of Hamburg and I could not stop thinking about him for a long time afterwards. Wherever I looked I saw misery and woe, desperate, suffering human beings whom nobody helped. Side by side with it I saw the active and carefree life of the well-fed rich.

Perhaps it was then that I first started thinking about becoming a priest. What can one individual do? You cannot empty the sea with a spoon. Only as part of the great Catholic Church can the individual help effectively, in the service of the gospel of universal love.

At that time the parents of a girl pupil came to Germany on a visit. They were owners of a coffee plantation in Honduras and they suggested that I should emigrate and come and stay with them as long as I liked. I declined without hesitation. Heavens, what life was there for me on a plantation in Central America? No, my road led in a different direction. I wanted to study, to understand and to help. Even if I was not yet clear in my own mind where and how.

In 1937 our headmaster, Dr Bondy, was forced by the Nazi authorities to go to Switzerland. The new head introduced the spirit of the Hitler Youth, and most of the elder boys left. I, too, left Marienau and went to Hamburg. My father wanted me to go to an interpreters' school. So I enrolled at Marricks on the Glockengiesserwall, but I hardly attended classes. I had put my name down for a Russian course, but next to me there sat a Luxemburg journalist, a rabid Nazi who spoilt all my pleasure in learning. And the French course was ruined by a bunch of silly, giggling young girls. What had I to do with all this?

No, my way was to be different. I spent days in the large quiet reading room of the State library, reading Catholic literature. I refreshed my stale Latin, and with a tough kind of resolution tackled the fat tomes of Thomas Aquinas's *Summa Theologae*. My imagination was kindled by St Augustine's superb vision *Civitas Dei*. I wrapped myself up in the ardent sermons of Eckhardt and Seuse.

At Easter 1938, I witnessed a Catholic service for the first time. The Bishop of Osnabrueck celebrated mass: soaring organ music, exulting choirs singing 'Resurrectus est', thick clouds of incense, brilliant robes – all this impressed me profoundly.

From now on I daily went to hear mass. I was in a condition of intellectual and spiritual high tension which it would be difficult to describe; I became oblivious of the world around me. I no longer took any notice of current events, and of politics; they were of no interest. More and more I sank my whole thought and energies in my ideal. Then one day at matins in St Mary's I felt sick, and on the point of fainting. I tried to drag myself outside, but my strength failed me. When I recovered consciousness I found myself lying in a little side chapel before the picture of the Virgin, surrounded by lit candles. On this morning I took a vow to enter holy orders.

I wrote to the general of the German Dominican Order in Cologne. At his suggestion I went to Berlin, where I received religious instruction for converts at the Turmstrasse monastery and was received, *sub conditione* in the Catholic Church. This was done in the chapter of the convent, in the presence of the prior, Father Count Arkenan, and the famous preacher of the Cathedral church of St Hedwig, Father Hoffmann, both of whom were very friendly to me. After that I took leave of my parents. I never saw my father again; a few months later he died of pneumonia.

I started my novitiate in Warburg in Westphalia. And here I was almost completely alone. There were only eleven novices, and personal friendships were not tolerated. Most of them were young and healthy sons of peasants, red-haired, freckled Westphalian men of an obstinate and tough disposition. Next to them I could not but feel nervous, weak and over-sensitive. It was a strictly secluded life such as novices of the Dominican Order have led for the last 700 years; a routine sequence of services, choral prayer, meditation and occasional instruction. This was entirely to my liking. I had resolved for the next few years I would see and hear nothing of the outside world. I wanted to live only in the world within me, gathering strength for whichever task the Order would allot to me later. The months passed peacefully and quickly.

But although I had cut myself off from the outside world, the outside world seemed to have other ideas. My peace and seclusion was roughly broken by the arrival of my military call-up papers. Exemption was granted only to priests in orders, and it was still more than three years before I would be a priest. This was the first indication I had of the impending danger of war.

The recruiting sergeants in the Munster barracks welcomed me ironically and changed my long black habit for a coarse grey uniform.

I reported for service with the auxiliary anti-aircraft unit 12 in Berlin-Lankwitz. There they had no use for the thousands of raw recruits they were sent, and so we were transferred to a 'pioneer battalion' where we had very heavy labouring work to do and were neither sworn in nor issued with arms. This fact was later to save my life.

We had to build a training camp for anti-aircraft units at Marienfelde, on the southern outskirts of Berlin. There were no living quarters there; during the arctic winter of 1939–1940 we often slept under canvas. We had a beastly time, following the best traditions of the age-old Prussian militarism. Most of those who had matriculated or who came from the universities were convinced Nazis, while the artisans and labourers, and especially the older ones among them were not very keen on either the Party or the war.

From my identity papers the men knew that I was half Jewish, and most of them kept at a distance from me. The one exception was a very young volunteer, von Arnim, whose father was standard-bearer in the SS and a major-general. Though we had little in common we took a liking to each other. Von Arnim and a few others were kind to me when I received a dressing down from the NCOs.

My corporal, a peasant's son from the Mark of Brandenburg, made no bones about his loathing of the Jews. He often addressed me as 'dirty Jew' before all the men, and was not content until he had me on special duties. From now on I had to be on guard every night from 10pm to 6am. In the morning I was on light duties, in the afternoon I was allowed to sleep, or rather I would have been allowed if the noise in the camp had not made sleep impossible. As a result I soon found myself completely worn out with my nerves jangling and unbalanced. The stupid narrow-minded trash that my comrades talked was an incessant irritation to me. Even the non-Nazis among them were so completely in the grip of official propaganda that one might have thought oneself in a lunatic asylum. It was all the fault of the Jews and Freemasons. The Poles had slaughtered the poor Germans; Britain had spared no pains to complete the encirclement of Germany. Her Secretary for War was a Jew bent on despoiling the German people … Such was their talk night after night, and they believed every word they said.

I soon found a way of leaving the camp at noon, when I came off duty. An old school friend of mine, who was now a soldier himself, had given me the use of his room near Nollendorfplatz in Berlin. When I was there I could breathe again and almost began to feel like a human being again. This was, of course, strictly forbidden, but for a time everything went well. But then as if a malign fate had been waiting for me, successive misfortunes fell quickly on my head.

On the night before my last illegal visit to town I had been involved in a lively argument. After a day of sickening and senseless drill, some of my colleagues had given vent to their feelings in very strong terms; they were German soldiers, but not slaves. They would not stand for such treatment. Why should they be treated worse than criminals?

Irritated and nervous as I was, I tried to show them the inconsistency of their attitude. I asked them why they had shouted 'Heil Hitler' for so many years. After all, they only got what they had asked for. This was not very well received, and I was reported to the sergeant-major the same night for having uttered 'remarks hostile to the State'. And then later, on my way to town, I was spotted and challenged by an NCO who, although he let me go on, reported me to the Company Office.

I shall never forget those hours: I felt frozen with terror and apprehension. My one thought was to run away. But where to? There was nowhere I could go, no one who would have sheltered me. Sooner or later I would be caught and shot as a deserter.

As night fell I dragged myself back to the camp with my heart in my boots. What followed now seems like a nightmare, like an unreal vision, seen through a mist; a glimpse of brutal faces jeering, questioning, writing. Where do you come from? Where have you been? What did you say? What did you mean? Like blows falling relentlessly and incessantly on my numbed brain. There was no escape. No relief. I was fighting desperately for my self-control. Desperately and vainly.

For about a hundred hours I had had no sleep; my nerves already raw now writhed and twisted in terror and agony. It was no use. I cracked, I shouted back, I screamed, sobbed and raved at them, I wanted to be left in peace, I was no soldier, I had never wanted to be a soldier, not here in this country, not among these filthy gangsters. This relieved my nerves and I felt calmer. But I had completely prejudiced my position.

I was now hopelessly lost. The drama moved on; the guard room, transport to the military prison, questions by the Reich war attorney. 'Disobedience … conduct prejudicial to political morale … death by beheading …' But my mind just would not grasp this. This was beyond belief. A quiet-voiced man in a neat grey uniform, smoking a cigar and saying: 'Your head will be chopped off.'

Bleak and dark days followed. In the next cell I could hear a prisoner run up and down without ceasing; at night he spoke aloud, sometimes he cried. He too had been sentenced to death. He was nineteen and had strangled his fiancée. He did not want to die. Twice every day I saw him in the corridor; I noticed how his blond hair had turned grey and his child's face looked as if drained of blood and feeling.

Early one morning I and four others were taken from our cells and driven to the penal servitude prison at Plötzbensee; our heads pressed against the bars, we were forced to watch four men being beheaded. As they dragged in the second one he screamed aloud; I remembered no more.

We had to shovel coal until we could no longer stand upright, and carry back-breaking loads; we slept in unheated cells through the worst of the winter. Soon my resistance was ground down. And then I was given the chance of recanting from my mutinous disobedience. The suggestion was backed by a beating by the NCO of a special squad and I recanted. My sentence was commuted to imprisonment.

During the next few months I sat quietly in my cell and had time for reflection. For the first time in my life I had had to submit to an overpowering superior force, for the first time I had had to humble myself, to stoop before people whom I despised. And all the time I was afraid: I had been threatened with a military hard labour battalion for the duration and then eight years' penal servitude. I know from reports that no one survived more than a few years of a military hard labour battalion. Meanwhile, my family had found out my whereabouts and had engaged counsel for the defence. He at once objected against the procedure: I had not been sworn in, hence I was not a soldier and, therefore, not liable to punishment for insubordination. Moreover, as I was a physical wreck as a result of overwork in the course of my duty, he demanded an examination in a nerve hospital.

Strangely enough he succeeded. I was removed to the military hospital in Tempelhof. A charming old doctor chatted with me for half an hour, then told me that I was quite sound and was, therefore, answerable for my insubordination; but I should not lose courage, he would help me.

At the end of April my case came up before the court-martial of the Luftgar III in Steglitz. I was driven to the court in a car; the last 100 yards I was taken, handcuffed and under heavy guard, through a group of about 100 little schoolgirls out to play. They giggled, pointed and grimaced. I could have killed the lot.

The hearing took four and a half hours in a suffocatingly hot court room. What endless formalities, what endless trite questions; 'What was in your mind?' 'Are you not aware that you have to serve your country loyally?' What was I to say in reply? 'Yes, sir, please sir, of course, sir.'

The doctor spoke at great length. Through his testimony and because in 1940 the army was still uninfluenced by SS and Gestapo methods, the sentence was unexpectedly light. The prosecutor claimed a four weeks' sentence; the court rejected this, declared the suit void, as I was in a highly nervous state, and terminated proceedings forthwith. This happened in 1940 before a German court-martial.

I was discharged; not only from prison, but also from the pioneer battalion, for in the meantime the Führer had issued a secret order in which Mischlings were declared 'unworthy to serve'. I remained in Berlin.

But the one man who was not satisfied by the verdict of the 'reactionary' Wehrmacht was Gestapo Commissar Sasse in the Headquarters at Burgstrasse, chief of the Mischlings' Division. I was summoned to a large, forbidding house on the banks of the Spree. From the windows I could see the islands in the river and the museums. The hearing took a long time; Sasse, a short squat man with a red face, wanted to know everything about the court-martial, even the opinions of the individual judges, and counsel for the prosecution. A few days later I was summoned again. Sasse briefly explained my position to me:

'Can't have scum like you in clean-collar work you know. Wouldn't do at all. Oh no. But you can help us to victory. Yes. Get those fine muscles to work – plenty of good healthy labouring jobs. Too good for you really. All right. See you get one. Now, go to hell!'

Two days after I took up work as a lorry driver's mate in a small paper factory, where I stayed for several months. I had a fairly miserable life there. During my imprisonment I had suffered greatly from hunger, and I still felt half-starved. And I was badly in need of a few weeks' rest; but that was not possible. At frequent but irregular intervals I was summoned to Burgstrasse. Sasse was playing cat-and-mouse with me. My nerves began to play up. I thought how I could escape. It would probably be best for me to leave Berlin. This was not explicitly forbidden, although Sasse had probably assumed that I would not dare to leave without telling him. At last an opportunity came. Some friends of my father who had an estate near Wuertemberg were prepared to engage me as labourer there. Trembling with fear and relief, I packed my bags and left Berlin and became a farm labourer.

The steward, his wife and three apprentice girls were a type of Nazi that I had not met in town. They were narrow-minded, humourless peasants. Their life of unremitting toil prevented them from thinking for themselves. They repeated uncritically what the Goebbels wireless told them, believed implicitly in the Wehrmacht communiqués and the speeches of the Führer. I had to sit at their table and suffer their second-hand claptrap in silence.

I was happier with the Polish slave workers. They were small peasants and farm labourers chiefly from the Krakow region who had been picked up in the street or in their houses and deported here. Those who were married had their families with them. All of them hated Germany and the Nazis, and they were all of them convinced that Germany would lose the war. But the Balkan campaign had just been concluded, Germany had invaded Russia, and nothing but victories were reported. And I had lost all hope. I knew that so long as the Nazis were in power I would always have to carry heavy weights, hew stones or cart dung. And I could see no end to it.

But Kasek, Ludwig and Andreas merely laughed at me. They held their grimy fingers near the ground as they said: 'Germany will come *so* low yet, so low!' One thing they all agreed; the campaign against Russia was good. It was all right that these two enemies should come to blows. They hated Moscow as much as Berlin.

Our work was terribly hard. I shall never forget the endless afternoons when rain and a biting wind beat against my face and I trudged behind the plough, cold and exhausted; or the intense heat at harvesting time and my useless struggle to keep up with the others, the carrying of sacks of potatoes across stubble fields. Again and again the thought occurred to me: everything is lost, everything has gone wrong. I'm finished, finished.

Strangely enough no one seemed to have noticed that I couldn't do the work properly without straining myself. Until the threshing when Andreas, the foreman, suddenly turned on me because I could not keep up the pace he set on the machine. We came to blows, and had to be separated.

Andreas and I were soon reconciled, and made peace over a bottle of schnapps. But the steward now had the chance he had been waiting for.

'There you are,' he said, 'this stinking yid is nothing but a troublemaker.' I was sacked.

I went back to a changed Berlin. The atmosphere was tense and ominous. I found the people even more obsequious and malicious than before. No one dared any longer to speak his mind, even among friends or family. Obedient, anxious and servile people gave up their overcoats and furs for the freezing troops in the east and worked the State war machine with downcast heads.

I resolved to take the first opportunity of getting back to the land. I told the official at the labour exchange this, and as a result I got a temporary job in a dressmaking factory in Spittelmarkt. Together with two others I spent the day packing girls' dresses and posting them at night. The work was relatively easy and pleasant, and we could talk without interference.

And we talked quite a good deal. I confined myself mainly to listening, while our 'foreman' – an elderly, typical Berliner – held forth on the whole range of political problems, from the Pacific to the North Sea.

Our foreman had a great respect for Britain and particularly for Mr Churchill. 'At least that's a real man, smoking cigars! Ours is a non-smoker!' His liking for Britain dated from the First World War when he had been a prisoner-of-war in a camp in Scotland where, among other things, he had learnt boxing. 'The British aren't what they used to be. Do you think in the old days they would have made a pact with the Bolshies? No, sonny, they wouldn't have done that!'

One day a ray of hope came from an unexpected quarter. The United States entered the war. Sitting around the wireless in the factory we heard what the illustrious Führer had to say on the occasion. There they squatted, my dear fellow countrymen, nodding thoughtfully when that hysterical paranoiac told them that on the other side of the globe a 'young nation – Japan – had arisen to make a new order.' Immoderate gibes at the Allies: 'That brandy-swilling British premier ... the paralytic in the White House ... patting each other on the back.'

Then came special communiqués: 'The American Navy was destroyed,' 'Japan had occupied the Pacific islands,' 'before long Australia would be taken ...' They all of them believed it. Not one of them thought of the immense material resources of the US or their millions of young, healthy, strong soldiers. I began to take hope again. The advance in Russia was halted; the United States rolled up their shirt sleeves. What did it matter if Rommel drove the British back into Egypt? Soon the tide would turn. Soon ...

I had an opportunity of working on an estate in Rostock in Mecklenburg, and took it. I had cause bitterly to regret my decision. The little estate was entirely neglected. The owner was away in the army, his wife was incompetent, and the Serbian prisoner-of-war who worked there was lazy and uninterested, not unnaturally. Everything was filthy, decayed and in ruins. In addition, my friend, Herr Sasse, had informed his Gestapo colleagues in Rostock of my arrival and soon I received an invitation to visit them.

I had had enough. These interminable, senseless cat-and-mouse interviews were grinding me down. Why didn't they leave me in peace? If I was so dangerous, why didn't they shut me up? What did they want of me?

I had to be free at last from the continual pressure, the unending fear. I had to get away. But how? Agricultural work was 'highly essential'; only two industries had a higher priority, mining and the merchant navy. I decided on the merchant navy. Surely on board ship I should be out of their reach.

I found myself on the SS _Colmar_ as a trimmer. She was a very old ship with three boilers and had plied for some years between Bangkok and Rotterdam in the Dutch service. My colleagues were a little wiry Chinese fellow, and Michel Fernand, a negro from Port-au-Prince in Haiti; he was my friend for my whole time on the _Colmar_.

We sailed for Norway in very bad weather; but even before we reached Oslo Fjord the second engineer noticed that I was no good in the boiler room; I could only just lift the heavy iron poker to break up the slag. I was sent to the focsle as a washer-up in the men's quarters.

This was the filthiest and lowest work on board. Every day I washed dishes, squashed bugs and cockroaches on the walls and scrubbed the latrines. 'You've done it now, my boy, now you're quite down. Scrubbing shit-houses, you can't get any lower than that.'

This boat had a colourful, wild crew on board: Dutch, Frenchmen, Balts, Serbians, Czechs who were forced labour, and Italians and Spaniards who went voluntarily. There were only a few Germans on board. All of us had this in common: a hatred of the Nazis and a love of liquor.

For one and a half years we boozed our way across the North Sea and the Baltic. I cannot remember any details of that time. Everything is fogged behind an alcoholic veil. This was really the lowest point of my 'career' – or so I thought. Sometimes we were momentarily aroused from our stupor by warnings of mines and torpedoes or air attacks, while we were rolling about near the Nordkapp [North Cape]. But that happened only rarely.

In those days I learnt to drink whisky from a bottle. The ordinary seamen could not afford this, but the engine personnel – of whom I was one! – were often completely drunk for a week or more at a time. And how the Letts and Estonians could drink! And when all the liquor, all the beer and Italian wine had gone, they showed us how to eke out half a bottle of beer with some alcoholic hair oil, how to make methylated spirit drinkable. They were right. Thus, and only thus, was life at all bearable.

On these ships which sailed for the glory of Germany there was no comradeship. Why should there be? We had all been more or less forced to go to sea, and none of us wanted to die for Nazi Germany. Our attitude was one of undiluted cynical egoism: 'Hang you, Fritz, as long as I stay alive.'

The Balts were completely cynical. We knew what the Nazis were like, but they taught us that the Russians were no better. Nazi or Bolshevik – it was all one. Often we listened to Moscow Radio. It was all propaganda. Don't believe it. Don't believe anything! Here, drink! Liquor is honest, liquor is true, and if we get a bomb and drown – who cares about us?

In the summer of 1943 we struck a mine near the Danish coast. We were badly holed above the waterline and our boatswain, who was crossing the deck with a bottle of gin in his hand, was torn to pieces. The _Colmar_ had to return to the Bloehm and Voss docks in Hamburg. I decided I had had enough of the sea. The merchant navy had by then lost so many ships that there were too many sailors. I was allowed to go without much difficulty.

The labour exchange directed me into a factory making motor tyres. I was to begin work at the end of July. What I did now was a matter of complete indifference to me. Tyres, all right, tyres. As far as I was concerned it could have been submarines or sandals. I was past caring. But as it happened nothing came of it. For several weeks the RAF had dropped leaflets over Hamburg calling on the citizens to leave the city. No one had left; everyone was too used to official exaggeration to believe anything very seriously. I still remember every detail of the hot, sultry July night when the first large-scale raid began. At first there was nothing unusual about it; people sat cowering in their damp cellars, children wept, the whistle of falling bombs, dull thudding hits, blasts of air which tore out windows and doors.

In none of this was there anything new. But what was new was the way in which it went on; while red flames still stood above the houses and the air was black with dust and dirt and the fire engines were clanging through the streets, the sirens went again. With a deep zooming sound the squadrons returned to the city. Again the sharp and clear bark of the 88mm guns alternated with the deep powerful hits of the heavy bombs.

At first I was not caught in the general mood of panic. 'The British don't mean me,' I thought. I had nothing to fear. Those men up there in the sky were fighting against the Nazis too; we had the same enemy. However stupid it may sound, I felt instinctively that no British bomb could harm me. I was firmly resolved to stay in Hamburg and see what would happen. I wanted to witness the death of the city.

Panic spread like a plague. People began to flee from the city in motor cars, in trains, in carts, on foot. Hamburg station was a seething mass of stamping, shouting people. They trampled each other down. Like ants they clung to the trains, on the running boards, on the roofs. Unending columns of despairing refugees left the city by road. Low-flying planes sprayed them with machine guns. Bombs took a ghastly toll of this closely packed mass of humanity.

As the planes turned back again and people emerged from their holes, yet new squadrons came to the attack. This went on without intermission, day and night. Hamburg's industrial and harbour districts sank in dust and ashes. Wave after wave, bomb after bomb, stirred up the existing rubble. Morning, afternoon, evening, night, day after day. And nature added a new horror. The myriad raging fires in so small an area made a natural blast furnace. A fierce whirlwind sucked the fires into white heat. Buildings crumbled into dust. The asphalt in the streets boiled and seethed and poured flaming into cellars and shelters. It was a second Pompeii.

And day by day the brilliant parching sun could scarcely pierce the heavy pitch-black dust clouds. There was a wan, unreal and ghostly half-light. There was neither water, electricity or gas. The city festered. Charred bodies, ridiculous in their short and dainty shapes, were lying among the rubble. Screaming figures scurried madly to and fro. The canals were filled with filth and corpses.

Epidemics broke out in the city. Typhus began. A dry wind swept it with dirt and dust.

The Hamburg disaster – which is still spoken of simply as '*die Katastrophe*' – had a terrible and widespread effect. The refugees spread panic throughout Germany. It was rumoured that Berlin was next on the list. Goebbels issued a proclamation to the population asking old people, women and children to leave the capital.

When I arrived in Berlin early in September the Lehrter station presented a spectacle similar to that on the station in Hamburg; utter confusion and a mass exodus to the open country. I had no belongings except the dirty, tattered clothes that I wore. Nothing, not even a suitcase was left. An old school friend named Joe helped me with the most essential things. He had not been called up as he worked in an armament factory as a designer; he had a little flat near the Hallische Tor, where I stayed with him.

At first he showed me to all his friends as though I were a strange beast, and let them marvel at me and my tales about Hamburg. They were all particularly interested, as a similar fate was expected for Berlin. On one evening he took me to a friend who had a book shop in Nürnberger Strasse and three girls who worked for him, and again I had to talk about Hamburg. Suddenly one of the girls turned on me and snapped: 'What an awful coward you must be!'

I looked at her. She was tall, slim with a pale oval face and large velvet eyes shining under a straight fringe. I agreed with her. I had never pretended to be anything else. Her eyes softened and I found that I couldn't think any more about Hamburg. I couldn't think about Berlin. I could scarcely think about myself. Her name was Bunny.

I saw her again the next day and after that we met frequently. She had a tiny flat nearby and I spent most of my time there. One afternoon, as we were having tea, the bell went. Outside were two men in light raincoats; one of them presented an octagonal tab – Gestapo.

I had several reasons for not wanting to get into the notice of the Gestapo. First there was my court-martial of 1940 which – strange as the ways of the German police are – might now lead to my arrest after three years, since I had been 'politically unreliable'. There was, further, my neglect to report to the police immediately on my arrival in Berlin which might be construed as an 'attempt at desertion', for although I was not 'worthy' to serve in the forces I was nevertheless obliged to report. But most of all I was in danger of being suspected of '*Rassenschande*' – racial pollution. Under the Nuremberg Laws Jewish Mischlings must not marry, but may have intercourse with German girls. In practice, however, the law was interpreted differently, and a Mischling reported to have such intercourse stood a good chance of going into a concentration camp.

We may have been denounced. I never knew nor shall I ever know. The Gestapo didn't do much talking and all I knew was that Bunny and I were arrested and taken to the nearest police station where Bunny was soon sent home, as her papers were all in order.

I was taken to Section 2a of the *Polizeipräsidium* [Police HQ] in Alexanderplatz. This was the receiving station, the popular name for which was 'grey misery'. I found good entertaining company there, most of them Gestapo prisoners, and we formed into small groups. We chatted away furiously so that we should notice neither the time nor our hunger.

We spoke of anything and of everything. For several days an antiquary, a young publisher, a pastor and I talked about the modern novel, where I remember stressing the supremacy of the Americans and praising Hemingway rather fulsomely.

But, however furiously I talked, at bottom I felt a deep and gnawing despair. Just now when Bunny had given me new courage, when, after the clean sweep of Hamburg I had meant to start afresh with her, my hopes were all crushed; the cat who had seemed to be asleep for so long had suddenly clawed the mouse back from life and held him starved and broken in her power.

There were no indications of what might happen to me. I was questioned once by an old friend, Commissar Sasse, who greeted me with a box on my ears. Evidently he did not know himself what to do with me but wanted to be sure that I was out of harm's way. He sent me back to 'grey misery'. The food was very poor, day and night we were tortured by hunger, and my strength began to decline.

The young publisher, Exner, one day returned pale with fear from a Gestapo interview. During a search of his house they had found British propaganda material and leaflets. That meant certain death. He was in the depth of despair. A short time before two young French boys, Pierre and Roger, had been sent to our section. They had broken into food stores at night and they, too, had to expect certain death.

The Frenchmen meant to escape. Their idea was to make ropes out of their bed linen and lower themselves from the latrine window into the interior of the HQ courtyard, after having sawn through the bars with an improvised file. In another part of the courtyard there was an iron ladder leading to the police radio station on the roof, from where they would lower themselves into Kaiserstrasse by means of their ropes.

After I had learnt of that plan I tried to persuade them to take Exner with them. It was his only chance. But Pierre and Roger would have nothing of it: 'We don't help a Boche!' But after a long and violent argument they agreed at last. As Exner did not speak French I had to act as an interpreter.

During the night while an air raid was in progress and the guards were in the shelter, they made an attempt to file through the bars. Next morning, by accident, it was discovered. The prison governor, a lieutenant in the SS police division, was in a towering fury. Exner, the French boys and I were taken away. I never saw them again.

I was given solitary confinement in a cell of the Gestapo building in Sophie-Charlotte Platz. The uncertainty about my future, and my increasing physical weakness, both wore me down. My mind churned incessantly over what might happen to me. Among the host of minor speculations two major fears stood out; concentration camp, where I would be tortured to death, or penal labour camp, where I would be worked to death.

One night I was taken back to the police HQ in Alexanderplatz. This time I fared worse. I was thrown in Section 2b among so-called 'transit prisoners' – common criminals, thieves, forgers, pimps and burglars who had already done several years' penal servitude and were now to be transferred to the concentration camp. In accordance with their usual policy the Gestapo had given them a sprinkling of 'politicals', for they knew only too well that nothing is more demoralising in the long run than to be with 'old lags'.

I enquired from the old hands about the camps to which I was likely to go. From them I learnt that labour camps were not much better than concentration camps; the main difference being that if you die in a labour camp you are buried, while in a concentration camp you go 'up the chimney'.

I was now completely 'down'. My physical strength was at an end and my perpetual hunger was verging on delirium. I was haunted day and night by visions of food, from whole banquets to crusts of bread and potatoes. My hair was shorn, my clothes were in rags. I had only trousers, coat and a pair of tattered shoes. I contracted the itch, a revolting skin disease. Countless bugs tortured me. I had lice and my whole body was stiff and sore from having to lie on the hard plank bed.

In a room which was intended for 60 prisoners 200–300 of us were continually crowded together in unspeakably filthy conditions. I fainted frequently. At night I would be torn by fits of nerveless sobbing.

I would not have got over this time if the other 'politicals' had not taken an interest in me and helped me. They were a colourful crowd: 'red' veterans of the Spanish Civil War, Alsatians who had declared their French loyalties, an ex-member of the French Foreign Legion, and a Catholic priest who had been a professor of fine art in Munich University.

It would be wrong to assume that these people, because they were all prisoners of the Gestapo and en route for the concentration camp, were of one mind. The communists in particular kept well away from all the others and rarely helped anyone outside their own clique. I discovered that almost all the Germans were intolerant, while the Norwegians, Dutch and especially the French were always kind and ready to help.

Typhus broke out in the prison in October 1943. We were put in quarantine; no one was allowed to enter or leave. The first deaths were in the subterranean holes, where Jews, gipsies, Poles and Russians vegetated in incredibly terrible conditions. All of us were so ill and weak that the epidemic had easy work with us. The mortuary vaults began to fill up.

Of my own circle only Karl, the Foreign Legionnaire, died. I caught the disease, but managed to pull through. At this time the air raids, during which we were locked in our cell under the roof became more intense. Sometimes I prayed that a bomb should put a stop to all this. Why hang on? There was no point in it.

On a cold November day I was called out. Again I went to Burgstrasse. This time Sasse was in a good mood. 'Aha, there you are. Had a nice time? That's fine, fine. Want your papers? Here you are. Have a cigar. That's right. Quite happy? All right. Go to hell!'

My release had come just in the nick of time. A few days later, on 22 November 1943, the RAF made their first really heavy raid on Berlin. Shortly after I learnt that Section 2b had got a direct hit and nearly all were dead.

When I returned to Bunny's flat she stared at me as though I were a ghost. She had heard nothing of me whatever and now I looked like one returned from the grave.

From this time I stayed with Bunny, although we would always be in danger of denunciation for racial pollution. But we could not bear to leave each other any more.

Bunny lived in one of those old Berlin houses in Alexanderplatz which had been erected at the time of Frederick the Great. The cellar was small, angular, damp, uncomfortable. When the raid began we had not wanted to go down. But an incendiary bomb which landed in the kitchen changed our minds.

When the raid had passed our flat was badly damaged; doors and windows were smashed, furniture ruined. Around us whole blocks of houses were in flames. It was as light as day and there was a scorching heat. I did nothing to help. I was sorry about every bomb that was not a hit. Was I not one with those warriors flying in the sky? Did we not have a common enemy?

While screaming people were running through the streets houses were blazing and ruins collapsed with a reverberating thunder. Bunny and I opened her father's 'secret' store of liquor. Sitting on the remains of the piano we laughed together and drank to the health of Eisenhower, Montgomery and Zhukov. Gay and excited and a little starry-eyed, we ran hand in hand through the burning streets, singing 'There's something in the air' and utterly oblivious to cares, dangers or other people. We felt a barbaric ecstasy. It was our own personal triumphant 'witches' Sabbath'.

To forestall the risk of another ·arrest we had to look round for a job for me. A friend of my father's wrote a letter of recommendation to the director of the AEG works in Seestrasse. I told him that I was allowed to work only as a labourer, but he was not worried. 'In this factory I am the boss!'

I was engaged as a clerk in the accounts division of the factory. My colleague was leader of the Dutch fascists in Berlin. He was an idealist who remained loyal to his opinions and later reported for service with the Volkssturm.

There were many other Dutchmen here and some Frenchmen who were living together in barracks on much worse rations than the Germans. I soon became friendly with some of the French after they had overcome the initial mistrust with which they view every German.

In the spring of 1944 Bunny found she was pregnant. Of course, owing to the Nuremberg Laws, we could not marry. In view of the intensification of air attacks, especially the day raids by the American Air Force, we thought it best for Bunny to leave Berlin. During the day I was in the factory while she was sitting alone in the cellar. Everything had to be concealed from the neighbours who would undoubtedly have denounced us. Therefore, she had to leave.

But where was she to go? Every weekend I trudged through the suburbs of Berlin from friend to friend, from acquaintance to acquaintance, begging for help. Refusal followed refusal. Humiliation followed humiliation. All these people called themselves anti-Nazis, they all listened to the BBC and hoped for an Allied victory; but they were not willing to take the risk of giving refuge to a woman who was having a child by a Mischling.

Finally, when it had become impossible to conceal Bunny's condition any longer, we managed to get a room in a small house in a village near Lubben in the Spreewald.

At first I went to see her there every weekend; sometimes I shared a compartment with SS men on their way to the extermination camp for Jews at nearby Lisbrone. Strange travelling companions indeed. Then later Bunny began to feel lonely and anxious and I used to catch the last train out, stay three hours and return to Berlin by the first train next morning. This put quite a strain on me, but it made things easier for Bunny.

Of course, it did not take long before the villagers began to smell a rat. The whole village was full of evacuated Berlin women whose time was taken up by prying into and speculating about each other's affairs. Whether Mr X got potatoes from a peasant on the black market; whether Mr Y was listening to British broadcasts; whether Mrs E had given a piece of bread to a French PoW. The young woman in an interesting condition who was visited at night by a dark foreign-looking fellow was a godsend to them. Now I could only leave the house in darkness; I had to use the back door or climb in through the window.

At that time the Nazis began a big drive against Mischlings, who were taken under guard to labour camps, as had happened to the Jews previously. I had kept this secret from Bunny for fear of upsetting her in her present state. In any case I seemed to have been passed over – either my papers had been burnt at police headquarters, or else my case had been forgotten. Everything might have gone well if a silly old woman had not told Bunny. As a result, Nina was born a month too soon, in October 1944.

During the winter the great Russian offensive began; the Russians swarmed into East Prussia, Silesia, Pomerania. It became extremely cold; refugees streamed in from the East, in endless columns on open horse-drawn carts. Slowly we realised what was in store for us.

I can still remember the day on which a long trek of several hundred carts, full of people and luggage, passed through the village. They had come from the region of Lissa and were utterly exhausted. There was a terrible snowstorm and an arctic wind swept across the high road. They halted in the village and unloaded some 40 children who were frozen to death. The little bundles were dumped in the gutter, pallid and stiff. Their mothers, mostly on the point of exhaustion, started to cook next to them, apathetic and unconcerned.

No one knew when the Russian advance would be stopped. Should we stay, or go back to Berlin? Would there be fighting here? Was there perhaps some truth in what the Goebbels radio was blaring forth about Russian atrocities? Contrary to the advice of all my friends I decided in February 1945 to take Bunny and the baby back to Berlin.

For four days we tried to get places in the Berlin trains. Even the carriage roofs were crowded with clinging passengers – and this in 25 below zero. It was impossible. Our only chance was to walk to the next main station. This was 20 kilometres away, and all the roads were covered with deep snow.

We wrapped Nina in all the woollens we had, and buried her deep in the pram with all our blankets round her. We could take only the barest necessities. The road was utterly deserted. In the open the storm howled in the telegraph wires; through the forest it screamed high over our heads dripping intermittent cascades of snow from the branches. Our pram was continually clogged with snow. Bunny was very brave. More than once my strength gave out and I wanted to sit down and rest. But she made me go on. So on and on we went.

Late at night we arrived at the railway station. A thousand people were already besieging the platform, but there was no train in sight. Struggling and pushing with all our might we managed to clear a place in the luggage room where Bunny could feed the baby. Then I had to leave her to keep our place on the platform.

On the afternoon of the next day a goods train bound for Berlin arrived in the station. Now came the real fight. Savage with despair, I finally secured a corner for us. The train rolled leisurely towards Berlin. We waited outside Königswusterhausen for three hours while an air raid was in progress. We were utterly exhausted, but very happy, for the baby was safe and sound.

When we arrived in our flat late at night we already sensed the atmosphere of panic in the city. An unspoken whisper of fear seemed to float through the streets: 'The Russians are coming!' In the middle of the night doorbells, including ours, were being furiously rung. 'All men outside at once!' I thought it best to go. Berlin was being put in readiness for defence and we had to build tank obstacles. Dog tired as I was I trotted along in a column of sullen, sleepy men. We were to tear up the pavements and build barricades out of rubble, paving stones and overturned tram cars. This was the 'Volkssturm', Germany's last line of defence.

I was determined not to stir a finger. After an hour I managed to get into an unobserved corner and from there to steal home. It was only a few hours before the work in the factory was to begin.

On that morning, however, both of us overslept and I did not go to work. As it happened, it was a good thing; on that day, 3 February 1945, Berlin experienced its, till then, heaviest air raid. All morning US bombers zoomed overhead. We sat in the very heart of the target area. We huddled close together over the pram. I was quite convinced that we would get it this time. Sticks of bombs, one after another, thundered down around us. But my premonition was wrong; we came through all right. Nina heard nothing; she had been sound asleep all through it.

In March all normal life ceased in Berlin. The factories were hardly working at all. We spent more time in the cellars than out of them. The Nazis became even more anxious, raved hysterically about 'wonder weapons' soon to go into operation, and of the immense hidden might of the Werewolf [secret Nazi organisation], while Russian tanks stood on the Oder and the American and British armies were pushing east across the Rhine.

In the factory I made bets with my French friends who would be the first, the Russian or Western armies, to arrive in Berlin. The general favourite was the Western powers. Patton was already attacking central Germany.

In the beginning of April I was drafted into the Volkssturm. My battalion consisted of a couple of hundred old gaffers, most of them over 60. The total armoury of our battalion amounted to two old Italian muskets and two cases of French ammunition of the wrong calibre. We had no uniform, not even arm badges. We were evidently expected to stem the onslaught of Russian tanks with sticks and stones and shovels.

We were taken by train to Fürstenwalde, and from there we marched on foot in the direction of the Oder. At intervals of 200 or 300 yards military police were posted with orders to shoot down retreating soldiers. We occupied an estate midway between Frankfurt and Küstrin, close behind the fighting lines.

The remnants of a tank battalion were already in occupation. They had run out of petrol and ammunition, but for some reason they still stayed on here. Our old men soon smelt out the reason – a completely undamaged distillery. And the fiercest fighting of the campaign now started between the surfeited tank men and our thirsty greybeards. The fighting got steadily feebler, and soon the entire battalion was dead drunk.

All the time we could hear the big guns booming from the front line; low flying aircraft sprayed us with machine-gun fire. One morning the Russians dropped an airborne sabotage detachment behind us, near Muncheberg. They were captured by the infantry, but all the same I thought the time had come for me to clear out.

My battalion commander was a shoemaker from Mulackstrasse and a Sturmführer in the SA. I had a serious talk with him and explained that though I desired nothing better than to lay down my life for Great Germany, I had to give up this ambition. I had been called up by mistake. As a 'Mischling' military service was '*verboten*' to me; Mischlings, as he knew, were unworthy of military service. However sorry I was to leave, I felt I had to confess – I could not let him be put in danger for me.

He was deeply impressed. I asked him whether he could honestly let honest German men march with something like me! This almost amounted to 'racial pollution'! He was terrified at the danger he had been in, thanked me profusely for my honesty and sent me back to Berlin in an ambulance with a rucksack of meat and sausage as my personal 'loot' from the campaign.

I was just in time. A few days later the Russians broke through and started the battle of Berlin. We had made preparations for living in the cellar for a fortnight; we had taken down a bed, the pram, some clothes and linen and all we possessed in the way of food.

Several dozen people were crowded into the few inadequate cellar rooms. It was hot, stuffy and foetid with the smell of human bodies. The only light was from flickering candles. Children screamed, fought and fell over each other in the chaos. Nina never stopped crying; she was teething.

Panic had reached its peak in the city. Hordes of soldiers stationed in Berlin deserted and were shot on the spot or hanged on the nearest tree. A few clad only in underclothes were dangling on a tree quite near our house. On their chests they had placards reading: 'We betrayed the Führer.' The Werewolves pasted leaflets on the houses:

Dirty cowards and defeatists
We've got them all on our lists!

The SS went into underground stations, picked out among the sheltering crowds a few men whose faces they did not like, and shot them then and there.

The scourge of our district was a small, one-legged Hauptscharführer of the SS, who stumped through the street on crutches, a machine pistol at the ready, followed by his men. Anyone he didn't like the look of he instantly shot. The gang went down cellars at random and dragged all the men outside, giving them rifles and ordering them straight to the front. Anyone who hesitated was shot.

The front was a few streets away. At the street comer diagonally opposite our house, Walloon Waffen SS had taken up position; wild, desperate men who had nothing to lose and who fought to their last round of ammunition. Armed Hitler Youth were lying next to men of the Vlassov White Russian Army.

The continual air attacks of the last months had worn down our morale, but now, as the first shells whistled over our heads, the terrible pressure began to give way. It could not take much longer now, whatever the Walloon and French Waffen SS or the fanatic Hitler Youth with their 20mm anti-aircraft guns could do. The end was coming and all we had to do was to try to survive this final stage.

But that was by no means simple. Everything had run out. The only water was in the cellar of a house several streets away. To get bread one had to join a queue of hundreds, grotesquely adorned with steel helmets, outside the baker's shop at 3am. At 5am the Russians started and continued uninterruptedly until nine or ten. The crowded mass outside the baker's shop pressed closely against the walls, but no one moved from his place. Often the hours of queuing had been spent in vain; bread was sold out before one reached the shop. Later one could only buy bread if one brought half a bucket of water.

Russian low-flying wooden biplanes machine-gunned people as they stood apathetically in their queues and took a terrible toll of the waiting crowds. In every street dead bodies were left lying where they had fallen.

At the last moment the shopkeepers, who had been jealously hoarding their stocks, not knowing how much longer they would be allowed to, now began to sell them. Too late! For a small packet of coffee, half a pound of sausages, thousands laid down their lives. A salvo of the heavy calibre shells tore to pieces hundreds of women who were waiting in the market hall. Dead and wounded alike were flung on wheelbarrows and carted away; the surviving women continued to wait, patient, resigned, sullen, until they had finished their miserable shopping.

The pincers began to narrow on the capital. Air raids ceased; the front lines were too loose now for aircraft to distinguish between friend and foe. Slowly but surely the T52 tanks moved forward through Prenzlauer Allee, through Schonhauser Allee, through Kaiserstrasse. The artillery bombardment poured on the city from three sides in unbroken intensity. Above it, one could hear sharply close and distinctly, the rattling of machine guns and the whine of bullets.

Now it was impossible to leave the cellar. And now the bickering and quarrelling stopped and we were suddenly all of one accord. Almost all the men had revolvers; we squatted in the farthest corner of the cellar in order to avoid being seen by patrolling

SS, and were firmly determined to make short shrift of any Volkssturm men who might try to defend our house.

Under the direction of a master mason who had been a soldier in Russia for two years we 'organised' our supplies. We made a roster for parties of two or three to go out and get water and bread. We procured steel helmets; under artillery fire we heaped up mountains of rubble outside the cellar walls in order to safeguard against shells from tanks.

The Nazis became very quiet. No one took the Wehrmacht communiqués seriously now, although Radio Berlin went on broadcasting it until 24 April. A tiny sheet of paper, the last newspaper of the Goebbels press, *Der Panzerbär* (the tank bear) announced Goering's deposition and the removal of the 'government' seat to Flensburg.

We left the cellar at longer and longer intervals and often we could not tell whether it was night or day. The Russians drew nearer; they advanced through the underground railway tunnel, armed with flame throwers. Their advance snipers had taken up positions quite near us and their shots ricocheted off the houses opposite. Exhausted German soldiers would stumble in and beg for water – they were practically children; I remember one with a pale, quivering face who said: 'We shall do it all right; we'll make our way to the north west yet.' But his eyes belied his words and he looked at me despairingly. What he wanted to say was: 'Hide me, give me shelter. I've had enough of it.' I should have liked to help him; but neither of us dared to speak. Each might have shot the other as a 'defeatist'.

An old man who had lived in our house had been hit by a shell splinter a few days ago and had bled to death. His corpse lay near the entrance and had already began to smell. We threw him on a cart and took him to a burnt-out school building where there was a notice: 'Collection point for Weinmeisterstrasse corpses.' We left him there; one of us took the opportunity of helping himself to a dead policeman's boots.

The first women were fleeing from the northern parts of the city and some of them sought shelter in our cellar, sobbing that the Russians were looting all the houses, abducting the men and raping all the women and girls. I got angry, shouted I had had enough of Goebbels' silly propaganda, the time for that was past. If that was all they had to do, let them go elsewhere.

Whilst the city lay under savage artillery and rifle fire the citizens now took to looting the shops. The last soldiers withdrew farther and farther away. Somewhere in the ruins of the burning city SS men and Hitler Youth were holding out fanatically. The crowds burst into cellars and storehouses. While bullets were whistling through the air they scrambled for a tin of fish or a pouch of tobacco.

On the morning of 1 May our flat was hit by a 21cm shell and almost entirely destroyed. On the same day water carriers reported that they had seen Russian soldiers. They could not be located exactly; they were engaged in house-to-house fighting which was moving very slowly. The artillery had been silent for some time when at noon on 2 May rifle fire too ceased in our district. We climbed out of our cellar.

From the street corner Russian infantry were slowly coming forward, wearing steel helmets with hand grenades in their belts and boots. The SS had vanished. The Hitler Youth had surrendered.

Bunny rushed and threw her arms round a short slit-eyed Siberian soldier who seemed more than a little surprised. I at once went off with two buckets to fetch water, but I did not get beyond the first street corner. All men were stopped there, formed into a column and marched off towards the east.

A short distance behind Alexanderplatz everything was in a state of utter turmoil and confusion. Russian nurses armed with machine pistols were handing out loaves of bread to the German population. I took advantage of this turmoil to disappear and got back home safely. God knows where the others went.

After the first wave of combatant troops there followed reserves and supply troops who 'liberated' us in the true Russian manner. At our street corner I saw two Russian soldiers assaulting a crying elderly woman and then raping her in full view of a stunned crowd. I ran home as fast as I could. Bunny was all right so far. We had barricaded the one remaining room of our flat with rubble and charred beams in such a manner that no one outside could suspect that anyone lived there.

Every shop in the district was looted. As I hurried to the market I was met by groups of people who were laden with sacks and boxes. Vast food reserves belonging to the armed forces had been stored there. The Russians had forced the doors open and let the Germans in.

The cellars, which were completely blacked out, now became the scene of an incredible spectacle. The starved people flung themselves like beasts over one another, shouting, pushing and struggling to lay their hands on whatever they could. I caught hold of two buckets of sugar, a few boxes of preserves, 60 packages of tobacco and a small sack of coffee which I quickly took back home before returning for more.

The second raid was also successful. I found noodles, tins of butter and a large tine of sardines. But now things were getting out hand. In order not to be trampled down themselves the Russians fired at random into the crowds with machine pistols, killing several.

I cannot remember how I extricated myself from this screaming, shouting chaos; all I remember is that even here in this utter confusion, Russian soldiers were raping women in one of the corners.

Bunny had meanwhile made me promise not to try to interfere if anything were to happen to her. There were stories in our district of men being shot trying to protect their wives. In the afternoon two Russians entered our flat, while Bunny was sitting on the bed with the child. They looked her over for some time; evidently they were not very impressed with her. We had not washed for a fortnight, and I had expressly warned Bunny not to make herself tidy, for I thought the dirtier and more neglected she looked the safer.

But the two gentlemen did not seem to have a very high standard as far as cleanliness was concerned. With the usual words 'Frau komm!' spoken in a menacing voice, one of them went towards her. I was about to interfere; but the other shouted 'Stoi' and jammed his machine pistol in my chest. In my despair I shouted 'Run away, quick'; but that was, of course, impossible. I saw her quietly lay the baby aside, then she said:

'Please don't look, darling.' I turned to the wall.

When the first Russian had had enough they changed places. The second was chattering in Russian all the time. At last it was over. The man patted me on the shoulder:

'Nix angst! Russki Soldat gut!'

Then they inspected the room, searched out belongings, took away a small watch, a fountain pen and an electric torch, grinned, mumbled: 'Auf Wiedersehen' and went out. They stayed a little while in the next room, which was only partially destroyed. I went to see what they had done; they had relieved themselves on the carpet. From now on I did not allow Bunny to leave the house and hid her and the child under the roof. This went on for days.

The whole city was now an evil-smelling rubble heap. In the heat of the summer an epidemic of dysentery broke out. There were orders not to drink water that had not been boiled, but the disease spread with alarming speed, the germs being carried by the swarms of flies which infested the city. There were no medical supplies. We were completely helpless against it. Milk was seldom available for children, and when it was it had invariably gone sour. Adults were not seriously harmed by the epidemic; but thousands of children died.

And now stories began to come in from the country about the behaviour of the Russians during the campaign. A few days after the occupation of Berlin Bunny's sister Ellen arrived from the east.

She lived in a village behind Landsberg-an-der-Warthe near the former Polish corridor. After her 60-year-old Father had been called up to the Volkssturm, Ellen was alone in the house.

When the Red Army pushed forward from the Vistula they had hardly noticed any traces of the hasty retreat of the Wehrmacht, for the village was too far away from the main road. By the time the Nazi authorities ordered the evacuation of all civilians, Russian tanks were only a few kilometres away. Train services were suspended, and the roads were blocked.

Many thousands of refugees tried, despite the deep snow, to reach the Oder in cars, on sledges or on foot. Mixed in with them were the retreating columns of the Wehrmacht. German tanks and lorries battered their way through, regardless of any refugees who might be in their way. Dead horses, dying men and women and derelict vehicles lined the road. Ellen tried to bicycle for a few miles, but soon had to give it up and returned to the village.

The first Russian columns swept in, but after they had satisfied themselves that no German soldiers were left in the village they moved on immediately. They were followed by motorised infantry and a cavalry brigade.

There were no young men left in the place; only a dozen old cripples and women and children remained. Like all of us Ellen had disbelieved the atrocity stories about the Russians. She had gone up to a pair of Russians in the street in all friendliness.

She was immediately seized and raped. When they released her she ran way into the woods and stayed there until nightfall.

The cold drove her back to the village where she hid in a barn. Her Russian 'friend' and his comrades had already been looking for her and finally discovered her hiding place. They took off their belts and beat her. Then they dragged her into a house where more than a dozen of them were billeted. All of them used her the whole night for their enjoyment.

Near daybreak they had reached such a state of drunkenness and enfeeblement that she was able to slip out and shelter with a neighbour who hid her in the stable. At noon they could hear drunken voices and knocks on the door. When there was no answer the Russians smashed it open with their rifle butts.

One of the children, a thirteen-year-old girl, was lying in bed with scarlet fever. A drunken Russian threw himself upon her and when she struggled he shot her through the throat. She bled to death. The oldest child was a girl suffering from almost complete paralysis who had been unable to move for years. Several of the drunken liberators threw her on the table, forced her paralysed legs apart, and raped her in turn. As she lay unconscious on the table they fired their revolvers into her from three paces' distance.

Just as they discovered Ellen four officers entered the house. They had only just arrived and were now looking round for the prettiest girls. Ellen saw that they were high-ranking officers and flung herself at their feet, hoping for their protection, which she was graciously granted.

Along with three other girls she was locked into a room in a peasant's cottage. The windows and doors were hermetically closed, the room continually lit by candlelight. They were brought food and forced to drink tumblerfuls of vodka. One of the officers had a festering wound which Ellen had to wash and dress.

These officers must have been very good friends, for they politely and calmly took their turn at sleeping with the girls. On one occasion there was a little jealousy and knives were used; but this was soon smoothed over with a few bottles of liquor.

For several days the Russians scarcely stirred out of the room. The air was thick with the fumes of liquor, sweat, the festering wound and Russian tobacco. The gramophone played continually. There was only one record – 'I can't give you anything but love, Baby.' One of the girls went mad, cried for her father, laughed, babbled nonsensically and twined rags in her hair. Ellen had some kind of alcoholic poisoning and vomited continually. The Russians 'cured' her by pouring more vodka into her.

On one occasion she managed to get away, but no sooner had she got into the High Street than two Siberians clubbed her with a pistol butt and raped her while she was unconscious. They then returned her to the officers' mess.

When, after a few days, the detachment moved on and was relieved by a new one, her 'friend' with the wounded foot gave her a glowing testimonial. The result was that she was at once taken over by the next batch of officers. The whole business started all over again, the only difference being that the new gentlemen were not such good friends.

She spent one night lying motionless on the bed, on either side of her a drunken Russian; both were clutching pistols and eyeing each other with mutual distrust. In the end the two cavaliers reached agreement and both went at her simultaneously.

The village was occupied by new relays of troops from time to time and always the same scenes ensued. After a fortnight she found she had gonorrhoea, and now she was driven twice weekly in a military car to the Russian military hospital where she received 'treatment' consisting of soap and water ablutions. The Russians were quite unconcerned.

In the end Polish troops moved in. Their discipline was far superior. There were no cases of rape. A Polish private who tried it was shot by order of the commanding officer. But to make up for this the Poles looted everything thoroughly, smashing anything that they could not take away.

But apart from the sexual angle, their treatment was much harsher than the Russians. Ellen had to wash their laundry in the courtyard. So intense was the cold that her fingers bled – if the blood dropped on the laundry she was forced to do it again.

The Poles did not stay for long. They were followed by Russians who were slightly better behaved. The women were now put on heavy work. All day long they had to unload wagons, lay cables and carry supplies. Those who did not work got no food. The only break was the customary visit to the hospital for treatment. Of course, all this was completely pointless; even if one of the girls had been cured she would have been re-infected within a matter of hours.

Heavens only knows what would have become of her if her father had not managed after a few weeks to come and take her away. He had managed to desert his unit and slip through as far as the Oder where he was held up by Polish troops. They took away everything that he had on him and put him into a labour camp. After a fortnight he was set free and was able to take Ellen back with him to Berlin. By now a few trains were running and they found room in one of them. On the way Russian soldiers moved in who flung several men and children out of the moving train in order to make more room for themselves.

One after another they used Ellen and another girl for their purposes while Ellen's father had to hold their luggage and rifles. Shortly before they got to Berlin they allowed the girls to dress.

For the first time now Ellen could go into hospital, but owing to lack of medical supplies there was no question of proper treatment. Only many weeks later, when the Americans and British moved into Berlin, could she be cured.

Hers was not an isolated case. Hundreds of thousands of young girls fared as badly as she. And thousands of them fared worse. Conditions in the city centre were such that we could no longer stay in our bombed flat. The heat was unbearable; there was dust and filth and gigantic swarms of dysentery-carrying flies.

Our problem was to find a new home in a less destroyed part of the town, preferably in a suburb. After several weeks' futile searching I was lucky. In Zehlendorf, a south-west suburb, there was a settlement of new buildings close to a wood, the 'SS Settlement Krumme Lanke,' which had been built by the Nazis for the sole use of

SS and police. Many of the SS families were still living there; only the men were in hiding, mostly in the British zone.

With the help of a friend of my father's, who was an official in one of the new public offices, we were given a nice little flat which had once belonged to an SS Oberscharführer. After having lived in the centre of the city, out here felt like paradise. Nina's health improved rapidly.

Now as we could slowly settle down to a peaceful life we began to realise just how our health had suffered during these last dreadful years. We both suffered from indigestion, sleeplessness and all kinds of nervous complaints. After a brief recovery Nina had a relapse which caused us much anxiety.

All this might have been bearable if it had not become clear, as time went on, that our unquestionable stand against the Nazis had been made in vain. It is true that on account of my political imprisonment I was recognised by the authorities as a 'victim of fascism'; but all this means is that my ration scale is advanced one group – from Class II to I. Apart from this the sole advantage is that my red card had earned me a 'special allocation' of ten pounds of cucumbers.

What we found particularly galling was that after the first shock the SS families could carry on without interference and soon found their feet again. In contrast to ourselves they had been well fed throughout the war. Our last remaining clothes were shabby and torn; but the wives of the SS officers wore elegant suits from Paris, furs from Norway and shoes from Czechoslovakia. Completely without shame or conscience they whispered behind our backs and sneered openly and smugly at our clothes and our wretchedness.

We had great hopes that with the arrival of the Americans things in general, and conditions in the SS settlement in particular, would show an improvement. Zehlendorf belonged to the American sector. It was occupied by the tank division, 'Hell on Wheels,' which had come from Italy. Despite their easy-going ways they made a very warlike impression; their coats were simply plastered with medals and decorations. They didn't give a rap about the non-fraternity rules, spoke to anybody and everybody and handed out cigarettes and sweets, evidently quite ignorant of such a thing as the black market. But they soon made up for this.

Our hopes were soon to be disappointed. A number of homes in the settlement had been filled by the authorities with recognised 'victims of fascism'. By now many SS women with their children had returned from the countryside where they had been safely and comfortably evacuated. They demanded their homes back. The German authorities naturally refused their claims and made them live elsewhere.

The ladies now appealed to the local American commander, one Colonel Trolp. This gentleman was obviously actuated by the most generous and noble thoughts. He was appalled at the sufferings of the SS wives. He said that America did not make war on women and children. Of course they must have their homes back. The 'victims of fascism' were told to get out. If they refused to go American military police would deal with them. Frau Obersturmführer and her SS lady friends had recovered their homes.

I have found that, on the whole, the British understand our situation much better than the Americans. While bathing on the beach of the Krumme Lanke I engaged in a conversation with a British soldier, a Manchester schoolteacher, who asked in a very business-like manner about the food situation and general conditions of life. He was evidently able to understand what it meant to live on a few slices of bread and a pound of potatoes a day. The Americans were quite different. Hunger seemed to them a purely academic and quite unreal idea. In this they differed not only from the British but also from the Russian. You can tell a Russian: 'I am hungry' and he will probably try to help you. From an American you get merely a gay and incredulous smile.

But not all of them were like that. In the early days we got to know a GI, quite a simple fellow who had been a bus driver in Boston. He was a driver in a transport company; his name was Francis Gallagher. He called on us one night and must have taken a liking to our little Nina. He did not stay long, but promised to return next morning. He kept his word. On the dot of nine he appeared, carrying a large bag full of sugar, flour, condensed milk, chocolate and oranges for the child. He handed those over not with the pompousness of charity but in such a nice and pleasant way that we could accept them without any feeling of embarrassment. From now on he called almost every day and always left a parcel in the corner, saying it was for baby. He never talked about and had never bothered about politics. In fact he helped us without any idea who we were and what we had done during the previous years. Unfortunately, he was sent home shortly afterwards.

The chief interest of GIs were 'Fräuleins'. They were by no means choosey about their girlfriends. Within a short time many of the SS women in the settlement had got American boyfriends. When we didn't know where our next meal was coming from, a succession of jeeps would stop at the house of Frau SS Untersturmführer and laughing, noisy GIs would jump out with heavy parcels under their arms. Dance music, laughter and clinking of glasses continued into the early hours of the morning. But it didn't wake us up. Hunger kept us awake anyway. Our baby got worse and worse. Instead of milk we were frequently forced to give her rye-meal dissolved in water, and instead of sugar, we would only give her saccharine. Through one of Francis's comrades I sent a letter to an aunt of mine in the US. She was a sister of my mother who had married an American and of whom I had not heard for a good many years. I described our situation, asking her to help the baby, although I had little hope of the letter arriving.

One day in October we placed Nina on the balcony for her usual afternoon nap. When we returned a few minutes later she was unconscious. The doctor diagnosed embolism of the lungs. He said that one of the valves of the heart was still working but he could not give her an injection which alone could save her, as German doctors had no strophantine. Bunny rushed off to the nearest American military hospital and ten minutes later the ambulance stopped outside our house. But it was too late. All that the two doctors could still do was to discover that meanwhile the heart had stopped.

We had a difficult time in the autumn of that year. In order to get an additional meal Bunny took a job in an office of the American military government. But she could not do the work for long, for she was far too tired and weak. Every day I went into the forest to steal wood and sometimes I went out at night with parties of several men. There were days when we stayed in bed because there was nothing to eat. Many people did likewise in the autumn and winter of that year.

The organisation for 'victims of fascism' could not be relied on for help because they had no money. The few surviving Jews were little better off; but at least they had various international organisations to look after them, and from time to time they received additional food from the United States, Sweden and Switzerland. No one bothered about us.

About a fortnight after the death of our child, Francis's friend brought us a huge parcel which had been sent to him by my aunt in the US. It contained a magnificent and sumptuous collection of things for baby, marvellous things which she had never tasted! Tinned milk, little tins of spinach, concentrated orange juice and chocolate – there was everything in it, everything that she could need, everything to have built her strength up to resist disease. But it came too late.

Despite our own great hunger we could not bring ourselves to touch any of the food. Months passed; but it was not before the beginning of December that, driven by hunger, we began eating from it. Then came Christmas. I had managed to get some onions and a little flour. All that was left of the parcel was two tiny tins of Spinach and some Horlicks tablets. This was our Christmas dinner. We decided to boil the whole lot up together and hope for some kind of pudding. Bunny warmed it in the saucepan and stirred it with a cheap tin spoon. She turned away for a moment. When she looked at the pan again the spoon had disappeared and the food was slowly changing into a silvery grey soap. The ersatz spoon had completely disintegrated in millions of little silvery particles. Then Bunny had a brilliant idea. She raced to the neighbours and fetched a magnet, which she slowly stirred through the mess. But nothing happened. Then I began to pour the whole lot through a handkerchief. This took hours. And only the liquid passed through while all the good food and the metal remained in the handkerchief. It was no good. The dinner was spoilt and had to be given to the cat. We went to bed hungry.

In the following months, undaunted by our appalling living conditions, I began to work on a novel. I showed excerpts from it to a publisher; he liked them and made a contract with me. At the same time he pointed out to me what little hope there was of bringing out a book in Germany within the next two years.

Nevertheless; I went on writing; it gave me something to do and helped me over the grey and endless months. Besides, I was earning money, for my publisher paid me advance royalties.

In the spring of 1946 I applied to UNRRA for permission to emigrate to the US. The procedure was easy for Jewish 'victims of fascism'; the Jewish community in conjunction with the United States Army Chaplain saw to it that their applications were making progress. In view of the regulations, which provided for facilities also for other victims of racial or political persecution, I was firmly convinced that my application would be successful.

After I had filled up a long questionnaire I was told by the UNRRA people to see the American consul in Dahlem. I had to queue up for several hours every day until I was admitted to the 'political screening'.

The vice-consul and an official of military intelligence were sitting in a small glass cubicle. The clatter of typewriters in the anteroom made it difficult to hear what was said. The viceconsul was in his early twenties, the intelligence man younger still. Both of them had arrived in Germany only a few months ago and neither of them spoke a word of German. My request for an interpreter was turned down on the ground that they had not got one. As a matter of fact he was sitting outside, where I had already spoken to him.

It was quite evident that these two had a low opinion of potential immigrants. Presumably they came from some of those ancient republican families who were on the beach to welcome the *Mayflower* on its first arrival in America. They behaved as though they were dealing with a criminal. The intelligence man glanced through my questionnaire and then turned to me with the words: 'We do not believe that you were a political prisoner. You must have been a thief. What did you steal?'

I had had enough.

'Half a dozen teaspoons!' I said, 'but don't tell anybody.'

This did raise a smile. But it was quite hopeless. They always came back to the same question: 'Why were you not in a concentration camp?' as if that were the answer to everything. They didn't seem to realise that it was easier to get into a concentration camp than to stay outside.

After a quarter of an hour had passed they were hardly listening any more. The vice-consul sat silently, chewing gum. In the end the intelligence men turned to him and said:

'Let's get rid of him, we'll be late for lunch.' The vice-consul stopped chewing and rose. I was suddenly gripped by a terrible fear. Bunny was waiting anxiously at home, and this was our last hope.

'Give me another three minutes,' I begged, 'All it matters to you is being late for lunch, but my whole future is at stake.'

With a deep sigh the vice-consul dropped back into his armchair, put his feet on the table and resumed his chewing. I spoke as fast as I could. I tried to explain every-thing to him, the pressure of the last few years, the eternal anxiety, the whole of our wretched existence: it was utterly hopeless. They simply did not understand me. They had spent their lives securely in a happy country, had a home, and ate porridge for breakfast. They did not even listen. In the end the intelligence man interrupted me.

'You have been with the merchant navy helping to prolong the war. You have worked for the AEG, an armament concern, and so you have fought indirectly against the United States. We only want the best types over there. We don't want your sort over there.'

In my despair I had to laugh out aloud.

'What you mean is that if I'd been gassed or shot through the neck I could emi-grate – is that it?' The intelligence man smiled. The vice-consul went on chewing. I was dismissed.

My nerves cracked and I began to shout at them. And then a cold fear suddenly silenced me. This had happened before. Time was playing tricks on me. This had happened before – the pale eyes devoid of understanding, the slow pitying smile, my own nerve-racked shouting. Then I remembered. And the cold fear became a band of ice round my heart. It *had* happened before – six years before. But then the pale eyes were German eyes, the pitying smile a German smile. Only I was the same.

Bunny made the best of it – as she made the best of everything. But it became clearer every day that they made no distinction between Germans and Germans. They are willing to forgive the Nazis their sins, at any rate the smaller Nazis. 'Give him a chance!' – that's their slogan; except for us. There is no one to give us a chance.

9

BARONESS MAUSI VON WESTERODE

We first got to know Mausi von Westerode in 1928 when my father began rebuilding and enlarging our house. Father was a great believer in giving young people a chance, and had given the job to a promising 24-year-old architect who in his turn had brought in the gifted and attractive Baroness von Westerode to do the interior decorating.

Mausi was blonde, blue-eyed and beguiling; she was also exceedingly efficient. Her clients invariably became her friends, and my parents were no exception. Whenever she came to the house, which she did quite often, she always had a celebrity of some sort in tow. She specialised in politicians and intellectuals of the left, and whenever she was around, politics was the main topic of conversation.

Although I found her exceedingly glamorous, and was deeply impressed by her clothes, her exotic perfume and her showy pink Mercedes car, I never paid much attention to her leftwing chit-chat until the arrival of the Nazis. After that I began to sit up and take notice, for Mausi was as outspoken as ever. She not only said things, but did things – if all we heard was true. And yet she managed to remain right on top socially as well as professionally and did a great deal of private decorating for the new masters.

She continued to visit my parents long after the rest of us had left Germany, nor did she ever bother to make a secret of it. It would never have entered her head to park her car a couple of streets away or to come after dark as most people did. In 1940, the last time my parents saw her, she was as self-assured and openly scornful of the Nazis as she had ever been.

There was little left of the gay, beautiful, egotistical Mausi in 1946. She was shabbily dressed and haggard, and had apparently lost all interest in her appearance. The only thing that seemed to interest her then was helping other people, and I was very much impressed by the change in her.

But when I returned to Berlin in 1947, I found that the Mausi of the 1930s had reasserted herself. She was certainly older, less attractive and more aggressively blonde, but the perfume and the chic, the well-informed chatter and the entourage of the 'right' kind of people were unmistakable.

Baroness Mausi von Westerode, born 1898

I was born at my parents' country house just outside Baden Baden in 1898. My father, Karl, Baron von Westerode, was a Privy Councillor and later became President of the Supreme Court of the Empire. He came from one of the so-called upper ten families and my mother was a member of a distinguished family of merchant bankers, which had been well known in Germany for centuries. The atmosphere of my home could hardly have been stuffier, more reactionary or more traditional. Luckily for me I was sent to school in France and Switzerland, which had the effect of broadening my mind at a very early age. I made friends with girls of all different nationalities. My best friend, Madeleine Leblanc, was French, and as her family were a good deal more aristocratic than mine, my parents had no objections to my spending some part of every holiday with her in Paris. In their house I met artists and writers, for Madeleine's mother was a great patron of the arts and was famous for her *salon*. I considered myself to be the only internationally-minded member of my family, and by the time I was fifteen I had already decided that I would leave home the moment I was grown up and travel about and meet interesting people of all nationalities. I was always, from the earliest age, vigorously independent and the idea of shocking people and defying the conventions always delighted me. I knew that I should be able to do pretty well as I liked as soon as I grew up, because my parents had been silly enough to tell me that I had my own money, left me by my grandmother.

When war broke out in 1914 my education abroad came to an end. I was terribly miserable and found it quite impossible to think of all my French friends as enemies. I hated the stern, confined atmosphere of my home and was unable to see things from my parents' point of view. There was a wave of Francophobia, not only for the people but for French things and words too. It even became an offence to use words like eau-de-Cologne. Anything and everything which was considered un-German was outlawed. My parents saw nothing wrong in all this, whereas I felt it to be utterly absurd. For the next two years I became steadily more and more out of touch with my parents and their ideas. Finally, when I was eighteen, I persuaded them to let me go and work as a military nursing sister at my aunt's Schloss near Hanover, which was being used as a convalescent home for officers. I had a wonderful time there, as my aunt, who was not terribly strict anyway, was far too busy to take much notice of me. I was the baby of the party, spoiled alike by the doctors and the patients. There was a hospital for wounded French officers nearby and I managed to wangle myself in there on the strength of my French and my 'good connections' as the doctor in charge was a terrible snob. I continued to stay with my aunt and work in the hospital until the end of the war, and the friendships I made amongst my patients made me more internationally-minded than ever.

In 1918 I was twenty, and Germany had lost the war. I had to return home. This seemed an alien world to me, and my parents seemed like strangers – and very dull strangers at that. I stuck it at home for another year, listening to lamentations, scoldings and reactionary talk.

In 1919, I was 21 and my own mistress. I came into my money and left home for good. To the horror and amazement of my unfortunate parents, I took a flat in Berlin and began to look round.

I suppose I had always been a Socialist and democrat, only I had not known it. But it did not take me long to find out when I got among free thinkers, who realised the desperate times we were living in. As soon as I met them I found the whole theory of socialism entirely fascinating; the more I thought about it, the more it appealed to me. It was the only political solution and at this time all the really exciting and worthwhile people that I met were confirmed socialists.

At first I was content to sit and listen to my new friends, but soon I wanted to take an active part in their work and so I went to Darmstadt where the Party was very active under the leadership of Dr Mierendorf and Professor Wrenger. Most of the people with whom I was working here were ex-soldiers who regarded socialism as the one hope for Germany. At the same time there were many extremists whose fanatic nationalist ideas were going to lead to trouble. Most of them were disgruntled officers (about the same age as myself) who had come home from the war and found it impossible to settle down again because they felt themselves to be 'outsiders' and 'misfits'. They were passionately and aggressively nationalist, far more so than the socialists, although they were not particularly internationally-minded either. But apart from their chronic discontent these firebrands had nothing to unite them except their fanatical nationalism. It was not long before we were having serious clashes with them in the universities and at meetings. Many of our leading socialists pointed out that if left to themselves, these tough national groups would be a potential danger to Germany and that we had to do everything we could to win them over to our side. But the trouble was that our programme was not sufficiently revolutionary and sensational to capture the imagination of these young malcontents. Also, I think, we lacked the tub-thumping technique which was needed to attract their attention. Our outfit was altogether too theoretical, too intellectual and too adult, and, from their point of view, much too complicated. They continued to remain an unsolved problem and one just had to hope that the more optimistic socialists were right; they claimed that these fanatical nationalists were merely hooligans who had such fun in the war that they did not want to stop, but that they would eventually outgrow their maladjustment.

But, then, in those days there was so much to hope for in Germany. As I listened to those wonderfully clever people expounding their theories of democracy, discussing economics, social science and planning the future of a new and better society, I felt that to be among them was the greatest privilege and the finest education that anyone could have. Once again I was very much the baby of the party; actually I was 22, but I looked sixteen. They all spoiled me just as in the hospital. I was madly enthusiastic and took everything deadly seriously. So it was natural I should come in for a good deal of teasing, which was good for me as it deflated my self-importance.

When I was 24 I decided to go and work in a factory. I felt that I could not be a good socialist without knowing what it was like to be a worker; also the idea of learning a trade appealed to me. It seemed to me the final smack in the eye for my upbringing and the tradition that I despised so much. So I went to Dresden and got a job in a furniture factory. Here the workers were very united and the socialist movement was strong. I liked the job and got on well. Of course, I kept the fact that I was a Baroness very quiet as I did not want my fellow workers to think of me as different from themselves, but the son of the owner of the factory found me out. He was very intrigued and amused and introduced me to his parents, after I had made him swear that my identity was never to be mentioned in the factory. I even temporarily converted him to socialism, and it was probably largely through this association with Georg that I became assistant designer in a comparatively short time. It was here that I discovered my natural talent for decorating and design.

I remained in Dresden for nearly two years, and when I decided to leave it was mainly on account of Georg, who was becoming more and more tiresome about wanting to marry me. We had a great deal of fun together, but to marry and settle down as the wife of an industrialist was the last thing I wanted to do.

What I did want to do now was to continue to study design at an art school. I had friends in Munich who had been wanting me for some time to come and join them and thither I went. Munich was incredibly gay and exciting. I worked at the Debschitz art school, and at the home of my friends I met writers, painters and politicians, and again I found myself sitting up all night setting the world to rights for, in spite of the gay and stimulating life we were leading, we knew very well how much the world needed improving.

It was some time during the first winter in Munich that I met Paul Hirschberg, who had recently been to prison with Adolf Hitler. We all knew of Hitler as the leader of one of the most reactionary groups and the tattered hero of the farcical putsch that had come to grief the year before. I was interested to meet Hirschberg. We had plenty to talk about and he introduced me to a number of friends, who were also in close contact with Hitler. Two of them, SA Führer Peter von Heidebeck and Gottfried Wagner, were very young and go-ahead and took it upon themselves to try to convert me to National Socialism.

We used to argue good naturedly by the hour. They were tremendously sure of themselves and so was I; it was quite natural that we should become good friends. Gottfried, especially, was so young and enthusiastic. He had a natural gaiety and freshness combined with a certain ruthlessness which I found most attractive. He and his circle were utterly different from anyone I had ever known before. I did not let him convert me to National Socialism but I had no objections to his falling in love with me.

This was no heart-stirring *grande passion*, but a gay adventure full of laughter and happiness. During the months that followed, politics tended to take second place in our relationship. Of course, he was as keen as ever about his work and I continued with my art classes and my political associations just the same, but in our spare time we went to the big Fasching fancy-dress balls together, motored up into the mountains for ice-yachting and skiing and sailing and swam in the Starnberg Lake.

Sometimes I used to tease Gottfried about the Nazi racial theories because they struck me as the silliest and most childish part of their programme. He used to get quite cross with me, pointing out that the National Socialist attitude to the Jews was only a minor detail that would certainly be dropped as the other difficulties were solved. He and the others were always reiterating that there were many points in the programme which were merely there as a window dressing and this was one of them. I remember one other thing that made him rather cross: Hitler's *Mein Kampf* was published during that summer [1925] and, of course, he wanted me to read it. I made a couple of attempts and then gave it up. He was dying to know what I thought of it. I told him I thought it was unmitigated balderdash. His smile faded. I added that it was also the dullest book I had ever read. He never forgave me for that.

Then I met Carlos von Löwenthal. He was living in Munich, sharing a flat with his sister, who was the widow of quite a well-known painter, killed in the war. Carlos had been in the Foreign Office until war broke out. He had been wounded in the lung and had not really been strong enough to do any war work since. He had tried various jobs, but had always had to give them up. When I met him he was preparing to sell their family house on the Starnberg Lake called Sonnenhof. The few transla- tions and articles he was able to write did not even earn him enough to live on, let alone keep up the house, which was deteriorating rapidly. I heard about it from some friends and I suddenly had a mad idea that I might buy it. I went to see it and fell in love with it. And when I met the owner I fell in love with him.

The house was a rambling eighteenth-century building with thick ivy framing the enormous arched windows. The gabled roofs were of pink tiles and wide, unkempt lawns stretched straight to the lake. Carlos was slightly built with large jet-black eyes, dark curling hair and a slim, decidedly Semitic nose.

The one thing I wanted was to live in that house with Carlos. But he was very dif- ficult to persuade as he did not consider that he was in a position to marry anybody and his pride would never allow him to marry a woman with more money than he had. I was used to getting my own way and this was a new experience. I found that his sister, Ruth, was an ardent socialist and set myself to getting her on my side. She was engaged to a young town councillor outside Munich, who was also a socialist, and I was able to point out how useful my political connections might be to him. But I grew to be genuinely fond of Ruth for her own sake. Now she, too, started trying to win Carlos over. The more opposition I encountered, the more determined I became, and for six months I worked harder than ever before in my life.

We were married in the New Year and for our honeymoon I took him to Switzerland. While we were there, I arranged for the main repairs to be done on the house, so that when we came back in the summer, we were able to move in. By the time I had fixed Sonnenhof the way I wanted it, it looked marvellous. This was my first full-dress interior decoration job and I think I never did a better one. Everybody who came to the house went mad about it, and I was, of course, very flattered. When my friends heard how little it had cost, many of them advised me to turn professional. Following this, I did one or two houses and flats for friends of ours. I found this great fun and Carlos was terribly proud of me and loved my doing it.

He was perfectly different now from when I had first known him. Then he had been bitter and reserved, perpetually on the defensive with a mordant and self-wounding sense of honour. Now he was really happy; he was back in the home he loved; he was much stronger and more active after the four months in Switzerland, and the feeling that he was soon to be able to work again had finally done away with his worries about being 'kept'. I think probably he was happy because he knew he made me happy. He got on wonderfully with all my socialist friends because, although he had been brought up in a conservative tradition, he was such an intelligent person and so tolerant that he was fundamentally the same as they were. Although he had always been far more interested in the arts than in politics, he found, as soon as he came into contact with them, an almost complete agreement with their views and philosophies. And, of course, I loved his friends, which meant that Sonnenhof was always full of people. Even my parents came down to see me. They were very surprised that I had married someone as respectable as Carlos; I am sure they never expected me to marry a gentleman, although it worried them a little that he was a Jew, and a good deal when they found out that he was tubercular. I believe my mother was secretly rather pleased by the idea of her daughter having a *salon*, although she would probably have disapproved strongly of some of the people who frequented it.

Gottfried was, of course, very upset when I left him for Carlos and I think that though he was always so broad-minded about the National Socialist racial theories, he deeply resented the fact that Carlos was a Jew. I did not see him for some time after I had married but I heard from him from time to time. Then one day in the winter, just before we were leaving for Switzerland, he arrived at Sonnenhof to pay a formal call. He was as gay and self-assured as ever and full of confidence about the future. Carlos was very reserved with him. I think he disapproved of his loudness and heartiness and probably disapproved of him for being a member of a professedly anti-Jewish party. But Carlos was quite polite and Gottfried certainly never noticed anything.

When we returned from Switzerland the following spring the mountains did not seem to have done Carlos so much good. The Swiss doctors were not so pleased with him as they had been before. Next year he had a bad haemorrhage in the late autumn and we went a month earlier. And then, in March 1928, it became obvious that Carlos would never come back to Sonnenhof. The doctors said his only chance was to stay in Switzerland indefinitely.

I went back to Munich and sold Sonnenhof lock, stock and barrel to the highest bidder. After that I moved to Berlin and started to set myself up as a professional interior decorator. With my social connections it was easier than I had ever dreamed. I took a showroom and offices on the Kurfürstendamm and my staff increased almost every week. I worked with architects, art dealers and wallpaper designers and gradually built up an extensive reputation.

A lot of money was made in Germany at that time and it was surprising how quickly the last war had been forgotten – at least by the well-to-do people. There was still unemployment but all the industrialists and also my socialist friends thought we had got over the worst. My friends were busy building up their careers. With most of us at this time there was a good deal more careerism than socialism. The initial drive and enthusiasm of the social democrats seemed to have petered out and the Party and its leaders lapsed into complacency and smugness. The fine idealism of our youth had been blurred and dissipated by comfort and success. This was brought home to me at a party given by socialist friends of mine. I met here a well known young lawyer, Dr Wolf von Kruger, who had been a prominent member of the Party for many years. He seemed so young and enthusiastic and real that suddenly I saw the others for what they were, and saw too how much we had changed and how much we had lost. Our fires had gone out. But mine was ready to be kindled again by him.

He said that everything really important that the Party had stood for had been forgotten. The Party had not bothered o keep the idea of democracy and socialism alive. People had forgotten why they were social democrats and as soon as anything went wrong, which he was certain would be very soon indeed they would turn to newer and more vital doctrines. The leaders of the Party were clever and intelligent isolationists. They had no connection with the ordinary people who made up the rank and file. The National Socialist leaders and the communist leaders went into the streets, into the cafes and into the homes of the people, and talked to them in their own language – that was why these parties would grow and increase and eventually would oust the moribund social democrats. For a moment I felt almost like taking up the challenge and throwing myself heart and soul into the propagation of these ideas. That evening I felt again the excitement of having new tremendous ideas inside me and of wanting to spread them.

But I was too busy to feel like that for long. Commissions kept pouring in and whenever I could snatch a few days I would go to see Carlos in Switzerland.

Trade had steadily improved since the inflation and people had been building up their careers and businesses without looking to left or right. Just when they thought that everything was running smoothly and the past could be forgotten, the whole economic structure broke down.

Every one of my customers and also my friends were completely shaken by the utter collapse of the fool's paradise in which they had been living for the past four years. Businesses, private banks, clubs, restaurants went bankrupt and the national banks closed down. Unemployment reached almost five million. In a panic all my customers and friends began to sell their cars and move out of their large houses and sack their servants. Everyone was talking about economising. Every conversation had something to do with the crisis; wherever you went, whatever you did, you could never get away from it. Everybody talked and talked and did nothing, and my Party was one of the worst offenders.

But I was luckier than most people in the luxury business as I was able to adapt myself to the changing conditions. I joined up with one of the architects I had previously worked for and who was now converting the stately homes of Germany into small flats. Where before I had designed palatial ballrooms and luxury boudoirs, I now did a very good line in bed-sitting rooms and utility kitchens. Before long I found myself miraculously weathering the storm.

I knew quite a few of the people who were in power now. They belonged to a coalition of centre parties, led by Bruening. Most of the members of this cabinet were blatant opportunists edging discreetly left or right, manipulating affairs, pulling strings behind the scenes, playing political cat's cradle just to suit their own private ends. Bruening's government did nothing to cope with the crisis. What particularly annoyed von Kruger and me was the complete inactivity and undecidedness with which the social democrats tolerated these conditions. After all, we were the biggest party in Germany and most of the civil service and administrative positions were filled by our men. And yet we shrank from responsibility and did nothing. Our leaders were frightened of losing their jobs if they opposed the Bruening Centre Coalition. They were frightened that if they did something on their own the right wing of the Coalition might join up with the Nazis and other national groups. They were frightened to join with communists because that might lead to revolution. So they did nothing. They just sat up grumbling, while things got worse and worse.

I had managed to save myself and my firm from the threat of bankruptcy, but even so things were beginning to be difficult. Work came in only slowly and one had always the dreadful bother of cutting prices and cheeseparing on expenses.

I went up to Davos as usual in 1932 to spend Christmas with Carlos. He was obviously very ill but he insisted on my returning to Berlin after three weeks to look after the business. Almost as soon as I had returned there was another government crisis, this time even more serious than before. The non-party Chancellor, von Schleicher, had been attempting half-heartedly to cooperate with the social democrats and the trades unions. [Kurt von Schleicher was the last Chancellor of the Weimar Republic and a prominent victim of the Night of the Long Knives, 30 June 1934, gunned down with his wife.] This was the opportunity the nationalist right wing had been waiting for. A German Nationalist bloc, with President Hindenburg and the Junkers, forced von Schleicher to resign and threw their weight on the side of the extremist National Socialist Party, who they thought would represent their interests. The leader of the Party, Adolf Hitler, then became Chancellor.

Wolf was in a terrible state and so were all my other socialist friends. But Wolf was the only one who suggested doing anything. Even he said it was really too late, but in spite of this everything had to be risked now, even civil war, if the Fatherland were to be saved. Only a few days later, socialists and communists were being arrested and beaten up. Wolf said there was nothing else to do but to fight it out in the streets. He was certain that once the Social Democrat Reichsbanner started the battle, the communist Red Front would join and the two together with the possible help of the Reichswehr and the trade unions, who could declare a general strike, might then be able to force Hitler from power and conserve a democratic form of government. It was the only hope. But however Wolf argued and pleaded, none of the social democrats would do anything. They did not seem to want to do anything, but instead hid themselves behind a smokescreen of wishful thinking. They said that Hitler would not last long anyway; that he and his Party were too incompetent to cope with the economic situation; and that his chief policy was simply a rearmament plan which would never be permitted by the foreign powers. They expected that Hitler would quarrel with the Junkers and that the German Nationalists under Hugenberg who had formed the government together with Hitler, would revolt. They were taking themselves into a fool's paradise of their own making. They would say anything, believe anything, rather than face the unwelcome possibility that they might have to *do* something. But even though the Party leaders and the intellectuals were so cowardly and ineffective I could not possibly imagine that the ordinary members of the Party would allow the Weimar Republic and democracy and everything they stood for to die without a fight. I felt that the ordinary German people, in whom I had always believed, would see the position in its proper proportion and save the country.

So I turned to the rank and file of the Party. I asked my employees what they thought of the situation. All of them had been with me for many years and I was on very friendly terms with them. But when I talked to them I found them quite as weary and resigned as I had found their leaders. Most of them were good trade unionists and social democrats and I had made certain that there were no Nazis amongst them. My carpenter, who had been with me since I first came to Berlin, would hardly talk at all. He said he had finished with politics. He had had enough. Whatever he and his mates said or tried to do in the past had never come off.

'I don't care; let someone else do the dirty work now.'

My painter foreman only said: 'Nothing can be worse than things are now,' and another one said: 'It don't pay; I've been backing the wrong horse for too long now and now the government puts you in clink if you so much as open your trap. One of my mates was taken to Goebbels' headquarters in the Hedlmannstrasse. He was only giving out leaflets for the Union meeting. He got a terrible beating up and they kept him there all night.' Others just said: 'Why should we worry, he won't last any longer than the others have done. Give him enough rope and he'll hang himself just like all the other reactionaries. Only socialism can save the situation. We can wait.' I got a worse shock when my plasterer, whom I knew to a very active Party member, just mumbled: 'Let's give him a chance. After all the Nazis are socialists of a kind.' Nobody seemed to be surprised at his statement. When I left the workshop, I knew there was not much hope for us.

A few weeks later I received an SOS from Davos, and when I got there the doctors told me that Carlos would only live for a few more days. He died a week before the elections. Now that Carlos was dead there was really no reason for me to feel that I must go back to Germany. Then I suddenly remembered that the next day was the general election and the one thing I had to do was vote. I packed hurriedly and left the same evening.

A couple of days later Wolf came round to see me. He told me that, although the Nazi Government had been confirmed by the election, he felt that he had to make the last attempt at saving Germany. He was going to tour Germany almost immediately to warn his friends and political contacts of the seriousness of the situation and try to persuade them to give up their official jobs and make a concerted stand. If he saw them personally, he might be able to dissuade them from working with the Nazis right from the start. I too felt this was the last chance and I asked Wolf if I could come with him. Obviously the more people we could persuade the better, and I had lots of friends too, all over the place. Anyhow I could do no harm and might do some good. Just then, I didn't care what happened to my business. I had nothing to make money for, now that Carlos had gone. Almost three weeks later we started on our trip.

None of my friends approved of this journey. They were shocked by my going off alone with a man so soon after my husband's death. And they were incredulous at my insistence that I was going because I felt it was the only thing to do. 'A little late, my dear, aren't you?' Most of them had resigned themselves to the situation. But because they felt a little uneasy and more than a little shamefaced at their own cowardice they turned on me and told me I was being a fool politically and implied that morally I was being something worse. I didn't care. I believed firmly both in our message and in Wolf.

The first man we went to see was Ruth's husband, Max Loebbecke, who was now the chief burgomaster of Esslingen. Wolf put the position to him very clearly. Would he, a man who had been working for the socialists and democratic idea for so long, help to further a programme like that of the Nazis by remaining in office? What they intended to do was there for anyone to read in Hitler's *Mein Kampf*. This explicitly demanded the overthrow of the constitution and the establishment of a totalitarian state; the censorship of opinion and the abolition of the rights of the individual; and the suppression or domination of the so-called inferior non-Aryan races – which meant that Ruth would be officially an outlaw. All this was quite openly admitted by the Nazis. Nobody could say that they had not been perfectly frank from the start. And now every German who cooperated with them would be to a lesser or greater degree responsible for their programme. He who was not for them, must be against them. No one could afford to be neutral. Max resigned then and there, and he and Ruth joined us on our crusade.

But he was unique, for as we continued through Germany calling sometimes at small villages, sometimes at larger towns, eve found hardly anyone who was willing to agree with us, plenty to talk, but few were prepared to act. And they all with one consent began to make excuses. The first said, 'I have bought a piece of ground and I must needs go and see it.' Another said, 'I have bought five yoke of oxen and I go to prove them.' And another said, 'I have married a wife, and therefore I cannot come.'

We said goodbye to Max and Ruth and motored sadly back to Berlin. At least we had tried. Now it was in the lap of the gods. Maybe our friends were right and the Nazis would overreach themselves and collapse. But we were unhopeful. We now turned to our own affairs. I had been in love with Wolf for some time and now that Carlos was dead there was nothing to stop our setting up house together. We were as happy as we could be in our small circle and tried not to think of affairs outside. But they intruded nevertheless.

Before long the Nazis began to make overtures to Wolf. He was a brilliant man and they knew it. They wanted him on their side and they did everything they could to win him over. They even offered him a ministry in the Wuertemberg Landtag. When he refused and they found bribery did not work, they tried blackmail. However, he was too clever for them and they never managed to prove anything definite against him. But they got their revenge by preventing him from working at all. Under a clause in the constitution which prohibited people classed as 'politically unreliable' from holding important positions, they had him dismissed from a number of appointments.

One night we had just finished dinner when there was a ring at the door. I was told that a lady had called who would not give her name. To my surprise it was Ruth. She looked terrified and could hardly be persuaded to take off her coat and sit down. She said she had left Max. Their life had been made intolerable by the Nazis. Because of Max's conduct in resigning and opposing the regime he had been taken away for questioning at the Party headquarters and they had returned him in the last stages of exhaustion and with his body a mass of bruises. They had warned him that unless he got rid of his 'Jewish concubine' they would put him out of harm's way for good. Ruth had known there was only one thing to do, and, without telling Max, she had done it. She asked me to find her somewhere to stay in Berlin. Of course, I said she must stay with us, and Wolf agreed. We had plenty of room and we were only too pleased to be able to help her. She said that if Max tried to find her we must say that she had gone abroad. But he never did.

Towards the end of 1933, trade began to revive, but the people who now gave me commissions were the big Nazis, who were beginning to feather their nests. They felt they ought to have their houses furnished and decorated by me, just as the leaders of other parties did in the past. It was difficult for me to refuse them but I kept to my resolution to have nothing to do with the new regime. But matters were brought to a head when Goering sent for me to do some of the interior decoration at Karinhall, his country estate. I did not know what to do. Even before 1933, Goering had approached me several times and asked me to do jobs for him, but I had always refused. Now it was different. This was an official request and to refuse it would mean hurting Goering's official vanity, and everybody knew what that meant. Night after night I sat arguing with Wolf and Ruth. But in reality I was arguing with myself and no one could help me. I knew that National Socialism was an evil, that innocent people of the highest rank and intelligence were being persecuted and imprisoned without trial; I had seen of their methods in what they had done to Wolf and Max and Ruth, and my fondness for her had made me nauseated and disgusted by the virulence of their anti-Jewish campaign.

On the other hand I loved my work: the revival of trade and the vast building programme meant assured success for my business. And then I had to admit that I loved my independent life and enjoyed so much being at the top of my profession that I could not give it up, which is what refusal would inevitably mean. It was not only myself I had to think of. We had to have some source of income. Neither Ruth nor Wolf was working and although Wolf had quite a large sum in investments one could no rely on this. But, of course, I could not discuss this point with Wolf. Finally, I made my decision and both Wolf and Ruth realised that I had no option. But we all felt very depressed about it.

From then onwards I met Goering fairly regularly and I must admit that he was a very pleasant and easy-going client. He could be completely charming if he liked a person, and he made it quite clear that he liked me very much. Before long there was nothing in connection with furniture and design he would do without me.

Goering was very impressed by my social standing and also by my independence. He knew exactly what I thought about the Nazis, but it never seemed to worry him.

All his personal acquaintances had sooner or later to pass one of his tests of bravery which he always enjoyed immensely and the result of which made or finished his friendship with him. Mine came when one day I was in his enormous sitting room. From the far side appeared his pet lion Caesar (he always had a pet lion called Caesar). He prowled stealthily towards me; knowing Hermann's peculiarities I forced myself to keep still and smile. Only when the lion was within six feet of me and was crouching ready to jump, did he send him back with a crack of the whip. Smiling broadly with genuine pleasure he said:

'I like you, my little Baronin Mausilein. You are as brave as you are beautiful.'

About this time Streicher's crudely anti-Semitic paper *Der Stürmer* had published an attack on me saying that I was living with a Jewess and a communist. I was absolutely furious and a little worried that it might prejudice my work, but Goering took no notice and instead entrusted me with the decor for his 'Grand Opera' wedding to Emmy Sonnemann.

Business in these days was amazingly good and the Nazis, contrary to all our expectations, did really seem to have pulled off the economic recovery of Germany. But their successes in other fields were less satisfying. When I wondered about those socialist friends of mine who were vanishing with such terrifying rapidity (one never knew when one rang up if they would still be there or not) my hair stood on end and I would break out in a cold sweat. I would storm and rant about it to Wolf, who seemed now to be strangely resigned to all the horrible things which were going on around us. Perhaps 'resigned' is not the word, but like Ruth he now adopted a kind of bitter silence and completely refused to talk or argue. As far as he was concerned the subject was closed; and, of course, he was right. The only possible attitude for people in our position was to turn our back on a situation we were powerless to help. Thinking about it, talking about it, got one nowhere. I threw myself more and more into my work. There is no doubt that success is a very effective dope.

Then, in 1935, the Nuremberg Laws were directed against Jews, half-Jews and quarter-Jews, and Ruth was officially classed as an unwanted outcast. Naturally we told her it could make no difference to her while she was with us. But the strange and dreadful thing was that Wolf was the first one to suffer from the effects of the new legislation. The Nazis now seized on it chance to pay him out for refusing to cooperate with them and daring to turn down their offers. Of course, everyone knew of our relationship, but now they pretended to believe that Wolf was really living with Ruth. This was not only very hurtful to my pride but was dreadful for Wolf, who knew it was no use even trying to deny it. Their persecution came in a series of sadistic pinpricks which they obviously enjoyed immensely. First came some more filthy jibes in *Der Stürmer*. Then nightly anonymous phone calls to Wolf: 'Throw the filthy Jewish slut out of your bed!' followed by threatening letters and obscene labels stuck to the windscreen of his car. We soon noticed that our flat was being watched, and we found that the servants and my employees had been questioned. And, before long, the Ortsgruppenführer of the local Party group sent one of his cronies to call. This gentleman pointed out that the Ortsgruppenführer had already several items on his files which could easily result in the most unpleasant consequences, and the Ortsgruppenführer would like a promise that Wolf would in future behave himself and give no further trouble. The Gestapo were, of course, also interested in this case and if Wolf would make a substantial donation towards the Party funds, the Ortsgruppenführer might see his way to put in a good word with them.

In all my dealings with them I had always found the older and higher Party members a fairly reasonable crowd of people. It was the newer type of people, the freshly recruited SA and SS men, the officious concierge in the block of flats, the. ambitious small tradesmen and petty-minded little people who were not even in the Party, who behaved most spitefully.

A little later Wolf was summoned to the Gestapo. There he was told that according to their information he was associating with enemies of the State and furthermore having irregular intercourse with a non-Aryan. He was kept there for six hours and then dismissed with a warning that if he continued with this blatant *Rassenschande* [racial pollution] he would know what to expect. But in spite of this dreadful and harassed life Wolf refused to allow Ruth to go away.

But it was obviously very unsatisfactory for her, and also a little dangerous for my own position. The Nazis these days were doing exactly as they liked, and if one of them had taken a fancy to my business they would have liked nothing better than to use Ruth as a lever. In fact *Der Stürmer* did try to suggest that as I had been married to a Jew and lived with a Jewess I was little better than one myself. So Ruth decided it would be best for her to leave Germany altogether. She had an aunt in Switzerland to whom she would go, and although it was difficult for her to get an exit permit I got in touch with Gottfried Wagner and he wangled one quite easily. Wolf was quite annoyed at my going to Gottfried, but after all it was only for Ruth's sake.

My business went on flourishing and increasing as the rearmament programme got into full swing during 1937. Big business men and industrialists and high Party members made fortunes, and unemployment was a thing of the past. We were moving towards a prosperity which the Reich had never seen before, and no one and nothing seemed to be able to stem the surging tide of German influence in all world affairs. But things were getting very difficult for Wolf. The Nazis were determined to get him. He was continually being sent for by the Gestapo and we even caught one of the maids taking down our conversation. Periodic attacks still appeared in *Der Stürmer* and we felt that our whole happiness was being poisoned.

We were both at the end of our endurance when Wolf suggested that we should leave Germany together and look around abroad for a chance to emigrate. But to leave Germany as late as 1938, even for a holiday, which was all we were officially proposing to do, was not going to be easy for either of us, and Wolf's passport had not been renewed because he was classed as 'unreliable' and mine had been retained by the Gestapo. For the next few weeks I pleaded, bribed and wangled. I went to Gottfried and tried to get his help, but he dared do nothing. Then I summoned up courage to go to Goering. I knew he liked me and he said he would help me. He could do nothing openly but he sent me to the smaller officials who could be trusted to take bribes. We received our passports eventually through the *Spionage Abwehr* [anti-espionage organisation of the Army]. The counter-espionage organisation of the Reichswehr was fighting a relentless battle with the Gestapo as to who should control the vast German secret service organisation. At that time, the Spionage Abwehr, under Canaris, was still powerful and Wolf got his passport ostensibly to work for them in Switzerland. All this was, of course, only a blind to deceive the Gestapo. By the summer of 1938 all was arranged and we crossed the frontier at Basle in my new supercharged Mercedes without any trouble whatsoever.

The next few weeks passed like a dream. We had forgotten what it was like to be on our own and free. For the first time in years there was no tension and fear in our lives and we were very happy. We motored slowly through Switzerland and into France. All the time we visited old friends, who were now living as refugees, to find out the best way to arrange our own emigration. But my hopes steadily faded. The more I saw of these refugees, the less I could imagine myself in their position.

None of them had been able to make a home in their new country and they were not even living as visitors or guests. They were looked upon as an unwanted and very tiresome burden. All these friends of mine, people who had the best brains of the German nation, who had held most prominent positions, now sat around all day in the cafes, isolated in their own little circles, talking of nothing but hatred and spite towards Germany. I knew I should not be able to stand this for long. After all, Germany was still my Fatherland, even if, at this moment, things were very deplorable there. I could not bear listening to their ever-recurring tirades of hatred and accusation. And then when I realised that I should not even be allowed to work abroad I knew that it was no use. I could not stand the thought of living in a furnished little room, doing nothing but sitting, talking and remembering, of being a poor, pitiful refugee from the country I could not help loving and calling my Fatherland. Wolf agreed with me that it was better to suffer in one's own country, the country one loved, than to be filled with hatred and resentment in an alien land. So we decided to return and face the old struggle once more.

But when we reached the frontier Wolf made me stop the car. I turned to him for an explanation. For a moment he looked into my eyes without speaking. Then – 'Goodbye,' he said, 'enjoy your lovely Fatherland.' I couldn't believe him. Then I pleaded, argued, cajoled, all for nothing. I pointed out how pitiful a refugee existence would be, I told him he was running away from his responsibilities, I told him I couldn't bear to go on alone, I even told him it was unfair to me – I should be blamed for his not returning. But he was as stubborn as an ox and I had to leave him there. I watched him receding in my rear-view mirror, and my eyes were misty with tears both of sorrow and vexation. It was so unnecessary.

And I was right about its being dangerous for me. I was summoned to the Gestapo headquarters and accused of conniving at the escape of an enemy of the State. I managed to bite back my automatic instinct to defend Wolf. It would have been no use anyway. I coolly answered that I was not responsible for Herr von Kruger's actions and managed get a threatening tone into my suggestion that they might ask *Spionage Abwehr*. This annoyed them very much but did divert their minds from me, and warning me that if I set a foot wrong in future they would see to me; they let me go.

Now that I was alone, with only myself to look after, without responsibility for anyone else, I felt I could make the best of the situation. I was terribly busy in my firm, orders for jobs came in as never before; I worked hard and played hard, and I did not want time to think. I started seeing Gottfried Wagner again. He used to take me out and come to my flat quite a lot, so did one or two others of the better-educated and more presentable Nazis. The Goerings still invited me and I stayed from time to time at Karinhall. I think Goering was very surprised that I had come back to Germany and I think he rather admired me for it. Courage was a fetish with him. We still talked about politics and it still amused him to argue with me, but from time to time he would toss in a warning and say: 'You know, Mausilein, I'll look after you as long as I can, but if you go too far you will end up in a KZ [concentration camp].' When I answered that I was prepared to risk it, there would always be someone to call off the lion at the last minute, he would roar with laughter and smack me heartily and playfully on my seat.

I was never afraid of Goering or of any of the high-up Nazis whom I knew personally. They were not in the least touchy on the subject of their credo. In fact I was always amazed at their cynicism about most of the Nazi philosophy. They admitted quite freely that the Hitler salute, the blood and soil, German sacred destiny, Jewish-communist world domination and the innumerable oaths of allegiance, were nothing but so much eyewash; necessary only for the masses, to keep them marching blindly in the right direction. They only gave lip-service to these things, because they were necessary and because they had proved to be eminently successful from the point of view of their own careers. It was also necessary that the masses and the rank and file of the Party should regard the Führer as a deity. But although these Nazis had an enormous respect for Hitler and were prepared to follow him unquestioningly, it was simply that they believed this to be a good thing and they were going to hold to it. I always found the frankness with which they admitted all this completely disarming.

I had been away for the absorption of Czechoslovakia into the Reich and so missed the excitement. But when the trouble over the Polish corridor brewed up I was in the thick of it. Gottfried proved to me how ridiculous it was for Germany to be cut in two by an arbitrarily imposed strip of Polish territory. But I thought it was going a little too far to go to war over it. But it did seem the only way out and could in any case not last longer than a few days. Gottfried was quite certain that it would end there; Britain and France had given in easily enough before, why should they fight now?

But fight they did and for a time everyone felt very apprehensive. Nevertheless, life went on. I was still working very hard and enjoying myself tremendously. Then came the shattering victories over Britain, France and Norway and everyone suddenly felt that a weight had been lifted. We celebrated night after night and were waiting only for the final victory. The Wehrmacht and the Luftwaffe were the heroes of the day and not even the Party uniform could compete with it. Gottfried had been promoted SS General and was stationed in Paris, where I was able to visit him from time to time. I tried to look up some of my friends who had been living there, but it was no use. They had all moved.

Most women were now being deluged with presents from their menfolk in the occupied countries. My typists and salesgirls appeared in silver foxes from Norway, shoes from Italy, silk frocks from France. Furs became so ordinary that I was tempted to stop wearing mine. There was so much French perfume that the whole of Berlin smelt like a hairdresser's. Girls who had never even seen a fur coat suddenly appeared dolled up like duchesses, looking like servants who had made free with their mistresses' wardrobes. Money was circulating freely and food and luxuries were flowing in from abroad.

I was showered with invitations. Horcher's and Kempinsky's were so full that it was impossible to get a table even if you were well known and had reserved in advance. People queued up to get into the nightclubs. I went often to the Tusculum, which was an imitation of Horcher's with candlelight and real Persian rugs. The food here was fantastically good – which was not surprising as the high-up leaders had taken to giving their official dinners here. I remember one night there with Gottfried who came back for a couple of days from Prague. He told me about orgies with Heydrich and how things had got so violent that even he could not stay the course and used to go home before the end. Gottfried was very candid about it and a trifle disapproving. But like everyone else he was enjoying the war immensely. The catchword of the time was 'Enjoy the war! Peace will be terrible!' It was impossible not to join in.

Everyone was having to employ foreign workers. There were Frenchmen and Belgians and Dutchmen and Norwegians and Poles and Czechs. One took them for granted as part of the wartime scene. Few people bothered about them or wondered about them. They were just there, representatives of an undercurrent of misery which nobody cared to think about. We were the conquerors and the foreigners were there to do the work. Germany was now becoming the Greater Germany in fact. The wildest prophecies of the Leader were coming true.

I saw a good deal at this time of Willi Muller – a charming and successful businessman. He had textile factories near Bremen and before the war had manufactured a number of my own furnishing materials. Now his firm produced most of the material for army uniforms. He had moved to Warsaw and was in charge of a group of factories in the Ghetto worked mainly by Jews. The orders were to work the employees unremittingly until they broke down. Willi was a member of the SS and had made his fortune very largely through the Nazis – but he prided himself on his humanity. He boasted that his workers were treated better than any others. He saw to it personally that they had better bread rations and an extra plate of soup. As a result they worked much harder and his production was always well over schedule.

Willi felt that he had done his duty by his own slaves and the misery of all the others was something he never thought about. I tried to point this out to him when we talked, as we sometimes did, but he was surrounded by a glow of self-righteousness and I could make no impression on him. I knew the Gestapo were always on the watch but I was quite sure that with my connections nothing could happen to me.

Every day things were getting worse for the Jews, just as they seemed to be getting better for us. The ones that were left were only allowed now to go shopping between four and five in the afternoon. They were turned out of their flats and life was made impossible for them, but they were not allowed to commit suicide. If, as they sometimes did, they managed to get Veronal [the first commercially marketed barbiturate] disguised as toothpaste, Jewish doctors would be forced to try to revive them.

It was not to be wondered at that those who minded about this sort of thing tried to think about it as little as possible. The best antidote was to celebrate the current victories as thoroughly as possible. We continued to celebrate the general victory and the imminent end of the war throughout 1940. Although England was still officially at war with us we hardly noticed that we were at war with England, except for pictures in the papers that showed how terribly the Londoners were suffering from our air raids. We had generally a soft spot for the British. They were our favourite enemy but, at the same time, the one of which we were most jealous. That we had beaten them showed more clearly than anything just how clever we were, for at no time had we ever regarded them as stupid. They were an enemy worthy of us and they received our admiration for remaining in the war without in any way worrying us.

In 1941 I spent my holidays at the Casino Hotel in Zoppot on the Baltic, which was packed with officers on leave, beautiful women and a delegation of Spaniards learning German. When the Russian campaign began, we were all a little startled but not really worried, and everyone continued to enjoy their holidays, drinking the best wines, eating crayfish, lobster and caviar, playing tennis, sailing and riding. And Berlin was as gay as ever when I returned, and I was as busy as ever. Our armies marched to within 70 kilometres of Moscow. The great hope that the Russian people were waiting to be delivered from communism and would end the war of their own accord did not materialise. This was disappointing. It meant that one could see no immediate end to the war which we had already considered to be finished.

Now people started asking questions about England again. Not that the air raids in themselves would be enough to win the war, but it was worrying to think that we might have to submit to them indefinitely. The propaganda services hardly ever mentioned England. When they did they were inclined to be contradictory. English ships seemed to have several lives and had a way of being sunk three or four times. One did not like this very much, because it indicated that someone was telling lies. It was worrying to think that there was anything to tell lies about.

When America entered the war it caused a lot of serious thinking. People said that once America was interested in Europe our prospects were not too bright. Many of these same people began as discreetly as possible to leave the Party and they were, of course, despised as rats leaving the sinking ship. It was about this time that Willi decided to leave the SS.

By the time the heavy English air raids of 1943 finally put a stop to the luxury life, our surface gaiety had worn very thin indeed. It was almost a relief to pack one's good clothes into an air-raid suitcase and stop pretending. After the big attack on Hamburg in July 1943, Berlin realised that it was next on the danger list. In this raid there were more dead than there had ever been before and many of the terrified survivors arrived in Berlin in their nightdresses. It had been terribly hot and the strong wind that was blowing at the time had helped to spread the fires. Goebbels made a speech after this raid and asked everyone who was not working to leave Berlin. And so began the great exodus to the east and safety. We who were left behind prepared for the worst. The SS and Gestapo were spying like mad. If anyone said anything they were arrested out of hand. But the people who were enjoying themselves most were the Luftschutz, who suddenly became the most important department. Everyone had to help with the building of the shelters and attend lectures about poison gas. Even the children were trained as air-raid helpers.

What caused a good deal of alarm was the news, first spread by the BBC, that the foreign diplomats were leaving Berlin. They were followed before long by other official services, most of which were transferred to East Prussia. We went on waiting and waiting and still nothing happened until 22 November. What we had not expected was that everything would come down at once. All the other air raids that one knew of had been longer but far less concentrated. This time the whole thing was over in half an hour. But while it was on it was like nothing one had ever heard before. I was dining with some friends in Lichterfelde that night and, although the main attack was concentrated on the Hansaviertel, about fifteen kilometres away, the noise was so great that we literally could not hear ourselves speak.

From then on the radio began its routine warnings about the arrival of enemy planes. All day long one would hear 'Planes coming over Western Germany. Planes coming over Western Germany.' It was a dreary accompaniment to everyday life. The best thing to do was to turn off the wireless and forget about it till it happened. The more cautious people who kept their wireless going night and day took their cue when the enemy planes got as far as Magdeburg. With their packed suitcases they would make off to the nearest shelter.

I called a meeting of my employees to decide if it would be advisable for our firm to evacuate Berlin. We were in the middle of discussions when my secretary burst in looking rather worried and asked me to come immediately because someone was there to see me. I went out and was politely greeted by two Gestapo men who asked me in all civility if I would mind coming with them for interrogation. My heart stopped beating and for a second I had a wild impulse to turn and run. They had chosen their time well. Goering had not been seen since the bombing and Gottfried was in Prague. A cold and numbing dread crept over me. It was my turn at last. The lion had sprung and there was no one to call him off. I asked them if I could use the telephone to let my family and my friends know that I was leaving. And I knew their answer before they told me. Like a chill nightmare I saw myself walk slowly out of my office and get into the big black Gestapo car that was waiting. I felt the terrified stares of my employees at windows and doors. Sitting between the two Gestapo men I was dimly aware of their loud and cheerful conversation. They were saying jocularly that there was nothing to worry about from now on, as everything would be taken care of by them. 'I'm sure you'll love it with us, Baronin. You won't have to bother about pulling strings and having affairs with the high and mighty. Everything is going to be arranged for you and we assure you you are going to be very happy.' They were still chuckling with laughter when we arrived at the Alexanderplatz prison.

I was led in front of a Gestapo official who inspected my papers. When I asked him why I was there he told me I was a notorious reactionary and had been known to have helped Jews and communists to escape and had spread subversive and lying opinions about the Nazi state. I knew better than to argue. They had got me and that was that.

I moved dully from room to room. In the first room all my rings and jewels were taken from me. A shiny-faced SS man tried my rings on and asked me if they were real. I told him his girlfriend would know. In the next room I had to sign a printed form: 'This is to certify that I donate all my money and all my belongings to the State to be used for social purposes.' In the next room they handed me another document to sign. There seemed no point in reading it. Then I suddenly noticed the words 'Old People's Home'. The form read 'I hereby declare that for the rest of my life I am willing to retire to an Old People's Home.' A grey terror took possession of me. I felt a great weight on my heart and a wave of self-pitying grief. They were going to bury me alive. From now on I did not care any more. I was pushed from room to room signing things, being searched, being examined and undressed and finally led to a cell.

Soon after I had a visitor who seemed to come for no other reason than to tell me that my employees from the firm had cried when they heard of my fate, and that they had packed two suitcases and sent parcels with food for me to take on the journey, and that the Gestapo was very grateful to have received these donations. According to him I was in luck all round. Didn't I realise that I was not being sent to a common concentration camp like Ravensbrück, but to Theresienstadt – the Gestapo's pride and showpiece, the model concentration camp in Germany? Now it slowly dawned on me that perhaps my friends had done something after all. At least it meant that I had a chance to survive.

A few days later I began my journey. I went by tram to the Anhalter Bahnhof with a Gestapo man at each side. As soon as I got settled in a first class compartment an SS officer came in and shouted that the Baronin von Löwenthal had to travel third class to the concentration camp. I didn't move. It was so long since I had heard my married name. Then I realised they meant me. I was pushed in with fifteen very old and very poor-looking Jews. I had never seen such a picture of complete and absolute fear and hopelessness. These people had been waiting for this year after year. It had been their only thought, their ever-present fear. And now at last it had happened. I felt suddenly young and normal and alive. During the last few years I had never thought about the future. I had been working and living and enjoying myself, always in the present. I had had no time to worry or be afraid.

I never had a chance to get any of my belongings and had walked to the station exactly as I was when I was arrested. No hat, no gloves, not even a handbag. But the other people in the compartment had managed to drag an incredible amount of trunks, parcels and odd possessions with them. I could quite imagine how they must have packed and unpacked and changed and discussed what they should take. This for them had been their last chance to keep something of the past with them. They were sweet to me and offered me all sorts of things. I remember a little old man who kept insisting on my sitting on his cushion. It was an ugly little thing with some faded *petit-point* embroidery, but I had to give in just to please him.

None of these people knew exactly where we were going, and I was glad to be able to tell them that things would not be too bad because we were going to Theresienstadt. Their faces lighted up immediately. For them this meant the same as it did for me – the chance to survive. Their spirits rose and they began talking and telling me about their lives, their suffering, their homes and their families. To these old people my news had almost the same effect as if they were set free and a new future was before them.

At Leitmeritz the train stopped and we were dragged out by shouting and bawling SS men. It was like being abruptly awakened from a dream. We had to stand in a row on the platform and a vicious-looking little SS Oberst swinging a cane strutted up and down the line, prodding and peering at us. He walked up to me and said: 'Hmm, our special case, the bawdy Baroness from Berlin,' and suddenly snarled: 'Stand straight, you old slut, who do you think you are?' I was so surprised that without thinking I shouted back at him: 'How dare you speak to me like that?' and to everybody's surprise his jaw dropped. Then he stuck his chest out and put on a very hollow-looking bravado act and warned me very sternly but quite civilly that it would not be long before I was put in my place and lost my superior manner. But, strangely enough, from then on he behaved quite decently to me and treated me quite differently from the others. I did not want to be treated as a special case and in reality this was rather a disadvantage because for a long time many people in the camp thought that I was a spy, especially as it was a camp almost entirely for Jews, which was another of the little ideas the Gestapo had thought out specially for me.

From the station we had a long, long trek to the camp. The old people would not have been able to stand this even without their precious bundles. But they were driven stumbling on and on through the muddy lanes and over fields, pushed, kicked and screamed at by the young guards. Many collapsed and were left to die where they fell. After twelve hours we reached the camp. The model camp, the place with so many advantages, the place that left us a chance to survive.

For many days I was in a kind of trance, unable to think either about myself or about my surroundings. My only impression during those first days was a swirling jumble of crowds and crowds of old people swarming sickeningly together like a plague of grey flies on some indescribable carrion. Wherever one looked one saw faces. Wherever one moved one touched arms and legs and bodies. Enveloping it all was a hideous sickly smell of utter and ultimate degradation.

After moving from hut to hut, each more overcrowded than the last, we arrived at last in a house where in normal times a family of eight or nine might have lived: Now there were 325 people locked up in it with no beds or furniture. There were only two lavatories, for which there was a perpetual queue day and night. Rows of old ragged men and women were lying on concrete floors without blankets or mattresses, so closely packed that one could hardly push through. Most of them were between 70 and 85, the youngest, apart from me, was 65. I now realised why I had had to sign a form for an old people's home. They had thought this up especially for me.

Theresienstadt was a complete town with separate parts for older people, children, for married people and for 'specials' – that was for people whose position or connections had earned them special consideration. Properly I should have been with them but the lower riff-raff of the Gestapo had been jealous of my influence with the high-ups for a long time and were making their revenge complete.

We had no lights or water. For the first time in my life I realised what it was like to live without the ordinary necessities of life. No soap, no wash-basins, no plates, spoons or knives, nothing. I noticed that, on the whole, people with a better background and education were able to stand these conditions better than the others. Many sank to the lowest grade of humanity and became little better than beasts. Men and women who had been married for years suddenly started avoiding each other, frightened that they might have to share their scraps of food. Sons and daughters let their parents starve so that there might be more for themselves. As soon as anyone died a horde of these creatures fought desperately to snatch their rags of garments, their shoes and their hoarded scraps of food. If some of us had not tried to keep order, they would have stripped the sick and dying, too, and would even have torn the withered flesh from their bones in their frenzy for food. It was natural that people here died like flies, but death had really no meaning any more. Some of them prayed for it every day. Typhoid swept through the camp and every morning we found some dead. The doctor did not even bother to come. There was nothing he could have done; there was no medicine and no other food than our staple pigswill. I started a desperate struggle for survival and knew that the first thing was to keep clean. I found a pump at the far end of the camp and was able to alleviate my condition a little.

Since I was the youngest and strongest in our house, I was elected foreman and tried to organise some sort of order. It was a heartbreaking responsibility. The only possible chance for those of us who could survive was to let the sick die as quickly as possible and use the food saved for those who were still well. As soon as we noticed that someone was going to die, one of my helpers had to stand guard to save their clothing and possessions and prevent their getting too much food.

This was the only concentration camp where there was a self-government by the inmates and where men and women were allowed to be together, and to walk about freely inside the camp. The camp guard really only bothered to hand out the food and a minute amount of other supplies. Otherwise they never interfered with us, except that every three months they collected together a party of a few thousand for transport to the east. A week before this the whole camp was terrified. Although we did not know exactly what was going to happen to those who were taken away, there was never any doubt in any one of our minds that it meant death. And the whispered name 'Auschwitz' struck a chill terror into all our hearts.

Apart from hunger and fleas, the most important aspect of life in the camp was sex. It was the only thing which could give us a sort of balance. The only chance to forget for a short while. And by this time we did not even bother about privacy. Couples would throw their ragged blankets over their heads in the middle of the crowded floor. We had no contraceptives and the great fear was pregnancy; we went to great trouble to avoid this danger. Pregnancy meant death and there were no clean ways and means for abortion. If any of the women were found to be pregnant they were shot. And if she gave the name of the man, he was shot too. Often in terror they would give the names of several.

One morning I was unable to get up. It was typhoid at last. I had lately been unable to keep clean from fleas and bugs and I was expecting this to happen. I had a very high temperature and was completely resigned. But one of my friends from the other side of the camp arrived to carry me into the hospital shed which was reserved for young people who had a chance of survival. People were lying on bare sacks of straw on the draughty floor. There was a crowd of sick people who had just been carried in and were waiting until someone died so that they could take their places on the ground. I did not have to wait long and without the sack even being turned I was laid on it. I was given more kindliness and attention than I had ever had in my life. The people who looked after the sick sacrificed themselves completely and mostly in vain. There was no special food and no medicine. For a fortnight I had to live solely on tea. But the miracle did happen and I came through. For several weeks I was too weak to move, and then slowly I regained my strength.

In the hospital I got to know the Jewish camp leader and other people who were running the camp. Through them I learned that there was a secret channel for sending out letters. Although I did not really believe that it would be any use, I wrote to Willi, to Gottfried and to several other influential people to tell them where I was and to ask them to do something for me if they could.

When I was well enough the camp leader asked me if I would like to take charge of the children in the camp. I was delighted to be able to do something worthwhile. The children were our greatest problem and the most important task the camp committee had to cope with. There were around 1,000–3,000 of them and it was everybody's aim to keep these children alive and create for them a world of their own. A special children's home was put aside for them and they were never allowed to come in contact with any of the horror that was going on in the camp surrounding them. This task was the most agonising but at the same time the most absorbing work that any human being could undertake. There was no time to think of oneself and the work put one into such a state of complete concentration that one forgot everything else. Our great preoccupation was to keep them isolated from the general KZ atmosphere of despair and decay. For this home we begged and scrounged in the camp, and when begging and scrounging were not effective we requisitioned.

In order to get the children their daily 1,350 calories we had to steel ourselves into complete ruthlessness. If they were to be fed, others would have to go without. What this meant in plain terms was that it was necessary for us to starve the old and the incurably sick to death in order that the young might remain healthy enough to survive. What was perhaps even more difficult and required even greater strength of mind was the fact that we had to feed ourselves too at the expense of others. It was obvious that we would be of no use to the children if we were so undernourished and lacking in energy that we could not continue to fight on their behalf. Every child of Theresienstadt who survived, represented the death by starving of many of the old and sick. It was this grim fact that made the SS propaganda about the 'Child Welfare Organisation' of their 'Model Camp' so ironical. They took credit for everything we achieved and patted themselves on the back for the happy and healthy existence of their little prisoners. Why some of the children were in fact happy was something the SS could never have known or understood.

One day when I was sitting in my office I heard a timid little voice behind me ask: 'Is Frau van Westerode from Berlin here?' I turned round and saw a little girl, about eight years old, whom I remembered immediately. She was called Claudia and came from a Jewish family in Berlin. Her parents had already been arrested by the Gestapo in the summer of 1941. Claudia, at that time, was spending her holidays in Pomerania with some anti-Nazi friends of her parents. She stayed on in Pomerania. In 1943, however, her foster-parents were arrested for illegal anti-Nazi activities and little Claudia was sent to Theresienstadt. I took her in my arms and told her how happy I was to see her. From now on I was going to protect her and she shouldn't be scared or unhappy. To my utter amazement she replied: 'But I'm not scared at all! For the first time in my life I am really happy. In Pomerania the village children used to tease me all the time and I was never allowed to play with them. Whenever I crossed the street they threw stones at me and said awful things about my being a Jewess. But here we all are alike and we get on splendidly. We play together and work together in the garden. Honestly, I like being here – so please don't worry about me!'

There was a strict ruling on education; the camp authorities did not interfere in general welfare or hygiene. If we wanted to make bricks without straw that was our business, but the children were not to be educated. I worked out a scheme to get round this. We introduced what was ostensibly organised games and storytelling and talks and under cover of this we were able to teach them to read and write, but this was all we could do. Nevertheless, this was at least a step in the right direction.

Yet all our scrounging and devising, all our scheming and plotting to improve the lot of these children was overshadowed and dogged by a perpetual nightmare which became a heartbreaking reality every three months. From the age of four upwards all children of Jewish parents on both sides and all orphans had to die. They were collected at three-monthly intervals in batches of a few hundred as required. If the numbers were short they were made up with half-Jewish and quarter-Jewish children, selected at random by the guards. The terrible part of it was that by hiding them and saying they were ill we were able to spare a few of the healthier children. This made our ordeal far worse, for it meant that the powers of life and death were rested in us. We knew a certain number of children had to die, but which children were chosen was to a certain extent for us to say. The most terrible torture the Gestapo could have devised was nothing compared to this, which ironically enough was of our own devising. It haunted us perpetually and there was nothing we could do about it.

News of the outside world filtered in; rumours of the progress of the war circulated round the camp; but our children's world was all we had time for. We had lost interest in everything that did not concern them. We had long ago dismissed the outside world as unobtainable; and because we never thought about it, we were able to forget our former lives and ourselves.

Even when I discovered why all the letters I had written to my influential friends had come to nothing I was only mildly disappointed. What had happened to me was that the SS had gone to the trouble of forging my handwriting. Willi had received a letter calling him by a nickname that I had invented and which said 'I am sure you are trying to get me out of here, but please don't as it is quite impossible. I am being kept as a hostage so please don't let anyone else try either. Try to understand that I want it this way.' That had done the trick. If I had known at the time I think I should have gone mad, but now it didn't seem to matter very much. My only reaction was to think that the SS had been rather more clever than usual, and anyway it was all such a long time ago.

But then slowly we began to realise that the war was coming to an end. There were more and more rumours and less and less food. The Nazi camp staff were disorganised and preoccupied.

Epidemics increased but there was an element of time in our battle now. We worked like maniacs to save as many lives as possible, for now the end was in sight. Our guards became less brutal and more uncertain of themselves. Some of the higher officials disappeared and, as time went on, supervision was reduced to a minimum. The camp staff, who did at times have to mix with us and walk through the compound, were more heavily armed than ever before and were clearly terrified. The human transports to the east had stopped and we realised that this must be because the eastern territories were occupied by the Russians. But we still had some new transports coming in from the west and this made life in the camp more and more difficult as the supplies became even more spasmodic. And yet our children and everyone in the camp who could be kept alive now had a future to look forward to.

The appalling thing was that the death rate was mounting faster than ever. Then we heard the rumble of artillery and knew that soon we would be in the front line. A few hours later a squadron of bombers appeared above the camp. At first, we cheered and waved because we thought these were the Allies to greet us. But instead of waving back the planes suddenly released their bombs. They were German planes trying to wipe out the camp, frightened of the retribution of the thousands of inmates. But the Luftwaffe's aim was not so good any more and little damage was done. Then suddenly the guards had vanished and the greyish brown uniforms of the liberating Russians took the place of the black SS. The Russians were marvellous; their first thought was for the children and before they had been there a day they started tackling the epidemics and cleaning up the camp.

There was no question of my leaving until everything could be arranged for the children: where they were to go, how to find their parents or their relations to whom they could be sent; a thousand problems to be dealt with.

Many of my old socialist friends had now taken official positions and I received offers of help from every side. Some of them even got a French officer to fly over to the nearby aerodrome with the idea of taking me back by air to Berlin. But there was still too much to do at the camp.

The day the last child left I began to make for my return to Berlin. All transport was completely disorganised and trains were quite out of the question. But I managed to book a place on a supply lorry. I went to say goodbye to the Burgermeister. This man, who had been put in by the Russians, had helped us a great deal in our work and I wanted to thank him personally before I left. He greeted me with the information that there was a warrant out for my arrest. Why, he could not tell me. All he knew was that the warrant had been issued and I was not to leave. I was staggered. I went straight to the Russian headquarters and demanded an interview with the commanding officer. I was passed from one room to another and saw about six people, all charming, but none of them knowing any more than I did. Finally, I went back to the Commandant of the camp. He knew nothing about it either, except that the police wanted me for questioning. He was a kind and considerate man; he knew all about the work I had done in the camp and because of this he said that as far as he was concerned I could leave with his blessing. In fact, he advised me to go as quickly as possible. But this I refused to do. I was hurt, angry and also genuinely curious; the whole thing seemed so entirely fantastic.

I cancelled my place on the lorry. Then I went to the police station where I was accused of being a Nazi spy and promptly imprisoned for six weeks. I was treated quite well, but these six weeks were more agonising and humiliating to me than anything that had happened before. To be branded as a spy after these years of fighting the Nazis and suffering from their vile methods, was more than I could stand. It affected my whole mind and body much more intensely than any physical strain and privation could have done. I can remember little about those six weeks. I had a complete nervous breakdown and only remember sobbing night and day, unable to think, to do anything or even to defend myself against the accusations.

The inmates of Theresienstadt, the doctors and the camp leader took up my case and slowly they unravelled the mystery of my arrest. What had happened was that the authorities had gone through the SS files and found copies of the forgeries which they had sent to Willi and to Gottfried telling them not to bother to do anything about getting me out. The officials had thought that I had really written those letters and that the only explanation was that I had been working secretly for the Gestapo in the camp. As soon as the mistake was realised I was let out and told that I was completely exonerated. I was too sick and disgusted and furious even to be pleased.

When I returned to Berlin I was appalled by the effects of the bombing attacks. The housing shortage was so acute that it seemed like a miracle when some old friends succeeded in procuring a five-roomed flat for me. It had been the property of a Nazi who had fled. The magistrate had confiscated it and it was allocated to me without further trouble, as an inmate of a concentration camp.

The circle of my friends had shrunk considerably. Some were dead; others had made their way to the west. The few who remained were eager to help. They too had suffered terribly during the war and many had lost all they had. They too laboured under the sorrow of the past. But their sorrows were different from mine, and in our conversations, in spite of all mutual sympathy, we rarely understood each other entirely. I had suffered a different and, as I believed, deeper spiritual hurt than they, and their eternal debates about guilt and atonement seemed to me beside the point. My own experiences, however, had driven me in a different direction, and I wished only to help and heal as I had helped the children in the camp. This seemed to me the most important thing in this metropolis of misery. My thoughts were with all my companions in misfortune now returning from concentration camps and prisons. I wanted to help them.

My meeting with Maria Wenthausen enabled me to put my purpose into effect. She was a communist who had spent ten years in prison and behind barbed wire, and she was now one of the leaders of the newly formed association of Victims of Fascism. This organisation had made it its task to help the inmates of prisons and concentration camps and the relatives of those who died there. The organisation was given an official standing and made a part of the department of Social Welfare of Berlin. Though I was in need of rest I began my work with this organisation a few weeks after my return.

At the very beginning it became evident that many people made themselves out to be victims of Fascism who, on closer investigation, proved to be impostors, or who had been in concentration camps as habitual criminals. It was often extremely difficult to decide how genuine our cases were. It was one long stream of pitiful and heartrending stories. A family of eight starving children, the father with TB as a result of eight years' imprisonment, the mother blinded by an explosion in a munitions factory, whose two-roomed flat had been made uninhabitable by bombing. Another one, emaciated, grey of face, ragged and bare-footed; a Jehovah's Witness, long persecuted as a pacifist, he had no home and slept now with one friend, now with another. 'I have no shoes and winter is drawing near.' Somewhere to live? No, he did not need that. His clothes too, were all right, but he needed shoes and, if possible, a permit to buy a pair of spectacles. A tall woman with two fair-haired children, a narrow, well-bred face with eyes which looked at me sceptically. All three comparatively well-dressed. 'My husband was a staff-colonel and took part in the plot against Hitler. He was hanged by the Gestapo. My brother, who was also involved, fled – I have no idea where he is. As his sister I was arrested as a hostage.' The new communist mayor had confiscated her entire property and thrown her into the street as a member of the Junker and militarist class. 'Am I considered a Junker or a victim of fascism?' A Jewess whose Aryan lover had served a long term of penal servitude was then transferred to a concentration camp. Now he had returned home, the right side of his body completely paralysed. She asked me for a bath chair, and for building material because the room in which they lived had been shelled and there were only three walls to it.

The misery of these people was without end and there was no help for many of them. The battle of Berlin had left little which could have been used to alleviate the suffering. At the same time the Nazis who had hoarded food and goods and furniture had mostly fled in good time with their loot.

But always we encountered a lack of understanding almost amounting to passive resistance. We were often asked 'Is a German who lost his sons in battle and his possessions through bombing any less a victim of Hitler's madness?' 'What do you mean by "victim of fascism"? We did not want this war either. We lived under a dictatorship and nobody asked our opinion.' This point of view greatly increased our difficulties.

There was an official order that victims of fascism were to be given every assistance. They had priority as far as lodging, clothes, food and employment were concerned. In addition, each one received an immediate payment of 450 marks and those who were incapacitated received a small pension. But how to obtain bath chairs or a pair of spectacles or false teeth, or window panes, building materials and the thousand and one things which were required? But any of these things could be obtained in the black market. When I returned home at night I saw people strolling along the Kurfürstendamm who knew nothing of these worries. Men in well-tailored suits and brand new shoes; women elegantly and fashionably dressed in fur coats and silk stockings; laughing girls at the side of American soldiers, oblivious of the past. They had rescued enough from the Holocaust to live comfortably and happily on the black market. My victims, however, had lost everything and their long imprisonment had made them unfit to find their way about in this new and corrupt environment.

Every evening I returned confused by the conflicting impressions of the day to my spacious and comfortable flat. It gave me a sense of physical wellbeing to feel a soft carpet under my feet and to look at solid furniture, good paintings and flowers. Above all I had room, room which was my own and private. I had my own bathroom, a bedroom to myself; no one shared my board whom I had not invited. All these things had become necessities for me, and only those will understand me who in full possession of their aesthetic faculties have lived for years in a concentration camp, where at every step one was surrounded by people and where there was not an inch of space that one could call one's own.

Gradually the organisation of the Victims of Fascism became a little more systematic. Our help for these people became more cohesive and better organised, although there was still not enough of it. But a new and very disturbing factor soon made itself felt. Even in the concentration camps the permitted camp leadership set up by the inmates had suffered from struggles for political power. The communists, in particular, used to try to gain all influential posts for themselves. Similar struggles now became apparent in the committee of our organisation. Communists, social democrats, national democrats and cosmopolitans opposed each other. Tension increased and frequently the true purpose of the organisation became obscured in the heat of the political debates. The Communist Social Unity Party was only interested in using the organisation as a political weapon. But leaders of other parties, too, most of whom had been victims of fascism themselves, seemed unable to differentiate clearly between a task of social welfare and a political organisation. This made work difficult and to me disagreeable.

Even here I was not spared political attacks. I was accused of reactionary tendencies in assisting intellectuals more effectively than the lower classes. I was even blamed for living in a five-roomed flat while others lived five and six in a room. They forgot all I had suffered. I was accused of being a friend of Goering and my friendship with Gottfried was held up against me. One dreadful woman even went so far as to say that had I not been married to a Jew I would have been a very good Nazi. These unprovoked attacks hurt me deeply. I was bitterly indignant and in the face of this spiteful ingratitude I resigned from the organisation. For years in the concentration camp I had devoted my unsparing efforts to the help of Jewish children. After my release I had refused to rest before continuing to help the needy. And this was my reward. I was deeply hurt and only now did I notice how I had overtaxed my physical strength. I lay in bed weeping with a raging fever, and for weeks refused to see anyone. One day, however, Maria came to tell me that all the accusations against me had been disproved and that they were prepared to offer me an apology and to ask me to return to my work. I hesitated for a long time. Finally I decided that such incidents might well be repeated. Intrigues and struggles for power were and still are the order of the day. I could not bear to expose myself to them anew.

As always, my one refuge was in work and slowly I started taking an interest in artistic matters. Instead of designing I began to deal in furniture and antiques, paintings and jewellery. My customers were British and American soldiers and the currency we used was as often food and cigarettes as money. With my connections I knew how to get hold of the things that were wanted better than the ignorant racketeers who also pretended to be dealing in jewellery and antiques.

At the same time I began to collect a *salon* of interesting people around me. At tea time and in the evenings there was a constant stream of guests. The business aspect was only of secondary importance. My drawing room now became a meeting place where Allied officers and officials could contact my German political friends. In my house they could talk informally over a cup of coffee about plans for the future and about the tragic German past. Sometimes I had difficulties in entertaining so many guests. But at this time I began to receive food parcels from America. In addition I had made enough money to be able to buy various things in the black market. My guests had to be content with a cup of coffee and dry toast with radishes, slices of cucumber and carrot paste. These things were cheapest in the black market. Cigarettes and alcohol they had to provide themselves.

But, after all, they had not come to eat and drink. What they enjoyed was the stimulating conversation. I was happy to be able to give them this opportunity and enjoyed listening to an official of the US Legal Division, a British officer in charge of denazification, a Swiss journalist, a German clergyman and the lord mayor of a large German town discussing the basis of a future judicial procedure in Germany. Visiting doctors discussed with leading members of German public health departments campaigns against starvation, tuberculosis and venereal disease. International currency problems were the subject of conversations between members of the DS Finance Department and German bankers. German artists made contact with cultural officials of the French Forces of Occupation. Publishers discussed their plans and difficulties with officers of the Allied Information Control, and details of the Nuremberg trial were reported by eyewitnesses. It was generally accepted, and I am very proud of the fact that the *salon* of the Baronin Westerode formed an exclusive and essential part of the political and cultural life of post-war Berlin.

CONCLUSION

Just as physical epidemics grow and multiply in hygienically primitive societies, so political epidemics develop most easily in a people who are politically immature.

Germany between the wars fulfilled the optimum conditions for a political epidemic. Having been completely ruled by the Kaiser, the German people were suddenly faced with the problem of ruling themselves. But against the dark background of a completely disrupted country in the grip of strikes, unemployment and economic upheaval, the Weimar Republic died before it had ever lived. What was more natural than that the German people should say: 'Let us try something new. Nothing can be worse.' The panacea they chose was National Socialism, a creed which was unequivocally undemocratic, repressive and reactionary.

There is no doubt that the Nazi Party appealed irresistibly to the German character. In almost every German there is a marked tendency to envy, and Nazism encouraged, developed and catered for this negative but powerful national trait. Another danger spot in the German mind is the leaning towards militarism. The Nazis did not have to teach militarism to the people; it was already there and only waiting for uniforms, guns, the panoply of marching and banners and shouting.

And after envy and militarism comes the worship of strength for its own sake. To many Germans the bully was someone to be admired, envied and respected. And the Nazi Party was founded on strength and strong-arm methods. No political persuasion could compete with the persuasion of the club-swinging, jack-booted SA man.

Envy, militarism, strength and next the ability to submerge their own morals and consciences in an entirely uncritical and fanatical enthusiasm for one cause and for one party – this mob hysteria makes them go always with the swim. Once the tide has turned they all turn with it – and at the same time turn their coats and their consciences. Moral issues are the responsibility of the party and the leaders. The individual is free to concentrate on personal issues and material gains.

And in this moral topsy-turvydom, good was made to serve bad. German loyalty, industry and integrity served the cause of German strength and success. I do not think there is any doubt that 80 per cent of the ordinary Germans who now blame fate and their leaders for the rise of Nazism, supported the movement wholeheartedly and were in fact the Party's greatest source of strength.

Dr Wertheim and Fritz Muehlebach are both typical rank and file party members, the former representing the bullying materialists, the unscrupulous go-getters; the latter, the sincere idealists, the meek and sheep-like followers who expected to be bullied and were.

Wertheim and his group put as little as possible into the Third Reich and took out all they could. When there was nothing more to be got out of the Party and there were signs that it was becoming unstuck they began dropping out. Dr Wertheim, together with most of the ex-Party members, now claims that he never really believed in National Socialism. He is quite right about this; he had no belief in Nazism – only in its usefulness to him personally. And yet Wertheim and his kind were Nazis before there was National Socialism; fundamentally they *were* National Socialism, much more so than the smaller group of idealists represented by Fritz Muehlebach, who believed absolutely in the Party doctrines and the leader.

Both Muehlebach and Wertheim found in the Party what they wanted to find, saw in it what they wanted to see and made of the Party what they wanted it to be. Today they will try to say that the opposite is true: that they were made by the Party into what the Party wanted them to be. The only Nazis of whom this is true are the younger generation represented by Hildegard Trutz and Erich Dressler, who were in fact moulded and shaped entirely by the Nazi Party.

Hermann Voss, Mausi von Westerode and Tassilo von Bogenhardt are typical of the fellow-travellers. Voss with his driving ambition and his love of power travelled furthest with the Nazis and derived the greatest gain from them. He represents the big shots, the majority of the industrialists and businessmen, few of whom were ever actual Party members and most of whom never even regarded themselves as pro-Nazi. These people disagreed with nine-tenths of the Nazi doctrine and had no use for the leaders; yet it was their support which guaranteed the success of National Socialism. Like the Wertheims; their reason for supporting the Nazis was personal gain; but they were shrewder than the Wertheims. They took a longer view and were careful to cover their retreat in case of trouble. This accounts for their refusal to take the final step of joining the Party. Instead, Voss found that the best way to ensure his peace of mind was to develop two consciences, one for private use and one for business. Few German businessmen were cruel or approved of cruelty; few were as ruthless as the Doctor. Most of them were opposed to war and when it started were by no means sanguine about the final result. But nearly without exception they supported the Nazis in their cruelties and they worked hard for the war. Their point of view was summed up in the motto 'business is business' and today they argue that any good businessman in the world would have done the same; did do the same, in fact, by continuing to deal with Nazi Germany right up to the outbreak of war.

Mausi von Westerode, on the other hand, travelled with the Nazis because of her inability to sacrifice her position – a position reached before and independently of Nazism. She represents those millions who always remained sincerely opposed to National Socialism and who fought a losing battle against the temptation of being drawn into the swim. Mausi's spirit remained strong but her flesh was weak. What is perhaps worse about her is that she need not have become a fellow-traveller. She was kind, honest and intelligent and her position was already assured; unlike Tassilo, it was not essential to her profession that she should accept the Nazis. But she was a snob and that was her undoing. Both she and Voss went with the Party out of purely selfish motives. But this is by no means true of Tassilo von Bogenhardt. It is as if Voss and Mausi von Westerode decided to travel with the Nazis, bought their tickets, and got into a first-class compartment of their own free will, whereas Tassilo merely woke up to find himself in the guard's van when the train had already started. It was only his strong sense of loyalty and a keen devotion to duty that prevented him from getting off. Von Bogenhardt is a typical product of the traditional professional officer class, the great majority of whom were strongly opposed to National Socialism – politically, morally and socially. They kept aloof from the Party and the Nazi military organisations, and were ready to destroy them as soon as their generals gave the order. But being typical German Army officers it never entered their heads that they themselves might take action. In this they stand guilty – but their guilt is not to be compared with that of the high-ranking officers who could at any time have expelled the Nazis from power. But their activities were confined to talking instead of doing. Not until the war was as good as lost and the Nazis on the verge of collapse did they make their futile gesture on 20 July 1944 – too little and too late – to excuse their apathy of the last eleven years.

Tassilo's character is of all the fellow-travellers nearest to the anti-Nazi. Had Tassilo not been brought up and educated from his early childhood as a Prussian officer, he might have become as conscientious an anti-Nazi as Werner Harz. Yet, by virtue of his occupation, the support he gave to the regime was considerable and much greater than that of any out-and-out Nazis.

Today, most of the German people seek to justify their direct or indirect support of the Nazi cause with the excuse that once it had started there was nothing they could do about it. They excuse themselves by claiming that had they not cooperated they would not have lived. But Werner Harz's story is proof that there were people who never cooperated and who were still able to live. Only a few – a chosen few. Theirs was a lonely road and few travelled it. But the road was there and it was an open road. Force was not the power which kept it empty – it was greed and pigheadedness and ambition and love of security. And the few pilgrims (they were pilgrims, not martyrs) who for fourteen years travelled this way, effectively destroy the excuse 'we were forced to do it.' Werner Harz was one of this small group; he is a completely ordinary young German with no special advantages and no passionate political convictions. He is only different in that he kept his mind healthy and independent in spite of the material temptations of National Socialism. The main difference between him and

Claus Fuhrmann, although both are anti-Nazis, is that the latter had no choice in the matter. He looks on his anti-Nazi attitude as an achievement, whereas Harz regards his as something quite ordinary, which any decent person should have done.

Of the nine representatives, five stand guilty of allowing and supporting an evil government to do evil in their country. They are Dr Franz Wertheim, Fritz Muehlebach, Baroness von Westerode, Hermann Voss and Tassilo von Bogenhardt, and they should stand for the vast majority of the German people. But the thing they are responsible for is now dead. It is dead because the power which raised it and quickened it had been smashed by the Allies. It was power and not ideas which was the life and blood of German's National Socialism. As soon as the physical strength was broken, the idea of National Socialism disappeared entirely and instantly from Germany.

In spite of all that has happened to them, most Germans today are still incapable of applying the simple laws of cause and effect to themselves. They live, as it were, in a permanent present of unrelated sensations. Their thought process might run: there was an economic crisis; the Nazis were in power; the war was lost; we suffer. Throughout, no blame or responsibility attaches to them personally. They are merely pawns in the grip of destiny – as innocent as they are powerless. And this delusion of innocence is one which can and does impress people outside Germany. It is a dangerous delusion.

We can only help and understand Germany if we see the Germans as they really are. We must be careful not to see them as they see themselves. Nor must we see them as the freak blackguards our war propaganda found it necessary to paint them. Before helping someone it is important to know not only what is the matter with him but also what he is – his weakness and strength. The German people must be assessed truthfully and objectively without sentimentality and without malice.

But as I have already said, we might have to look for the disease of Nazism not only in Germany but in the world … perhaps in our own hearts. Well, gentle reader, now is the time for you to look.

Louis Hagen's childhood home in Potsdam before the war.

Louis Hagen's home after the war. When he retuunred to visit after reunification, he found it had been used by the Stasi Water Police.

Louis Hagen's grandfather's villa 'Karlshagen' in Potsdam before the war.

Louis Hagen's grandfather's home in Potsdam where Louis returned after the war. It had been used as a cancer clinic.

INDEX